LESSONS LIFE TAUGHT ME,
UNKNOWINGLY
AN AUTOBIOGRAPHY

Live Life!

Anupam Kher

By the same author

The Best Thing about You Is YOU!

LESSONS LIFE TAUGHT ME,
UNKNOWINGLY

AN AUTOBIOGRAPHY

HAY HOUSE, Inc.

Carlsbad, California • New York City

London • Sydney • New Delhi

Published in the United States by: Hay House, Inc.: www.hayhouse.com®
Published in Australia by: Hay House Australia Pty. Ltd.: www.hayhouse.com.au
Published in the United Kingdom by: Hay House UK, Ltd.: www.hayhouse.co.uk
Published in India by: Hay House Publishers India: www.hayhouse.co.in

Cover and design: Hay House India • *Cover photograph:* Atul Kasbekar • *Interior photos:* All photographs used are from the author's personal collection.

Library of Congress Control Number: 2019947578

Hardcover ISBN: 978-93-88302-04-3
Tradepaper ISBN: 978-1-4019-5972-2
E-book ISBN: 978-93-88302-05-0

10 9 8 7 6 5 4 3 2 1
1st edition, August 2019
1st US edition, October 2019
Printed in the United States of America

To
Those who dare to dream.
And succeed!

CONTENTS

Memories of who I was and where I lived are important to me. They make up a large part of who I am going to be when my journey winds down. I need the memory of magic if I am ever going to conjure magic again. I need to know and remember, and I want to tell you.

—Robert R. McCammon, *Boy's Life*

Prologue

$\mathcal{I}$ started writing my autobiography at the age of 10, way before I became an actor, a movie star or an award-winning performer. I unconsciously stored vignettes of memories of my family, my early childhood and encounters with other actors, directors and performers in the years to come—soaking in every experience.

I have steeped myself in the adventure of living, in the highs and the lows and most importantly, in the arduous, exhilarating and creative process of acting.

Because I have lived my life so fully, I developed an almost photographic memory of most events—recalling at will both big and small encounters and events, visuals and voices, sounds and smells.

It is pure magic that my autobiography is now organically gaining a voice, shedding light on the people who have touched my life and holding a mirror to my existence—a pulsing chord that links the ten-year-old to the person I am today.

Aptly summed up by the legendary Colombian writer Gabriel (José de la Concordia) García Márquez who wrote in his autobiography *Living to Tell the Tale*: 'Life is not what one lived, but what one remembers and how one remembers it in order to recount it.'

In my mind's eye, it all started with the survival instinct of being born into and raised in a lower middle-class family. Reading the renowned Russian masters like Maxim Gorky, Anton Chekhov, Fyodor Dostoevsky or even Charlie Chaplin, I realise a major impetus was their resilient instinct to face life at every twist and turn, overcoming every hurdle with grit and determination.

Even today, I remember how special it felt when at the age of three, my maternal grandfather, Lambodhar Kak, gifted me a gold coin, though I did not fully comprehend its worth. I remember everything vividly and have forgotten almost nothing—the first time my mother slapped me, my first day at school, the first time my class teacher beat me with a cane, my first love, my first rejection, the first theatre role I got, the first film role, my highs and lows, the successes and failures.

As I narrate my life, it is not as a flashback, but it is pulsating alive and in the moment. I am living it in telling it. It is not presented as a one dimensional photograph but as a happening, breathing, evolving multi-dimensional moment to be shared.

Retrospect gives its own perspective. In March 2016, I received the prestigious Padma Bhushan from the President of India, Pranab Mukherjee, in the glittering, spectacular and hallowed halls of the Rashtrapati Bhavan.

On that occasion, I was elated by a sense of achievement but also humbled as I held the award in my hand—poised at the pinnacle, savouring the moment but remaining grounded as I recalled my roots from where I had sprung.

If I were to sum up my life in what I hold dearest to me, I would choose the strength of family, vitality of optimism and the energy of the creative process. My chosen career melds all three in a way that enriches both my performance and my persona. At every turn, one or all of these have been my beacon, illuminated my pathway, pulled me back from the abyss, propelled me to dizzying heights and made me the person I am—the entity the world knows as Anupam Kher.

My childhood was shaped by living with my grandfather, Pandit Amar Nath Kher, and I infused a lot of him into my first major film role in Mahesh Bhatt's *Saaransh* (The Essence) portraying both his physical and mental characteristics. My family and film career blended seamlessly with *Saaransh*—a watershed in my life and after years of struggle and disappointment, this film launched my career, my stardom and my first major award.

I recall as if it were yesterday, the day I delivered the mahurat shot for *Saaransh* in 1984. My first shot was a slow-motion scene of me getting the news from America that my son has been murdered in a senseless act of violence in a subway in New York. Director Mahesh Bhatt briefed that dramatic sequence to me, as to how the phone rings, I pick it and hear a voice from the other side say: 'Aapka beta mara gaya hai' (Your son has been murdered) and what my expression should be for the camera. In any case, I was obsessed with the story of the film . . . with the role of B. V. Pradhan and for that particular shot, I distilled all the frustration, all the heartbreaks, all the humiliation that I had faced through the years. Even after the shot was completed, it took a while to shake off the pensive mood from my psyche.

The shoot was to start at 9.30 that morning. As the set was being prepared, I went up to Mahesh Bhatt and said: 'Now that we are launching the film which I was thrown out of and signed back on (a story of uncanny destiny that appears in later chapters), I would like to know what demonstrates my character, the defining emotion of B. V. Pradhan, because I want to make that emotion the most encompassing one—is it disappointment, compassion, love, what is it? Who is B. V. Pradhan? How do you summarise his spirit?

He answered simply: 'Compassion.' And that became my guiding post.

Saaransh was not just my personal obsession. It was a gift to prove myself, to make my dreams a reality. During the entire filming, Mahesh Bhatt too was passionate about finding his groove having done the film *Arth* before this in 1982 with Shabana Azmi, Smita Patil, Kulbhushan Kharbanda and Raj Kiran in the lead. Whenever we spent time together, whether travelling, during our morning walks, on the sets or in the office, anywhere and everywhere, all our conversations centred on the film. We would reinvent the scenes, recompose and rewrite them.

This is how the iconic scene where Pradhan goes to the customs office to collect the last remains of his son was conceived. It's a scene that has been discussed threadbare. A pivotal scene that is both the essence of the protagonist and one that spotlights the core of the tragedy.

Many, including critics and film buffs, later said to me: 'So you too got into method acting.' The reality is that though I am a trained actor, when I perform, I tap into a reservoir of personal associations that ring true to me.

I had to cry out of helplessness and frustration in that crucial sequence. Initially, I was at sea as to how to bring that scene to screen without being melodramatic. I was not married at that time, neither could I relate to the loss of a son. How could I dramatise my feelings on receiving the ashes? Instead, I created my own reality and gave free rein to my imagination.

As I grappled with the creative process, first the sequence from Francis Ford Coppola's *Godfather*, based on Mario Puzo's book, came to mind where Marlon Brando on seeing his Sonny boy's bullet-ridden body says: 'What have they done to my Sonny boy?' What a scene. Truly iconic. That look, that expression by Brando when he looks at the body of his son is worth watching the film over and over again. But as I mulled over it, I realised that my scene was totally different. I had to come up with something more nuanced because Pradhan's grief builds up as he is shunted from officer to officer, room to room of a corrupt system, to get the same reply curtly: *'Aapko TV lena hain, aap upar jaayie'* (You have come to collect a TV, go to the upper floor). Finally, he meets the assistant commissioner of customs:

> Pradhan: *Main apna samaan lene aaya hu, koi bheek mangne nahi aaya hu. Aur na hi koi is tarah . . .* (I have come to collect my goods, not to beg, nor to . . .)
>
> (Gets interrupted by the officer, who says curtly): *Dekhiye mister, yahan sabhi ko apna TV lene . . .* (Look here mister, everyone comes here for his TV . . .)
>
> (Gets interrupted by Pradhan): *Main TV lene nahi aaya hu. Main apne mare hue bete ki asthiya lene aaya hu. Ek baap ka apne bete ki raakh pe koi adhikaar hain ya nahi? Ya uske liye bhi mujhe neeche rishwat deni padegi? Aapke paas itni fursat toh hogi ki aap*

mujhe mere bete ki asthiya dilwa dijiye. (I have not come to collect any TV. I have come to collect the last remains of my son. A father has a right to his son's ashes or not? Or, for that too, I have to give a bribe downstairs? Would you have the time to get me my son's last remains?)

It's a brilliantly crafted scene where the surprise element is when Pradhan says to the assistant commissioner of customs: '*Main TV lene nahi aaya hu. Main apne mare hue bete ki asthiya lene aaya hu*' (I have not come to collect any TV. I have come to collect the last remains of my son).

Initially I was not able to strike the right emotional chord for the scene. I feared that the outburst would ring false instead of being the highlight of the film. So, I told Mahesh Bhatt: 'I am turning my back towards the camera. I will prepare myself and when I give a signal with my hand, take it that I am emotionally ready to give the shot. We will try that out and take it in one shot . . . no retakes.'

Kudos to Mahesh Bhatt, who without any hesitation, placed his trust on a young upcoming actor. When I turned my back towards the camera, I was not thinking that B.V. Pradhan's son had died. I evoked the humiliations, the slights I had encountered, the hardships that my father had faced trying to raise me just to let me realise my dream to be an actor. I felt the pressure of everyone waiting for me to perform the dramatic scene, acutely aware that this was my do or die chance to prove myself. The summary of my feelings reached a crescendo when I gave a signal with my hand to Mahesh Bhatt and the camera rolled as I turned and emoted my scene, giving it my all, spurred by my past failings, sadness, homelessness, sleeping on the railway platforms, losing the love of my life, all humiliations big and small. It was all shot in one take. The only take!

It flowed as a passionate, remarkable scene and even though I say it myself at the risk of sounding like I am boasting, I still think that it is one of the ten best scenes of all time in Indian cinema.

Saaransh meant a great deal to me at a personal level too. It taught me how to live life; it gave me my guiding principle—empathy. It opened the doors of my heart and mind to understand another individual's point of view. *Saaransh* afforded me not just a great platform to perform but it became a trajectory for the future—it gave me a life to live and directed me on how to live that life. B. V. Pradhan has lived with me since, in countless ways and deepest thoughts.

It is both a blessing and a bonus that nearly 35 years later, I am becoming like Pradhan. Though Pradhan did not believe in the afterlife while I am a firm believer in karma, his honesty, audacity and the complete absence of fear as he took on an entire system without seeking to be popular, is a great lesson for me. Today, if I am able to speak up for my country, vocalise what I believe is right or wrong—it is because of what I have somewhere imbibed from B.V. Pradhan. I am emboldened to take a stand, learnt to live with being dubbed 'politically incorrect' since B. V. Pradhan taught me to stand up for what I think is right or wrong. Being in his character took a lot out of me, but fulfiled me too in ways that go beyond words—I was a 28-year-old boy, born in a disadvantaged family, in the remote town of Shimla, who was able to catapult beyond his circumstances and become an actor without borders.

Teachings from my grandfather, Pandit Amar Nath Kher, have seeped into my spirit. Most of my childhood went by and I never even realised that we were poor. I had learnt the most important lesson that is even more priceless today—money does not buy happiness.

A good storyteller starts at the very beginning and I have an interesting story related to my birth that leads me to believe that mine was not just a routine birth. I was destiny's special child.

Part–I

THE EARLY YEARS

—◆◇ ⚬⚬ ◇◆—

If you carry your childhood with you,
you never become older.

—Tom Stoppard

1

IN DEMAND FROM DAY ONE

So why an autobiography?

I believe that by telling my life story, I can illuminate the people I've crossed paths with and our experiences shared and apart, which in turn will highlight the influences and lessons imbibed. My sense of wonder and joy for a life well lived is only multiplied in its sharing. Truly, in life, *kucch bhi ho sakta hai*! (Anything can happen!) This would later become the title of my autobiographical one-man play, which premiered on 8 August 2005, but the first instance of this truism presented itself on 7 March 1955, my entry into this world, in room number 3 of a 95-bed Lady Reading Hospital. This hospital is now called the Kamala Nehru Hospital, in Bemloi Estate, below Oakwood, which was once the summer residence of the Maharaja of Patiala (now in Punjab, India) but is presently Himachal Pradesh chief minister's official residence in Shimla.

I was born at 9 p.m., the eldest offspring of my parents. My cherubic features very typical of my ancestry, peaches and cream Kashmiri skin with an angelic smile that evidently not only charmed my mother, but also enchanted the attending nurse immensely. Having taken quite a fancy to me, the nurse lost no time in asking my mother, in a clipped British accent: 'Is this your first child?'

My mother, then only 19, was an illiterate traditional housewife and hence, totally unfamiliar with the spoken English language. She looked at the nurse, nonplussed; having no understanding of what the nurse was saying or asking. Apparently, in her bewildered state, she gave a gentle nod of the head, prodding the nurse to communicate another way. Instead, the nurse took this as an affirmation to go further, and in an excited tone stated her desire in a low, gentle and courteous demeanour: 'My dear, you are so young, just 19 . . . and so beautiful . . . you can . . . and I am sure you will have more children . . . I request you with folded hands . . . I beg of you to give me this child . . . please let me adopt him, as I don't have any child of my own . . . I can't have any'.

Obviously, my mother could not understand a word of what the nurse was saying but her sixth sense cautioned her that something was apparently not quite right. Somewhat tense, she called out to my father (who was waiting outside the room) for providing 'translation facilities'.

My father who also only had a meagre grasp of the Queen's English, somehow managed to figure out what the nurse wanted. Pleased and surprised at the quality of his product, he was also taken aback by the request since it was the first time he had witnessed a Britisher plead in such a manner. Initially, he did not know how to react for he just couldn't believe that a Britisher was requesting him, a commoner—for a favour; something totally unexpected, something that was happening at least to them for the first time . . . and that too a boon that only he could grant.

In that perplexed and puzzled state, he slowly translated for my mother the nurse's request to adopt their firstborn. With tears in her eyes, my mother, an otherwise meek, gentle, easily imposed upon young lady, mustered enough courage that day to categorically shout a firm 'No . . . Never . . . not even for all the riches in the world'. The nurse walked away.

I don't know if my mother really loved me more than 'all the riches in the world', though I have a sneaky suspicion that at the back of her mind was the prediction of an astrologer she had once met and the forecast she had taken to heart: 'Your first-born would be a son who would solve all your problems . . . He will be the one to bring joy into your life!' Probably that was the reason why she was always very patient with me. When I say to you *kucch bhi ho sakta hai*, you'll understand that I truly mean it!

After the agonies of childbirth had subsided, the English nurse on duty handed me over to my mother who looked at me and proclaimed: '*Mera Bittu!*' (My Bittu), as she hugged me and with eyes filled with tears of joy planted a tender kiss on my forehead. The pet name 'Bittu' stuck to me and for the family and those close to me I am Bittu to this day.

It is not in my nature to look back or indulge in what-ifs, but just imagine what if I had been adopted by the Britisher; I could have become the Prime Minister of Britain or a guard outside Buckingham Palace or even a British actor.

My life lesson has always been there is no point in thinking of what could have been—for I lay great store by John Lennon's quote: 'Life is what happens to you when you are busy making other plans'. But one thing I know for sure, I would not be narrating this story to you about how sought after I was from the moment I was born.

2

THOSE WERE THE DAYS

My earliest childhood memories are of fourteen of us extended family members confined to a small one room in a Shimla tenement no more than 12 feet by 14 feet in size. Three generations lived almost literally on top of each other—paternal grandfather and grandmother, five paternal uncles of mine, some of whom were married with their spouses and children, a paternal aunt and the rest of my family all cramped together. There was no luxury of beds and everyone had to spread out beddings on the floor at night and then roll them up in the morning. It was like living in a small army barrack. We did not have the luxury of privacy to feel depressed. Even otherwise, if anyone felt down in the dumps, there was always one relative or the other to cheer him or her up.

So, in contrast to modern nuclear families, I grew up with an assortment of Khers of all ages, which gave me a head start in learning the lessons related to sharing, tolerance and respecting diverse viewpoints and ideas. In fact, when I hear the generation of today say they are 'bored', I am always very surprised and ask myself: How can anyone be bored in life—there is so much to be observed and so much to be absorbed all around us!

We were Khars, later changed to Kher, when my uncle P. L. Kher changed his name in 1958. My parents, Pandit Pushkar Nath Kher and Dulari Kher, both hailed from Kashmir. My father used to call my mother Dura, though her name before she got married was Jayshree. When I was born, my father, then just 24 years old, was a run-of-the-mill lower divisional clerk in the Forest Department and knew only a smattering of English.

My parents were married in Srinagar, Kashmir, on 11 October 1953. Soon after their marriage, they moved to Shimla where my grandfather, Pandit Amar Nath Kher, had relocated years earlier because of his job as an employee at the Public Works Department (PWD). This means that the Kashmiri Pandits have been shifting homes ever since. It was to be a long journey for them—over 400 miles (650 kilometres)—first by bus to Pathankot, where they halted for the night in one of the rooms of a *dharamshala* (inn) where my mother found Rs 80 which, in those times, was a lot of money. Presuming that my father had perhaps dropped it, she innocently asked him if the money was his, which it wasn't. But, as a man of the moment, he quickly replied: 'Yes, yes, yes . . . thank you very much!' Suddenly with the ill-gotten money in his pocket, he felt rich . . . very rich. The train journey was to be made on 'third-class' tickets from Pathankot to Kalka. Yes, few will remember that those days, the Indian Railways had what was known as 'third class'—the lowest rank of train travel in compartments which, as Mahatma Gandhi had once described were 'evil-looking, [with] dirt lying thick upon the woodwork and I do not know that it had ever seen soap or water.'[1] As can be seen in the 'second class' compartments of today, there would be utter confusion and an awful amount of din and chaos among the passengers, each trying to find a place to lie down or sit, in a compartment already choked to the brim. And yet, once the train started, everyone would somehow squeeze in.

With the new-found cash in his wallet, my father decided to upgrade the status of travel to 'first class' and therefore, gave my mother the deluxe experience of travelling in great style and comfort—a luxury my mother remembers to this day.

Two years later, on 11 September 1957, there was an addition to our family—another son, Vijay, known to one and all as Raju. Even though we were not born into an affluent family, yet Raju and I were raised in a content home with an easy happy-go-lucky atmosphere.

I had a joyful childhood mainly because many of my relatives were an unusual lot—comical characters who proved to be a source of constant entertainment and amusement. I had and still have a gift for looking at people from a humorous point of view. For me, not only my family members, but also my neighbours, my friends, and my teachers, were all akin to comic book characters.

One of the most influential persons in my growing up years was my grandfather, Pandit Amar Nath Kher. My memories of my grandfather are very visual because he was physically very different from everyone else in that large family of ours. For example, none of my uncles or other senior male relatives, used to wear the *safa* (turban) or the *achkan* (the long traditional coat buttoned at the neck and also called the bandgala); only my grandfather did. Besides, there was a ritual that he alone followed—performing the difficult *shirsh asana* (the headstand in yoga) and other complex asanas that Baba Ramdev has now made popular. He also used to practise water therapy and was an expert in inhaling water through one nostril and taking it out of the other.

As children, we would be fascinated by these asanas and today, when I look back, I certainly marvel at the fact that at his age he did all those intricate and tough asanas, which I can't even think of performing. So, if we needed to talk to him while he was positioned upside down, we would have to do so by going down on all fours too and placing our heads next to his on the floor! If a visitor—a friend or neighbour—happened to drop by to witness this scene you can be sure they would burst into fits of uncontrollable laughter.

My grandfather was a very spiritual person who taught me some very pithy phrases. I looked up to him as a saint—the most disciplined person I ever knew. He followed a strict daily routine, a timetable for every activity. Like a Buddha in a crowded house, he would be the least affected by the people clamouring around and all the noise, din and chaos surrounding him. He often said, 'When you are very poor, the cheapest luxury is happiness.'

Surprisingly though, he was not a strict person. He used to laugh a lot. I remember his laughter clearly because I used to make him laugh a lot by mimicking my grandmother, my father and mother, my uncles and aunts, the neighbours, the teachers, everybody.

My childhood was shaped by living with my grandfather and I poured a lot of him into my first major film role in *Saaransh* portraying both his physical and mental characteristics. His love rescued me and let me dream of a bigger reality than the one I was living in.

In the years to come after I moved to Chandigarh, Delhi or Lucknow and eventually even Bombay (now called Mumbai), letters were my means of communication with him. He used to write very well. After staying with us in Shimla for the first 15 years or so of my growing up years, he shifted back to Srinagar in Kashmir, coming home only to visit us during our summer break.

When I was studying theatre at the National School of Drama (NSD) in Delhi, I would never miss an opportunity to meet my grandparents at the Old Delhi railway station when they were on their way from Shimla for a pilgrimage, say, to Allahabad (now called Prayagraj). My grandmother would never fail to bring me lovingly home-made food and snacks.

Even before movies became an integral part of my life, I was a very visual person. I viewed everything in the form of frames, backdrop effects and musical scores. My vivid optical of my grandparents was of them as one unit—of them always being together. By the time I was in the third year in NSD, my grandmother passed away and my grandfather became very lonely. And that was the first time I saw him sad. When they got married, he was 11 and she was 10 years old. Their relationship was deep-rooted in friendship and companionship. I recall being told that after the birth of their third child, he had become a disciple of a Hindu mystic and saint, 'who had experienced spiritual ecstasies from a young age and was influenced by several religious traditions.' Apparently, before the swami made him his disciple, he had questioned him: 'you have come to this ashram (hermitage) while you are in 'ghrahast ashram' (family hermitage) also . . . you have a family. Why should I trust you? You should go back and rejoin them so as to continue carrying out your duties towards them as head of the family. Ashram life here is very tough and not easy to take."

'I will be okay here. I know what it means, and I have thought about it and come,' he answered.

The swami said: 'If you are sure then your test is that you go stark naked to the sweetshop in the market and get me some curd (yogurt).

My grandfather must have been around 30 years of age at that time. He took off his clothes, walked through the bazaar completely naked and got the curd. He stayed at the ashram for over eight years and then returned home. What was the reason for the sudden change of mind no one knew—to this day I am curious about the reason for his return.

My grandfather's room on the third floor of his house in Nai Sadak, Srinagar, was more like a shrine. *Us kamre ki khushbu jaisi duniya mein koi khushbu nahi thi* (There was no fragrance in the world as there was in that room). The fragrance of incense was always there. The room was filled with religious scriptures like the Vedas, the Bhagavad-Gita, the Ramayana, and many others. Don't misunderstand me. That room was not a mere temple. It was an abode of knowledge. During the summer vacations when we would go to spend our holidays with our grandparents, I used to run up the staircase to that room and hide there. It was my favourite hiding place, where I would very often go to sleep. The special kind of energy and vibe the room emitted lingers in my memory to this day. I would descend only when my grandmother would call us down for meals which she would prepare in the traditional clay ovens and serve in large brass bowl dishes from which we would all serve ourselves. She used to proclaim always: 'A family that eats together stays together.' A timeless life lesson. Last, when I visited Nai Sadak in 1995, the house was not there anymore. I became emotional and returned with tears in my eyes.

I think living with grandparents is the most significant factor in the growth of any child. At least, it was for me and my brother. Today, with extended family units no longer the norm, for whatever reasons, in my opinion the children are rather dysfunctional.

Sadly, when my grandfather passed away on 19 September 1984 at the age of 84, I was very busy with my back-to-back film commitments. I didn't even have time to mourn his passing. That's why, when I deliver motivational talks at various forums, most of my conversations are about my grandfather and me. That is also the reason why I dedicated my book, *The Best Thing about You Is YOU!*, 'to my grandfather Pandit Amar Nath', because I think that all my awareness and my native wisdom came from him and I want to acknowledge his influence on my life for all posterity.

My grandmother, Kalawati, was a frail lady, just 4 feet 5 inches 'tall'. She was rarely ever visible around the house and being of a docile nature, her voice too could hardly be heard even if she spoke loudly. And if no one responded to what she said, not because of any disrespect but just because she had not been heard, she would immediately go into a sulk. Another major characteristic of hers was that whenever she would get angry, which was pretty often, she would rush off to the nearby temple. One of my uncles would go cajole her and bring her back. This image of my uncle carrying her back like an innocent child was in great contrast to how I would normally view my grandmother. Such a striking visual has stayed with me to this day reminding me of her inherent childlike innocence—a graphic I still carry within me.

In contrast to my grandfather, my father, Pandit Pushkar Nath Kher, was not a very learned person. He was superstitious by nature. One morning he discovered that he had won a lottery worth Rs 50. It so happened that, before winning the lottery, he had seen the face of the local bread and bun seller who would visit our locality every morning on his rounds. Later that day, on reaching office, my father, already feeling 'good' about having won the lottery, got the news that he had been promoted and that too from a lower division clerk to an upper division clerk. He was thrilled . . . as happy as he could be. He was convinced that the good luck was all due to the bun and bread seller and that if he saw that fellow's face the first thing in the morning it would always bring him good fortune in some form or the other. The bread vendor had become my father's lucky mascot!

Since that day, every morning my father would eagerly wait to catch sight of his 'good luck charm'. As soon as he would hear the vendor's proclamations on the streets, while passing by the house, 'HOT BREAD AND BUNS', my dad would jump up and hurriedly walk towards the door in great excitement but with his eyes closed. Of course, on the way he would step on the faces, stomachs, backs or other anatomy parts of everyone who was in his path fast asleep on the floor! How he never ever tripped over someone asleep on the floor remains a mystery. He would open his eyes only when he could hear the bread and bun man speak directly to him. Unfortunately for him and the rest of us, one day my father overslept and missed the vendor. The whole day he was in a sullen mood, impatient and snapped at everyone. From that day onwards, my brother Raju, and I were entrusted with the task of bringing that bread and bun seller to our home first thing in the morning.

You can well imagine the bewildered state the vendor was in. Here were two young Kashmiri kids, waiting daily at a particular corner of the street that led to our house, taking him home every morning before he could start his rounds of the different localities he was assigned! And why did Pandit Pushkar Nathji not open his eyes until he was positioned in front of him? The mystery carried on for a few days. But the truth had to come out one day, and it did. When he realised the truth, he raised the price! One bread loaf would now cost 40 paise instead of the earlier 30 paise.

Over time, Raju and I got bored with our father's morning routine. In any case, during the cold winter mornings of Shimla who wanted to get out of the comfort of the warm quilt? My father soon realised that we could not be trusted with the job given to us but for him to see the vendor's face first thing in the morning was very important. So, he decided to get back to the routine himself once more. And he did, again with his eyes dosed, stepping on someone or the other. One day Raju got a solid kick. So, we decided to play a prank. Around midnight, we got up, went out and from behind the door, I imitated the bread and bun seller and shouted: 'HOT BREAD AND BUNS!' And as expected, my father immediately dashed to the door, with closed eyes, expecting to see the bread seller by which time, we had run away.

Predictably, there came a time when he stopped believing in this routine due to a hilarious turn of events.

A few days later, he went to his office in a happy mood for, as usual, he had seen the bread and bun seller's face in the morning. As he was the store in-charge of the office, the keys to the storeroom were in his custody. Unfortunately, he had misplaced the keys that day, so he was at the receiving end of a solid firing from his superior for his 'irresponsible behaviour' in front of the entire office staff. Low and dejected, sad and dispirited, that evening, on his way back home, while he was shopping at the vegetable market in Lower Bazar, a *kachhar* (mule) that was transporting sacks of vegetables to the market, kicked him for no apparent reason. With his bag on the ground and most of his shopping fallen out, the mule having walked off most unconcerned, my father, a picture of total misery, kept on looking at him as if to enquire: 'You donkey, what was that for?' Some youngsters started laughing as a passer-by helped him collect the fallen vegetables. By the time he reached home, he had worked himself up to a real state. But that was not the end of his misery that day. Just as he was about to enter the house, a crow passing by shat on his tweed jacket—the only one he possessed. By the time the sun set that evening, my father's obsession with the bread seller was also a thing of the past. But the bread seller never lowered the price of his good back to 30 paise!

Just to get him out of his bad mood my brother and I decided to persist with our old routine of yelling 'HOT BREAD AND BUNS!' Perhaps, it would amuse him, we thought. However, our effort just boomeranged. In a fit of anger, my father virtually screamed in Kashmiri: 'Stop this hot bread and bun nonsense!'

Kashmir has been considered a conflict zone for the past three decades or so due to the regular clashes between the police and the other security forces on one hand and the militants on the other! But much before that, in our house in Shimla, every time my father lost his cool, he would lapse into Kashmiri and trigger a conflict.

As I mentioned above, my father was one person who was a simple man with very simple wisdom. Let me recount an incident involving my father that was to become one of the most impactful lessons of my life: In his own quiet way, he taught me how to handle failures. His thoughtful action has stayed with me all my life. This is an example I share with my audience wherever I speak . . . and whenever I speak.

As children of a lowly paid government official, outings to restaurants were unthinkable for me and my brother Raju. Like our fellow Shimlaites, we siblings used to regularly loiter on the Mall Road and watch with awe, from outside the expensive restaurants such as Davicos or Kwality, each at the opposite ends of the Mall Road, and wonder if we would ever afford to go inside and eat there. After my father got his promotion and became an 'upper division clerk' he took us out for a treat— not to Davicos or Kwality, but to a not as 'fancy' but still popular restaurant called Alfa just opposite the Scandal Point. It still exists today and remains as prominent as ever. My father noticed how his two sons enjoyed that evening. That night, my father made a momentous announcement: two times a year, we would be treated to a meal at Alfa: just me, my brother, my mother and my father.

I cannot overstate what this meant for us at the time: these two treats a year were bigger for us than Diwali, Christmas, Holi, or any other holiday we celebrated. This was our time together as a family and a very special indulgence for us to be together—just the four of us away from the joint family. Every time we went together, our menu was fixed: a mutton samosa (the largest of its kind I have ever eaten in my life), a pineapple pastry and espresso coffee for each of us. These visits became high points in our otherwise frugal pattern of life. At the end of the treat, my father would tip the waiter eight annas (50 paise)!

Both Raju and I first studied at the Lady Irwin Primary School at Phagli in the south of the town, and later in the local DAV (Dayanand Anglo Vedic) Higher Secondary School in Lakkar Bazar, on the Ridge. I was good neither in studies nor in sports. Neither were extra-curricular activities like debates, dramatics on my horizon.

Obviously, the biggest humiliation for any student was failing in the final examinations. In Shimla, because of the extreme winter months, annual exams were held in December and vacation ran through February. However, to keep up with the rest of the country's schools' schedules which had annual vacations in the summer—students in Shimla were allowed to continue to the next grade even before the test papers were evaluated. So, students went on to join the next grade but if they failed, they went back, after two months in Class XI, to the previous class, sitting with students who were your juniors just a couple of months back. As you can imagine, this was the most mortifying disgrace that could happen to a student.

A day or two before my Class X results were to be announced, my father came to the school and sought leave from the teacher to take me out. How highly unusual I thought! My father was a simple man, and as previously mentioned, our life was frugal and mundane, this had never happened before. Nothing much was spoken between us as we left school and curiosity was gnawing me from the inside. Naturally, I was quite inquisitive to know why, how, for what reason, where to . . . my imagination was running wild as we left the school premises.

My father asked, 'Kuch khanna hai kya?' (Do you want to eat something?) I suggested Nathu Halwai (a popular sweets shop in Lower Bazar), because I knew we had another four months before our favourite bi-annual trip to Alfa Restaurant. But to my surprise, my father was ready to go to Alfa again! We were soon on our way there. Once seated, he proceeded to order our usual items for each of us: a mutton samosa, a pineapple pastry and an espresso. I was completely dazed and wondered what motivated this out-of-turn celebratory treat: Had my father received a promotion? Had someone bequeathed him a fortune? Had he brought me here to tell me that he was leaving and separating from my mother, as he had threatened in his anger during a fight with her a couple of days earlier? Why this indulgence when we were here just two months back? Too many questions were cluttering my mind, and no answers were forthcoming from my father.

Finally, after we finished eating, he disclosed the truth: 'Bittu, this morning I went to the education board and I found out through my source that you have failed in the matriculation examinations.'

I was shocked, but before I could defend myself, he continued: 'You are probably wondering why I brought you here, to our favourite restaurant, to have our favourite meal. I did this so that you never forget this failure or any other failure you will encounter in your life. Why? I want you to remember that failure is an event, not a person.' That day my father tipped ONE rupee to the waiter.

That was my father Pandit Pushkar Nath Kher, celebrating failure with a 16-year-old boy, long before it became a fashionable philosophy!

When the fear of failure is taken away from you in any situation at such a young age, you can handle any adversity! It's been a great lesson which has stood me in good stead through the years and I have my father to thank for it. I will also never forget how artfully he taught me that lesson not with a loud lecture but with an unforgettable gesture. Even today, when I meet with a so-called 'failure', I go back to my age-old comfort food: one mutton samosa, a pineapple pastry, and an espresso.

As I grew up, I realised that there was something extraordinary in him. He was a very good human being—warm, friendly and straightforward. A good father. The ultimate example of a good parent. My best friend.

I would often test how far I could push my relationship with him. Once, when I was in the second year of the National School of Drama in Delhi, my father had come to visit me. While we were waiting for an autorickshaw outside the gate of the school complex in Bahawalpur House on Copernicus Marg, I decided to challenge my father, my friend. So, I asked him seemingly innocently: 'Dad, I have a small problem. Whatever the mode of transport, whether I am travelling in a car or riding a cycle or a motorcycle or bus or train, I get a hard-on! What do you think is the reason?'

'It's hereditary', he replied calmly. That pithy answer summed up my father and his take it easy attitude to life.

He used to discuss everything with me. He was also my greatest fan, right from the first time I appeared on stage. He would always sit either in the third or the fourth row and his expression never changed till the last minute I was on the stage. For him, I was the best son in the world. In our home in Shimla, he had a trunk that no one was supposed to open. No one knew what valuables he stored in it. After he passed away on 10 February 2012, when my brother and I were in Shimla to immerse his last remains in the Sutlej River at Tatta Pani, we debated whether we should open that trunk or not. We were curious and decided to open it. It contained only clippings of my drama and film reviews, press cuttings, my certificates, bounced cheques, my pithy letters, and in some cases, just my name mentioned in some publication or the other. Each was relevantly underlined. It was fascinating.

He was an ordinary person with an extraordinary life. An average human being who imparted amazing lessons on how to deal with every aspect of life. Today, I miss him the most even as I see him clearly in my mind's eye. His going away made me aware of death. Before him, whenever I lost someone in the family, including my grandfather, it never created a vacuum. My father's going away has

Financially and academically, my mother's side was better off than my father's. In short, they were more affluent. My maternal grandfather, Lamboodhar Kak, was a senior assistant in Registrar of Co-operative Society. The only memory I have of him is that he was a tall man. My maternal grandmother, Arandatti Kak, was a jovial, roly-poly person. I loved staying at my maternal grandparents' home at 84, Karan Nagar, Srinagar, because of the luxury of a better lifestyle, better houses and better neighbours around. I remember being sent to the nearby National School, even though I was on my summer vacations. I still remember the first two lines of my morning prayer in Kashmiri:

Gulshan wattan chu sonoui
Bul-bul wanaan chu poshun

My maternal uncles were educated and dignified. The elder one, Mohan Lal Kak, was a professor in the Government College for Women in Srinagar. The one next to him, Makkhan Lal Kak, was a senior official in National Sample Survey. Both were disciplinarians but kind and affectionate. Moti Lal and Krishan Lal, the younger brothers of my mother, were both overseers in the government service. My maasi (mother's sister), Sheela, fondly called Dida by us, was a bright person. My aunts (mamis), Rani, Pyaari and Nansi were the best cooks and believed in feeding the ever-starving us (me and my brother, Raju) till we went into a food coma, almost. My youngest aunt Karuna, who was a teacher, was much younger to me and more like a friend. However, the great difference between my mother's family and that of my father was that the latter had an inherent comic perspective.

Now let me introduce you to the other members of the family who all lived under the same roof. There was Dwarka Nath Kher, who had earned the unenviable distinction of failing seven times in the eighth grade in school. In fact, the oft-repeated sentence by the teachers was: 'His head is as thick as the desk he sits on.'

There is the issue of the landmark 'achievement', the totally helpless school principal, on the unanimous recommendation of the teachers, who by then had no idea what to do with him, promoted him to the ninth grade on what was described as 'compassionate grounds' because his classmates had started calling him UNCLE. He was the only student in his class who needed to shave!

Every new teacher, and even a new principal, would often get very confused as they couldn't distinguish the class teacher from my uncle. You will be amazed to learn that my uncle's 'academic record' has not been broken for the past 65 years and I imagine it will remain that way for the next 65 years too. In fact, pondering over his mark sheet once, the new principal of the school realised that he would never get to read a document of this kind, ever again. He felt that that in itself was enough reason to read out the report card before the entire school in the morning assembly. Hence, the next morning, the principal stood there, with my uncle next to him and read out:

Mathematics: Out of 100 marks, required to pass is 35, Dwarka Nath has scored ZERO.

Social Studies: Out of 100 marks, required to pass is 35, Dwarka Nath has scored TWO-AND-A-HALF.

General science: Out of 100 marks required to pass is 35; Dwarka Nath has scored SIX . . .

This means that out of 750 marks, required for passing 265; Mr Dwarka Nath has scored EIGHTEEN.

Years later, I creatively incorporated a reference to my ignorant uncle in a quirky scene in Aditya Chopra's 1995 blockbuster, *Dilwale Dulhania Le Jayenge* (The big-hearted will take away the bride), where I introduce my son, played by Shah Rukh Khan, to his ancestors through the picture gallery.

The only 'regular' people were my father and my grandfather. I grew up surrounded by a medley of amusing relatives, in a light-hearted atmosphere filled with much laughter. They were ordinary folks but with heart of gold, filled with native wisdom—always there for each other as one big family unit. To this day, I don't like solitude even in holiday destinations. I like being around people and love crowded cities like Mumbai, Delhi, New York and London. Unlike some of my friends, I don't like the concept of a holiday in isolated destinations like the Himalayas or in a desert.

Uncle Dwarka Nath was married to Tosha, a much younger village girl from Badarwa, a very *chulbuli* (perky) personality who was ready to marry Dwarka Nath despite his academic misfortunes. His only consistent article of clothing was his Kashmiri pyjamas that had his *nada* (string) hanging loosely to be seen by one and all. I can still recall a very funny visual of Dwarka Nath and Tosha: he used to have a funny habit of shutting his eyes completely whenever he had a temper tantrum. That means he would yell at her with his eyes closed. In the middle of tirades, Tosha, being the much more playful half, would jump away from the direction of Dwarka tirade. As soon as he opened his eyes again, he would be caught unaware and be staring at a blank wall, turn to Tosha once again, and re-start his lecturing, closing his eyes once again! My brother and I would be watching from the other room, struggling to keep our laughter in check, while Dwarka Nath himself would struggle to keep his head straight—let alone his tantrums! He was just one of the many humorous personalities I've had the pleasure of growing up with, who I still remember vividly to this day.

I had another uncle, Mohan Lal Kher, who had lost one eye to plague in Betul (now in southern Madhya Pradesh), and therefore used to wear dark glasses (or goggles as we used to call them). He had an answer for everything. He sported a 007 belt and would do a poor imitation of the Special Agent, so we used to refer to him as James Bond. His wife, my chachi, Rupa, was a character straight out of a funny movie or a novel. Middle-aged, plumpish and possessing a very jovial nature, she had two teeth missing in front. Hence, she used to lisp while talking and, naughty as we were, we used to make her laugh a lot and, in her laughter, she would release a lot of air from her mouth. It was a hilarious sight and we children would burst into peals of uncontrollable laughter. But she was a good sport and would laugh with us which encouraged us even more. They had five sons.

Brijnath Kher—whose wife's name was also Dulari—a junior officer in Baramulla Match Factory, was a man who always insisted on speaking in English—even within the family, where hardly any of us knew the language. He sported this small moustache that was fashionable at the time, having seen the 1939 American epic historical romance film, *Gone with the Wind,* adapted from the 1936 novel by Margaret Mitchell, and imagining himself as our family's own Clark Gable. But the biggest asset he left me with was his passion for collecting family photographs. All the pictures I have today of those times are from his collection only, and I will forever be grateful for his diligence in keeping these memories in safe storage throughout the years.

Brijnath had two sons and two daughters, one of whom we call affectionately Kakaji, who was worried that he was losing hair after noticing that Lux soap bar in the house had more hair than soap. As it is, we come from a family prone to losing hair, and so he resorted to a curious fix for fighting nature's way: every night, Kakaji used to sleep with a comb, a mirror and hair spray under his pillow. And in the middle of the night, he would get up, adjust his hair, and sleep peacefully thinking this was doing him a service for his scalp! Needless to say, I didn't try and pick up this routine, but the thought still tickles me.

Pyarelal Kher is the youngest of my uncles, and also the most intelligent. He was the first official graduate of the family and today lives in Delhi. Pyarelal was the editor of the SDB (Sanatan Dharama Bhargava) College magazine and presented me my first novel, Maxim Gorky's *Mother*. In those days, many were translated in Hindi under the Indo-Russian treaty. I remember Pyarelal as a very strict person also. Not only was he married to Neelam who is hands down the best cook in the family, he was also very particular about his habits—aristocratic even—and always wanted his *aloo tikki* (vegetable cutlet) with his meals. He worked in the Intelligence Bureau (IB), a great source of pride for himself and our family, and always had a very cultured, educated demeanour. He struck me as someone very learned, and I was fascinated by his office work. He used to write letters and would use extremely verbose and flowery language, at times bombastic. He would challenge us to interact with the world outside of our little bubble. Today, as the only eldest surviving family member of my father's generation, his very presence in my life makes me feel immensely blessed.

I must mention my bua (my father's sister), Raj Mohini who we affectionally called Tit-gigri. She was one of the most affectionate and loving people I knew and played a big part in my upbringing. I remember this incident when my mother gave me a bath, and I got some soap stuck in my throat. You cannot imagine the kind of protective instinct this induced in Tit-gigri, who got very upset with my mother on my behalf.

Tit-gigri's husband was Narayan Kaul, a very tall man compared to my Bua. He was a very dignified man with a dry sense of humour. We used to go to their house often for delicious food. One day, he said to us, '*Kheer banayi hai tumhare liye*' (We've made some delicious *kheer* [a common Indian dessert made of milk and rice] for you). We arrived to find the tables with tall cups filled to the brim with delicious kheer. While we dug in, we were jolted to find that the cups weren't as deep as they looked, and the kheer was more a teaser—a small morsel rather than a mouthful, and somehow this episode gave Narayan a joy to no end.

I didn't appreciate this humour at the time, but looking back, humour was ever-present throughout my family. In those days, decorum and etiquette weren't things we discussed, only things to be experienced and learnt from. We did not operate under ill-will or any bad intentions, but instead accepted each other as we were, and managed our day-to-day lives with a dash of mischief and mayhem.

I admit that family did, and does even today, matter to me a great deal. I recall a proverb relating to parenting told to me by a friend that has stayed with me all these years: 'In our quest to give our children what we didn't have in our childhood, we forget to give them what we had!' He was referring to parents neglecting to narrate the epics such as the Ramayana and the Mahabharata, or reading bedtime stories, to their children in these days of electronic gizmos and the almost ubiquitous presence of television and Internet.

I was fortunate to have grown up in a pre-television era. The radio was our window to the world, though the elders invariably tuned in only to the news bulletins or *bhajans* (religious songs). In that era, the patriarch of our family, my grandfather, would regularly tell my numerous cousins and other relatives including my brother and myself spiritual and moralistic tales from the aforementioned epics, with each story having a lesson. Chanting a hymn: 'Do all deeds to the best of your ability and care not for the results,' was one of his favourite sayings, whose source is the eternal Bhagavad-Gita—the holy book of the Hindus. This is the karma yoga concept. Another memorable saying of his, which I quote frequently is: '*Bhiga hua aadmi baarish se nahin darta*' (a person who is drenched does not fear the rain).

However, even in those days, we kids sought fun and entertainment and didn't relate to such lofty concepts as elucidated by my grandfather. It is only now that I recall these invaluable lessons with pride and affection! Indeed, at that young age, we preferred stories from my grandmother, Kalawati!

My grandmother's oft-repeated story began thus: 'Children, once there was a king who had three daughters, but he never loved the youngest one.' Apart from this beginning, every other detail in the story kept on changing, with every recitation. The king's name was Abhijeet Singh one day; the next day, it was Vikramaditya. The third day it could be Harishchandra. The daughters' names too kept varying. One day they would be Kamla, Bimla and Nirmala. And if grandmother had kept a fast on a particular day for religious reasons, then the names were specifically Durga, Saraswati and Lakshmi (after the three main Hindu Goddesses).

Whatever their names, in the story, the king never loved his youngest daughter. But it was this very daughter who looked after him in his ageing days, when almost everyone had deserted him. In the 1970s, during my training days at the National School of Drama in New Delhi, I realised that my grandmother, throughout my childhood, had been repeating simplified versions of William Shakespeare's highly acclaimed tragedy *King Lear* with different names for the characters each time she narrated it.

Grandmother also enjoyed telling us ghost stories, changing her voice to suit the character. They would be related in a staccato manner and would invariably start like this: 'Children, it was a full-moon night and there was darkness everywhere . . .' In spite of a full moon, why was it dark all around? We never asked her to clarify that detail as we didn't want to disturb her flow! She went on: 'The princess was alone in the palace. All the servants were off for the day and the king [her father] and the queen [her stepmother] had left on a pilgrimage. She was sleeping in her bedroom. Suddenly, a wolf howled, and the bedroom window opened with a bang. A gust of wind entered the room. The princess woke up with a start. She noticed that the frame of her stepmother's portrait on the wall was shaking vigorously. The princess got very scared and tried to light a candle. She somehow managed to do so. But the candle got extinguished due to the strong wind.' While the story would remain the same every time she narrated it to us, she would go on to complete the tale, with a different ending each time!

Power failures were a common occurrence in Shimla and the nights were inky dark. (We used to study by candlelight or lantern light whenever the electricity performed a disappearing act.) Whenever grandmother came up with ghost stories, we children, out of fear, would sleep close to her at night. Once, grandmother thought she really saw a ghost and screamed out loudly only to realise, a little later, that it was her own shadow on the wall projected by a lantern's light that had freaked her out!

In the hustle and bustle of life, grandparents are the ones closest to the children as they have all the time in the world to satiate the curiosities of the little minds. They are also the repository of family values. Thanks to them, my grandfather in particular, I was exposed to a lot of authentic qualities, some of which I have imbibed. He was a civil engineer; one of his important projects was the construction of a helipad in the Shimla area. To swing the deal his way, a contractor, offered him a bribe of Rs 30,000, which was really a huge sum in the 1950s. In fact, the president of India's monthly salary was just a third of the amount! But do you know what my grandfather did?

Next morning itself, he penned his resignation letter. When his boss asked him why he was quitting, my grandfather replied: 'Sir, today I am not in need of more money, and that is why I would never accept a bribe. But what if someday I may need the money . . . and have to accept bribes? Hence, to avoid such a situation in future, I don't want a job in which I may be tempted to accept a bribe!'

Perhaps unbelievable, but true! I proved to be a fitting heir to my grandfather when in early 2011, in different parts of India, I found people constantly complaining about corruption, but doing very little about it. *Have we become cynical to life around us*? I would often ask myself. Or is that we (the highly successful lot in various fields, including politicians) have become very selfish because we do not want to stick our necks out and stand up for principles and values as we are scared that our possessions would be snatched away from us and we would have to start our journey all over again. So, I decided to step forward and in April 2011, took a stand and came out openly in support of Anna Hazare the Indian social activist who led movements to promote rural development, increase government transparency, and investigate and punish corruption in public life.

My disappointing experiences down that path I have described in detail in subsequent chapters.

Looking back, there is no reason why anyone should find it difficult to stay close to their roots and remain grounded even after they taste success. The friends you make during your childhood remain the closest to you throughout your life. They have organically melded with you as a person, evolved through the growing up years. They are the ones who have seen you in all evolving avatars: laughing and crying; fighting or retreating; in success and in failure; in the classroom and in the playing field. They are the ones with whom you have shared your darkest secrets, fears, likes and dislikes. You never feel the need to hide anything from them.

These are your buddies in the truest sense of the word. They can be as close to you as your underwear and as comfortable as your favourite old T-shirt. Yes, you may make friends in your later years, in college or in professional circles. In their company, you can peel away your outer layers and just be *yourself*. Yet, many of us choose to drift apart from our buddy gang when we become more successful than the rest of them. In the process, we are casting away our anchors and cutting loose from perhaps the only group of people who can hold a mirror to us and keep us truly grounded. It is often said that success makes us lonely. That is because we choose to become lonely. We have no one to blame but ourselves. My childhood comic book also comprised our neighbours who were an essential part of our lives. Our immediate neighbour (in 4/3 Nabha House) was R. K. Sharma, who worked at Gainda Mull Hem Raj, the famous departmental store on the Mall Road. His wife was chachiji (aunt) to us and they had two sons Kewal and Raj and a slightly plumpish daughter, Bholi bhenji—a sister to all of us. It was quite customary in those days that all neighbourhood girls were given the status of sisters. Adjoining them was the S. K. Malhotra family comprising of five daughters—Gogi, Bubbly, Pinky,

Kanchan and Sunita. I used to like Gogi. I was about ten then, but I do remember that though Gogi was not the best looking of the five daughters, she was the most outgoing one and when we played games she would allow me to hold her hand. This always thrilled me. Another neighbour Mulk Raj and his wife Mulki who remained constantly unwell and instead of tying a muffler she would tie a sweater on her head—a very comic couple.

At 6/4, Nabha Estate, lived Mrs Bajaj, who appeared very strict but, in reality, was kind-hearted and was liked by one and all. She was our school principal and I would normally carry her bag to school and would feel very important and privileged doing this. She would be pleased too and blessed me every day. I think I instinctively learnt how to get on the good graces of people.

Then there were Kashmiri pandit families—the Rainas, the Mattos, and the Pandits among others. Matto saab and his wife Rani aunty had three daughters with truly unusual names—Lovely, Pupli and Baboo (the latter name is a common male name) and the story went that Matto saab desperately wanted a son after two daughters but when the third daughter was born he decided to give her a male name.

Then there was Uma aunty who had this peculiar habit of glaring at us with her huge, bulging eyes even under normal circumstances. And they grew even bigger and more menacing when she flew into a rage. We were terrified of her until one day a monkey helped to dispel those fears. Monkeys were rampant then in Shimla as they are even now. Hordes of them used to swoop down from the nearby trees and snatch away many of the garments that were hung out to dry on the clotheslines. This seemed to be their favourite pastime. One had to engage in a subtle art of negotiations with them: gesture and offer rotis or bread so they would imitate you and return your garments. Mostly everyone was well versed with this tactic.

One day, a bunch of us happened to witness Uma aunty's 'parleys' with a somewhat aggressive monkey to get her saree back. The simian somehow sensed, quite rightly as it turned out that she was not going to part with the bread. As she lunged forward to snatch the saree from his left hand, while withholding the bread, he landed a tight slap on her face with his right hand and fled. Uma aunty was completely rattled by the monkey's action. She was so dazed that she began spluttering incoherently. From that moment, we stopped being petrified of her.

Every home was open to all the neighbourhood children at all times. There were no restrictions and we could share their meals or snacks or games. The lives of people around us was similar to ours. Nobody was better off, or worse off, for that matter. And even if there was one, one could not see the difference. India had just attained Independence less than 10 years back, causing an enormous amount of upheaval in everyone's lives and families were still dealing with the aftermath. To our young eyes, people were still patriotic, sharing their joys and reservations with each other.

I was not a reclusive child, but a very outgoing and carefree one. That's because I grew up in a content atmosphere where the inner and outer worlds I inhabited coexisted in harmony with each other. The inner circle of my family lived in harmony even though we could barely make ends meet and this gave me a great sense of security. My world outside too seemed to ebb and flow in unison. My stable childhood taught me above all it is family I treasure the most. Even today, when confronted with severe trials and tribulations in life, I recall the humour-laced milieu that I was raised in and draw sustenance, confidence and inspiration from it. I have learnt, that whatever be the adversities one faces, if one approaches the situation with a humorous perspective, then one is spared the angst, the tension and the stress that are nowadays part and parcel of day-to-day life and living.

Friends who have known me since decades are always wondering why I never lose my cool. My closest associates . . . my family . . . my office staff . . . has never seen me lose my temper, or react harshly, whatever be the circumstances. Humour has been a handy tool for coping with, and overcoming, many crisis-ridden situations in my career. Most certainly, unknowingly this has been the most valuable life legacy from my childhood.

Now you know why I call my childhood a happy one—because I never felt that we were very deprived. Instead of paucity, I was sustained by the warmth of togetherness.

3

SHIMLA—THE ONE-TIME QUEEN

Shimla, once commonly known as the 'Queen of Hill Stations' is located at an altitude of over 2200 metres (about 7250 feet). It is a quiet, quaint, picturesque hill station and used to be the summer capital of British India in the pre-independence era (before 15 August 1947), right through the 1950s and 1960s. It was renowned as 'an exquisite and sensitive place' where artistes and writers painted and wrote. Shimla was the subject of wonderful odes by well-known English novelist and poet Rudyard Kipling (1865 to 1936) and the noted Mexican poet Octavio Paz (1914 to 1998). In 1945, Henry Sharp (an English official) wrote in his widely read book, *Goodbye India*, 'Anyone who visits Shimla for the first time is bound to be struck by two things: it is silent, it is scenic. Its silence you can get nowhere else, and when it is scenic, I mean it wears the appearance of a stage-setting, for example as in the first act of a light opera.'[2]

With the advent of the 1970s, the hill station started losing its earlier charm and elegance and began deteriorating rapidly. With the passage of time, coupled with the pressures of the local population explosion as well as the rapid influx of tourists virtually year-round, the age-old infrastructure was simply unable to cope with the demands of the changing times. I was horrified to learn that in late May and early June 2018, the city faced a massive water shortage and the common people were forced to stand in long queues with their buckets and jerrycans to get a meagre quota of water from tankers! Tourists—a major source of income for the state (Himachal Pradesh)—were advised to stay away. This saddened me deeply.

In most hill stations, one can actually feel the romantic atmosphere, given the delectable and fabulous climate apart from the myriad bounties of nature. Shimla was no exception. Back in the 1950s, all of us, my relatives and friends included, were enthralled by all that Shimla offered. The vertiginous snow-clad peaks, the deep verdant forests, the magical mountain streams that sparkled when touched by the sun's rays, the maze of lanes and bylanes, the splendid and architecturally unique buildings and, above all, the city's 'centrepieces'—the Mall Road and the Ridge, with its stately and imposing 1857-built Christ Church, the Shimla Municipal Library with its Tudor style of construction with sections of the woodwork in the roof left exposed, the Band Stand and the Boy's Scout Hut.

The Mall Road (about 6 km long) is studded with showrooms, departmental stores, shops selling a wide variety of curios, handicrafts and jewellery, restaurants and cafés and theatres. On this road, stands the historic Gaiety Theatre (set up in 1887, the golden jubilee year of England's Queen Victoria), the long-surviving India Coffee House, which was, and still is, my favourite haunt, and what is known as the 'Scandal Point'. The last mentioned derived its name (so the story goes) from the scandal that resulted when a former Maharaja of Patiala (now a city in Punjab, India) eloped with a viceroy's daughter during the British rule.

Our official address then was: 4/4 Nabha House, Shimla 4. As time rolled by, on Independence Day (15 August) 1972, the postal index number (PIN) code was introduced by the Indian Posts and Telegraphs Department and the scraggly '4' became a more respectable '171 004'. As I mentioned earlier, our house had just one long hall, a kitchen and a bathroom. All 14 occupants shared the common bathroom and toilet which were located outside the house. The bathroom was situated at the entrance to the house, but the common toilet was situated some distance away—a common practice in those days. You can well imagine the 'competition' for gaining access to this vital 'outlet' was nothing short of fierce, especially in the mornings.

The main hall, which had a small prayer area in one corner comprising of several idols and images of various gods and goddesses installed by my highly devotional mother and grandparents, was a multipurpose and multi-utility area. It served as a sitting room during the day and a bedroom at night.

Framing the back of the house was a wooden veranda the length of the house. The view from here was breathtaking since it overlooked the majestic and grand Shivalik range of the Himalayas covered with multitudinous vegetation. Sitting there for hours together on a *takhtposh* (wooden bed), I would watch the tall oaks, surging up to the skies and enjoy listening to the chirping of the hordes of birds.

A small path in front of our house led to the base of a nearby mountain, again, studded with trees and a variety of plants and bushes. Mother Nature seemed to embrace our family lovingly!

As I grew up, I came to learn that my ancestral home and the adjoining ones, all were said to be part of the Nabha Estate which was originally used by the erstwhile rulers of Nabha, Maharaja Hira Singh and his son, Maharaja Ripudman Singh Nabha—the surname derived from the former princely Phulkian dynasty in the Punjab that was merged into India in 1948. (Nabha is now a city in Punjab, India.)

All the houses were built on a sharp incline; so, if we had to visit the market or elsewhere, we had to climb a steep path to reach the main artery of Shimla called Cart Road. Our primary school was close to our home and so was the railway station.

I recollect that there used to be a naashpati tree and a babugosha tree near our house—the two varieties of pear. I was partial to the latter since it was sweeter and more succulent. As children, all of us used to liberally climb these trees to pluck and gorge on the fruits, as often as we could. Some of us used to secretly build tree houses complete with a provision for padlocks to store our valuables such as rare coins, colourful matchbox labels or stamps of different countries. I recall the unique one paisa coin with a hole in it—similar to a doughnut, though much smaller. One could string 20 or so together and fashion a necklace.

Of all the flowers, I loved the hydrangeas because of their popular large heads which had various shades of white, blues and light purple and also the passion flowers (Passiflora) which produces regularly showy flowers with a distinctive corona. As youngsters, we used to call them *ghadi phool* (clock flowers) because they had on the inside three or four strands resembling the hands of a clock. Another favourite were the rhododendrons with their evergreen and somewhat leathery leaves, long and thin, growing alternately on the stems—the upper surface dark-green and glossy, the underside fuzzy. As soon as the snows started melting and the air turned warm, hundreds of clusters and dark red flowers in the shape of bells bloomed. I used to wait a whole year for this season.

The plant that I, like all my friends, detested the most was the stinging nettle known as *bichu butti* in Hindi. '*Lag jaye to current marti hai*' (Touch it and it gives an electric shock) was the oft-repeated warning. It certainly had a scorpion's sting to it for wherever it touched the skin, it led to swollen rashes that felt itchy and painful for hours on end, and at times, could go on for days.

During summer and winter holidays and whenever we got the slightest opportunity, we used to rush outdoors and play for hours on end. Among the most preferred games was *gilli-danda*—a popular street sport played with a *gilli* (a small, oval-shaped piece of wood) and a *danda* (a long wooden stick). This game was dubbed the 'poor' man's cricket. Other games included lagori or phittu (seven stones) and the two most popular traditional tag games in the Indian subcontinent: kho-kho and kabaddi. The best part was that none of these games required any costly equipment or specialised kits. All that one needed were skill, stamina and perseverance—all useful qualities.

We also used to spin tops with reckless abandon and play a variety of games with marbles, where accuracy was the key requirement.

Of course, like all youngsters, we used to squabble amongst ourselves about seemingly trivial matters, shamelessly cheat over points in a game, push each other, throw the weaker person on the ground, but by the next morning, we made peace with each other and were inseparable friends again. Events of the previous day were forgotten. All these activities led to an unmistakable sense of bonding and camaraderie, which proved useful in later years. Those were innocent days; we made do with so little and were easily satisfied and always appreciative of everything we had.

As time went by, I did try my hand at other sports such as cricket, hockey and badminton in school but with little success. Any team I was selected for would look for the first available excuse to throw me out. I recall that once when I was selected for the cricket team, the captain ensured that I was the twelfth man. And, by default, if I did get a chance to swing the bat, I would always come up empty-handed. Yet despite these failures, I myself did not feel like a failure. I was a positive young person, always full of boundless energy and seeking new outlets.

Like most hill stations in India, Shimla too, had been blessed with stately mountains, dense jungles, lush waterfalls and spectacular landscapes. Every time I think of Shimla, I recall vividly the small, sparkling streams that ran through the hill station or down the mountainsides, adding to the beauty of the scenery, which lets one's imagination soar to poetic heights. I am here reminded of the highly acclaimed shayar (poet) Sahir Ludhianvi's exquisite lines:

> *Parbat upar khidke khole, jhaanke sundar bhor, chale pawan suhani*
> *Nadiyon key yeh raag raseele, jharon ka yeh shor, bahe jhar-jhar pani*[3].

Atop the mountain, with a window open, dawn peeps out and a pleasant breeze wafts by,
The notes of the river are lush, the waterfall creates a din and the gurgling water flows by.

From the veranda that wrapped my humble home, I would look at the world outside and dream of the vast possibilities that lay beyond. It spirited me to a different world and where I could soar without wings, dream unlimited, visualise endless possibilities while I watched the clouds in the sky. With the changing seasons my imagination continued to meander. In the winters, I watched the snow-covered mountains even as the snow slid off the giant ancient trees. Every once in a while, I would see a helicopter landing on the army's Annandale ground or taking off from there. The tin roofs of the houses painted mostly green or at times red, the monkeys jumping on them and creating a massive racket, the raindrops hitting the tin roofs, all created a music of their own. This was my little world—a world of some realities but plenty of dreams and numerous fantasies! My childlike awe and keen sense of observation for the world around me enriched me immensely both as a person and my craft as an actor. To this day, it might be the reason I feel very proud of the fact that Shimla is my home and I never get tired of introducing myself with these words—I am Anupam Kher from Shimla.

A short distance from my house was my favourite *halwai* (sweet shop) owned by Santosh who had given his son a very odd name—Mirchu. Mirchu was born cross-eyed and Santosh was very upset about it and had nicknamed him Chabakka (which seemed even odder). Santosh was partial and generous to me of all the youngsters in the neighbourhood since he secretly wanted a son like me—fair skinned with a pleasant smile. To get his father's approval, poor Mirchu, who was just 6 or 7 and hated his name, would try hard to adjust his eyes. I would often see him retreat into a corner and practise fixing them.

Also etched in my mind are the two barbers of our locality, Tinchu Ram and Polu Ram, especially the former for 'introducing' my brother Raju and me to the stage. While Polu Ram, was a kind and gentle person, Tinchu Ram, was a crafty salesman, who was in the habit of taking on a client, cutting half his hair and, if a new customer came, he would immediately attend to him leaving the first one stranded in the chair! Years later, I discovered that even in Tirupati, barbers use the same practise so as not lose any customer. Tirupati is a pilgrim centre located in southern Andhra Pradesh, thronged by multitudes of devotees throughout the year, many of whom 'sacrifice' their hair as an offering to Lord Balaji the principal deity.

Polu was serious by nature, whereas Tinchu was a natural comedian and a remarkable storyteller. His features were like a caricature: a long, hooked nose on a slightly twisted face. At the local Ram Leela (the dramatic folk re-enactment, according to the ancient Hindu epic Ramayana of the life and times of Lord Rama) during the annual Dussehra festival, he used to perform a few hilarious acts in between the Ram Leela enactment. He soon became some sort of a legend in Shimla. His group was called Tinchu and Company.

During one of the Dussehra celebrations, Raju and I were thrilled to be a part of the Ram Leela in the role of Vanarsena—Lord Hanuman's monkey brigade as a *vanar* (who helped Lord Rama in his epic battle with Ravana, when he had abducted Sita, Lord Rama's wife). In those growing years, I also remember clearly my first role on stage—that of a vanar-monkey—at the local Ram Leela performance. You might ask, why such a vivid memory of a token role? Well, the whole idea was to get closer to Tinchu Ram who used to puff away at a beedi before going onto stage.

What a strange sight, seeing Tinchu Ram in white pyjamas, and Sita, who was my best friend, adjusting 'her' saree and blouse, which had two small apples (yes!) inside to function as her breasts. Sita used to see Tinchu Ram's act from the wings and laugh out loud, all day long. One day, when the *Lanka Dahan* (burning of Lanka) scene was going on, I threw a fit because I wanted my tail to be burnt, just like that of Lord Hanuman! 'Why should only Hanuman's tail be burnt and not mine?' I shouted. Those around me tried to pacify me by saying that Hanuman, the great leader of the Varansena (monkey army brigade), had a tail long enough to set fire to Ravana's kingdom. But I was ready to compete even with the great legends, for there has always been that fire in me to be noticed above and beyond what others saw of me. I truly believe that, if we keep making space for everyone else, on stage and in life, we will never make space for ourselves. Just the other day, I was reminding an up-and-coming actor about this very lesson, one that I continue to follow in the work I do today.

I recall an incident which seemed insignificant at the time, and only now do I fully understand how mature and non-judgemental my parents were. They taught me by example showing me how they treated other people, regardless of their background. I was about seven or eight years old then. Balasaram used to clean our toilets, which in those days were very rudimentary brick facilities with no flush and a pan from which human waste had to be collected and cleaned out every day. Balasaram and his ilk used to live in a separate colony on the outskirts, where they decided to hold a Lav-Kush play. Lav and Kush were the sons of Lord Rama and Sita. It was a sequel to the Ram Leela production. They cast Raju as Sita and me as Lav. After the play, they graciously offered us dinner and topped off the meal with halwa—a dense, slightly gelatinous dessert, made from semolina (*suji*) whose primary ingredients were clarified butter (*ghee*), flour and sugar. We gleefully accepted this sumptuous meal. When we came home, my father asked us to sit down for dinner and we told them we had already eaten at Balasaram's home, at which point, I noted my parents exchanging some glances, but they did not utter another word to us. During those years, the majority of parents had certain preconceived notions about which household we were allowed to eat at, but my family never held such judgements. It is because of their tolerance that I have maintained my open-mindedness to people of all walks of life, regardless of their differences in background or culture.

My mornings in my childhood home used to be amazingly peaceful. In front of our house, there was a temple, in close proximity to the St Michael's Cathedral dating back to the Victorian Era (precisely 1886). Its architecture was of a typical French-Gothic style. Adding to the morning chantings was the nearby gurdwara with the *shabad kirtan* (hymns) sung well before dawn. I could hardly follow the words of the verses recited in Gurmukhi, but the music ensured that my day would start on a very serene note. The sounds of *bhaijees* (devotional singers), singing to the accompaniment of the harmonium and the tabla from the gurdwara, coupled with the intonations inside my home as my grandfather recited his lengthy daily prayers, accompanied by short ones by my father, have remained with me to this day. This juxtaposition of sounds from the gurdwara and those from within my house created a blissful atmosphere all around me.

It was perhaps because of such a tranquil atmosphere as a child that I experienced no weighty stress or pressure. In fact, contrary to the children of today, one did not even know what it meant to feel that emotional burden.

Snowfall in Shimla was a very profound event for us youngsters. It was sheer magic. We would go to sleep like on any other cold wintry night and wake up to a town painted white as though by a spell . . . snow all around . . . like the clouds had descended on earth. In the cold, freezing temperatures, one could feel a great deal of warmth and at two different levels—first being the warmth of the people, shaking hands, hugging and wishing each other, particularly during the first snowfall and then there was the warmth of the heavy woollens. I recall six of us children sleeping on one mattress and I would try and be the first one to occupy the middle position—not always successfully—so that with the others on my two sides, I would be well protected. Each snowfall would produce overnight many artistes among us and that too of different kinds—good, bad and indifferent. Though I was very poor in my art class in school but to the surprise of many, I was very good at making snowmen and would receive many compliments. I would make them about three to four feet tall, with puffy cheekbones and well-chiselled facial features. I would use round coal pieces for the eyes, marbles to show the nostrils, carrots for the nose and the stones of the *rithas* (soapnuts) for the teeth. Into the mouth, I would insert a piece of chalk for a cigarette.

Even though Shimla has now deteriorated beyond recognition, my love for it has not diminished. My spirits lift whenever I revisit the city. It will always occupy a very special place in my heart as virtually every street and every lane and every nook and corner holds numerous memories of an irretrievable past. In addition to our five senses, our sense of childhood is one that stays with us forever. Even to this day, the smell of the pine tree anywhere in the world will instantly transport me back to my roots in Shimla.

My sense of nostalgia is succinctly summed up in that famous Mohammed Rafi melody:

Yaad na jaaye beete dino ki
Jaake na aaye jo din, dil kyun bulaae unhe?[4]

The memories of past days do not go away
Why does the heart beckon the days that have gone by and do not come back?

4

SCHOOL DAYS

$\mathscr{I}$ remember going to Lady Irwin School in Phagli located in the south of the town. Even though the name was Lady Irwin, there was nothing lady-like about the environment. It was a standard school where I studied for the first five years of my life. Of the many incidents that I can recall of my time there, one stands out. I was in the fourth standard when one of our teachers informed us that a much-revered holy baba (godman) was to visit the school the next day and to receive his blessings, we had to offer him something. My mother gave me five paise to offer to the baba—five being an auspicious number.

The next day in school, I discovered that though many students were giving their offerings to the holy man, there were some who had not and yet, they were not being punished. This caused me to change my mind and I decided not to offer him anything and instead, chose to spend the money on myself. I used up two paise on *churan ki golis* (small digestive balls made of asafoetida) and safely hid the balance three paise in my school bag. That afternoon, back at home, my mother asked me to sit down and finish my homework. Even though illiterate herself, she always made sure that my brother and I study as much as possible and wanted to ensure that we did not lag behind. And while doing so, since I could not find my 'rubber' (which were called erasers in those days), she turned my bag upside down and instead of the eraser, the three paise rolled out. She looked at me and I stared back at her. She then looked at the three paise. While I gazed at the coins, she asked: 'Where did you get this money from?'

Petrified and somewhat with a stammer, I answered: 'I don't know . . . somebody must have put it there.'

'Why would anyone put three paise in your bag?' she asked sternly.

'How would I know?' I answered somewhat defiantly.

'Are you sure?' she asked, this time threateningly.

'Yes, I don't know who put it there,' I replied.

She then said in a grim tone: 'Okay . . . so you won't tell me . . . I will teach you a lesson.'

With her nostrils flaring in anger, she took my clothes off and pushed me out of the house— literally stark naked—and yelled: 'Only when you remember how this money came into your bag, can you enter this house.'

Imagine how a nine-year-old boy would have felt standing in the buff outside his house, trying hard to maintain some semblance of dignity. Neighbours and strangers who were passing by, including a gaggle of giggling girls, gaped at me! Mirchu, who was also passing by, came up with an obscene comment. Fortunately, it was summer; imagine my plight if it had been winter!

I stewed over my predicament, wondering how to tell my mother the truth! Perhaps, I would have done so if I had an inkling of the severity of her punishment. But now that I had told a lie, I was determined to stick to it. The afternoon and evening hours went by at a snail's pace and the sunset happened gradually around 7 p.m. My father came back from office and was horrified to see me in that peculiar predicament. He shouted at my mother through the closed door, 'Open the door.'

She responded, equally angrily: 'You want me to open the door . . . you want to bring him in? In that case, you too stay outside.'

So, my father asked me what had happened. When I related the details, he said in a serious tone: 'The only way this problem can be solved is when you tell me the truth; otherwise she's not going to let us in.' He went on to say: 'The sight of you naked, with me beside you, out on the street is not a great optic. Because of you even I am feeling insulted, because now it is common knowledge that my wife is also punishing me. Moreover, my father is inside the house. What will he think? So, let's have the truth.'

I saw his reasoning and revealed everything.

He then asked several questions: 'But why didn't you tell this to your mother? What was the problem? Why didn't you tell her that many others too did not give offerings and hence, you spent two paise?'

'I would have got a thrashing,' I replied.

'But this,' he pointed out, 'is worse.' He added: 'Okay, now let me talk to her.'

He banged on the door and told my mother the real story. She said: 'No that is not sufficient . . . I am not going to let him forget this incident. He has to be taught a lesson . . . a moral he will not erase from his memory.

She opened the door, plucked the dreaded bichu buti (stinging nettle) plant that grew all over and hit my naked bottom with it. As the spikes of the plant pierced my skin, I jumped and howled in pain. Some of the neighbours witnessed the scene, but no one came to my assistance. Not a single family member showed any sympathy. The rashes remained for about three days. My bottom was itchy during that time, but I dare not scratch it in front of the others. I was hurt . . . felt degraded . . . humiliated . . . every time I stepped out of the house and faced someone. I held a grudge against my mother for a long time, almost a year or so, and did not talk to her in a normal manner. *How could she be so cruel? How could she do this to her own son?* I would ask myself. My cousins too were surprised at the treatment meted out to me for such a 'small' matter. For them, it was normal to tell white lies of this nature quite often and their parents too would take it in their stride . . . it never used to make any difference to them. *So why me* was the question that haunted me for a very long time.

The truth is, my mother taught me a lesson that day that has stayed with me throughout. The lesson was that unnecessary lying was not permitted with family as there were some values, you just didn't lose sight of. There's a saying that to whom much is given, much is tested, and I couldn't help but relate it to this incident. My mother disciplined me so much because she cared about me enough to make even this small incident, a lesson. That incident and the lesson learnt from it have stayed with me to this day.

Looking back, I think it was my mother's way of separating me from the other cousins in the house. They were all wonderful people but were singularly unmotivated with no goals, no ambition in life, and no desire to achieve something one day. My mother had great aspirations for me and Raju. She had married young, having given birth to me when she was just 19. As a young girl in her teens, she was burdened with looking after the entire household and performing numerous chores and errands. However, she was looking beyond the narrow confines of her universe and seeking a world of infinite possibilities for me and my sibling.

My father would leave for work at 7.30 in the morning, walk for almost 10 km to Chhota Shimla (where his office was located) and trudge back in the evening because during those days, there were no other means of transport. Those days when father returned home after a long day's work, he just wanted to spend a little time with the family, especially the children, without having to face any tension or friction. He certainly didn't want to encounter the sort of incident my mother did that particular evening. My father was seemingly different from my mother in the sense that he was not very keen on knowing what subjects I was studying, or whether or not I was involved in sports and games. Normally, he would just sign my report card without even looking at it. However, I remember once when I was in the seventh standard, as always, I gave him my report card to sign. He looked at it as if for the first time and said: 'Very low marks . . . against the 35 per cent pass cut-off, you have secured just 36-37 in every subject. Your highest is 38.' At the bottom of the report card, he saw my overall rank, which was 59. Then he asked me: 'How many students are there in your class?'

'Sixty,' I answered.

I remember clearly the scenario that followed. He sat down in the corner chair and, as he took off his woollen muffler, I thought he was going to slap me or punish me and was not going to sign my report card for never in the past had he taken so much time to study it. Breaking the long silence, he said: 'I want to tell you something.' In the short silence that ensued, a hundred thoughts went through my mind: *Oh, my God, what is he going to say . . . my report card is the same . . . similar . . . nothing different at all . . . with the same grades I have always scored. So, why is he scanning it today?* Finally, he observed: 'A student who stands first and tops the list is always tense and under great pressure because he or she has to score high to come first every time . . . to score the highest. He or she is always under pressure . . . stressed. Even if he or she comes second in the class, they feel disappointed. But a person who comes 59th can always score more marks to come 46th, 36th, 27th or 18th. So, try and come 46th next time.'

An unbelievable lesson I was taught that day and that too by a simple man—a mere clerk in the Forest Department of the state government. It reminded me of the renowned Austrian neurologist (and founder of psychoanalysis) Sigmund Freud's words: 'I cannot think of any need in childhood as strong as the need for a father's protection.'

In contrast to parental pressures one comes across almost everywhere nowadays, I had a gem of a father who had a wonderful sense of humour, which I appreciated a lot. His magnitude was reflected in the way he handled delicate situations. Once, during my teens, when I was walking down the Mall Road in Shimla with a girl, I suddenly saw him coming towards us from the opposite direction. Seeing my anxious and awkward and somewhat scared stance, the girl asked me what had happened to me suddenly. I told my companion that the man approaching was a neighbour and then greeted him loudly: '*Namaste uncleji!*'

Without missing a step, he shot back: '*Namaste beta* . . . Give my regards to your father!'

In my motivational speeches, I never get tired of mentioning that I am only 8 years younger than my beloved country. I feel a close kinship with my country as an elder brother and have experienced at close quarters, the pre- and post-Independence era struggles of India. Since it happened at an impressionable age, it made a lasting impact on me and probably that is why I am infused with a 'nationalistic fervour' which many question today.

During the school assembly at Lady Irwin School in Phagli, we all used to sing Muhammed Iqbal's famous patriotic song:

Sāre jahān se acchā, Hindositān hamārā,
Ham bulbulen hain is kī, yih gulsitān hamārā.

Better than the entire world, is our Hindustan,
We are its nightingales, and it is our garden abode.

It kept that spirit alive in my heart. During the 1962 China war, I would watch the soldiers of the Western Command Headquarters which was then located in Shimla as well as all the activity in the army barracks. I was only seven years old when I heard the sirens blare piercingly and we had to hide in the trenches outside our homes.

On 27 May 1964 afternoon, Mrs Bajaj called a special assembly of the school and announced with misty eyes and a choking voice: 'I want to tell you all that Chacha Nehru is no more.' I have a vivid visual of being dressed in khakhi shorts and a green and white check shirt, standing in the corridor and being affected enough to burst into tears. *Chacha Nehru nahi rahe* (Chacha Nehru is no more), I was muttering to myself. *How can it be that our beloved prime minister has left us? Oh my God, what will happen to us now?* (Prime Minister Jawaharlal Nehru who was affectionately known as 'Chacha' [uncle] was considered indispensable for the country at that time.)

Through my college years, I continued to imbibe the patriotic fervour all around me. Once, an army major came to address everyone and urged us to donate blood for the soldiers. I was so caught up in his passionate appeal that I found myself in a hypnotic trance that made me go inside the van where the blood was being drawn. Now, if you recall, I was very skinny. In fact, I was so thin that I could see through a keyhole with both my eyes. But nothing was going to hold me back that day! In the van, I was asked repeatedly that if I was sure that I wanted to donate blood. I was quite adamant. And lo and behold, I donated blood and promptly fainted and had to have a transfusion instead! That is how I found out that my blood group was 'O+'. We were all offered snacks that consisted of a boiled egg, some special biscuits and coffee along with a token sum for the blood donation.

Unlike many who were born years after me and have only heard stories of independent India, I lived through it and my involvement has only grown through the years. My *desh bhakti* (love for my nation) is rooted in my childhood and developed quite organically.

A boy named Nav Prakash Parihar was my first close friend. He was a resident of Ramnagar—an adjoining colony—and was in the same class as me in primary school. The son of an affluent public works contractor, he always showed me immense kindness. His lunch box contained a variety of food or snacks, unknown to most of us. One day, he brought something known as 'cutlets'—quite a novelty for me. There was three of them in his tiffin box. He gave me one which I found very delicious and then wished I could have more. He looked at me and, as if reading my thoughts, offered another one saying: '*Khaa le, khaa le yaar*' (Eat it, eat it buddy).

'But, let's share it equally—one-and-a-half each,' I said hopefully.

'*Arre, mein toh roz hi khaa lunga. Tu aaj khaa le. Aur tu bol toh tere liye roz le aaya karunga*' (Oh, I can have it every day. You eat it today. If you say so, I will bring them for you every day).

What an unusually genuine and kind gesture for a child, I think back to myself. Nav Prakash has remained a lifelong friend. His numerous generous offerings throughout the years make me think ordinary does not always mean 'not achieved anything'. Sometimes ordinary contains the extraordinary, and some people make their life more meaningful, thanks to their large heart and openness of mind. When I last met Nav Prakash a few months back, he was partially blind due to an eye ailment, but he was still as warm as always and as open-hearted as ever. He remains to this day an important link to my childhood. I can never forget his acts of kindness when we were both young impressionable students in the fifth standard.

I was a very average student in school and did not exactly shine in academics, but I had an inner, burning desire to succeed in life. So, with hardly any noteworthy achievements in academics or in sports, my only recourse for shinning in the spotlight on myself was to be on stage. Even here, my initial forays were nothing short of hilarious.

Though I have mentioned earlier my acting stints during the Ram Leela festivities, my principal moment of excitement came when I went up on stage in school for the first time. Mrs Bajaj our principal and fifth-grade teacher elected to stage a historical play for us to perform. It was based on the life of Prithviraj Chauhan, the courageous twelfth-century king, who repulsed attacks by Muslim invaders in North India. Those days, true to our colour prejudices, kings were always portrayed as fair-skinned! Hence, being the fairest student in the class, I bagged the title role.

And a milk vendor's muscular son, Nand Kishore (Nandu), played the role of Jaichand, the king of Kannauj. Nandu was five times my size and I was three times skinnier than what I am today.

According to the twelfth-century A.D. legend, Prithviraj Chauhan falls in love with Jaichand's sister Samyukta and takes her away despite fierce resistance from Jaichand. Jaichand then seeks the support of the Ghurids from Afghanistan in his fight against Prithviraj Chauhan. Jaichand's name has thus become synonymous with treachery. I had invited my whole family to watch the play and so had Nandu. My father knowing the end of the play was ecstatic. He knew I was going to be triumphant. Consequently, as the script went, I had to push Nandu down three times during the course of the play and my dialogue was to repeat this line thrice (at different points of time) when Nandu had to fall down each time:

Chala ja . . . chala ja . . . naa bakwas kar tu, Nandu gir!

Go away . . . go away . . . don't talk rubbish, Nandu fall!

After Nandu took the second fall, and I had just started speaking the dialogue for the third time (*Chala ja . . .*), his father stood up in the audience and suddenly interrupted me. He shouted for one and all to hear:

Nandu, ab ke gira toh tu ghar mat aiyoo.

Nandu, if you fall this time, don't you dare come home.

After that resounding threat, history was rewritten that evening on the stage of the school. Nandu turned the script on its head and gave up his submissive demeanour. And 'Jaichand' lifted 'Prithviraj Chauhan', threw him into the audience, almost into my father's lap and then asked his father:

Yeh lo bapu. Ab ghar aaoon?

There dad. May I come home now?

The audience, mainly made up of parents of the students, was in splits. The schoolteachers did not know what had hit them. And poor Mrs Bajaj never came to school for the next week or so!

That night, my father, disturbed after seeing his son being thrown into the audience by a classmate, told my mother: 'Bittu has become very weak. You should give him milk and almonds every morning so that both his body and mind can improve.'

My mother who had heard the same dialogue earlier too and was sceptical about the results it might produce and gave him a very sarcastic look and said in a low voice, as if to herself, 'If only we could afford them I would. But I am not sure they will make a difference.'

My father was a typical man of his times offering solutions which were not truly practical while my mother was always the more hands-on and down-to-earth person.

After the fifth standard, as my time at Lady Irwin primary school drew to a close, my family debated which school I should attend next. Various names were tossed around. I heard someone in the family suggesting St Edwards High School, not because of better education but only because it was on the way to my father's office near Chhota Shimla, which would enable us to go together. It was too expensive and hence rejected. Then the Harcourt Butler School, above the Ridge, was suggested and rejected, because it too was for the more affluent. This conversation would normally take place in the evenings among my parents, my uncles and my grandfather, all throwing in their two bits of advice for whatever it was worth. Finally, for financial reasons, it was decided that I would be going to the DAV (Dayanand Anglo Vedic) Higher Secondary School.

I was very thrilled that I was going to walk from the south of Shimla to the north of the town—a distance of about 8 km. The fascination of walking from Nabha House till Lakkar Bazar on the Ridge and passing through the grandeur of Shimla, comprising of numerous beautiful old buildings filled me with joy. First came the railway station where one could see the five-compartment, small narrow-gauge toy trains as well as the white coloured rail motor car which ran between Kalka (now in Haryana) and Shimla on the 56-mile (about 86 km) track passing through 103 tunnels. Then, there was the grand structure of the Gorton Castle built in stone set in lime (from 1901 to 1904) with a red galvanised iron roofing. This was followed by the 1896-97 cast-iron and steel Railway Board building. After that came the historical State Bank of India structure and then the six rectangular-shaped, spotlessly clean, green tin-roofed horizontal structures with the Indian Army flag flying in the breeze and where the guards stood in attention in their shining uniforms—the headquarters of the Western Command. These sights were always a great delight to watch. The other 'attractions' included the Mall Road, the famous India Coffee House, the Scandal Point, the Alpha Restaurant, the statue of the respected freedom fighter, Lala Lajpat Rai (1865 to 1928) and on the Ridge, one of the father of the nation, Mahatma Gandhi. They are all part of the unforgettable memories of my growing up years. These long-lasting, evergreen memories of my childhood capture the true beauty of my small-town roots. A place where the slow pace of life allows one to soak in all aspects of the environment—its sights and smells, until they all become an integral part of one's psyche.

In my new school, my uniform evolved into white shirts, blue sweater and grey trousers. The sixth standard for me started in the month of March and two years went by quickly without anything of significance. There was still nothing 'remarkable' about me. I had the same grades, the same humdrum subjects, as well as the same rankings in class.

DAV was, though, a much larger school than Lady Irwin and with more students and more teachers came more interesting personalities. Here I had a new audience with which to experiment with my comedy, but also various characters who provided comic inspiration! Satya Prakash, a tall, well-built man with a grim face, took his role as the school principal very seriously. I distinctly remember Sada Singh, our PT (physical training) teacher who habitually directed inappropriate comments at me. A few such incidents come to mind, and I mention them to highlight where I come from and the type of culture that was the norm in my little corner of the world. I look back on these moments as experiences that have moulded my behaviour. My current approach to life, my frequent 'political incorrectness,' my unwavering sense of wonders and determination to break the mould, they've all been a product of my culture and my surroundings.

And, indeed, even someone such as Sada Singh influenced me in that respect! Once, he saw me competing in a race during a sports class and cursing in Punjabi: *B*** ai ladka agar kalla daude ga tab bhi second hi aayega.* (Even if this *** runs alone, he will still come second). Of course, it was certainly derogatory, although the comment stuck with me more because of its humour than its intended offence. Even Sada Singh knew how to deliver a solid turnaround joke, and I kept these little nuggets squirreled away to serve me in my work in later years.

Another interesting anecdote: one afternoon, when I went to the school toilet to pee, I saw Sada Singh standing there. Not wanting to be disrespectful, I waited my turn, but upon seeing me he said: *'Aa kaka, tu wi aaja'* (Come son, you also come). It was too late to pretend to have never appeared and come back later, and I was quite embarrassed. Think of the situation, a teacher and a student in the school urinals, which unlike today, had no partitions between them. I went through the motions as one would expect, but my teacher, standing there well before me, was trying his level best but obviously was not able to urinate. I zipped up and left, and when Sada Singh came out, I pretended everything was normal and greeted him with a normal expression. He looked at me and said in Punjabi: '*Honda hain. Meri umar wich jad ponchega, te peshab karn which time lagu ga*' (It happens. When you reach my age, it will take time to pee). Direct as it was, but in Punjabi, it sounded cruder than it really is. In fact, there was clearly no subtlety in those days and that's how I grew up! Teachers or even parents were quite matter of fact in these matters and would say things like: '*Tatti kar laeyi?*', '*Peshab kar lita?*' and '*Lulli saaf kiti ke nahi?*' ('Did you shit?', 'Did you pee?' and 'Did you wipe and clean your penis or not?')

The peculiar traits of my teachers in school compensated for the humdrum happenings at home. In those pre-family planning days, I had a Hindi language teacher, Munni Lal Sharma, who had long forgotten how to smile and had seven daughters and a son, Arun. This, in a country like India, where the birth of a female child is still considered a big burden ... where the female infanticide is still a major cause for concern, having seven daughters was considered more of an encumbrance those days. I suppose he had only himself to blame for his libidinal excesses. Understandably, he was always worried about how he would get them married, because a daughter's wedding in India entailed then, as now, a huge expense. He would constantly scout the school premises for a potential son-in-law. Whenever any student's parents or guardians came to the school to meet him or any of the other teachers, he would always ask: 'Do you know a good groom for my daughter?' His biggest opportunity to grab a good catch was on the annual sports day or the Founder's Day, when hundreds of parents would gather in the school. His situation often reminded me of Stanley Donen's 1954 musical, *Seven Brides for Seven Brothers*, with that exceptional musical score by Saul Chaplin and Gene de Paul. The only difference was that here the roles were reversed and Munni Lal Sharma's story could have been *Seven Brothers for Seven Brides*. I presume that he must have found seven sons-in-law for his seven daughters over the years. But, were they seven brothers? If so, it would have been too much of a coincidence.

My geography teacher, Jai Ram, was one of a kind. His sole source of happiness every day came from thinking of fresh ways to somehow make students trip up in class so that he could punish them . . . and punish severely at that. Yes, in those 'Jurassic era' days, corporal punishment was a much-lauded, recommended practice as it was considered an integral part of enforcing a strong sense of discipline— not just at my school but in the code of schools nationwide. If Jai Ram couldn't find any fault with us, he would ask us convoluted questions in an even more confusing tone. For example, he would pick out a student randomly and ask in a stentorian voice: 'Is India within Asia . . . or . . . is Asia within India?'

The student would confidently answer: 'Sir, India is within Asia.'

'Think carefully and answer again . . . Is India within Asia . . . or . . . is Asia within India?' he would growl menacingly.

The student would ponder for a while and reply: 'Sir, I think India is within Asia.'

The teacher would then scream: 'You idiot, how many times do I have to ask you . . . Is India within Asia or is Asia within India?'

After being questioned three times, any student (even an otherwise bright one) would naturally start doubting himself and would blurt out: 'It is Asia that is within India, sir.'

As soon as Asia went into India, oh my God! It meant that Jai Ram's aim for the day had been painstakingly achieved and after which, the worst would come. 'Wrong!' he would shout. After which, he would give a tight slap to the student, pull him out of his seat while simultaneously twisting his ear, take him into a corner where all the students could see him and say: 'Asia in India . . . I will now teach you where Asia is . . . *Ab murga ban*' (become, i.e., sit like a rooster; it is a form of punishment).

The poor student, who had initially answered correctly, but was threateningly misled by the teacher, had to then take a position resembling that of a rooster, by squatting and then looping the arms behind the knees and firmly holding his ears, with the buttocks raised high—a position which itself is as painful as it is embarrassing. The teacher would then gleefully cane the lad four times on his backside. Only after this exercise had been completed, the teacher's urge to whack students for that day would be over.

Then there was the famous Hardarshan sir. He was fat . . . as fat as one could be. And to us, the students of the school, he looked like a cross between the Hollywood actor Oliver Hardy (one half of the legendary Stan Laurel and Hardy team—a comedy double act during the early classical era of American cinema) and roly-poly Asit Sen (the prolific Indian actor and comedian of the Hindi film industry who spoke his dialogues with a typical drawl). He was in the habit of pulling up his trousers as they would keep on slipping down as no belt could hold them. Finally, he switched to *galles* (suspenders) and became even more of a sight. Like a cartoon, when he walked with his feet to one side, his huge tummy would flop over to the other. One or two buttons of his shirt were always undone as his shirts could never quite fit him. On most days, his very sight brought out giggles all around.

But as soon as Hardarshan sir would enter the class, he would ask a question and then say: 'Those who know the answer, be seated . . . and those who don't, please stand up.' If you didn't know the answer and were standing, you would be caned four times. And if you didn't know the answer and were sitting, you would be caned eight times! I had found the easy way out—stand up to be caned four times, instead of eight. I did so for an entire year claiming that I did not know any answer to any question, which may or may not have been true!

In those times, many routines became games, and the games from my imagination interested me more than the tests that came with the curriculum or what was being written on the blackboard that we were told to copy word for word. What interested me were the characters, the behaviours, the quirks and the idiosyncrasies of the people around me—Nav Prakash Parihar, Nandu Kishore, Sada Singh, Jai Ram, and Hardarshan sir—all coexisting in their own insulated lives. My natural sense of observation and my fertile imagination etched everything vividly in my own mind's musings. The melting pot that was my school days remains the source code of my imagination, the fire behind the will to constantly mould truthful, universal characters.

5

Growing Up

All too soon, I realised that I was growing up. One day, as the neighbourhood boys and girls were playing a game of hide and seek, I hid in the bathroom. Soon a girl with the green eyes and a voluptuous figure too came in and huddled next to me. Every time she moved suggestively and her breasts brushed me, I was titillated and experienced my first erection and felt both embarrassed and excited. I tried my best to create some distance between her and myself. When we finally came out of our hiding place, she looked at me with a knowing smile as if to say, 'how risque'. For several days, I tried to avoid her while she, it seemed, needed no excuse to look out for me. At least, that's what I felt! My childhood innocence was dissipating.

The radio was to us what the internet is to teens today—our entire universe. Binaca Geetmala, a weekly programme of the top Hindi film songs from Radio Ceylon compered by the famous announcer Ameen Sayani was the highlight of our week. His baritone style of addressing the listeners with the words: '*Bhaiyo aur behno*' (Brothers and sisters) mesmerised generations for decades with its medley of songs interspersed with his inimitable style that brought joy into millions of homes. Years later, when I came to Bombay, meeting Ameen saab, face to face, was like meeting God.

Just as iconic as the Murphy radio, which relayed the strains of Binaca Geetmala, was the Murphy calendar depicting the chubby little cute toddler, which was often hung on the wall above the radio. Calendar art was an integral part of household decorations and calendars depicting various Hindu gods and goddesses was an endearing part of my growing up years.

Unwittingly I used my innate comic sense to my advantage. By the time I reached the ninth standard, I was quite a popular student. I could mimic effortlessly and make everyone laugh. On the first day in the class, I was deciding where to sit when I chanced upon an undersized nondescript boy sitting on a bench in the fourth row. I decided to sit next to him, simply because I didn't want to be seated in the first row, conscious of my low grades. Moreover, given my sense of fun, I knew there that I couldn't indulge in any pranks under the watchful eye of the teacher. Neither did I want to sit on the back bench which was automatically reserved for the worst students—a title I was not going to award myself. So, I went over to the somewhat timid looking boy and asked: '*Main baith jaaon idhar*?' (Can I sit here?).

He answered: '*Teri marzi*' (Your wish).

Quite magnanimously, I answered: '*Meri marzi chhod . . . teri marzi kya hai?*' (Forget my wish . . . what is your wish?).

Pat came his answer: '*Nahin*' (No).

I was taken aback but I shot back: 'Why?'

'I don't know, but I don't want you to sit next to me,' he answered nonchalantly.

'In that case, I will sit here only,' I said taking the seat and added. 'By the way, you will remember this day . . . remember it throughout your life.'

Yes, this is exactly what I said to him.

Then, as I sat down, with the needle of the compass from my geometry box, I carved my name Anupam Kher on the hard-wooden desk and told him: 'Whosoever will sit on this bench in the coming years will remember that once Anupam Kher sat here.'

He looked at me and did not know what had hit him. 'Can you write your name too? Come on, will you write your name on this desk?' I asked.

'No, you've written it,' were the only words that came out of his mouth. This sums up his personality just as my actions spelt out mine.

This was my first meeting with that student—Vijay Sehgal. The year was 1967. Over half-a-century later, he is still my best friend, my buddy, my touchstone who keeps me truthful.

Vijay was, and remains to this day, an easy going, laid-back person who is very content leading a normal, simple life. He retired as the head cashier of United Commercial Bank, Pitampura branch, Delhi, in 2014. He was quiet, self-effacing and studious while I was an indifferent student, loud and attention seeking. He was most unpunctual then as he is even today. I am very particular about time. Hence, in a word we were polar opposites. He was my partner in crime and leant me unquestioning support through every crucial event especially during my struggling years. The fact that nothing ever fazed him was a source of great strength to me. I always appreciated his great sense of humour. My mother would joke and say when he came home, '*Hanumanji aa gaye*,' (Hanuman, the devotee of Ram has come). Such was his devotion. And my mother elevated me to status of Ram was an entirely different matter.

Memories of attending his wedding in Delhi on Saturday, 11 February 1984, still bring a smile to my lips. I still remember his home address, 74 Bharat Nagar. By this time, I was basking in the aftermath of the success of *Saaransh*. I was late reaching the venue, but as was customary, there were several weddings going on in the same street and I stumbled into at least four venues until I reached Vijay Sehgal's festivities. He was thrilled to see me and urged me to dance at his *baraat* (groom's wedding procession) and even though I am not a good dancer, I did my best. My buddy was thrilled. He is an honest critic of my films but never hurtful and if he did not much care for the film he would say, '*Theek tha yaar*' (It was okay).

His family was my family, his home (C-52, Phagli) was my home, and vice versa. His father, Shri Ram Seghal, who used to work in the army canteen of the Western Command headquarters, was a warm-hearted man but a strict disciplinarian. Once he gave me a hard slap, something my own father had never done. But those were the days when even neighbours had equal right on all the children.

Their house was an extension of mine and I would be there most of my school and even college years. I recall how his mother, Raj Sumitra, used to make the most amazing chutney out of fresh *dhaniya* (coriander) and *pudina* (mint) and *rotis* (Indian bread) with a few drops of ghee. Once a month, on a Sunday, Vijay's father would cook mutton curry which was a ritual in itself. Three days in advance we boys would start talking about the fact that 'uncle' was going to make mutton curry. On that Sunday morning, he would take an early bath, wear a crisp kurta-pyjama, then prepare, clean, chop the mutton in a precise manner since he was quite an expert at it. Next, he would mix the various spices and herbs; and finally, he would put it all in a large brass pot and cover it with a steel lid, finally sealing it to the pot with fresh flour dough. By the time it was getting cooked on a low fire, he would order us children to take a bath. Yes, that was the unwritten law—no lunch without a bath. Once bathed and ready, we would sit in the kitchen itself on wooden *chowkies* (slates) which was the norm in those days. He would then serve us, one by one, taking out the delicious mutton pieces while Raj aunty would serve freshly cooked rotis. It was all done with immense love.

Satish Malhotra was another one of my childhood buddies that I hold dear. Vijay, Satish and I used to hang out together—quite like the three musketeers. Sometime in 1977, we had watched in the local Regal Theatre the Sergio Leone directed star-studded English film *The Good, the Bad and the Ugly* and immediately after the film assumed each of the roles from it. I naturally took on the role of Clint Eastwood as 'the Good', Satish was Lee Van Cleef—'the Bad' and Vijay as Eli Wallach was 'the Ugly'. We bought cheap cowboy hats and walked down the Mall Road in Shimla whistling the film's popular signature tune composed by Ennio Morricone. We were so inspired by the film that we wanted to do something outlandish and soon we spied a single train boogie parked in tracks. We pushed it and it suddenly started moving since it was on a slope. We promptly ran from there but for the next few days remained petrified even at the sight of a policeman. Satish, who was three years older to me, was already employed and worked at the State Education Board. Thus, he was cash rich to finance our indulgences likes movies and eating out. I was an avid reader of James Hadley Chase and had borrowed some books from the college library and promptly lost them the same day. At the end of the academic year, I needed to get a clearance certificate from the library and instead of paying the fine from the money borrowed from my father on false pretences we decided to steal the books from Batish and Sons on The Mall. It was decided that I would engage the shopkeeper in conversation and distract him. Vijay was tasked with stealing the books because of his nondescript appearance and hiding them under his shirt and Satish was to serve as the lookout and whistle at the first sign of trouble. While Vijay was stealing the books, someone kept winking and smiled at him which he mistook as an encouragement and was emboldened to walk out of the shop. However, the person, a professor in the local college, went and reported to the shopkeeper. When Vijay left the shop, he was chased by the shopkeeper's son. Fearing the wrath of his father he soon threw the stolen books on the side of the road. I too began chasing him. But my aim was different. I wanted the cinema tickets that Vijay had in his pockets, which had been purchased from the money given by my father. Eventually because of our failed 'mission', Satish had to step in and purchase the James Hadley Chase replacement books for me.

I devoured these books and they made a big impact on me with their vivid descriptions and colourful exploits, storing a lot of the material read in my memory. Over the years I have used it in various forms, in my numerous film portrayals.

These childhood friendships have been precious beyond what words can capture. They hold up a mirror to me, genuinely delighted in my successes, ready to embrace me during my failures. Cheerleaders and advocates, I can always come home to them. In today's world, such relationships are rare.

Among the other memories of my school days is one relating to my brother Raju, who, used to start developing a stomach ache around 8.30 a.m. every morning when we were about to leave for school. The pain would increase in intensity by 9.00 a.m. when the school bell would ring and the gates would be closed! After that, the latecomers were not allowed inside. The moment he would hear the bell, his pain would vanish! But during that half-an-hour, the pitch of his howling increased in proportion to the persistence of the elders forcing him to go to school. But, as time went by, my parents discovered this mischief and Raju had no choice but to give up such tantrums and began attending school regularly.

For my part, I used to love going to school and relished virtually every moment. The most beautiful memory I treasure is that of my mother, who (during summers) used to bring *dahi* (curd) with cooked rice mixed in it and wait outside the school (during the lunch break). There was this huge, rock-like stone and we (Raju and I) used to sit on it and tuck into this tasty dish.

My brother and I have always shared a very close relationship. He is the most important person to me in the world. My strength comes from the fact that he has been a silent pillar who has stood by me all my life. We do not know what sibling rivalry is and my success has never created a barrier between us. He has always been free of complexes—never in competition with his 'famous brother'. On my part, everything I have done has been first for him, whether it be owning a house, a car, or whatever the case may be. He has been with me every step of the way and when I asked him to join me in Bombay and find a job when I began my struggle in films, he just came and asked no questions. He used to manage the household and was a great cook with his favourite dish being *rajma chawal* (red beans and rice) and *aloo mattar* (potato and peas). He worked in a tin factory—a job Sikandar's father, Gautam Berry, procured for him.

I must admit that I have always been very protective towards Raju. He has had various health issues—ailments like skin problems, dental issues and in later years his struggle with cancer. I have always been by his side to take care of him. He is a great giver. In mythological terms, I see him cast in the mould of Laxman, the brother of Lord

Ram. He is not overtly in your face and happy to be one step behind me. He lets me bask in the limelight. For a short period, he was also my secretary. Like me, he has a good sense of humour. His greatest asset is that he possesses a pure heart.

He has a wonderful wife Reema who we all affectionately call Chanu. She is also an amazing cook. She too has accepted me and treats me in a very balanced way which I really appreciate. She had played a very important role in taking care of my parents who too loved staying there with their two wonderful children—Vrinda and Pranit—one a fantastic dancer and the other presently working in a special effects company, respectively—who are my great joys.

Raju was the executive producer of one of my first TV serial *Imtihaan* which I produced for Doordarshan in 1995. One day, when one of the actors didn't turn up for shooting, I suggested to my brother to step in and act: 'Do it . . . it is only one scene, be confident.' He found his own niche and today I am so proud that my brother has his own successful TV career.

While performing my play *Kuh Bhi Ho Saktha Hai* I had to get teary-eyed. During the interval, I would think of different incidents from my life to get my emotions going. Initially I used to think that something had happened to my father (then that also happened in real life). Then I started thinking of my brother having cancer. When I was honoured with the Padma Shri award in 2004, I called my brother to share the good news but he did not pick up the phone. After a few hours, he called back to inform me that he had cancer of the bladder. I was devastated and hated myself for being an actor, of having associated pain with my work. The reality cut to my inner core. When he went in for surgery, he gave me a thumbs up sign and that day I saw how courageous he was. Today, with His grace, he is fine.

6

ROMANTIC INTERLUDES

In most hill stations, one can actually *feel* the romantic atmosphere and given its verdant location, Shimla was no exception. I was finely tuned to my surroundings and reaching puberty, so it wasn't long before I was caught up in the throes of romantic interludes both real and imagined.

Anything can happen in love. And many things did happen in my case! Contrary to common perception, love and courtship do not cast their spell only in the rarefied circles in cosmopolitan cities. Even in the lives of hillbillies, there are many romantic escapades! In the small-town Shimla in the 1960s and early 1970s, there was little excitement in our daily lives. Our days were quite monotonous and predictable, forcing us to create our own forms of entertainment and amusement. Many times, we had to stage-manage events. Sometimes, we were plain lucky! More often than not, events backfired and took a completely unexpected turn.

My first crush I would like to believe was the result of my magnetic personality. And Bollywood actor of yesteryears—the popular Manoj Kumar[5]—unwittingly played a significant role!

The Family Planning Department of the Government of India (set up in the mid-1960s, essentially to create awareness to control the growing population was screening a movie in our Nabha House hall, through a 16 mm projector during the festival season—a popular ploy to reach the masses. It was Manoj Kumar's 1967 blockbuster film, the multistar *Upkar* in which the hero, originally a farmer, becomes a soldier, who defends his country when attacked by the enemy. The narrative was based on the theme of Prime Minister Lal Bahadur Shastri's stirring slogan: *Jai Jawan, Jai Kisan* (Victory to the soldier, victory to the farmer).

During the screening, a young girl was sitting next to me. Let me mention here that even in those days, we kids were really not as innocent as we seemed to be. While watching the film, during a romantic scene, I surreptitiously held her hand—yes, there was one such scene even in the patriotic film. After the film came to an end, the girl left the hall and so did I. But things did not end there; they actually gained momentum. The next day, the girl's younger brother brought a letter for me. In our neighbourhood, virtually everyone knew everyone else; so, locating me in school did not exactly require the qualities of a Sherlock Holmes. He said that his sister's exams were going on and that she had sent me a letter and sought a reply.

I opened the letter, which was in Hindi (written in the Devanagri script). The words sprang up at me:

My dear Anupam,
Since the time I have seen you, my nights are sleepless, and my days are restless . . .

There was more penned in a very dramatic manner. Contrary to general opinion, I believe Indian films have had a good influence on kids. They at least taught them to write love letters, among the most famous being that of hero Rajendra Kumar (also known as 'Jubilee Kumar', as many of his movies celebrated silver jubilees) who wrote it to his beautiful heroine Vyjayanthimala in the 1964 Raj Kapoor's famous film *Sangam—Yeh mera prem patr padkar . . . ki tum naraaz na hona*[6] (After reading my love letter, you should not get angry). I read it again as the girl's brother tugged at my sleeve and whispered: 'Make it fast, how much more time will you take to read the letter?'

I responded with a curt: 'Shut up!'

I then took that letter to my friend Vijay Sehgal—who has 'starred' in almost all my escapades, romantic or otherwise! He read the letter and made a very profound observation: 'Hmmmmmm . . . this is a love letter! Somehow, we have to get a few books on poetry and pick out a poem from there to write it out in a letter to her.'

Our efforts were successful, and we selected a poem, which became part of my first love letter:

> Some wear diamonds in their ears,
> Some wear it around the neck,
> Why am I concerned about diamonds?
> My loved one is a diamond in itself!

My love letter, in my opinion, was certainly more dramatic than hers. As soon as the letters were exchanged, we automatically 'fell in love'. The next logical step was to exchange photographs. So, I rushed to Shimla's popular Mall Road and had my first official photograph clicked at Roshan Studio.

That day, a musical play based on the Ramayana was being staged. A perfect setting to continue our love story to the next level. I was blissfully unaware of the fact that my mother was seated in the audience watching the play too. I was seated in the balcony and my mother on the ground floor. So, when my girlfriend handed me a photograph of hers, I too took out my photograph from my pocket and was about to give it to her when the audience started clapping loudly on seeing the Lord Ram break the famous bow in the court of King Janak and my elbow was jolted suddenly and the photograph slipped out, and amidst all the applause, landed—of all the places—in my mother's lap!

Mom, out of curiosity, picked up the photograph and realised it was mine! She then turned the photo over where I had poured out my heart thus:

> Your body is as smooth as sandalwood,
> Your smile is so beautiful,
> Oh world, do not blame me, if I fall in love with you.
> Lovingly yours,
> Anupam

Mom looked up angrily, scanning the faces in the balcony in order to spot me. I was trying my best to hide behind my friend Vijay. That evening, the phrase, 'Oh Mother Earth, split and hide me in your womb,' was expressed by two people—Sita in the play and me!

After the play, for quite some time, I wandered here and there in a daze trying to delay my return home. Ultimately, I had to go back and face the music, rather the cacophony. That night my mother yelled at my father tauntingly: 'Yes, now you give him more milk and almonds so that his creativity can blossom, and he can do better in school . . . better in school with writing "your body is as smooth as sandalwood, your smile is so beautiful . . ."'

My dad was, understandably, totally baffled . . . and had no idea what the allusion to body and the sandalwood was all about. He asked: 'What's the reference to context?' He was greeted by a stony silence. That was the last day of my first love! But lady luck was on my side, quite literally . . .

It seemed a scene directly out of a B-grade Hindi film!

When I reached the eleventh grade, a very beautiful girl moved into our neighbourhood. I soon found out that she was the daughter of an army officer, recently posted at the headquarters of the Western Command in Shimla. She studied in an English-medium school. She wore miniskirts and to me looked like an angel who had descended from paradise! Without disclosing her identity, let me give her the imaginary name Urvashi, after the gorgeous apsara or nymph in Hindu legend who 'first appeared in Vedic texts as a celestial maiden in Indra's court'. As expected, every lad in the neighbourhood wanted to win her over. Vijay Sehgal and I were no exceptions; we were rendered stark, raving mad with thoughts of her. We began to follow her around, like puppies. After almost two months of such 'pursuit', by which time Vijay had gallantly given up his 'love' for me, and then virtually pleaded: 'I can't bear this any longer . . . why can't you clearly tell her that you love her?'

But at that stage, I was assailed by doubts and was not ready to proclaim my love . . . for fear of being rejected.

After another month had gone by, I finally mustered enough courage to whisper to her at a secluded spot (in Hindi): 'Hello lady . . . hello lovey . . . hello sweetie . . . I . . . I . . . I love you!'

She replied coyly (in English): 'Really? Me too!' And fled.

The ubiquitous Vijay translated her words!

Her reply caught me off guard. I had thought that she would get angry and yell at me or, as depicted in numerous Indian movies, take off her footwear to whack me. Nothing like that happened. Vijay then sagaciously advised me: 'The next time you meet her, tell her, "I want to kiss you".'

'Are you insane?' I shot back. 'If I say, "I want to kiss you", she will definitely slap me.'

Vijay's response was nonchalant but down to earth: 'A few slaps are not a big deal in exchange for a kiss! Accept them as compliments!'

I resumed my courtship in earnest all over again at another romantically secluded place with just a few words added to my previous dialogue: 'Hello my young lady . . . hello my lovey . . . hello my sweetie . . . I must kiss you.'

I immediately braced myself for the slap! But instead, came the reply: 'Alright . . . but after my school's annual day function.'

My heart was brimming with happiness and my fantasies knew no bounds! I couldn't sleep that night. It is only in the harsh reality of the next day that I realised that annual day celebrations were another eight months away.

As this truth seeped in, I rushed to find Vijay again and narrated what had transpired and almost whined in a dejected tone: 'She said she would let me kiss her only after *eight months*.'

He tried to uplift my sagging spirits with his characteristic élan: 'Tell me, how many girls have you kissed so far?'

My subdued answer: 'Not a single one.'

Vijay's apt rejoinder: 'So can't you wait for eight more months for your first kiss? Till then, practise your kissing skills and hone them to perfection.'

'Practise my kissing skills? How?' I queried.

'Use a drinking glass for that.'

My dear, idiotic friend of mine did not specify that I should use a stainless-steel tumbler and not one made out of glass! I started practising with a glass tumbler and, as my passion got the better of me, the glass shattered, and my lips started bleeding and soon became swollen. Being quite naïve then, I thought this was what naturally happened while kissing. Many years later, after achieving a bit of proficiency in the amorous activities, I discovered that the results actually depend on how you kiss!

During the next few months, time which would normally fly by, at least for me, moved excruciatingly slowly. It certainly tested my patience to the maximum. A few days before the annual day function, the bewitching girl Urvashi, called me aside and, in an enticing tone, laid down a precondition: 'Listen . . . I'm going to wear a saree for the function. And you must wear a suit.'

A suit? In seven generations of my family, no one had ever owned a suit. I told her so. But she insisted: 'Listen carefully . . . you *must* wear a suit to compliment my saree.'

Off I ran once again to my saviour Vijay and disclosed the new twist in the love saga.

Once again, as all too often in the past, he rose to the occasion with his no-nonsense approach: 'If you want a kiss, I suggest you ask your dad to fork out the amount to pay for a suit.'

That night my entire family was seated for dinner. My father had just picked up a morsel of food in his hand and was about to transport it to his mouth and my brother was sipping water from a glass and my mother was about to place hot curry in my father's plate, when at that precise moment, I piped up: 'Dad . . . dad . . . I want a suit.'

My father's jaw dropped noticeably, and the food fell out of his hand. Raju gave me a look as if the water he had sipped was about to shoot out of his ears, if that was possible. And my mother, instead of putting the hot curry into my father's plate, dropped it on one of his thighs. He went ballistic and started screaming and demanded, '*Why* do you want a suit now?'

I had my response ready: 'Dad . . . there is going to be a prize distribution ceremony in our school . . . and I am being given one as well. But the principal has said that only if I wear a suit will I get the prize.'

Dad, turned livid and roared in his native Kashmiri language (we normally spoke in Kashmiri at home): 'Is the principal out of his mind? Has he ever worn a suit in his life that he is insisting on you wearing one?'

My mother, not wanting my father's blood pressure to rise, tried to mollify him in a soothing voice: 'The poor boy . . . if he is asking for a suit, why not get him one.' At this moment my brother, not to be left out, demanded petulantly: 'If he is getting a suit, even I want one.'

My father took some time to recover from this distressing situation. After pondering for a while, he said: 'Okay, I will get you both new suits, but you will not get new shoes to go with them.' He negotiated still fuming with anger.

Having won this round, I then assured him: 'Don't worry about the shoes. I have an old pair of brown sports shoes. I will polish them black to match the dark-coloured suit that I have in mind.'

On the day of annual day function, Urvashi and I had an understanding that we would meet below the railway bridge at 8.00 p.m. Early that morning, before the town awoke, Vijay and I removed all the light bulbs (most of which were non-functional anyway) under that bridge as we did not want anyone to witness the kissing incident. Mercifully, there were no CCTVs, hidden cameras or smartphones during those 'medieval' days.

On the dot at 8.00 p.m., as befitting an army officer's daughter, Urvashi arrived at the designated spot. She was draped in a pink saree, with a matching pink blouse and not to mention, the pink lipstick, which was the focus of my attention. She was looking radiant. I noticed that her midriff was exposed . . . it was a slender one. Her blouse exposed a shallow cleavage between her young, firm breasts. *Has she exposed it purposely by draping the pallav of her saree at a certain angle*, I wondered. She looked all around and then sat down on the bench under the bridge.

I was wearing what I thought was a well-fitted suit (navy blue with white stripes) and brown sports shoes, polished black.

I sat myself down on her right side. Silence settled down all around us and the air felt heavy and I could hear my own heartbeat rapidly. A million thoughts raced through my mind and suddenly ten minutes had passed. In the dark, I was biting my lips. At the same time, through the corner of my eye, I was trying to locate Vijay Sehgal, who was on the lookout for any strangers on the bridge and entrusted with the vital task of sending warning signals by whistling the tune of the evergreen hit film song: *Mere desh ki dharti sona ugle, ugle heere moti . . .*[7]

We also faced an additional hitch as Urvashi's house was close to the bridge. But in my inward eye I was not concerned about it since in our sleepy town in that pre-TV and pre-Internet era, almost everybody normally was in bed fast asleep by half-past-eight at night.

I realised then that between Urvashi and me, there was a gap of about one-and-a-half feet. Edging closer, I placed my hand on her knee. At exactly that moment, a goods train blew its horn and crossed over the bridge above us. Due to sudden distraction, I withdrew my hand and placed it on my knee.

Now, each passing second felt like an hour. I began to experience an out-of-body experience as my lips moved towards hers. She drew close to me. Our lips were just about to touch, when, unexpectedly, the front lights of her house came blazing on. Her father stepped out of the house, apparently, to stretch his legs and have a smoke. And from the top of the bridge, I heard Vijay screaming (the whistling totally forgotten): 'OYE . . . DON'T DO IT!'

The girl turned her head to locate the sound of the screaming and my lips landed hard directly on her right ear with her earring half in my mouth! She virtually yelled: 'You moron! What are you doing kissing my ear? You don't even know how to kiss properly.'

I said in a sincerely contrite tone: 'I'm really sorry . . . by mistake my mouth went in your ear. Let me try again.'

But the spell had been broken. She was holding her ear, as if she was in pain, and said: 'Get away from here . . . just leave me alone

. . . idiot.' After those words, she walked away, leaving me alone in the inky darkness.

Finally, after some moments, I too started to walk towards the bridge where Vijay was waiting. He could hardly control his excitement and curiosity. He asked: 'How was it?'

I replied enigmatically: 'Terrific, now she can't marry anyone.'

He became alarmed and queried: 'Why? What did you do to her?'

I replied: 'I kissed her in such a manner that she will never ever forget it in her lifetime.'

Following my bombastic pronouncement, we continued our trudge home in silence.

After this fiasco, for many days, I studiously avoided Urvashi. But, eventually, she cornered me behind the school cafeteria and whispered in my ears: 'Listen . . . come here . . . kiss me.'

From the kitchen, wafted the overpowering odour of deep-fried dishes. I was amazed that she wanted me to kiss her then and there!

I asked, with a mischievous grin: 'Without my suit and matching shoes?'

She said, with an infectious laugh: 'Don't be silly, stupid. Come on, come on . . . kiss me.'

I took her in my arms and kissed her . . . slowly . . . gently. As she wrapped her arms around me, my tongue darted into her mouth. She hugged me tightly; our kissing became hard and fierce, full of youthful passion. That was my first kiss ever. But I kissed to my heart's content! And so did she. I was transported to dizzying heights. Our intimate moment became my little secret and one I did not want to share with anyone . . . not even with my buddy Vijay Sehgal!

Indeed, *kucch bhi ho sakta hai!* (Anything can happen.)

Decades after this incident, when I was shooting for Mahesh Bhatt's *Marg* (which never got completed) in Shimla, with Vinod Khanna and Hema Malini, my assistant, Dattu, informed me that a lady had come to see me.

I turned around and saw a woman standing at a distance along with a group of onlookers. She was wearing a pink saree with a matching pink blouse and pink lipstick. I could catch the whiff of a very familiar perfume. *Was it Urvashi?* I asked myself. Yes, it was! Time, it seemed, had not been kind to her: slimness and she had parted ways perhaps, many years ago. She had aged prematurely, and her face appeared tense. She was accompanied by her husband and three children. When I went closer to her, I noticed a sort of uncertainty in her eyes, not because she thought I would perhaps talk about that kissing episode in front of her family, but she was desperately hoping that I hadn't forgotten what had happened between us.

I welcomed her and her family warmly. I arranged for their photographs with both Hema Malini and Vinod Khanna and the other stars working in the film with me. The entire family was overjoyed. Yet, I could sense that there was something on her mind an unspoken need, a hesitant tension. Eventually, the mystery was solved when Urvashi asked for a solo photograph with me as a souvenir for old times' sake. And then she was gone forever—back to the normal life that was her lot.

That evening back in my hotel room, I mulled over the day's event and was flooded by memories of the past; the precious moments treasured forever—my first kiss, intimate, virgin, stolen sexual escapades that linger for a lifetime. I never forgot the following magical words that reverberated in my mind:

Waqt ne kiya kya haseen sitam,
tum rahe na tum, hum rahe na hum.[8]

What a beautiful injustice has time done,
You are no longer you, I am no longer me.

Anyway, after that momentous episode with Urvashi in the school canteen, I was unable to concentrate on academics anymore. Not that I had any sterling record to keep up with, but my rank dropped to 28th/29th from 25th/26th. My father kept up his ranting in Kashmiri about feeding me more milk and almonds. But milk and almonds were hardly going to remedy this situation.

My second stint on stage also proved to not be noteworthy. This time I mauled William Shakespeare, no less.

It all happened because it was the dream of one of my teachers, Hardarshan sir, to direct an English play some day. But in our Hindi-medium DAV School, not a single student could speak English fluently enough to stage a play. However, one particular year, eight students from a nearby English-medium school, who had failed to make a mark there, joined our school.

Thinking that destiny had sent him a sign, Hardarshan sir decided to achieve his life's ambition and set his sights on William Shakespeare's *The Merchant of Venice*—a sixteenth-century play in which a merchant in Venice must default on a large loan provided by a Jewish moneylender.

Since I had mastered the art of sweet talking all the teachers by serving them tea and snacks during rehearsals, I bagged a small role to perform as the clerk of the court who gets to read out the charges. In the scene which I had to enact, the judge would announce: 'Clerk of the court, read out the charges.' That was my cue. I had to read eight lines: 'The charges against you [the protagonist Antonio] are the following: Charge no. 1 . . . Charge no. 2 . . . Charge no. 3 . . .' (till Charge no. 8).

During the final dress rehearsal, I 'notched up' twenty-seven mistakes while delivering those eight lines. The school principal, Satya Prakash, who had been watching the proceedings, virtually stormed on to the stage and almost began cursing:

Pagal ho gaya hai mainyawa . . . is nu actor kisne bana dita hai . . . satiye galtian aath linyan wich . . . bar kado isnu . . . kal deputy commissioner the hor wade log aa rahe ne, te tu school di badnami karen lagan hai. Saade school di grant band jo jayegi . . .

('You ... get out of here! Have you gone mad! Who has made him an actor? . . . 27 mistakes in eight lines? Throw him out . . . Tomorrow the deputy commissioner of Shimla and many other dignitaries are coming to see the performance. The school grant will be stopped . . .)

And he literally delivered a solid kick to my backside that sent me rolling off the stage.

I immediately rushed over to Hardarshan sir and fell at his feet. I beseeched him: 'Sir . . . Sir ji . . . Please don't exclude me from the play. I have invited my father, mother, neighbours, friends, family members and everyone I know. If I don't feature in the play tomorrow, it will be very embarrassing for me and my entire family . . . I will be ridiculed in my school and neighbourhood.' Those days, a student could melt a teacher's heart by merely begging for forgiveness.

Hardarshan sir melted and took pity on me, and in an attempt to convince the principal, stated: 'He is a decent boy and he comes from a good family. Let's not exclude him from the play. We will change it so that he will be on stage, but all the dialogues will be given to the judge instead. Let the judge say: "The charges against you are the following . . . "'

The principal reluctantly agreed and Hardarshan sir informed me: 'Hey lad! I have spoken to the principal and with great difficulty he has agreed. You are now part of the play again. But remember you will not have any dialogues to speak . . . only keep *nodding* your head. Okay? Will you remember that?'

I nodded my head! I was excited and relieved to be back on stage.

The next day, at the scheduled time, the play started. In the front row, the principal, the deputy commissioner and other dignitaries of the town, were seated. My esteemed invitees were in the eighth row. My parents were desperately waiting for the curtain to go up, praying that along with the stage curtain, my fortune would also rise.

Since my lines had been taken away from me the previous evening and I was not to speak any more, unlike some of the other students on the stage, I was feeling very relaxed—free from all tension and anxiety. As instructed, I was just nodding. Suddenly, I heard the judge say: 'Clerk of the court, read out the charges . . .'

I just kept nodding my head.

But the judge kept looking at me and repeated in a loud voice: 'Clerk of the court, read out the charges . . .'

Realising with a start that the judge was addressing me, I was taken aback! Obviously, Hardarshan sir had forgotten to tell the judge that we had altered Shakespeare's script. Thinking quickly, I stammered: 'Thou read out the charges . . . the Teacher said that yesterday.'

The judge, however, repeated: 'Clerk of the court, I want *you* to read out the charges.'

I persisted: 'Thou read out the charges . . . the principal said yesterday eight lines . . . twenty-seven mistakes . . . idiot.'

The judge paid scant regard to my plea and repeated firmly: 'I want *you* to read out the charges.'

I looked at Hardarshan sir standing in the wings and gesturing towards me to proceed.

I asked desperately by miming: 'Should I read?'

He signalled: 'Yes.'

I didn't have the paper in which the charges were written, so, impromptu, I used my own imagination and the dialogue and what emerged from my mouth was as follows:

> You bloody Shylock, what do you think of yourself? He [Antonio] is ready to give you your money but all you want is your *pound of flesh . . . pound of flesh.* Hah! Accept the money; if not, I'll take my shoes off and hit you with them!' (My sincerest apologies to the Bard of Avon.)

In retrospect, I can be sure if William Shakespeare had a chance to heed my charges he would have jumped out of his grave and protested loudly, 'Hey, you Hindi-medium boy, thou shall now stop.'

I did.

I was thrilled that I had spoken my self-created dialogue and to my delight most of the audience laughed and laughed hard. My parents enjoyed the spectacle the most. And as they looked around to see people laughing heartily, they thought how amazingly I had performed a comic role! That day, the clerk of the court was the most applauded character of all! But you can well imagine what Hardarshan sir went through during my performance. How the principal Satya Prakash and the deputy commissioner of Shimla felt about my performance or rather my non-performance.

That night, the fact that my father was laughing heartily revealed that he was very happy! He proudly told my mother: 'Bittu did a fantastic job today as a comedian . . . it was so much fun . . . he was very good . . . in fact, I think he was the best of the lot. No need to feed him milk and almonds anymore. Raju needs them now as Bittu is about to finish school.'

Even though I completed my schooling with a third class, scoring a forgettable 38 per cent against the pass cut off of 35 per cent, I was still riding high on a wave of triumph based on my play performance, audience feedback and especially my father's appreciation!

Part–II

THE CURTAIN RISES

Success is not final; failure is not fatal:
it is the courage to continue that counts.

—Winston S. Churchill

7

FROM THE ABYSS TO THE SUMMIT

When I joined the Government College, Shimla, it was the beginning of a new journey—even though I did not recognise the fact immediately. I was emerging from a low point and things could only get better. College was a learning experience for me in more ways than one. All my life I had studied only in a Hindi medium all boys' educational institution and the likes of us were treated as virtual pariahs by girls from English-medium schools like Tara Hall, Auckland House, Convent of Jesus and Mary and St Thomas.

Being in a co-educational college was a novelty for me and naturally, I was drawn to and promptly fell in love with a girl from an English-medium school who tantalised me with her sensuous pout. She, of course, paid no attention to me but that did not deter me from following in her footsteps all over town.

Just by being in a college I seemed to have gained a second wind and developed a sense of self-confidence! When walking down Mall Road, if I would spot any girls from the English-medium schools coming my way, I would try to impress them by saying the well rehearsed Newton's third law in a clipped English, 'To every action, there is equal and opposite reaction.' But none of the girls were ever impressed and showed no interest in me whatsoever. Recalling this memory now, I am filled with laughter but then I was brimming with self-assurance and no one could shake it.

I was selected to play the lead role in the play *Balidan*. It was staged at a competitive drama festival in Shimla's famous Gaiety Theatre. The girl was not acting but came to see the final dress rehearsal. After the curtain call, she met me and said, in English of course: 'That was very cute.' I was bowled out just hearing her voice though I had no idea what 'cute' meant.

Later my friend Vijay Sehgal asked: 'What did she say?'

'She said, I'm very queet,' I replied.

My happiness knew no bounds. I noticed that when she enunciated my name Anupam, her accent made everything seem more sexy and long drawn out like 'nupam' and 'oo' instead of 'you'. With her around, my world was complete. Without her, I felt 'lonely'.

Many years later in 1998, in Karan Johar's highly successful film, *Kuch Kuch Hota Hain*, which had Shah Rukh Khan, Kajol and Rani Mukerji in the lead, I played Principal Malhotra, who on meeting Ms Briganza, played by Archana Pooran Singh, says: 'You are very queet'—a sequence that drew a hearty laugh from audiences.

Finally, the day came for *Balidan* to be staged at Himachal Pradesh inter-college drama competition. I was playing the role of a dashing police officer. From the wings, I noticed that quite a few of my friends were there to cheer me, and most significantly, the 'girl' was there too. *She has come specially to cheer me . . . see the performance of her hero*, I thought and was inspired. The fact that my parents were sitting in the auditorium—as usual in the eighth row—became secondary. I decided to put in my best performance and impress the 'girl' by winning the best actor's award.

There was thunderous applause once the curtain came down on *Balidan*. I visualised the 'girl' cheering uncontrollably for me! *She was surely mine now*, I thought.

I was certain of bagging the top award—that big, shining trophy which was displayed on the stage that evening. After the speeches, the results were announced in reverse order. First, the best supporting actress . . . then the best supporting actor. . . then the best actress. I clapped for each one, waiting for my name to be announced: *And the Best Actor Award goes to Anupam Kher from*

Government College, Shimla. I was convinced this was going to be truly my moment. I could imagine the whole scenario in my head—my friends cheering, my parents clapping and the 'girl' rushing to give me a hug and then saying: 'I always knew you would get it. You are a great actor . . . the best of them all.' I was aroused by my own thoughts when came the announcement: 'And now for the final award of this drama festival—the Best Actor's Award.' I got up and looked at her sitting a few rows ahead and was about to proceed to the stage, when the announcer said: 'And the Best Actor award goes to . . . from Government College, Chamba.'

I was devastated. *How will I face my parents now? What would my friends say? And she, what will she say?* I thought to myself. I headed straight for the restroom and fainted.

When I regained consciousness and opened my eyes, I saw her looking at me. She said: '*Itna bhi kya dil pe lena*' (Why take it to heart). And I looked straight into her eyes and answered: 'I love you'. She was shocked as were the others standing around us.

The next year we staged *Sawang*—a comedy based in a mental asylum. This time I bagged the Best Actor Award and overnight became famous. This propelled me to another level. Quite convinced that I was invincible, I decided to apply for admission to the National School of Drama (NSD) in Delhi. I applied with Suman Tiwari, my rakhi sister. At NSD we were interviewed by Frank Thakurdas, Sheila Bhatia, Ebrahim Alkazi—the giants of India's theatre world. Suman was selected. I was not. I couldn't believe it. Once again, it felt like that I had been dealt a bodily blow. *How could this be? I am a far superior actor than her, certified as the best actor of Himachal Pradesh*, I asked myself numerous times. But unbeknownst to me, my life was waiting in the wings for me.

Knowing my limitations as a student and given my flair for comedy and penchant for the spotlight, theatre was a natural outlet for me. But in a small town like Shimla, being in theatre offered very slim pickings. After graduation most students opted for safe government jobs. I was determined to try my hand at something a little different.

I decided to seek a career as a 'casual' announcer in All India Radio, Shimla which seemed like a good compromise. In AIR parlance, a casual appointee meant a temporary job and being paid daily wages. Today, it would be known by the fancy term RJ! Here, I must express my gratitude to the renowned santoor maestro, Pandit Shiv Kumar Sharma, who was responsible for making me an actor. For the first time in his life, Pandit Sharma can claim to have made a nobody into somebody without teaching him music!

My first shift was for three hours—from 6.30 to 9.30 in the morning. In my customary style of making sure I had an audience, the previous evening, I had implored everyone I knew to listen to my captivating voice on their radio sets.

On the dot, at 6.30 a.m., from my cubicle, I announced: 'This is All India Radio Shimla. We will begin our day with a programme on . . .' and I suddenly found myself stuttering and stammering . . . 'bhajans (religious songs).'

On observing my nervous condition, the paan-chewing duty officer, Gupta, came into my cubicle and told me in a soothing tone: 'If you face any problem, switch off the mike and play this signature tune.' He showed me what to do.

At 6.55 a.m., I was supposed to announce the day's programmes and schedules thus: 'This is All India Radio Shimla . . . the day's schedule is as follows: News at 7 a.m., agricultural programme at 7.20 a.m. and at 7.30 a.m., Pandit Shiv Kumar Sharma will play Raga Shankara on his santoor.'

But my version came out this way: 'This is All India Radio Shimla . . . the day's schedule is as follows: News at 7 a.m., agricultural programme at 7.20 a.m. and at 7.30 a.m., Pandit Shiv Kumar Sharma will play Raga Shankara on his santoor . . .' and I started stammering again.

Nothing could ease my nervousness. The furious Guptaji came inside my cubicle, slapped me soundly on the back of my head and unceremoniously showed me the door. Now, imagine if I had announced Pandit Shiv Kumar Sharma's performance correctly, then I would probably still be working in the radio station and wouldn't have become the Anupam Kher you all know!

Later that day, I asked my dad the question that had been bothering me: 'What is to be done now?'

He replied in a matter-of-fact manner: 'Now that you have completed your initial studies, you should find a job.'

But the rebel within me became restless. I did not want to find a job; I did not want to live in a small town; I did not want to lead the humdrum life of a faceless, common man; and I definitely did not want to become one amongst a crowd. I wanted people to look at me and say: 'Look, there goes Himachal Pradesh's best actor, Anupam Kher.'

A few weeks later, Vijay Sehgal showed me an advertisement in the *Tribune*—a well-circulated daily English newspaper published from nearby Chandigarh. That advertisement called for walk-in interviews scheduled for two days later issued by the Department of Indian Theatre at Panjab University, Chandigarh. It stated that successful candidates would be offered admission to the one-year diploma course in acting with a monthly stipend of Rs 200. An eternal optimist that I was, I could already envision the doors to becoming an actor opening! But, before that, there were a couple of rather tricky hurdles to be crossed.

The first hurdle was actually making it to Chandigarh and that too without my parents' knowledge. I knew that if I asked my dad for the bus fare even before I could have completed my sentence, he would have thrown a fit and I would have to bear the brunt of a lecture delivered in native Kashmiri.

I recall the bus ticket at that time was Rs 9.50, one way. That would be Rs 37 for the two of us (Vijay and me) including return fare. In addition, I needed additional funds to actually make it from the bus terminal in Sector 17 to the university's sprawling campus in Sector 14 and back home. And of course, there was also the small matter of eating lunch during the day.

Like most homes in India, my mother too had created a small but conspicuous prayer corner (mandir) in the house adorned with framed colour photographs and brass idols of various gods and goddesses avidly seeking their blessings. Every month, on festive occasion like Shivratri, Holi and Janamashtmi, my mother would make a small offering to the deities. There was always a decent amount of money in the temple. In my desperation and as a last resort, I decided to raid that treasure chest. That evening with a slight feeling of guilt, I took the risk and entered my mother's sacred sanctum and found a total of one hundred and eight rupees.

Feeling both guilty and driven, I counted out eight rupees with a sense of reverence and put it back into the chest and took a total of hundred rupees and put it in my pocket. Vijay and I planned to leave for Chandigarh by bus the next morning. But, as it happens in numerous Bollywood films, when I was about to leave the house, I bumped into my mother at the front door. She asked the most obvious question: 'Where are you going?'

I replied promptly: 'My friends and I are going on a picnic and will return by the evening.'

And Vijay and I were off to Chandigarh in a rickety Himachal Pradesh Road Transport bus, which for some reason charged each of us two rupees more than we had budgeted for.

The Panjab University's Department of Indian Theatre established in 1972, has been housed since its inception in the rear part of an open-air auditorium sandwiched between boy's hostels No. 1 and 2—named Mehr Chand Mahajan Hall and G. C. Chatterjee Hall, respectively. There were a large group of boys and girls who had come for the interviews. When my turn came the department director, the multifaceted Balwant Gargi, asked me what piece I was going to perform. I thought that since all the boys would naturally enact a male-oriented scene, I should do something offbeat: a female role.

I replied: 'Sir, there's a play in Sanskrit called *Mrichchakatika* (*The Little Clay Cart*[9]). I shall perform a scene from it of the female protagonist Vasantasena.' Many years later the well-known actress Rekha performed this role in the film *Utsav*, in which I too played a minor role of a silent character. I put my heart and soul into my performance that afternoon. But, after I had finished, Gargi Sir exclaimed: 'Very bad! But very daring!'

After this disappointing response and with a feeling of utter dejection, Vijay and I left Chandigarh and returned to Shimla by bus. As we trudged towards my house, we noticed a crowd of mainly our neighbours gathered outside. My first reaction was that perhaps there had been a death in my family, or why else would there be a crowd outside the house. Soon, I realised that there was massive chaos inside the house, triggered by the theft from the mandir. Most of my relatives were running helter-skelter, searching for the money. Those days, losing 100 rupees was as good as losing a child in a public place. The child could be found later, but not the 100 rupees! My mother was howling while beating her chest with her hands and was in a bad shape! When she saw me, she asked in an agonised tone: 'Where are you coming from?'

'As I had told you in the morning, I had gone for a picnic with my friends,' I replied.

She was apparently not convinced by my reply and then asked, looking at me with great suspicion: 'Have you stolen the money from my mandir?'

'Money? What money? No mother, what will I do with your money?' I answered quite indignantly.

She then stared at Vijay with the same degree of suspicion. Perhaps, at some point of time, she must have seen him lingering around the mandir. He, too, denied it, point-blank.

A week or so after that incident, I was at home, when my father came in after work and asked in Kashmiri (an ominous sign): 'Where were you on the day the money was stolen from the mandir?'

I knew that I was now as good as dead for the gods must have somehow come in his dreams to inform him of the robbery by his own son! I felt as if I was now truly trapped in my own web of lies! I revealed, stammering, the truth: 'D . . . Da . . . d . . . Dad, I had gone to Chandigarh.'

'For what?'

'To give an audition to qualify for admission to an acting course at the Panjab University.'

Upon hearing my words, my mother standing nearby screamed: 'And from where did you get the money to go to Chandigarh?'

I had no option but to confess: 'Mother . . . I stole the money from the mandir.'

Mom, who by now was crying, slapped me hard on my face. Before she could lunge at me and take another swipe at me, I took a step back.

'I am sorry. I don't want to become an actor,' I mumbled to no one in particular and I sat down, a picture of dejection. I blurted: 'I will try for the job of a clerk in the government.'

After that, I kept on repeating: 'I don't want to become an actor . . . I don't want to become an actor . . . I don't want to become an actor . . .'

Dad then said: 'Shut up and get up! You have been selected.'

My mother, still crying, queried: 'But what about my hundred rupees?'

My dad, who had evidently read the selection letter, then told her: 'You also shut up. He will get a monthly stipend of 200 rupees, so he will be able to return your 100 rupees.'

On 27 July 1974, as a raw 19-year-old, I began my journey to train to become a professional actor and my personal goal of a new life.

As was the custom then in villages and small towns, the entire neighbourhood turned up to see me off at the Shimla bus terminal. Vijay, who helped me put my tin trunk and the hold-all comprising my bedding on the roof carrier of the bus, became rather emotional, took me aside and whispered in my ear: 'Hey, Bittu . . . once you become a big actor, don't forget me!' I gave him a tight hug and assured him that I would always remember him. As was the family tradition, I bent down to touch the feet of the elders to get their blessings. And then I boarded the bus, which began lumbering towards Chandigarh.

Three main languages were spoken in Chandigarh: English, Punjabi and Hindi, in that order. English was the most prominent everywhere be it the secretariat building, the university campus, a dozen colleges, hospitals, clubs or the main shopping centres. Ironically, even the seminars on Punjabi were conducted in English. All those who proudly fought for and propagated Punjabi ranging from the powerful ministers to the rich village zamindars (headmen), sent their children to the best English-medium schools.

On joining the Department of Indian Theatre at Panjab University I soon realised that the stage too suffered from a linguistic complex. A majority of the plays staged were 'imported' from 'high-brow' cities such as London, Paris, New York and Berlin. Some of them were translated, while others enacted in the English language itself.

The dramas in Punjabi and Hindi were negligible. Western theatre dominated. Even visiting directors like Joy Michael or Amal Allana from Delhi, preferred plays in English or those translated from European languages into English.

The Chandigarh stage was an easy-going place with relaxed but attentive audiences. They enjoyed the theatre and engaged with the actors. They were open to even minor actor trying to make a mark, irrespective of whether the play itself was good or bad. A flimsy or shoddy set did not seem to bother them, and in the presence of real talent, they were appreciative, laudatory and just present without question. Looking back, it was the most perfect place for me to start my education and career as an actor—yet another Grace in my Life that I appreciate in retrospect.

About fifty plays were being staged annually by more than two-dozen cultural groups that functioned in the city with politicians and retired high court judges as patrons. The activities of these groups ranged from sponsored Red Cross and family planning *melas* (jamborees) to glamorous potpourri with a 'play' or two thrown in. Governors or ministers from Punjab or Haryana or the chief commissioner of Chandigarh inaugurated these shows complete with speeches and media coverage, making them full-fledged events.

Besides local groups, theatre activity was supplemented by visiting ensembles from different parts of the country or from the UK and the USA, courtesy the British Council and the US Cultural Center (now known as American Center), respectively.

Drama reviews in the press, in the true sense, were unheard of, but the media of course covered the activities extensively in as much a laudatory language as possible, keeping both the organisers and the participants happy.

At the Department of Indian Theatre, Balwant Gargi's first lecture was on 'how to serve tea'. I was shocked and said to myself: *What is he talking about? I have come here to learn theatre, and he is, of all things, teaching us how to serve tea and telling us that in Japan there is a six-month course on the same.* I was a little disappointed. A couple of months later, when we were immersed in our studies, I asked him: 'Why did you give the first lecture on how to serve tea?

'Because, serving tea teaches one patience and patience is the most important aspect for anyone who wants to go in for acting,' he replied.

How true his teaching was I realised once I joined films and learnt that we actors get paid more for patience than for talent.

It was during my early days at the department that I happened to meet Ashok Chopra a journalist who was also from my hometown Shimla. He had worked with Balwant Gargi as his chief assistant director on a number of plays earlier. Rumour had it that theatre was quite a passion with him but he had quit out of sheer 'disgust'. My first impression of him was that he was a ladies' man and an 'elitist snob'. Supporting a well-trimmed, intricately chiseled beard, at a time when beards were least in fashion, he was always immacutely dressed. He was soft-spoken with impeccable manners. Obviously, girls loved him; we men did not. In any case most, including me, hesitated to approach him, for he kept us at an arm's length.

He was working for the *Tribune*—the only English newspaper published from the city, which was influential because of its massive circulation in the northern states of Punjab, Haryana, Jammu and Kashmir and Himachal Pradesh. He also reviewed plays, apparently as the first 'drama critic' the paper ever had. Actually, he had been set as a cat among the pigeons. He changed the rules—no more glorious reviews, no photographs of inaugurations, no more reporting of the speeches by the chief guests and no more pampering of the directors and their productions. He wrote what he saw and felt—just a succinctly, straightforward and a crisp review of the play. I don't know why, perhaps out of sheer respect or fear, most of us called him 'sir' despite the fact that there was little age gap.

Sometime in August 1974, Amal Allana was invited to the theatre department as a guest faculty member along with her husband, Nissar Allana, a young doctor who had left practice to join theatre, basically for designing the sets. During her stint there, she produced *The Exception and the Rule*, a play by the noted German playwright and director Bertolt Brecht, who had set up the world-famous Berliner Ensemble, a post-Second World War theatre company that created a revolutionary new form of drama called 'epic theatre'. I was selected to play the leading role.

The opening night was a gala event by Chandigarh standards and the play, going by the audience response, was appreciated. And yet, we were all somewhat nervous as to what Ashok Chopra would write in his review. I vividly recall Monday, 23 September 1974, the day his review was published in the *Tribune*:

> In the weak theatre season so far, which has been full of bad and hopeless theatre productions, hopes soared when the billboards announced the [staging] of Bertolt Brecht's *The Exception and the Rule* directed by Amal Allana for the Department of Indian Theatre at the Panjab University campus here . . .
>
> The production was a rich theatrical experience. Amal who mounts frighteningly lavish productions is a creative collaborator

with student actors of the theatre department. The result of her highly accomplished direction was enlightening. With it, she has given Chandigarh a new actor—Anupam Kher—whose performance as the merchant is brilliant. Mark my words, he is an actor to be watched, whom we are bound to notice, much more of, in the years to come.

Not only was I thrilled but now I consider it a prophetic statement.

The review was supplemented by a photograph of mine in a scene from the play. In Shimla, someone saw my picture and the review and informed my father. Soon, the news of the 'local boy' earning his spurs in Chandigarh spread like wildfire. As Vijay Sehgal read the review, tears of joy flowed down his cheeks. Everyone from my neighbours and my schoolteachers read it too and in my heart of hearts I was hoping my principal, Satya Prakash, who had once ordered me off the stage in a fit of temper using cuss words was literally eating his words! There was apparently so much joy generated all around that my father immediately bought a dozen copies of the paper and kept on showing the praiseworthy review to everyone he met for days after that.

Six months later, on Wednesday, 19 March 1975, came the big dampener. Ashok Chopra's review of Amal's second play—which was more of a studio production—*The Threepenny Opera*, also by Brecht, was not all that glowing. In fact, he tore it apart. I was, once again, the main male lead, Captain Macheath—Mac the Knife. Chopra, however, was appreciative of my performance. He wrote:

This production was not only a major let down from Amal Allana but was exceptionally boring and quite terrible. Though, at certain points, the play does work well, especially the compositions and the light arrangements, but for all that, it certainly fails as a whole due to the faultiness of the structure and attitude and unbridled theatrics. Musical compositions were below average and played a major part in making the play fall. Lacking in power, it was very disappointing to have so unique a work reduced to a minor event by such an ill-prepared performance.

The only redeeming grace was, once again, a brilliant performance by that youngster from Shimla—Anupam Kher, who saved the play from [becoming] a total waste. He commands our immediate attention as he performs with real conviction. He is terrifying and touching. One does not love Kher but is greatly moved by him. In an earlier review, a few months back, I had mentioned that he is an actor to be watched. Perhaps that was an understatement . . . Kher is indeed a genius.

I was happy. Amal Allana furious. Balwant Gargi livid. Apparently, Gargi even went to the extent of strongly complaining to the *Tribune* editor, R. Madhavan Nair. However, Nair did nothing. In any case, the damage had been done.

One's first review is like the first love that you dread to lose. I have preserved both issues of the *Tribune* to this day, even though the paper has turned woefully yellow and somewhat brittle with age. And as I write these lines, a *sher* (couplet) comes to my mind:

Yeh pehli mohabbat ka jaadu hai shaayad
Ke woh waqt-e-rukhsat mujhe yaad aaye.

This is probably the magic of first love
That at the time of departure [from this world] I remembered her.

Who knew then that I would connect with Ashok Chopra years later and this time in an author-publisher relationship—a rapport that would create a unique and a strong bond between us.

In Chandigarh (1974-75) I was given a room in Hostel No.1— Bhatnagar Hall— which I had to share with another student Swaranjit Singh. This was my first experience of life in a hostel and also of having a roommate. Swaranjit was psychologically a little unstable. Every morning, when I got up, I would discover that the laces of my shoes were missing. And one morning I noticed that my shoes were torn. Soon I found out that Swaranjit would get up around midnight in his sleep, take the shoes out of the shoe rack, tear them and put them back.

His fragile world was further threatened shortly afterwards. He fell madly in love with a student of our theatre department, who went on to join the film industry and earned some critical fame. Apparently, she laid a condition for reciprocating his love—'you have to shave off your long hair'. Swaranjit came from a fanatic Sikh family. That night he told me the story of his love: 'She has ordered me to cut my hair . . . how can I? After all, it's a part of my faith . . . my religion. If I do it my parents will kill me. I mean it. But I love her very much . . . she is the love of my life.' He was obviously very torn between his family and his love.

The next day, when I came back to the hostel after late evening rehearsals at the department, Swaranjit would not open the door. Even after I came back from dinner over an hour later, he would not let me in. I tried in vain, I shouted at him, I banged the door, I called him names but without success. Finally, well after midnight, with great difficulty, I entered the room through the balcony and what do I see: a clean-shaven Swaranjit Singh. He had dared to defy his faith, his religion and his family to possess his love. Who says determination does not move mountains! But the story did not end there. He was unable to secure his love. She refused to see him, let alone talk to him. Seeing his crazed state of mind, I went to the girl's hostel to meet her and ask her to reconsider. Instead, her answer shocked me: 'If a man can listen to me so much, how can I be in love with him.'

The next evening, the performance of Bertolt Brecht's play, *The Exception and the Rule*, directed by Amal Allana was on, in which Swaranjit was playing the role of a judge who comes in the last scene. But that evening, Swaranjit lost his voice and the whole public performance was in danger of collapsing. Every time he opened his mouth only a humming sound came out. Amal, like all of us, was shocked. But the show had to go on and finally, it was decided that his lines would be read out by someone from the behind the wings as he moved his lips in sync, as is done by film stars in movies when they lip-sync to the voice of a background singer.

One day, many years later, after I had joined the film industry, I got an early morning call. It was Swaranjit Singh: '*Main bhi aagaya*

(I too have arrived). You have made it. Now, I will also make it. And this was after a gap of over 10 years or so. I could tell right away that something was amiss. The same nervous laughter, the same hurried manner of speech.

Before I could say anything, he repeated: 'I have also come to do what you did . . . if it can happen to you, it can happen to me also.'

'What can happen? I asked.

'Success . . . my friend, success. I will also achieve success like you . . . I've come with my luggage to stay here.'

I was shocked. *Where to put him up . . . with whom?*

I was still lost in my thoughts when Swaranjit asked: 'Where should I come?'

Without another thought, I asked him to join me at an outdoor location called Giri Kunj where I was shooting that day. We had just about started work when Dattu, my assistant, informed me that somebody had come to meet me. I knew it was Swaranjit. As I saw him being led in my heart sank. He looked so dishevelled, with stained clothes, unkempt stubble and a strange glint in his eyes. Hugging me he said: 'You have to introduce me to Mahesh Bhatt today itself. I have come and that's it. I've come to be as successful as you'.

'Okay . . . okay,' I tried to assuage him. 'But, it's not as simple as that to meet Bhatt saab. I will have to check where he is . . . when would he be free to meet you. Meanwhile, I suggest take this money to buy some nice clothes for yourself.'

'No', he replied. 'What is wrong with these clothes . . . I must meet Mahesh Bhatt . . . you have got to make me meet him.' He kept insisting.

Somehow, I was able to convince him to ride in my car and check into the Hare Rama, Hare Krishna temple guest house where I had made arrangements for him to stay. That evening I called Bhatt saab and said: 'A friend of mine from the university days, is coming to meet you, please be kind to him. He wants to be an actor. Don't say much to him as he is somewhat disturbed.'

A couple of days later Bhatt saab called me in the morning and said: 'Anupam, are you mad or what for sending that chap to me?

In one thousand years he won't become an actor. In fact, he will not become anything in life. He is a madman. Get rid of him. You'd better tell him to go back. You'll be kind to him and do him service if you honestly tell him to go back.'

Later that morning, I went to have breakfast with Swaranjit at the guest house. The minute he saw me he asked: 'What did Mahesh Bhatt say? Is it done? When am I shooting?'

'These things take time Swaranjit . . . have patience', I replied. I just did not have the heart to tell him what Bhatt saab had said.

The television boom was just beginning and Doordarshan had acquired the satellite rights for making some serials. Bhatt saab along with I. K. Behl, started making a series on *Aungulimala Daku*—the powerful and athletic serial killer who features prominently in Buddhism. We were in an outdoor shoot in China Creek, about 40 km from Mumbai when the actor who was playing Aungulimala's guru did not land up. I knew that he just had to chant three words 'Buddham Sharanam Gachami'. So, I told Bhatt saab: 'This is nothing, just put beard on Swaranjit and give him the three words to speak after which I, as Angulimal, have to just touch his feet and push him so that he falls. Just one scene . . . it does not require much work and he would have the feeling of having acted and that too under you.'

'Okay, call him', Bhatt saab agreed.

I called the guesthouse and told Swaranjit: 'Take a taxi fast and come to China Creek. I have got you a role in Bhatt saab's serial. It's just about an hour's drive. Just hurry.'

After about an hour-and-a-half Swaranjit came and straight away hugged me: 'Thank you, thank you very much. Now you see . . . after this I will be a star, I will also have a house . . . everything will be fine.'

Make-up done, the three words and the scene rehearsed, Swaranjit was ready to face the camera—his life-long ambition. Bhatt saab said: 'Action'. But no words were coming out of Swaranjit. He was just producing the same old sound of 'hmmmmm' and 'mmmmmm'. His voice was gone. Bhatt saab looked at me and shouted: 'We are losing the light needed for filming. We can do this scene tomorrow, but I need to shoot the other scene—the pushing scene—right now.

In it, I had to push Swaranjit so that he would fall next to a stone, then turn around and look at me with a feeling of great hurt. But unfortunately, for this silent shot, he could not coordinate his fall even after nine retakes. The fight master briefed him numerous times and with great patience but to no avail. Finally, I took him to one side and explained: 'It is a very simple shot where all you have to do is fall, put your hand between the stone and your forehead, turn back and look at me.'

That did it, or so I thought! He looked at me triumphantly, and then at others making everyone feel that it was simple and this time he would do it.

Bhatt saab shouted: 'Camera ready? Action.'

As per the scene, I gave a gentle push, Swaranjit fell down but removed his hand from the head and banged it on the stone and as he turned, we saw to our shock that his forehead had torn and he was bleeding profusely. But Swaranjit was unconcerned about it. He looked at me and said: 'I did it. I did it na? Was it okay?'

Bhatt saab took me aside and ordered: 'Leave him . . . You leave him immediately. He will commit suicide or even murder you. Look at what he has done . . . what he is capable of.'

That was the last time I saw him. Till today I have no idea about his whereabouts! A sad hiccup in the strange journey to stardom.

Theatre historian, Balwant Gargi, had earned fame early at home and abroad. Always wanting to shock people, his plays in Punjabi, for example, *Loha Kutt* (The Blacksmith, 1944), about the double elopement of a daughter and mother in a blacksmith's family, was a real shocker for its time. *Saelpathar* (Petrified Stone, 1949), *Kanak Di Balli* (Stalk of Wheat, 1968), *Dhuni Di Agg* (Fire in the Furnace, 19770) just to name a few—each highlighting filial hate, sex, violence, betrayal and death, all of which, in fact, were his obsessions. His 'life seemed to be a kind of template of how a Bohemian artiste should behave. Unconventional dress, iconoclastic social behaviour, and his tempestuous marriage to the beautiful Jeannie, his erstwhile young student at the University of Washington in Seattle . . . was the stuff that fed our imagination . . . He would tell us stories about his life, his travels, the plays he had written, the ones he was going to write; all the while urging us to move ahead untrammelled by our history and tradition. He exhibited disdain for convention, community or family. I did not understand what was being said, but each sentence sank somewhere within me and remains with me until today.'[10]

Gargi normally chose difficult plays like the French writer Jean Genet's *The Maids* or his compatriot Jean Anouilh's *Antigone* and built up discussions around them. Shunning the traditional theatre of word acting and method acting, he wanted a stage alive with stunning images, abnormal shapes, strange visions, esoteric chants and surreal music. In visual terms, his theatre would be like a vibrant painting. One of the oft-repeated stories in the department was that while casting for a production of the seventh-century Sanskrit play *Bhagwad-Ajjukium* (The Harlot and the Monk) he asked his female students: 'Who wants to play the harlot?'

All the young women (from well-to-do families) who had come for the audition shrieked: 'I do.'

Gargi replied: 'Yes, that's how it should be . . . a noble girl should play a harlot . . . a harlot a virtuous lady . . . a judge should play a criminal . . . a beggar a king . . . a coward a bandit. We should all play our opposites on the stage, to get rid of our repressed wishes . . . our nightmares . . . our dreams. Things we dare not do in life; the players can act out on the stage. Acting is an art of transformation.'

To find the English word that would best describe Indian prostitutes of those days, he quizzed the students: 'What types of prostitutes are there?'

They sounded out the types: 'courtesan, concubine, strumpet, slut, streetwalker, hooker, harlot, whore, tart . . .'

Finally, they chose 'harlot' because it implied historical distance and appropriate characterisation. ('Hooker' was American and too casual, 'streetwalker' too modern and 'courtesan' too refined).

'Actors are the big judges of words,' he would remark. 'They spin a word and know by its ring if it is counterfeit . . . they know its exact weight, its associations, its rhythm, its colour. They feel words because they transmit feelings through them.'

My next brief stop at the Panjab University, on the track to becoming an actor, was indeed a memorable one. I recall that shortly after joining, Balwant Gargi wanted me to walk on stage. As I did so, he looked at my movements and asked, with a big frown on his face: 'What makes you think you can become a good actor?'

I was deeply hurt by this question. Here I was visualising myself as Himachal Pradesh's best actor and I was told that I could not even walk properly on stage. I then decided to hone my talents and worked seriously on improving my skills. I first made a beeline for the library, a vast and essential repository of knowledge for a newcomer. I devoured books on a variety of theatrical genres (both ancient and contemporary) with an emphasis on Greek theatre, Roman theatre, Indian theatre (including rare material on Sanskrit theatre)! My constant companions were giants in the field such as Jerzy Marian Grotowski (from Poland), Bertolt Brecht (from Germany), Konstantin Stanislavski (from Russia; credited with evolving the technique of 'method acting') and George Bernard Shaw (from Ireland). I literally absorbed their works like an enormous blotting paper.

That one year in Chandigarh whirred by in a swift sequence that involved acting in an assortment of plays along with many wonderful people apart from participating in a slew of workshops and seminars. And from the abyss of a mere third class when passing out of college, I reached the summit at the university by standing first and being awarded the Mohan Rakesh Gold Medal.

It was a glorious period for me and the first rung in the ladder that catapulted me upwards and beyond.

Incidentally, I did return the one hundred rupees to my mother, but only in instalments, sometimes it was ten rupees a month and twice I was able to pay her with a twenty.

8

GRADUATING IN THEATRE

After being taught and trained by Balwant Gargi and Amal Allana, my natural progression was to move on to National School of Drama (NSD), New Delhi. This time I gained admission.

In Delhi, I discovered that theatre was at the crossroads. The 1960s had marked the heyday of theatre in the nation's capital. After that, the nation entered a state of turmoil in 1974-1975. Prime Minister Indira Gandhi imposed internal Emergency on 25 June 1975, which lasted till end-March 1977. I shall not go into the details, since they are only too well known, except to say that freedom of expression was drastically curtailed. It became a dark period in the history of our nation—something which has not been forgotten to this day. Theatre was laid under siege, but its spirit was not destroyed.

Over three dozen theatre groups mushroomed in Delhi, but they had little in common vis-à-vis their objectives, their audiences or outreach. Just as in Chandigarh, these Delhi groups were patronised by influential industrialists, powerful ministers or mighty bureaucrats. Each season a plethora of plays were performed, but most of them were just not up to the mark. Talent on stage was also a highly misused appellation; it was bestowed on those with a knack for being unduly flamboyant or crassly melodramatic.

Delhi theatre was both linguistically and seasonally divided. Hindi and Urdu plays as well as English plays existed as distinct entities. Productions 'hibernated' in summer because of the scorching heat and sprang back to life by October and continued to buzz with

113

activity till the end of April during which time audiences would crisscross the city shuttling from one venue to another.

The vernacular theatre followed closely on the heels of its Hindustani counterpart. The Bengali, Tamil, Malayalam and Punjabi stage drew upon community appeal, mixing culture with regional politics and social issues. It solidified its reputation for presenting interesting and in some cases, innovative plays. But it was the Punjabi theatre, mainly in the Sapru theatre auditorium—by and large crude, vulgar and loud—which, though very popular, did the greatest harm. While discerning audiences chose other theatres, the crowds thronged the Punjabi stage performances to see plays such as *Dhi Jawan, Gavandi Pareshan* (Daughter Grows up, Neighbours get Disturbed), *Budi Ghodi, Lal Lagham* and *Chaddi Jawani Buddhe Nu*.

Here I must also mention *Ram Leela* of the Shriram Bharatiya Kala Kendra, founded by Sumitra Charat Ram, a respected patron of the fine arts, and later taken over by her daughter, Shobha Deepak Singh. One could not help but admire the admirable blend of poetry, music, dance, ceremonials, rituals and superb building of tension in this saga. Like Kavi Kalidas' works or Kabir's dohas (couplets), *Ram Leela* had also become a classic. With its discipline, punctuality and lavish sets, the Kendra was, for a long time, the only complete theatre in Delhi, holding its audiences spellbound.

English theatre in the capital did not touch the lives of ordinary Delhites, yet it enjoyed a great deal of popularity, perhaps because the Queen's language has become an essential and integral part of our urban existence. This theatre became a subject of controversy for several years and later, the butt of ridicule among a few sophisticated aficionados. This attitude could perhaps be attributed to the fact that what was presented was just hastily patched up trivia. At one stage, it was more or less on the brink of collapse. Many considered it good riddance, but I felt that it was both a dangerous and a destructive attitude, for it was the English language theatre that was mainly responsible for whatever stage traditions Delhi had. It also provided a level of professionalism to both the performance and production.

English theatre had retained some quaint characteristics. The artistes going on the stage after the show for a 'curtain call' was, and still is, a must. The artistes did tend to perform nervously the classics penned by William Shakespeare, George Bernard Shaw or Anton Chekhov or even the energetic French farce.

The father of the English theatre wave in the capital was a Jewish director-professor-linguist, Charles Petras, who died during a hunger strike in support of the theatre. Petras rented the first floor of a Connaught Place building and staged the noted French playwright Jean-Paul Satre's *No Exit* on a bare platform with the audience on three sides. Later, he also produced some fabulous plays like the well-known French writer Albert Camus's *The Misunderstanding* with impressionistic colours and a crazy decor. Theatre enthusiasts such as Joy Michael, Michael Over and Jamila Verghese worked under this cigar-smoking, paunchy, black-bearded French-style, director.

After his death, his theatre disappeared, and a restaurant appeared in its place, which spewed out blaring music in the name of entertainment.

The Little Theatre Group (LTG) under the leadership of the ageing I. L. Das had been steadfast for almost thirty years and was the only group to have built its own theatre, providing a tremendous boost to the movement. It exists even today on New Delhi's Copernicus Marg, named after the renowned Polish astronomer, Nicolaus Copernicus (1473 to 1543).

The theatre movement got the real impetus when Yatrik was founded in 1964, under the leadership of Joy Michael, who remained its director for 40 years. During this period, Yatrik collaborated with eminent theatre personalities such as the Royal Academy of Dramatic Art (RADA) trained Ebrahim Alkazi (the director of the National School of Drama from 1962 to 1977) and Alyque Padamsee, and emerging talents like Roshan Seth, Sushma Seth, Barry John, Marcus Murch, Kulbhushan Kharbanda, Prabha Tonk and Kusum Haidar, all of whom were passionate about theatre. Within a short span, Yatrik surged ahead. Its productions became 'a must' for the elite theatre-going crowd of Delhi and provided enough material to the critics to write about.

However, as it happens in many cases, its sudden and enormous success was short-lived and it soon began stagnating. Instead of moving upwards, it moved horizontally. There was a clash of personalities. Roshan Seth quit and Marcus Murch and Barry John took to producing plays for educational institutions.

And then came, the one and only, Ebrahim Alkazi. As the director of the National School of Drama (NSD), 'he revolutionised Hindi theatre by the magnificence of his vision and the meticulousness of his technical discipline . . . A strict disciplinarian, who did rigorous research before producing a play, leading to important advances in scenography design, his standards later became very influential.'

The next three years at the NSD—which went by in the blink of an eye—marked one of the most fascinating periods of my life. I began discovering the magic of international cinema. I entered the wonderful world of legends such as Sir Laurence Olivier, Sir Alec Guinness, Clarke Gable, Charlton Heston, Marlon Brando, Gregory Peck, Anthony Quinn, Charlie Chaplin, Arthur Miller, Tennessee Williams, Cecil B. DeMille, David Lean, Francis Ford Coppola, François Truffaut, Akira Kurosawa, Vittorio De Sica and many others.

Closer to home, I came to know quite a bit of the art of theatre through respected stage personalities such as Manohar Singh, Habib Tanvir, Uttara Baokar and Surekha Sikri. I watched with rapt attention the works of noted Indian film-makers including Bimal Roy, Satyajit Ray, Mrinal Sen, K. A. Abbas, V. Shantaram, Mehboob Khan, Chetan Anand, Guru Dutt, Raj Kapoor, Hrishikesh Mukherjee, Vijay Bhatt and Adoor Gopalakrishnan.

At the NSD, from the very start of the first academic session, I was a star who was acting in every single play in the lead roles. In my second year, I met Sukhdev, the famous documentary film-maker who selected me to do the lead role in his first feature film, which was never made. A number of known foreign teachers would come as guest lecturers on the faculty. Lots of plays were being staged and I was devouring everything as a valuable gift. Here I was truly in my elements.

Besides, unlike many others, I knew modern Indian theatre and had read many drama books. I was very excited about learning.

. I was learning make-up from Indu dada, Yoga from Sharmaji, Modern Indian Drama from Nemichandra Jain. We had Mohanty dada as our music teacher. Rita Kothari was our movement teacher. Nibha Khanna was our classical Indian drama teacher. And, there was the great, the one and only, E. Alkazi himself. My seniors were the likes of Pankaj Kapoor, K. K. Raina, Naseeruddin Shah, Raj and Nadira Babbar, Ranjit Kapoor, Anil Chaudhary, Om Shivpuri, Om Puri to name just a few from the long and illustrious list. We were exposed to the performances at the Kamani Auditorium, Shri Ram Centre, Little Theatre Group auditorium and Triveni Kala Sangam. There was enormous talent . . . an amazing richness all around.

However, there were two other aspects to my life in Delhi that were running on parallel tracks. One was the stay in the hostel of Vakil Lane, next to Bengali market and study in Bahawalpur House. Life was full. But something in this 'full life' was taking over, which was to consume me later.

Once again, I had fallen in love!

At the NSD, there was this girl who entered my life and fell in love with me. Instead of revealing her name, let me give her the name Radha. She was possessive and very proprietorial to the point of being obsessive. My Radha tried to commit suicide twice to prove her love for me. And if any girl tries to kill herself twice for your sake, you are convinced that she has been handpicked by God to be your life partner. In reality, Radha and I would always struggle to keep our relationship on an even keel since we were forever clashing and at cross purposes. If I would say the colour white was good, she would retort that white was bad and black was good. If I ever said that an apple a day kept the doctor away, she would forcefully say: 'No! Apple is no good; it is the banana that is better and keeps the doctor away.' And God forbid, if I would persist with my viewpoint, she would pick up a knife and cut herself. In other words, Radha was very emotional and volatile by nature and every reaction was in extremes. And worse, Radha would occasionally see a ghost when there was not even a shadow around. Let me explain.

One evening, after having spent a day together, Radha and I decided to see a late-night movie together at the Regal Cinema. Before that, we went out for dinner to Volga, a popular restaurant in New Delhi's Connaught Place (which was then a 'happening place'). Just as we sat at our table, three girls, whom I didn't even know, were sitting two tables away from us making conversation amongst themselves and laughing merrily.

Seeing them laugh, suddenly, Radha flared up and asked me: 'Which one of them is your girlfriend?'

I was taken aback: 'My girlfriend? You are my girlfriend, sitting in front of me.'

She then raised the decibel level by shouting: 'Shut up! I am sure you must have invited them here.'

A couple at the next table began staring at us. I tried to pacify her: 'No, certainly not. I don't even know them.'

She then wanted us to switch seats. I told her: 'If we do that in front of everyone, it will look odd.'

On seeing that she had started clutching a knife, I quickly agreed: 'Okay, okay. Keep the knife down and let's switch places!'

I told her that I would pretend as if I need to wash my hands and go to the washroom and she should order the food in the meantime. When I returned, Radha was seated in my place, facing the rest of the clientele and I sat in her seat, facing the wall. Soon the food arrived as per her gourmet choice—sweet corn chicken soup, boneless chilly chicken with gravy, fried rice with egg and hakka vegetable noodles.

We were just about halfway into our soups, when the girls laughed again during their conversation.

Radha abruptly threw a tantrum: 'Anupam, we will not eat in this restaurant.'

I literally cooed in her ears: 'What do you mean sweetheart? We have had such a nice time since morning. After dinner, we plan to watch a film as well . . . I have the tickets . . .'

But my attempt at pacifying her did not make any difference. 'I will count till ten. If you don't get up, I will throw all this food on your head,' she threatened.

As my luck would have it, at that particular moment, those girls laughed for the third time. Radha began counting: 'One, two, three, four, five, six . . .'

I did not take her threat seriously and remained seated, but she continued: 'Seven, eight, nine, ten.' She looked at me. I asked her to start eating. Then seething with anger, her nostrils flaring and face intense, she stood up and abruptly yanked the tablecloth and flung the entire contents of the table all over me. And then she walked away from there.

You can well imagine my plight . . . and visualise my hapless sight—sweet corn chicken soup had accumulated in my lap, the boneless chilly chicken with gravy mixed with the egg fried rice was dribbling down my T-shirt in splotchy waves and the vegetable Haka noodles were dangling from my head the way a traditional *sehra* (headdress) hangs from a bridegroom's head. The only difference being that while the sehra adds a royal splendour to the groom's overall looks, mine could not have presented me in a worse state . . . it was pathetic, miserable and abandoned.

A sudden hush descended on the restaurant. All eyes were on me. The three 'laughing girls' seemed to have been silenced like Egyptian mummies. One could have heard a pin drop all around. People were not even breathing (or so it seemed to me) and I was the centre of all that unwanted attraction. They were waiting for me to react . . .

After what seemed an eternity, I calmly stood up, picked up a couple of serviettes from my table and a few from the next one to clean the soup from my clothes, patted away the chilly chicken and fried rice and wiped the noodles off my head and my shoulders. Noticing that everyone was still staring at me, I told the shocked diners: 'What are you all staring at? Enjoy your food.' I then left the restaurant. In my shocked state, I forgot to pay the bill. In any case, the bill was not forthcoming either.

Walking out, suddenly the title of William Shakespeare's play *All's Well that Ends Well* came to mind. And then, as if I was in a dialogue with the great master, I murmured to myself: 'All does not end well, Mr William Shakespeare!'

As most of you would have experienced, 'a human voice in song is capable of expressing an unfathomably complex blend of feelings'. That night, as the shadows lengthened, I sat feeling miserable and wretched in my room. Soon, I could hear echoes of the voice of that gifted playback singer with 'an intuitive sense of beauty, charm and grace who had a unique, elegant and profoundly artistic style of singing', Talat Mehmood, and began to hum softly to myself his evergreen number:

Shaam-e-gam ki qasam aaj gamagi hai ham
Aa bhi jaa aa bhi jaa aaj mere sanam
Shaam-e-gam ki qasam
Dil pareshaan hai raat viraan hai
Dekh jaa kis tarah aaj tanahaa hai ham
Sshaam-e-gam ki qasam.[11]

I swear on this sorrowful evening
I am today melancholic
Please come, please come today my love
The heart is troubled, the night is desolate
Please come and see how very lonely I am today.

Completely exhausted and confused by my situation, I thought that my only solution to the complicated relationship with Radha was to run away. So, during my holidays, I stole Rs 100 from my classmate Ananth Desai's pocket and went to the ISBT (Inter-State Bus Terminus) and caught a bus without even checking where it would take me. I landed in that ancient and sacred city of Haridwar—an important Hindu pilgrimage centre on the banks of the river

Ganges. I went to an ashram, shaved my head and became a kind of monk. I began to function as if on auto mode. My job was to get up at 4.30 in the morning and serve food to numerous pilgrims who would assemble there every day. But I soon realised that this was not the place for me simply because I was not made for that kind of world. My thoughts were neither pious nor was I a practising person, nor was I able to adjust to the morning and evening prayers and the various rituals required of me. My entire chemistry was so very different. Without informing the management of the ashram, I ran away to Nainital, a scenic hill station, set around a giant lake in the Himalayas, to meet up with my teacher B. M. Shah, who was the director of the Little Theatre Group.

Since I was in a state of flux, my stay in Nainital too was short-lived.

I was clearly at a crossroads in my life. Back in Delhi, I used to aimlessly walk the lengths of various roads like Copernicus Marg, Raj Path and Feroze Shah Road. I found I had no plan and sense of the future.

I knew that my experiences in Chandigarh and Delhi had changed my outlook towards life. By contrast unfortunately, whenever I went back to Shimla, I would feel low and disheartened—simply because the lives of the people there had not moved forward. Santosh halwai's life was the same. Mirchu had gotten married otherwise his life too remained stagnant. Tinchu Ram had passed away. Sharmaji, Raina saab and all the others of their age-group had retired. Seeing a certain amount of ennui in peoples' lives there, I realised that life is 90 per cent monotony and just 10 per cent excitement. I would just run away as fast as I could either back to Chandigarh or Delhi where, in contrast, there were Balwant Gargi's uninhibited but rich conversations or Alkazi's theatre productions of Shakespeare's *Hamlet*, Dharamvir Bharati's *Andha Yug* and Girish Karnad's *Tughlak*. In that world of mine, life was unbelievably exciting and full of immense possibilities.

My own experiences have taught me that tragedy and trauma teach you a lot and makes you aware of who you are if you don't indulge in self-pity. Actually, come to think of it, even self-pity, moulds you. It may be a cliché to say that catastrophe and distress makes an artiste. That's because artistes, in any field, be it art, writing, poetry, cinema and drama, music, are all acutely tuned and sensitive to whatever is happening in and around their lives. I don't think that people like Santosh halwai or say Polu Ram ever questioned their lives. They accepted it for what it was. I and my ilk on the other hand intellectualise trauma, tragedy and loneliness. Spurred by my survival instinct, I somehow kept alive the small flame of optimism.

I know what solitude is. But the world of creativity is so wonderful, so engulfing, so consuming, so overpowering there is no time to indulge in loneliness. Creativity is a great stimulant. It is like sex—the more you experience it, the more you seek it. It is just so fascinating. As I grappled with my depression during that period thinking: *God, why me* . . . and questioned what my life is all about, there was still a part of me very alive and buoyed by my years of creative study. Reading the Spanish playwright and poet Federico Garcia Lorca or the Russian master Anton Chekhov, I felt I could identify with them. Even Charlie Chaplin's life I felt was like mine. You may laugh at this, but I strongly feel that the American playwright Eugene O'Neill's life was similar to mine. As an artiste, it was like holding a mirror up to my own life and finding a kinship reflected back. This is the true greatness of creativity—it builds a fraternity; it rescues you when you are lost.

In this my chosen life, I was surrounded by kindred souls. I recall going to that small, one-bedroom house of Balwant Gargi, on Curzon Road (now known as Kasturba Gandhi Marg) and meeting the greatest minds in the field of literature, art and culture—Elia Kazan, M. F. Husain, Khushwant Singh, Ved Mehta, Satish Gujral, Yamini Krishnamurti, Uma Sharma and many others. His house was a treasure trove of knowledge and information, gossip and news, making for engaging dinner conversations in the course of an evening. I had never seen before such a social engagement. I was suddenly getting exposed to the richness of art and culture. My mind and soul were being fed.

Those three years in the drama school were the richest years of my life even though one year was also the most traumatic. But I was evolving into who I would become in the years to come. My friend Ashok Chopra once told me that if God was to ever grant him one wish for his next life, he would without hesitation say: 'The same life all over again, with all its ups and downs, successes and failures, because each failure has been beautiful and enriching with a lesson of its own.' How beautiful!

I think, if given an opportunity, I too would want the same life all over again including the trauma.

An unfortunate incident took place during my third year at the NSD. For the first time in its history, an agitation started against Alkazi. A group of students got together complaining against his 'autocratic' ways of running the NSD and levelled a charge that he was a 'dictator' and that the institute needed democracy.

It was unbelievably shocking that a man who had built a school with sheer blood, sweat, hard work, determination, fervour and passion, into a prestigious institute since 1962 and placed it on an international map was being questioned in such a manner. Today, I realise that there are some such students in every institute, every university and every organisation. Soon the agitation caught momentum and about 80 per cent of the students were made to join into what came to be known as the 'Young Turks Group'. Just about a handful of us remained 'loyal' to him. How could we not? What we were and what we are today is because of him. Alkazi was a Goliath. The rest of us were mere pygmies.

Personally, I was shocked, disheartened and demoralised. The important fact is that theatre needs discipline and that is what Alkazi had created at the NSD. That's why those giant, spellbinding productions were launched. That's what gave the institute its name and prestige. Yes, in the world of theatre, as in cinema, one needs a strong leadership. Today,

I run my acting school—Actor Prepares—which is very successful but that doesn't make me an Alkazi. We are all miniature Alkazis. A legend like Alkazi is born only once in a lifetime. And lucky are those who can be taught by him . . . learn from him . . . follow in his footsteps. And I must admit that it was his discipline that has made me what I am today. If today Anupam Kher is here in New York, working in the NBC serial *New Amsterdam*, whatever I have achieved nationally and internationally, it is because of what Alkazi taught me, imparted to me. For me, his attitude towards art and theatre automatically percolated to cinema. Nobody else could have taught me all about aesthetics, about the difference between being an actor and an artiste. You can be a successful actor but remain aesthetically very mediocre.

In the final analysis, the agitation against Alkazi was not Alkazi's loss, but a terrible loss for the institution and also, for those so-called 'Young Turks' who unfortunately are nowhere in the theatre, or for that matter, in any scene today. Little could they achieve in their lives. A pity indeed! Perhaps they had forgotten the age-old saying: '*Bin guru gyan kahan se paon*' (Where can I get the knowledge without the guidance of a teacher).

Here I am reminded of a very interesting incident from those days. Because of my emotional state of mind, I had not been able to submit my western drama project on *Pier Gynt*, the five-act play in verse by the Norwegian playwright Henrik Ibsen. Alkazi, always somewhat dramatic by nature, said to me: 'If tomorrow, by 2 o'clock you don't submit your project, then you're out of the school! Don't even waste your energy in coming here . . . just leave the school at 1.45.'

Given my frazzled nerves, I could not finish the project. So, I wished my class fellows goodbye with the words: 'It was great being with you . . . goodbye friends . . . I will be leaving today as I have been asked to leave the school.'

However, one of them cautioned me (I believe it was Satish Kaushik): 'I suggest you attend Mr Alkazi's class and tell him personally. After all, he has been your teacher for so long.'

I agreed!

Often, if he wanted to make a statement, Alkazi would come to the class in a put on bad mood which put the fear of God in all of us. He said: 'Okay. So, let me ask you one final time. How many of you students have completed the western drama project?' Out of fear, I could not say anything, so I just kept quiet. He said: 'Let me check with each one of you. Suhas Khandke, have you done the project?'

'I have done sir.'

'Anang Desai, have you done the project?'

'I have done sir.'

'Kavita Chaudhary?'

'I have done sir.'

'Anupam Kher?'

'*I will do sir.*'

'Satish Kaushik?'

'I have done sir.'

He didn't say anything to me. The class continued. I finished the project that night with the help of Satish Kaushik. I imagine that I had successfully slipped something by my 'guru'.

Many years later, while I was shooting for a film in Pahalgam in Kashmir, I learnt that Alkazi was also holidaying there. I decided to meet him. By this time, he had quit the NSD and theatre for good. And I was a recognised actor in my own right. On meeting me, he said: 'Well done, Anupam. Very good. I am very proud of you. I saw your film *Saaransh* in the Regal Theatre ... it's a very good film. And you were very good ... brilliant. I'm glad ... By the way, I am planning to go for a picnic why don't you join me?'

For me, going for a picnic with Alkazi was like going to the moon with Neil Armstrong. I said yes without any hesitation. We went to the riverside and found a quiet corner where he had some cold beer bottles. I used to hardly drink at that time, and even today, I am more of a 'social drinker', but that afternoon, I was very happy about the fact that I was actually having drinks with my teacher whom I adored, admired and revered like God. After a glass-and-a-half of beer inside me, I said: 'Sir, I have been wanting to tell you something for a very long time and, I think, today is the day to say so. You remember the incident about that class project on western drama, which I couldn't do on time? Well sir, when you were checking who all had completed it, I was able to trick you. Because that day, you had questioned each one of us about who had done the assignment and while all others said, "I have done it sir . . ."'

Alkazi interrupted and said: 'You said, "I will do it . . ."' He looked at me and said with a light smile: 'Anupam, what makes you think I did not notice it? I remember you said, "I will do it sir". But, if I had pointed it out and stopped there, you would've not been sitting here and sharing a beer with me now.'

In a word that was the magnanimous Alkazi, who through his sharp and crisp memory remembered a minor incident like this even decades later. Precious lessons learnt at every turn.

As a part of our curriculum at the drama school, the students had to go to the prestigious Film and Television Institute of India at Poona (now Pune) for six months of study and training. Those were the most amazing six months of my student life. I watched outstanding films of the great international masters one could come across those days, under the guidance of Satish Bahadur, who was the professor of film appreciation: Akira Kurosawa from Japan whose films influenced cinema the world over, the Italian Federico Fellini's 'highly idiosyncratic visions of society' through films which 'are a unique combination of memory, dreams, fantasy and desire' and which were labelled as 'Fellinian' or 'Felliniesque', the French film-maker Jean-Luc Godard who was 'the pioneer of the 1960s French new wave film movement', the Greek-American Elia Kazan who was described as 'the most honoured and influential director in Hollywood history', the Swedish director Ingmar Bergman to name just a few.

In addition, I worked in 21 small film projects—in different roles and scenes, worked closely on diploma films, tried to understand the technique of shots, lighting, compositions, and such. This created a lot of jealousy amongst my other classmates to the extent that one day, my dear friend Satish Kaushik came to me in a drunken state and picked a fight: 'What do you think of yourself . . . that you are a big star or something here? Remember, just because of your fair skin and good features you are getting good roles and not because of any talent or anything.'

I count as one of my singular achievements to be the chairperson of both these institutes—National School of Drama and the Film and Television Institute of India. It's an honour close to my heart, and a treasure worth more than words can describe.

I allow myself the luxury to say it myself, but I did the most unbelievable work at the NSD. It was the high point of my life. An appallingly poor student in academics, who barely made it through school but then went on to outdo himself—first at the Department of Indian Theatre at Panjab University in Chandigarh and later, in National School of Drama, the country's highest and most prestigious institute of theatre.

I had conquered the world.

I felt wealthy—very rich. Opulent without riches.

For those in the creative arts, life is very uncertain. Those who choose this path have to be prepared for the challenges and the isolations inherent. You can be a great painter, a great writer, a great poet or a great actor and yet live in penury because you have not been 'discovered'. The talents of many greats in these endeavours have usually been discovered decades after they have passed away. It is only a few 'lucky' ones who achieve both fame and monetary success in their lifetimes. In such trying circumstances, one finds strength in angels (not necessarily from heaven). This has been a great life lesson for me. Given the challenges of this field, it is not surprising that an artiste can get diverted from the path and lose sight of the goal. If luck holds, someone appears, as if from nowhere, to hold them and guide them back on the right path.

Here, I would be failing in my duty if I did not mention the three hands . . . the three guardian angels of my life—my drama teachers, who guided me, groomed me and moulded me in my self-discovery as an actor. Each one taught me lessons that have stood me in good stead in my journey of life. The first one, as you may have guessed, was Balwant Gargi, who opened my eyes so that I could envisage the magnanimity of theatre in general and life in particular. The next was Amal Allana who taught me how to bring to life on stage the characters from the page of a book.

And, finally, the one and only, the NSD director, reputedly the 'king of Indian theatre': His Excellency Mr Ebrahim Alkazi. He taught me that the grander your vision, the larger will your world be! And the deeper you feel from your heart, the more humanity you will exude!

In June 1978, my education at the National School of Drama came to an end. I was completely free. And I was ready to enjoy my total freedom. But I began to feel suffocated by this freedom . . . I was like a ship without a rudder. Until then I had a scheduled routine to follow. But, suddenly, there was nothing to do. Where should I go next? What prospects lay ahead for me?

Every morning, I had nowhere to go. It was a very strange feeling—a feeling of emptiness. Also, suddenly after residing comfortably in the hostel, I had no place to stay. Finally, I took a small room on the fourth floor, in the dhobi colony, behind Bengali Market. The owner of the house was an alcoholic who, after getting drunk every night, would pee from the fourth floor and the victims would be anyone and everyone sleeping or sitting on the ground floor or just passing by. A train of filthy abuses would follow from both sides. Suddenly, my life, instead of being full of drama, had become dramatically chaotic.

I went from Alkazi's highly disciplined schedules to a point where there was no discipline, no schedule. From the world of make-belief, I fell into the real world. And there was no scholarship . . . which meant no money, which I needed badly.

Luckily, I got an assignment from the Modern School on Barakhamba Road to direct its annual play. I directed the French playwright Molière's (actual name being Jean-Baptiste Poquelin) play *The Doctor in Spite of Himself* (*Le Medecin malgre lui*)—a farce, in which I gave the boy's role to a girl—Radha Sahni, who apparently got an award for it. It got me another assignment, this time from the Kamala Nehru College, near Siri Fort area. I did John Millington Synge's three-act play *The Playboy of the Western World*. But nothing significant was happening in my life. My class fellows were going to Bombay to try their luck in cinema, but I was stuck in Delhi. I too wanted to go to Bombay but not as a pauper, without having achieved much. I wanted to be someone before landing there as I had a feeling that it would be easier to establish myself with a name and a first-rate reputation attached to it.

Just to create a routine for myself . . . go somewhere . . . I decided to do a three-month massage course from a 'beauty parlour' operating in Shankar Market. Looking back, I see how inventive and curious I was, eager to be always doing something. This inherent survivor quality has always kept me resilient.

9

A Rendezvous with Sir Richard Attenborough

In life, often we are swayed or falsely buoyed by moments. When we achieve a degree of success, we convince ourselves and believe that Lady Luck will be a constant companion for a lifetime. Providence is very capricious and can desert us on a whim. When that happens, one experiences gloom and misery. It is easy to sink into despair and believe that success is destined to elude us. The inherent reality, however, is that all things pass. Change is the only constant.

To be a truly successful human being, I believe in and adopt the principle of a 'karma yogi' according to the Bhagavad-Gita. We should be selfless and not be motivated to seek the fruits of our labour. In other words, we must remain unwavering and composed if our efforts go unrewarded. Karma Yoga advocates the path of unselfish action. It teaches that we should act according to dharma, without being attached to the fruits or personal consequences. Be in a state that purifies the mind.

As an artiste who engages with the world, I embrace this principle and try at all times, to engage in the large reality. I am guided by joy as I pursue my endeavours. In fact, the concept of karma yoga is not restricted to doctrines alone; even the eminent English poet Rudyard Kipling (1865 to 1936) echoed it—as a sagely advice from a father to his son—in his legendary poem 'If':

If you can keep your head when all about you
Are losing theirs and blaming it on you,
If you can trust yourself when all men doubt you,
But make allowance for their doubting too;
If you can wait and not be tired by waiting,
Or being lied about, don't deal in lies,
Or being hated, don't give way to hating,
And yet don't look too good, nor talk too wise.

If you can dream—and not make dreams your master;
If you can think—and not make thoughts your aim;
If you can meet with Triumph and Disaster
And treat those two impostors just the same;
If you can bear to hear the truth you've spoken
Twisted by knaves to make a trap for fools,
Or watch the things you gave your life to, broken,
And stoop and build 'em up with worn-out tools:

If you can make one heap of all your winnings
And risk it on one turn of pitch-and-toss,
And lose, and start again at your beginnings
And never breathe a word about your loss;
If you can force your heart and nerve and sinew
To serve your turn long after they are gone,
And so hold on when there is nothing in you
Except the Will which says to them: 'Hold on!'

If you can talk with crowds and keep your virtue,
Or walk with Kings—nor lose the common touch,
If neither foes nor loving friends can hurt you,
If all men count with you, but none too much;
If you can fill the unforgiving minute
With sixty seconds' worth of distance run,
Yours is the Earth and everything that's in it,
And—which is more—you'll be a Man, my son!

So universal is the appeal and so widely hailed is Kipling's advice that two lines from the poem—which reflect its central theme—are engraved, quite aptly, above the players' entrance to the famed Centre Court at Wimbledon, London, the epitome of all things British:

If you can meet with Triumph and Disaster
And treat those two impostors just the same.

That is what I believe we should all be aiming to achieve: a kind of detachment from the vicissitudes of life. As far as I am concerned, I have tried to consciously achieve this delicate balance and that is how I have been able to overcome the many reverses I have encountered in life.

One of them was when I was turned down for the role of Pandit Jawaharlal Nehru (independent India's first prime minister) in Sir Richard Attenborough's film, *Gandhi*, based on the life of Mohandas Karamchand (Mahatma) Gandhi, released in November 1982 and which won eight Oscar Awards.

It was the multitalented Dolly Thakore (an actor, a casting director and a BBC-trained journalist) who was my contact person. She put me in touch with the internationally respected director and actor in late 1980. I had seen a few movies in which Sir Attenborough had acted, for example, *The Great Escape* (1963; directed by John Sturges) and *Shatranj Ke Khiladi* (1977; directed by Satyajit Ray in which Sir Attenborough played a cameo). Much later, in 1993, he also featured in the Steven Spielberg-directed trendsetter—*Jurassic Park*.

My meeting with Dolly was very positive. She virtually gushed: 'Anupam, I have seen many of your plays. You are a brilliant actor.'

'Thank you, Dolly.'

'You see, Sir Richard Attenborough is in town [New Delhi] and he is casting for *Gandhi*. I have suggested your name to him.'

'For Gandhi's role?'[12]

'Not quite. I was thinking of Nehru since you resemble him a lot.'

I observed: 'Maybe because he was a Kashmiri and so am I.'

After that, I started earnestly preparing for Nehru's role. I shaved off my luxurious moustache and beard, which I had carefully grown and nurtured till then. I managed to obtain a white achkan (a knee-length coat buttoned in the front) and tight pyjamas, similar to those Nehru usually wore. Affecting Nehru's favourite fashion accessory, I affixed a red rose in the lapel. I meticulously studied Nehru's mannerisms and style of speaking from archival films (YouTube was non-existent then). I even fashioned a paper boat resembling Gandhi cap on my head. In addition, I memorised and rehearsed innumerable times—the poignant speech that Nehru had delivered after Mahatma Gandhi's assassination on 30 January 1948 (here is an excerpt):

> Friends and comrades, the light has gone out of our lives and there is darkness everywhere. I do not know how to say and what to say. But our beloved leader, Bapu, as we called him, is no more. Perhaps it's wrong of me to say that, but nevertheless, we will not see him again as we have seen him all these years . . .

A few days later, Dolly called me again: 'Anupam . . . Richard Attenborough is staying in New Delhi's Ashok Hotel. You must come and meet him.' She gave me the room number and the time. I donned my elegant Nehru costume (with the customary rose in the lapel) and headed towards my destination with my childhood best friend and partner in many 'crimes' Vijay Sehgal (who had, by then, taken up a job and had just been transferred from Shimla to New Delhi).

Along the way I kept on muttering: 'The light has gone out of our lives and there is darkness everywhere . . . The light has gone out of our lives and there is darkness everywhere.' Vijay knew that I was rehearsing my scene for the forthcoming audition, but I wonder what the cab driver thought of my odd behaviour. I was very confident of bagging the role. In fact, there was never a doubt in my mind . . . after all I was a gold medallist from the Department of Indian Theatre . . . Moreover, Dolly had personally recommended my name. In fact, in my mind, I had already bagged an Oscar for playing Nehru's character.

At the Ashok Hotel, Dolly and a British casting director were anxiously waiting for me in the lobby. Vijay took me to a corner and whispered excitedly: 'You've made it . . . You have really made it!'

Dolly Thakore introduced me to the British casting director who looked at me rather appreciatively further encouraging my feeling of being cast as Nehru in the film. The three of us boarded the lift, which began its ascent to the floor where my meeting with Sir Attenborough was to take place. As the lift moved up, my spirits too rose, and I felt that the day had come, and I was literally 'moving up' in life. The lift operator was a tall bloke with rugged features. I noticed that the Englishman was continuously staring at him. The operator deferentially took us to the fifth floor. Just as we got out of the lift, I saw the impressive Sir Richard Attenborough appear in front of me. I was dumbstruck. He had his arms around a man's shoulder, saying, in a delighted tone: 'I'm so happy to meet you, Roshan! I have finally found my Nehru.'

I looked questioningly at Dolly, who immediately turned her face to avoid me and pretended to be focusing her attention elsewhere.

When Sir Attenborough saw me, he asked Dolly: 'And this young fellow is here for what role?'

Instead of her, I replied: 'Sir, I am Nehru. I am Pandit Jawaharlal Nehru.'

He said: 'Sorry young chap; I have already finalised Roshan Seth for that role.'

Involuntarily, a series of questions flew out of my mouth: 'How could you finalise somebody else for that role? You have not even auditioned me? Have you seen my screen test? Have you seen me performing as Nehru?' I then added for good measure: 'This is absolutely unprofessional, not expected from a Britisher . . . and that too from a person of your stature.'

As we walked to his room, I could hear a din in my head and a voice running through my head: *The light has gone out of our lives and there is darkness everywhere . . . The light has gone out of our lives and there is darkness everywhere . . . The light has gone out of our lives and there is darkness everywhere . . .*

Suddenly, I heard Sir Attenborough say: 'Okay, perform Nehru.'

But as soon as I heard those words, my mind went blank!

I had rehearsed and practised for so long, but when I had to prove myself in front of a world-famous actor-director . . . the one who had the power to open the doors to my future . . . the one whose direction would get me an Oscar . . . I just froze. As moments ticked by, I said instead: 'Okay, forget Nehru. Give me another role.'

Sir Richard Attenborough kept toying with the telephone for a while. Then he looked quizzically at Dolly.

'Give me the role of a person, who actually participated in the freedom struggle of India,' I persisted.

Sir Attenborough then went to consult with the British casting director and even though I could not hear what he was saying, I added desperately: 'I'm not asking for Gandhi's role . . . not Sardar Patel . . . not Nehru and never Jinnah,[13] but someone who actually participated in the freedom struggle of India.'

Sir Richard flipped through the casting file (which the Englishman had just given him) and said: 'Okay, you play Khan Abdul Ghaffar Khan.'

'Frontier Gandhi?'[14]

He nodded in the affirmative. I thanked him for his offer.

But then, just as I had started feeling elated to have bagged a role in the film, the British casting director butted in to state: 'Sorry Richard, I have already finalised somebody else for that role.'

Sir Attenborough asked: 'Who may that be?'

'That lift operator. He is taller and bulkier and fitter for the role.' (The real Khan Abdul Ghaffar Khan's height was 6 feet 5 inches and was robustly built.)

Sir Richard Attenborough then said ruefully: 'Sorry, young chap . . . I tried.'

I responded this time a bit philosophically: 'It happens . . . That's what life is all about. Thank you for your time.'

After my rendezvous with Sir Attenborough, I went down to the hotel lobby where Vijay was waiting for me with eager anticipation. I don't know why, but I was too embarrassed to face him. But I could not avoid him either. Vijay, who had been by my side in many such situations, instinctively, knew things had gone awry. Friends don't need words to express themselves; silence is sometimes more eloquent than speech. Vijay came up to me, placed his hand on my shoulder and said reassuringly: 'It's alright Bittu . . . *Chal roti khate*

hain' (Let's go and eat something). Vijay Sehgal's famed formula to get over a setback was always to fill one's stomach and invariably, it worked!

Yes, that rejection by Sir Attenborough for a role in his film *Gandhi* certainly *did* hurt . . . and hurt deep.

But I have drawn strength and courage from a lesson my grandfather, Pandit Amar Nath taught me, which still helps me in challenging situations. It forces me to adopt a stoic attitude in times of setbacks. His advice was to make me count to twenty-five before responding to anything critical. A friend later amended it to counting in reverse order, as the exercise inculcates mindfulness! My grandfather would also never give any knee-jerk response to any occurrence. Sometimes, he would wait for days to respond. If anything would happen, which would necessitate a strong response, he would tell me to make a note in my diary and reply after a gap of ten days. That delay, I have realised, helps take the sting out of the moment. It helps us regain our equilibrium, reprogramme our inner balance and get on with life.

10

To the City of Nawabs

Apart from the rejection by Sir Richard Attenborough—a painful experience that I managed to soon shake off—there were other trials and tribulations that lurked ahead. One of them, once again, involved the heart.

After passing out from the National School of Drama in June 1978, as was the unwritten norm, many of my classmates left for Bombay to try their luck in the film industry. Some others, who remained behind in Delhi, joined the Repertory Company at the National School of Drama to keep on acting in a variety of plays. My destiny too would eventually lead me to Bombay, but there was a detour via the sarzameen of Lucknow—the captivating capital of Uttar Pradesh. Once the haunt of nawabs and shayars (poets), known for its refined *tehzeeb* (culture) and etiquette . . . whose ambience, mood and the elegance have been exquisitely captured in verse by the noted Urdu poet-lyricist Shakeel Badayuni in the song *Ai Lucknow ki sarzameen* . . . from the famous Guru Dutt, 1960 film *Chaudhvin Ka Chand*, rendered superbly by Mohammed Rafi and set to tune by the highly talented composer Ravi (Ravi Shankar Sharma).

It was in this 'multicultural city that flourished as a North Indian cultural and artistic hub, and the seat of power of nawabs in the eighteenth and nineteenth centuries' . . . which gave us Mirza Hadi Ruswa's famous biography of the courtesan, Umrao Jaan Ada. The story that 'elaborately portrayed the city's decadent society in the mid-nineteenth century and its moral hypocrisy where Umrao Jaan also becomes the symbol of a nation that had long attracted many suitors who were only looking to exploit her'. It was in this historic city, which was once the capital of the Awadh region, controlled by the Delhi Sultanate and later the Mughal Empire, that yet another riveting love story took shape that was to change the lives of two young lovers.

And in this love story, yours truly was the protagonist!

Finally, luck turned, and I got a job offer from Raj Bisaria of the Bhartendu Academy of Dramatic Arts in Lucknow. On 12 September 1979, I reached Lucknow and took up my first employment. I was only 24 and had become a 'lecturer' which was a very big deal for me. There was a great deal of romanticism attached to being a drama teacher.

Raj Bisaria, head of the Academy was a very learned, thoughtful, cultured, well-mannered and warm person. In short, a thorough gentleman. Very different from Balwant Gargi who was earthy and raw, who would communicate more in a vivid explosive language. From Bisaria saab I learnt what taste is all about . . . what it means to be a refined person. His wife, also kind and a soft-spoken was the princess of a small estate. They literally adopted me into their family with the result that every other evening, I would be a guest at their beautifully decorated home in Lal Bagh, filled with priceless artefacts. Over drinks and Oudhvi (home-made dishes), he would supplement my education with his immense knowledge of art and literature, plays and playwrights, poets and writers, composers and singers. It was he who introduced Johnny Walker Black Label to a person used to an occasional rum, or at the most, Solan No. 1 or Peter Scotch. And mind you, those days, scotch—leave aside Black Label—was a luxury and not easily available. And if it was, it was only for those few who could afford it. Bisaria saab was perhaps one of the very few in Lucknow who could!

It was at the Academy that I met Hemendra Bhatia, my colleague who became a friend and a confidant. Years later, on 5 February

2005, when I started my school Actor Prepares, I called him to join the faculty and design it. He is a fantastic designer, a little short-tempered, but a good, compassionate human being.

I liked the steady job and my daily routine. I directed plays, and at times, acted in them also. The salary was good—Rs 3500, which was a pretty decent amount of money in those days. For the first time, I had a decent accommodation, first in Indira Nagar and then in Nirala Nagar.

Food, always my weakness, was out of the world. I had never before tasted cuisine the likes you could chance upon in Lucknow. 'Tunde ke Kabab' were far better than those of Malook's that I used to love in Shimla. The Nihari Kulcha at Rahim's, the Biryani at Idrees in Raja Bazar, the paans (betel leaves) of Ram Ashrey in Hazratganj, were all to die for. The only problem, or rather two problems, if one can call them so, were: first, my old flame from Delhi, Radha, who apparently had not given up on me, would land up in Lucknow every now and then; second, once again, I fell in love. And, as always, once again, *madly* in love.

In Lucknow, I was doing William Shakespeare's *The Merchant of Venice* (Remember the earlier reference to it from my school days, when I took a few liberties with the original?) when I lost my heart and mind to this young girl who was also acting in it as Jessica. Graceful and good looking, convent educated and with an independent mind, she was a complete contrast to Radha. Given the regular interactions between 'Jessica' and me, she fell in love with the director. And the director's condition was such that he was fully ready to reciprocate. To keep matters discreet, let's give 'Jessica' the name Meera, after the revered sixteenth-century poetess-saint from Mewar (now in Rajasthan), who gave up all worldly comforts and possessions and became a loyal devotee and went in search of Lord Krishna up to Dwarka (now in Gujarat). If she was Meera, then I was naturally her Giridhar Gopal (another name of Lord Krishna, which Meera frequently used in her poems). Both of us fell deeply in love with each other. I was totally mesmerised by her. She was totally intoxicated by me. Whenever we met, we seemed to float into a state of trance and did not realise how fast time flew by. I forgot all my problems and worries in her company and felt that the following lyrics penned by Raja Mehdi Ali Khan and composed by Madan Mohan in a song from the 1965-film *Neela Akash* were written for just us two:

Tere paas aake mera waqt guzar jaata hai
Do ghadi ke liye gham jaane kidar jaata hai.

When I come close to you my time goes by
For a few moments, I never know where the sorrow goes.

Every night when I went to bed these lyrics reverberated in my mind. It seemed that Mohammad Rafi and Asha Bhosle had sung it especially for Meera and me and not for the film's lead pair, Dharmendra and Mala Sinha.

Soon, I had become this young, mystic hero of Lucknow who supported a light brown beard and went around attired in a kurta and jeans, with a khadi bag slung around the shoulders. In fact, it would be no exaggeration to say that, in many ways, I had conquered Lucknow. The rich, the famous, the well-to-do, the academicians, the bureaucrats and technocrats, the cultural aficionados—in short, all those who mattered, knew me. They talked about my theatre, my performances.

Meanwhile, my affair with Meera too was at its peak for by then she was, as the saying goes, 'head over heels' in love with me. This despite the fact that Radha had appeared on the scene and had tried to create a lot of misunderstandings and confusion, once even telling Meera to her face: 'You are committing the biggest blunder of your life.'

As soon as I got a chance, I took her to Shimla to meet my parents. Both of them liked her very much and, in fact, my mother offered her blessings to her future daughter-in-law with a customary shagun.

So far so good. But soon we ran into the proverbial stumbling block—Meera's parents, especially her father, who was a senior police officer posted in Lucknow. He was high-handed and rigid in his views and opinionated. When he came to know about our 'love affair to remember', he vehemently opposed it on the expected lines:

'An ordinary, low-class, poor, good-for-nothing ordinary *nauttanki wala* (theatre person), *jhole wala, daadhee wala* person . . . wanting to marry my daughter? How dare he? . . . I will never let this happen.'

You have seen such clichéd reactions in many Bollywood films countless times or have read it in some novel or the other, but they do occur even in real-life romances also.

But Meera was reliving her sixteenth-century role. She was firm in her stand and asserted: 'He is my true love. There will be no one else. If I marry, it will only be Anupam Kher! If not, I will die a spinster.'

At that stage, I decided to purchase the first vehicle in my life: a brand-new, shining, blue-coloured Atlas bicycle (a proud moment for me). But the police officer was not impressed.

He continued to repeat like a parrot (with a minor addition): 'An ordinary, low-class, poor, good-for-nothing ordinary nautanki wala, jhole wala person, who goes around on an ordinary bicycle . . . wanting to marry my daughter? How dare he? No . . . Never!'

With the passage of time, I knew I had reached a saturation point in Lucknow. It was time to move on as I could not spend my entire life doing plays at the Academy. But where to go was the main question.

Then, one day, I saw an advertisement in the *Screen* newspaper—then a prestigious film weekly from the *Indian Express* group of newspapers, published from Bombay. It was from an acting school who wanted to recruit teachers on its staff. Well-known actors were associated with it including Om Puri, Naseeruddin Shah and Shabana Azmi being on the board of advisors. I applied and got selected. Besides a salary, I was to also get a lecturer's accommodation. Now I was torn between the new job and my love—Meera. But it was she who encouraged me to consider this option.

One breezy evening, Meera and I were sitting on the stairs outside a Lucknow church, chatting aimlessly and muttering sweet nothings. Suddenly, Meera told me in a serious voice: 'Anupam, you should go to Bombay and prove yourself. This is your big opportunity. Don't leave it. Go. It's for our future. I will wait for you.' She added, with conviction: 'You must show my father that you *can* achieve success.'

As she spoke, I saw tears in Meera's eyes. They were tears of encouragement!

I gently held her hands and said: 'Okay. I will go to Bombay but only on one condition. I will write a letter to you every day and you too will reply daily.'

She then said: 'Don't be ridiculous!'

I thought that she would say, *'How can I write every day . . . I can't . . . but will do so regularly . . . whenever I can . . .'*

But her response bowled me over. 'You write one letter to me daily and, in reply, I will write you two letters every day,' she declared earnestly. 'I am always here for you! You will *live* in my letters.'

I then asked hesitatingly: 'What about the police officer?'

She answered, confidently: 'Don't worry about him. I will handle him.'

On 3 June 1981, I landed in Bombay.

Part–III

READY? ACTION!

To grasp the full significance of life is the actor's duty,
to interpret it is his problem, and to express it his dedication.

—Marlon Brando

11

IN THE CITY OF DREAMS

In its communication, the acting school of Bombay had informed me that a messenger would be at the Victoria Terminus (VT) railway station (renamed in 1996 as the Chhatrapati Shivaji Maharaj Terminus) to pick me up and take me to my allotted accommodation. I waited there for what seemed like endless hours, but nobody came, and my worst suspicions came true. No school existed—my hopes had been dashed. My last and only resort was to go to my friend, Suhas Khandke's home. I must tell you an interesting story about Suhas.

In Delhi, one was always short of money, but one also felt that one could borrow. There was my aunt, Dr Sheila Datt, whom I could visit to enjoy a hearty homemade meal, or we could eat at Nathu Sweets at Bengali Market and say: '*Kal de dengein*' (Will give tomorrow) and never pay him for a week or at times even longer, but he never, ever asked for it. I can't tell you how many meals of delicious parathas one had at Satish Kaushik's home. I recall how Satish travelled an entire night just to give me 80 rupees which I needed desperately and then travelled back. Twice he travelled the whole night, simply because I was not in a position to do so.

Suhas was from Mumbai, and he was my 'bank' in Delhi. Whenever I needed financial help, I would approach him. Kind-hearted and generous, Suhas was also a man of principles. For my first loan, I went to him and said: 'Suhas, I need a hundred rupees.'

'No problem,' he said. '*Dega kab?*' (When will you return it?)

'In one week,' I replied.

'Take your time. Let's make it one month. Today is the third of the month. Next month, on the third, you return. If you forget, I will ask for it.'

Of course, I forgot. So, on the next third at 12.05 a.m. he woke me up: 'You remember hundred rupees?'

'Yes, I will give it to you,' I replied, half asleep.

'No, no . . . you have to give it now.' He insisted and went on to tell me that 'friendship was one thing and accounts was entirely another matter'—a pithy lesson I will forever associate with my buddy Suhas.

Suhas was the first person who allowed me to stay in his house in Mumbai and treated me like a family member, which meant the world to me at that point in my life.

In Shimla, I never used to think of myself as being poor. In Chandigarh and Delhi, I was a student. In Lucknow, I was a teacher who had gained respectability. But now I discovered that suddenly I had become an adult. And I was forced to face life as such. Living in Bombay made me feel anonymous. I felt like I had to reinvent my identity all over again. It was all very bizarre. But my indomitable spirit kept me moving forward. I knew that indulging in despondency would not help me. I had the strength of my dreams. I was propelled forward by an unseen force, by a mysterious inner strength. I also was aware that this was my chance to seize.

Soon I realised that Mumbai is a unique, large-hearted city with a remarkable character. It does not interfere in your life, a free for all state that allows people to live and let live. The city is inclusive and eclectic. Nobody judges you unless you judge yourself. It makes you feel small because of the sheer enormity of its size, and the overwhelming numbers of successful people that inhabit it. It is a city of contrasts; just take a look at the tall buildings and small huts, the posh colonies and the jhuggi settlements, coexisting side by side. It has its own singular charm. In Mumbai, you are always assaulted by a sense of speed. And the challenge is how to survive in the medley and come out a winner. To my mind, a good analogy are the local trains—standing on the side of the platform trying to get into a local train as you are pushed in, pushed out and pushed around, all at the same time. How you finally manage is conditional on you. Surviving in Mumbai whether it is riding the train or the industry itself is another life lesson learnt.

In Bombay, one of the first places I went to was Prithvi Theatre. It was the opening night of Satish Kaushik's play, which was a Hindi adaptation of *A View from the Bridge,* a drama written by the American playwright Arthur Miller. Prithvi Theatre had an electrifying atmosphere. Its culture was superb; the most amazing place for an educated actor. It was a sacred place that made you feel respectable. I count it as one of the greatest contributions of Shashi and Jennifer Kapoor. It was the only art place in Bombay which did not become an *adda* (joints for out-of-work actors) for the struggling actors though they were ever-present. Unlike Delhi, which has a lot of places ranging from Kamani Auditorium to Triveni Kala Sangam, Prithvi Theatre has great dignity. One met a lot of people from the world of theatre there. During that visit, I saw Shabana Azmi and Alok Nath and some others, all talking to each other on a first-name basis. *Am I in the right place?* I questioned myself. But I was determined to make a name for myself . . . come what may . . . whatever it took. From a steady life in Lucknow, my struggle to fit in had begun all over again!

These addas—there was one in Pamposh on Bandra Linking Road—would all be crowded in the evenings. A couple of times, I too joined with seven to eight other 'struggling actor' friends in a *desi sharab ka theka* (country liquor joint). As I've mentioned, I never used to drink much, but often you indulge for a sense of belonging. To feel, 'we are brethren's, comrades'. I remember everyone ordered something called 'Koofy' (not to be mistaken for a coffee), which was a strong locally brewed liquor. It was horrible tasting and awful smelling. And the kind of conversation taking place was nightmarish . . . frightening. One of them said: 'Yaar, I have been struggling in this city for the last seven years. Listen to me because I know what is to be done . . .' For me, it was the most unbelievable demoralising losers' conversation. I thought to myself: *This idiot has not been able to get any work for the last seven years, so now he is enjoying being the senior most struggling actor.*

I realised that this wasn't meant for me . . . I couldn't be part of this situation. I decided it's better to be lonely, better to be frustrated and even better to be dejected than sit with people who will certainly never ever make it. They were natural losers and would remain so. I was resolute to make it and I determined to forge ahead. I was filled with a strong sense of purpose because of my inner knowledge . . . my inner voice . . . my core conviction that I was good. Mind you, it was not a false realisation of my capabilities. Theatre was my grace; its training has shaped both my craft and my character. I never used to call myself 'a struggling actor' because that meant I would limit myself with those words. Just say the words aloud and see how it feels. Imagine if you ever asked someone the question: 'Who are you?' and the reply was: 'I'm a struggling actor'. Too much negativity is generated. It goes into the other and comes back to haunt you and shrouds you.

Hence, whenever I was asked, I would say: 'I am an actor, presently without work'. At every step, I held on to my optimism and surrounded myself with a halo.

Coming back to my arrival in Bombay, not only was I without a promised job, but I was also bereft of a place to stay in this mammoth city. I had outstayed my welcome at Suhas's home and began looking for a place of my own to stay. Finally, I was left with no choice but to shift in with three students in a little *kholi* (room) belonging to a widow who worked as a *bai* (washerwoman) in various homes during the day. The kholi had a kitchen, which she would share with her son and two daughters while the four of us shared the room which was partitioned from the kitchen with a skimpy curtain. It was a less than desirable situation, but I did not have any options. I remember asking one of the students the address of the kholi so that I could inform Meera so that she could reply to my letters and also my parents, in case they needed to ever get in touch with me, though I had not told any of them of my miserable circumstances.

The address was given to me written in Marathi. I couldn't believe what I read. It was:

Anupam Kher,
2/15, Kherwari,
Kher Nagar,
Kher Road,
Bandra East,
Bombay.

I could not help but smile as I read the address—it was surely a sign from the Gods I whispered to myself. My hour of reckoning was upon me.

One day I remet Dolly Thakore by chance, who had tried to help me bag Pandit Jawaharlal Nehru's role in Richard Attenborough's *Gandhi*. She said: 'Anupam, you have come to the right place . . . the right city. I want you to meet somebody. Come with me.'

That somebody was Alyque Padamsee—the well-known actor, theatre personality as well as a brilliant ad film-maker.

Unfortunately for me, Alyque Padamsee was in an awful mood the day I met him. Dolly said: 'Alyque, I want you to meet Anupam.'

As I extended my hand with a slight bow, Alyque said: 'Dolly, don't you realise I am late for the play. Fuck it, let's just go.'

And he left. Dolly just followed him. I felt insulted and ignored.

Today, when I look back at that incident, I don't perceive it the same way. Over the years, I have cultivated a more open-minded perspective. Perversely, such incidents and events, instead of creating bitterness have made me gentler and kinder. When one reads about the life of the well-known personalities, from any field, specifically the field of art and culture, one realises that the same experiences have happened to others too especially the ones who finally made it big in life. Read any biography, any memoir, any autobiography and you will see and feel the truth behind what I say. Read about the lives of Elia Kazan or the legendary Dutch painter Vincent van Gogh. My favourite being Irving Stone's *Lust for Life*, which was also made into a film by Vincent Minnelli starring Kirk Douglas and was nominated for four Oscars, coupled with Nikolai Ostrovsky's *How the Steel was Tempered*. So, today I look back at my interaction with Alyque very philosophically: I went there, but there was no place for me. That interaction taught me that I should be prepared for ups and downs but not let anything drag me down.

One of the first persons from the world of Hindi cinema that I went to meet was the famous poet and dialogue writer Rahi Masoom Raza. He was very nice to me and very encouraging but could not give me any work. He was a writer and a poet. But in those early day, it was important to go and sit with such erudite artistes—there was much I could imbibe. Manmohan Desai, the immensely successful producer-director, known for his multi-starrer blockbusters, also met me with courtesy. He was the man who taught me: 'Remember Anupam, this industry does not respect talent. It respects how difficult it is to get your dates and you will get more films *only* by signing more films.'

Mukul Anand, who died at a young age of 45 (7 September 1997) too taught me a very important lesson: 'Make yourself secure with money . . . you will need it at all times. In this industry, good times don't last . . . bad times always do.'

I was able to meet the great showman Raj Kapoor who offered me a foreigner's role in his *Ram Teri Ganga Maili*. 'But sir, I'm an Indian, how can I do a foreigner's role.'

'But look at you . . . you look like one. Do it. It's a good role, powerful role', he said.

'No sir, I cannot.' I yearned to work with the great showman but wanted to work in a substantial role otherwise felt it was okay to pass up the opportunity. In life, I have taught myself to hold out for the best—it will come to you.

The evergreen hero and my teenage idol, Dev Anand, owner of the famous Navketan banner that had produced some of the biggest hits in Hindi cinema, and the Anand dubbing studios, was unbelievably cheery and bright. A joyous place of energy and happening. For him, it seemed as if I was the biggest star ever. As I entered his office room he said in his typical tone and voice: 'Anupam, *aaja baithja, aaja . . . dikha kya kiya hain tune . . . Tereko koi takat nahi rok sakti. Tu bahut kuch kar ke dikhayega. Tu ek din mere saath kaam karega . . . aur zaroor karega, mein vade ke saath keh sakta hoon. Abhi mere paas kaam nahi hain, lekin jaldi, bahut jaldi* (Anupam, come and sit . . . show what all have you done . . . no power can stop you. You are bound to achieve a lot. You will work with me one day . . . certainly, you will. At present, I don't have any work for you . . . but one day I will). In two minutes, he gave the kinetic energy that could boost anyone's morale—work or no work. He was a thorough gentleman.

Then I met the scriptwriter and director, Shyam Benegal, who too met me agreeably and informed me: 'I am making a film *Mandi*—a 'satirical comedy on prostitution and politics' which has a heavy star-cast comprising, amongst others, Shabana Azmi, Smita Patil, Naseeruddin Shah. I have no role for you in it right now, but I suggest that you come with us to Hyderabad, where we are shooting and stay with us for about two months or so and I'm sure something will work out.

I recall telling him: 'Sir, my time may not be really important for you but for me, it is very important.'

He liked my frank answer and said: 'Oh, that's very good. I'm sure you would do something good with it.' Once again, I yearned to work with Shyam Benegal but could not wait in the wings hoping for something. I knew that good work would find me.

I went to meet the famous writer-producer-director Ramanand Sagar, but landed up meeting only his 3rd or 4th assistant at Natraj Studio in Andheri—one Chaubey or Dubey saab, I forget his name now. He looked at me and said to my face: 'Look at you! So thin a body and balding. Maybe you can become a writer or an assistant like me (he was also bald) but forget about being an actor.'

'How long have you been an assistant,' I asked him.

'Ramanandji *ke saath pichle unees saal se kaam kar raha hoon*' (I have been working with Ramanand sir since the last 19 years).

'Sir, I don't want to tell the world after 19 years, that an aspiring actor is still working as an assistant,' I replied.

Of course, he has shocked at my impertinence. Out of sheer hate which was so very visible by now on his face, he shouted: 'Get out of here.'

Years later, when I went to shoot a film at the same studio which housed Ramanand Sagar's office, my first instinct was to taunt him. But my upbringing had taught me to be the bigger person. He did not remember who I was. I folded my hands and said: 'Uncle, *namaskar. Kaise hain aap? Aapne shayad mujhe pehchana nahin. Main aapko pehle bhi mila tha. Aapne bahut hosla diya tha aur kaha that ki main kuch zaroor banunga*' (Uncle, greetings. How are you? Perhaps you have not recognised me. I had met you earlier also and at that time, you had encouraged me a lot. You had told me that I would make it big one day).

He was shocked at 'his own goodness'. For me, it was very important to behave that way—somethings in life are better dealt in less obvious ways.

There was nothing working out on the work front and gradually I seemed to be losing out on my optimism. As they say, 'I was going fast but nowhere'. I was doing an occasional play after which people would come and say: 'Very good actor', 'Well done', 'Great work', etc. etc. but work was not coming.

In Bombay, I was expecting to be showered with offers from film producers and directors and production banners. Regrettably, nothing of the sort happened. I started teaching students—wherever and whenever I got the chance (sometimes even on beaches at odd times)—just to earn enough money to feed myself. But that option was short-lived. Soon my savings were exhausted, and I was forced to quit my tenement as I could not afford to pay the rent and, for twenty-one nights, I slept on the railway platform at the Bandra-East station (in western Bombay).

Despite my relentless efforts of doing the rounds of studios tirelessly, I failed to make any breakthrough. I used to travel by the local trains, which were packed beyond their capacity during rush hours, with many intrepid commuters dangling precariously! Here, I came across a 'mini-India': people from all over the country mingled seamlessly. I keenly studied the mannerisms, styles and accents of a variety of individuals and used them later in my films.

I couldn't possibly go back to Lucknow and face the barb-like taunts of the police officer's sharp tongue. I often visualised the scene and heard voices in my head: 'An ordinary, low-class, good-for-nothing poor actor . . . You have again come back here . . . you loser.'

In short, my condition was bad. I was very miserable. During this phase, I sought out the ever-reliable Dolly Thakore. Realising my predicament and in order to help me, she said: 'Anupam, the dubbing of the English dialogues of *Gandhi* in Hindi is going on . . . Would you be interested? You will be paid one thousand rupees for the one sentence you have to speak.'

The next day, I reached the B. R. Dubbing Theatre (named after the respected producer-director B. R. Chopra, known for his theme-based films), three hours in advance to dub for one sentence (the Hindi version), which is as follows:

Non-cooperation ka ek hi matlab hai, sarkar ko ukhad bhenkna hai . . . Uska mehet baghavat hi raasta hai . . . Is liye na hum sulah karen gey, na sulah ki baat hi mane gey. Kya aap ne yeh nahin likha?

Non-cooperation has just one aim: to overthrow the government . . . sedition has become the only path to this . . . which is why we will not talk about compromise . . . nor expect to be offered a compromise! Do you deny writing this?

Can you imagine the irony of the situation? The cocky chap who dreamt of bagging an Oscar for playing the role of Nehru in the movie *Gandhi* was now thankful for a single—just ONE dubbed line in the film! It was as if my fate was telling me to *stay grounded* because *zindagi mein kucch bhi ho sakta hai* (Anything is possible in life). I managed to rent a tiny room with the amount I got for the dubbing. At least I had a roof over my head!

Muzaffar Ali was a talented, multi-faceted film-maker, fashion designer, poet, artiste and music lover. He belonged to the Muslim Rajput royal house of Kotwara and it was he who gave me my first break. It was in *Aagaman*, a film that was being produced by the Uttar Pradesh Sugarcane Seed Development Corporation which was to be shot in Lucknow and Kotwara—Muzaffar's hometown. Suresh Oberoi and Saeed Jaffrey were also in the film. The first time I met Jaffrey, with whom I travelled to Lucknow, I noticed that he was wearing a brown corduroy jacket which Balwant Gargi also used to wear. For some unexplainable reason, for me there was something about this jacket—only a good actor or an intellectual was supposed to wear a brown corduroy one. I recall that Jaffrey, a British-Indian actor, was very courteous but very talkative. His *lahza* (tone), his *zubaan* (language), his pronunciation of Urdu words, *amma miya!* Initially, I was in awe of him. His 'fluency and versatility in various languages allowed him to straddle radio, stage, television and cinema' with equal ease. He was much sought after by the British, American and Indian film-makers.

Aagaman never got a proper release and hence, did little for my career. Even so I was aware that one never forgets their first break, but as soon as it was over, I was looking for my next role.

In 1982, I got a little role, without any dialogue, in *Utsav* (based on *Mrichchakatika* [*The Little Clay Cart*] by Sudraka) which was being made by the debonair Shashi Kapoor and directed by Girish Karnad. It had a huge star-cast led by Amitabh Bachchan and Rekha. Then because of certain unexplained reasons, Amitabh's role was taken over by Shashi Kapoor himself.

A successful actor who had a chain of Hindi and Hollywood films behind him, Shashi Kapoor, 18 March born, a Piscean, was an exceptionally charming person. He was also very kind-hearted. I have shared some great moments with him. I recall once when we landed at Palam airport in Delhi on our way to Bharatpur in Rajasthan where the shooting was to take place, Shashi Kapoor noticed that my car hadn't come. He said: 'My car is there, and I am alone, so you come with me.' I couldn't believe that Shashi Kapoor had invited me to join him in his car. It was a special moment for me.

I wanted the whole world to look into that car and see that Anupam Kher was sitting with Shashi Kapoor. The minute Shashi sat in the car, he went off to sleep. That didn't deter me at all, for at every traffic light, I was almost shouting for attention for everyone around to see who I was with.

While in Bharatpur, junior artistes like me, Satish Kaushik, Rajesh Puri, all had some minor role or the other. In fact, being the attendant of Shashi in the film, I used to joke that 'I have a running role' because I was constantly running behind Samsthanak, the role Shashi was playing. We were put up in some nondescript hotel. Shekhar Suman (playing the role of Charudutt) and Annu Kapoor (as masseur who is trying to be an ascetic) were staying in a better hotel simply because they had bigger roles. Every evening, when we met at our underprivileged hotel, both of them used to make us feel even worse off. Annu would walk in with a Dunhill packet and Shekhar with a 555. Was it truly the real Dunhill or 555? Suffice to say we had our strong doubts for the shape and condition of the packet never changed. They would always boast as to how Shashi Kapoor does not eat without them and how Rekha did this or that. Perhaps their intention was not to run us down, but just show off and glorify themselves. Whether they intended to or not, we were made to feel even more like cast-offs.

For the outdoor shoot, our job was to be ready by 7.30 with full make-up including a beard, long hair, dhoti etc. *every morning*, regardless of if we were necessarily in the shot or not. I had just two sets of underwear with me for the shoot, Victor brand. Only those who have worn Victor brand regularly in those days know that if worn for about six months or so, they develop a hole in the front which pretty much renders the garment useless. Hence, I would wash one every day and wear the other one.

One day, it so happened, that Dubey, who was Om Puri's secretary, said with great confidence: 'Relax, the shot will not be ready till 11.30 . . . guarantee you are not working till 11.30 today.' So, that day I decided to wash both my underwears and put them on the wooden railing outside my hotel room. I was feeling relaxed after many days when suddenly around 9 o'clock, an assistant came with the summons to rush as the shot was ready. I was in a panic. I just picked up one, which was still a little wet, put it on and rushed for the shot. As the shoot was in progress with Shashi Kapoor and me following him as per my role, suddenly I screamed at the top of my voice holding my crotch. Everyone was baffled. They were all looking at me. The shot was ruined. I rushed to the washroom only to realise that hundreds of small brown ants had gotten into that wet underwear, when it was hung up to dry and they had bitten my crotch. Everything had swollen down there. The more pitiful thing was that no one had any sympathy for this accident. Instead, they all had a good laugh at my expense, especially, Shashi Kapoor. Thank God, Rekha was not there for shooting that morning!

Underwear reminds me that I would always envy the ones that Shashi Kapoor used to wear which one could notice through his see-through dhoti. I would say to myself: *When I become a star, I will wear the same brand of underwear.* Shashi was a kind-hearted man with a big heart. He treated everyone in the unit—big or small, junior or senior—the same way. I think he had a soft spot for those who were theatre trained. I also believe that in the course of the journey between Palam airport in Delhi to Bharatpur, we exchanged some interesting conversations, with me expressing my views on theatre and cinema, had created a favourable impression on him. One evening, while the underwear incident was still fresh on everyone's mind and Shashi seemed to be in an exceptionally good and happy mood, I asked him: 'Sir, if you don't mind can I ask you a question?'

'Yes, do that,' he replied.

'The underwear that you wear, where are they from?'

He laughed, perhaps remembering the reference to the context from the ruined shot: 'They are from Marks & Spencer.'

I had no idea what Marks & Spencer was and where was it, so I asked: 'Where is it?'

'In London, you will find one easily on Oxford Street,' he told me.

Many years later, when I went to London with Kishore Kumar, for a 'Kishore Kumar Nite', I remembered that I had to buy the same underwear. But I forgot where to get them from. Only Shashi Kapoor knew. By that time *Saaransh* had been released and I had become a known actor. I called Shashi's office: 'Can I please speak to Mr Shashi Kapoor, this is Anupam Kher. I am calling from London.'

He came on the line: 'Sir, I am sorry to once again ask you a rather personal question. Since I can now afford them and am presently in London with Kishore Da, I thought I should also wear the same underwear that you used to wear during the making of *Utsav*. But I don't remember the place you told me to get them from. Can you help me please?'

There was a stunned silence for a few seconds and then I heard him laugh: 'Go to Marks & Spencer on Oxford Street. On the first or second floor, go to the men's section, and you will see a whole area designated to men's' undergarments. That's it. And by the way Anupam, since you are there can you pick up a few for me too. My size is ***. Good luck!' He laughed again as he put down the receiver.

On the topic of Kishore Kumar, I would like to recall an interesting incident, lest I forget about it later.

I am not too sure of the dates now, but if I am not mistaken, I think it was in 1985-86, when Kishore Kumar was to perform two shows at the Wembley Arena in London with Kalyanji-Anandji as the music directors. For some reason or the other, I too was invited to be a part of that show, perhaps because of the success of *Saaransh* and another film or two, because of which I was now considered as 'an actor on the rise' and people were talking about me. I too had to perform a couple of items, including the singing of a song with Shabana Azmi: '*Itna na mujhse tu pyara badha, ki main ik pagal awaara . . .*', an evergreen song from the 1961 Hindi film *Chhaya* directed by Hrishikesh Mukherjee with Sunil Dutt and Asha Parekh in the lead. The song, written by Rajendra Krishan and composed by Salil Chowdhury, was based on Mozart's 40th symphony and sung by Talat Mehmood and Lata Mangeshkar. Besides that, I had to do a funny item on baldies titled 'Balchand' about the various stages of baldness, which was always popular with the audience.

Before this event, I had met Kishore Kumar once. I had gone to the Mehboob Studio for the shooting of *Saaransh*. As I was getting out from my taxi and paying the driver, I saw a man in crisply starched white dhoti-kurta, come next to me singing:

Taxi, taxi, taxi, taxi.
Tum utro taxi se, main baithunga
Han jee han, Tum utro taxi se main baithunga.
Aur paise bhi main doonga,
Tum utro taxi se, main baithunga.

It was vintage Kishore Kumar. It was, as if, he was singing only to me! But before I could collect my wits and introduce myself or say something, he sat down and left. That was my first true encounter with him.

Now, here I was at the Wembley Arena waiting for the great singer to arrive for the rehearsal. It was already late afternoon and a few hours later, was the show. Kalyanji-Anandji, too were waiting with their 150-piece orchestra. I had finished rehearsing my song with Shabana who had left. After about half-an-hour, Kishore Kumar entered strangely with a miner's torch around his head and suddenly, the orchestra, with a cue from Kalyanji, started playing. He started singing one song after another: '*Mere naina sawan bhado, phir bhi mera man pyasa*' from Shakti Samanta's 1976 film *Mehbooba*, which had Rajesh Khanna and Hema Malini in the lead and music to which was given by R. D. Burman to the lyrics by Anand Bakshi; '*Mere sapno ki rani, kab ayegi tu*' from Samanta's biggest ever hit in 1969 *Aradhana*, which had Rajesh Khanna and Sharmila Tagore in the lead, music for which was composed by S. D. Burman to lyrics by Anand Bakshi. In fact, it was *Aradhana* that made Rajesh Khanna a superstar. I was sitting in the front row enjoying the magic of Kishore Da's voice. Then he started singing the popular song from Shekhar Kapur's 1987 iconic Indian science fiction blockbuster *Mr. India*: '*Zindagi ki yahi reet hain, haar ke baad hi jeet hain*'. Written by Javed Akhtar its music was composed by Laxmikant-Pyarelal. It was my favourite song because it had positivity in it, it had optimism in it, it had an elevating quality about it. I loved it and very often hummed it. I had come to know the lyrics backwards.

While singing, Kishore Kumar was changing the tune of the song and I was quite sure that he was singing wrong. My small-town naive and innocent mind asked: *Should I point out to him or not, and if I do point out to him will it be taken in the right spirit?* I decided to tell him because I couldn't let him sing the wrong way. So, sitting in the front row, with the orchestra playing on the stage, Kalyanji-Anandji conducting it, Kishore Kumar singing with great intensity, I interrupted: 'Dada . . . Dada.'

Suddenly he stopped and said: *'Bolo?'* (Yes, what?)

The orchestra had stopped. Kalyanji-Anandji, were looking at me, horrified that how come I had dared to stop Kishore Kumar in his singing . . . and what was so important that I had to say, and that too in the middle of the rehearsal. I just wanted to tell him that the tune was different, but what came out of my mouth was: 'Dada, dada, sorry for interrupting you, dada, but you are singing it wrong'. Pin-drop silence followed. Everyone was staring at me. I am sure Kalyanji wanted to order me out. Given an opportunity, every musician, whatever instrument he was playing, wanted to throw it on my head. Anandji quietly hid behind Kishore Kumar.

Kishore Kumar looked at me and said with a light smile: *'Aacha* (Oh really)? I am singing it wrong? Oh! I see. And where, I may ask, am I wrong?'

I explained, as best as I could, how the original song is somewhat differently sung to what he was singing right now. I continuously kept using the word 'galat' (wrong). Kishore Kumar listened to me with great patience and asked: *'Kya naam hain?'*

'Anupam Kher, sir.'

'Original *kaise hain?'* (How is the original sung?) he asked me.

I sang a bit of how he had sung it originally in the film *Mr. India.* He smiled again and I thought: *How considerate of him to sort of humour me.* He then looked at me, smiled and said: 'Anupam Kher of *Saaransh* fame ji, who has sung the original song?'

I said: 'You sir.'

'Who is singing the wrong song?' he asked.

I said: 'You are.'

'*Toh aapke baap ka kya ja raha hain?*' (So what loss is it of your father?), he replied and resumed his singing.

For me, it was the most amazing experience with the mesmerising, inimitable Kishore Kumar. The one and only Kishore Kumar! This was my special interaction with him that spurred me on to be bolder and passionate about the one precious life we have been given.

I don't know if I did the right or the wrong thing. However, at times, your disastrous stories become the most memorable stories to narrate—a lesson I learnt early in life.

Let me resume my recollections about the suave Shashi Kapoor. After completing the Bharatpur shooting schedule, we were on our way back to Bombay, with a stopover in Delhi to attend the premiere of Govind Nihalani's *Vijeta*, which Shashi Kapoor had produced to launch his son Kunal. Once again, I happened to travel with him in his car, but this time along with his elder son, Karan. A room had been booked at the Taj Mansingh Hotel for a quick shower. Shashi said: 'Boys, we have just half an hour, so just rush, freshen up and come down quickly. We should be in the lobby in exactly thirty minutes. We must reach Siri Fort Auditorium on time.'

This was my first ever visit to the Taj Mansingh. In fact, it was the first time I had stepped inside a 5-star hotel. Karan and I were sharing a room. Karan came out in just five to seven minutes. Then I went in, took off my clothes but just could not find the shower button. So I got into the bathtub, put-on the tap full, lay down with my face down, then turned on my back, and after wiping myself with the finest, soft and white towel I had ever used, came out as if I have had the best shower. After the premiere and downing one drink, I told Shashi: 'Sir, this being my first time in a 5-star hotel, therefore I did not know where the shower button was. So finally, I just laid in the bathtub, first face down, and then turned on my back and immersed in the water.'

To my surprise, Karan, who was standing next to us said, 'That's precisely how I too bathed.'

We all had a good laugh. That evening, I learnt that it's always better to say what you feel. There is a great charm in honest expression.

Utsav came and went. It did not do anything for my career. But the opportunity to meet and interact closely with Shashi during the car trips were my big reward, my real prize. An invaluable lesson I learnt was that such interactions were priceless, fulfiling and enriching in a way that was hard to quantify but one that built the most far-reaching bridges. It was less real than getting actual work, an actor got work which he was destined for but this was an invaluable treasure. I was an educated actor, a student of cinema, a dedicated teacher but in these incalculable ways I was learning valuable life lessons.

And then I met Kiron Thakur Singh, who was married to the businessman Gautam Berry at that time. She was very warm and unbelievably nice to me. We decided to collaborate to do plays together. But more of that later!

12

REJECTED, ONCE AGAIN

In my life, time and time again, destiny has intervened only this time it took an abrupt twist.

All of a sudden, I stopped receiving Meera's letters from Lucknow—my lifeline, my sustenance. I would stand for hours on end at my doorway, expectantly waiting for the postman—who played a vital role in our lives in that era. I would even walk across daily to the local post office to check if my letters were being delivered to the wrong address. But that was not the case. When there was not a single letter from Meera for eighteen days, I rushed to the telephone booth at Bombay's Santa Cruz airport to make an emergency call. In those days, only airports and possibly a few railway terminals had phone booths installed to make long-distance calls. I called my friend, Hemendra Bhatia, in Lucknow. The connection was terrible, full of static and rumbling sounds, but I persisted. This is how the conversation went:

'Hello Bhatia saab, hello Bhatia saab . . . can you hear me?'

'Yes, I can but not clearly. Hello . . . hello . . . Kher saab, where have you been all this time?'

'Bhatia saab, I haven't received any letter from Meera for many days . . . is everything alright?'

'Kher saab, actually Meera is getting married . . .'

My voice seemed to crack as I asked: 'Meera is getting married? When?'

'Within the next three days.'

'Bhatia saab, why didn't you stop her? We have been seeing each other for three years . . . And it was on her pleading and encouragement that I came here . . . Bhatia saab, what about my parents? What will I tell them?'

I quickly cut the connection. I had just 100 rupees in my pocket and I noticed that the phone tab was already at 97 rupees.

I could not believe my ears. Meera was getting *married*? *That's not possible*, I thought. I was sure some misunderstanding had taken place. Or, maybe her father was forcing her to get married to a groom of his choice, given his one-track mind and authoritarian behaviour. I was determined to stop the wedding. But how could I bring this about? I did not even have the money to buy a train ticket from Bombay to Lucknow.

Immediately I thought of approaching my friend, Satish Kaushik, who lived in Santa Cruz locality. I pleaded with him, 'Satish, please give me some money. Meera is getting married in Lucknow three days from now and I need to somehow stop her.' Unhesitatingly, he came up with 400 rupees and told me to hop on to a train immediately. But it was risky travelling by train, because of the huge distance between Bombay and Lucknow (about 1380 km or 860 miles) and also due to the paucity of time. Many trains in India were notorious for running well behind schedule. One day, it could be because of floods inundating the tracks; the next, it could be because of some sundry political outfit's 'rail roko' (stop trains) agitation. I *had to* take a flight but was desperately short of cash in that pre-credit/debit card era in India. Then I dashed to see Kiron (now Kirron), who was one of my best friends.

I was panting and in panic when I told her: 'Kiron, Meera is getting married in three days' time in Lucknow and I have to stop the marriage by going there . . . Can you please lend me some money?' She gave me 700 rupees. Now I had 1100 rupees in my pocket. With that amount, I managed to buy an air ticket and flew to Lucknow. When the plane landed late in the evening, like my mood, the whole city seemed to be drowned in darkness. I have noted that whenever we are faced with an impending tragedy in life, the gods of electricity follow suit and fail us.

From the airport, I went straight to Mrs Roy's house who was our contact for delivery of my letters to Meera. On entering, the first thing I noticed was that my last 17 letters were lying on the side table unopened by Meera. On enquiring, Mrs Roy said: 'Please forget her.' I then somehow found my way to her friend Ritu's house. I told her, in a desperate voice: 'Ritu . . . somehow inform Meera that I am back.'

She pleaded: 'Anupam, please keep me out of this.'

Then I asked her: 'What should I do? How should I meet her?' But she remained mum. I then left her place, wondering what to do next. Because of her father's complete disdain for me, I had to tread cautiously without her parents knowing about my arrival in her life again.

Suddenly, I remembered Meera was pursuing her PhD. I thought I should contact her guide, Ms Rao. (I cannot recall her first name). I requested her also to please immediately inform Meera that I had reached Lucknow.

She replied: 'Mr Kher, please leave her alone.'

I virtually yelled: 'I can't leave her alone . . . I can't lead the rest of my life thinking that she was perhaps waiting for me.'

She responded: 'Mr Kher, if a girl has decided to get married, then it's her decision.'

I was in no mood to give up. I went on: 'Not quite possible! What if she is waiting for me to stop her from getting married? Can you please, please help me? I just need to meet her once and, if she turns me down, I will walk away.'

On witnessing my desperation, she telephoned Meera and fixed a meeting for me to meet her at the landmark Kwality Restaurant at 10 a.m. the next day. I thanked Ms Rao and left. I spent that night in Mrs Roy's home and my mind was in a state of turmoil.

Tense and stressed out, I reached the rendezvous spot at 9.30 the next morning. She arrived on time at 10.

In my heart of hearts, I felt that Meera was being forced into the marriage and with my arrival, she would be would not only be glad but thanking God that I had come to rescue her. But I was wrong!

As soon as I saw Meera, with a spring on her step and a glow on her face, I instinctively realised that it was her own decision to get married. She wasn't being forced to tie the knot! On seeing me,

Meera's face turned pale. And I don't know why, but I suddenly felt relaxed . . . at ease. All that tension and stress of a few moments ago had gone . . . simply disappeared.

She came straight to the point and said softly: 'I am sorry, Anupam, but I have consented to get married . . . It's my decision.'

The actor in me responded, somewhat dramatically, with the Shakespearean line: 'Hold on . . . Before Rome banishes me, I banish Rome!'

She tried to explain why she had decided to marry someone else: 'I resisted a lot, but, as you know, my mother has not been keeping too well and is now in quite a bad shape. I did not want to break her heart.'

I countered: 'What about my heart? Is it okay to break my heart?' Then, I impulsively said: 'We are going from here.'

'Where?'

'Shimla.'

'I *can't* come to Shimla; I am getting married in two days.'

I was boiling inside . . . thinking is this the girl I loved . . . my big hope . . . the one whom I banked on in my life presuming her to be my life support when nothing was working out in Bombay. Thoughts . . . words . . . expressions . . . were running fast in my mind. I was feeling claustrophobic. I then pointed out: 'I can't sit in this restaurant and talk freely . . . you want to put an end to this relationship then at least allow me the dignity of doing so.'

After that, Meera and I stepped out of the restaurant only to find that it was raining heavily. We then sat in a cycle rickshaw and headed towards the church in Lucknow where we met often. There were two rear-view mirrors fixed on the handlebar of the rickshaw and I could see my features in one of them; hardly an encouraging image. My face was dripping wet, the head was semi-bald and food stains formed a peculiar pattern on a white T-shirt. Meera, on the other hand, remained poised, composed and graceful.

After reaching the church, I did not know what to talk to her about . . . what to say . . . what to ask. Without intent, some words came out of my mouth: 'What does your husband-to-be look like?'

She immediately opened her purse and showed me a photograph of a young, good-looking man with a smiling face! Then I looked at her and thought about a life without her. I don't know why, but I lost all my remaining confidence and I started crying.

In between sobs, I implored her: 'Meera, don't do this to me. Just give me some time. I will become somebody. Just give me six months; I will achieve something in life . . . in your life . . . in our life. But don't get married to this guy. Or for that matter, any guy, because if you get married to somebody . . . it will shatter my confidence. Please give me a little time. I know I am a nobody today . . . I look just an ordinary person like so many others on the streets that you see or don't even look at, but I promise you, I will become somebody . . . somebody you will be proud of one day.'

After a few moments, she said: 'Anupam, I think you're right and I was wrong. I will not get married. Let's run away tomorrow morning. You get ready at 7 a.m.'

As promised, she came on time but there were three cars and a jeep in her tow. I noticed that her father was sitting in the first car. She came to the hotel lobby and told me: 'Anupam, I tried a lot. I can leave you but not my parents . . . they mean everything to me.'

Outside, her father was continuously honking. I said: 'Meera, wait here for a minute. I'll be back.'

I went to her father and said: 'Sir, I request you to please leave. Your daughter will return back to your place after an hour.'

Seeing his nostrils flare and anger well up across his face, I knew he was about to say something nasty or threaten me. Before he could say anything, I said: 'Sir, I have many letters that your daughter has written to me. And one of them was penned when she spent a night with me at a hotel in Delhi. I will read the first line for you. If you still don't leave, I will read the rest of it to her husband-to-be. It's for you to take the final call.'

The first line I read was:

Dear Anupam,
Since the last night, I feel as if I am married to you . . .

He stepped out of the car and said forcefully: 'This is blackmail. I can send you to jail for this act.' However, realising the consequences of his daughter's letters reaching the wrong hands, better sense prevailed and he abruptly changed his attitude. He then decided to concede to my request and leave. His car and the other vehicles soon drove away.

Of course, I would have never shown those letters. It was just not in my nature to do so. It was just a simple threat to be alone with Meera for some time . . . to make a last attempt, even if futile, to reason things out.

I coaxed Meera to sit down and think calmly. I assured her that I would not force her to do anything against her wishes. In fact, I was just breathless . . . incoherent . . . and just blabbering.

And once again, I spelt out to her what a tremendous success I could become in the future. I then declared: 'Meera, what you are doing is wrong. I admit that I am not a doctor, an engineer or a businessman. I am an actor and I can tell you today that after you celebrate your first marriage anniversary, your husband will come out of the bathroom wearing his bathrobe. You will offer him a cup of tea in a tray and in that tray will be a newspaper with my photograph in it. You will walk the streets of the city with your husband and there you will see large posters of mine. There won't be a single theatre in your city that wouldn't be screening my film. Remember, I will never leave you. I will haunt you all your life . . .'

I soon realised that I was out of control and was venting my anger and frustration. But the fact is that it was because the forsaken Anupam was totally shattered. He knew that now he had only one option: to return to his small house in the small town of Shimla to lead the life of a small man.

The deafening silence carried on. Completely composed, she said: 'Anupam . . . I can well understand your feelings and emotions. I wish you good luck for your life, but now I must go.' Then she got up from the chair and slowly walked out of the door and my life. Forever.

I did not stop her!

As I mulled over the situation and faced the bitter truth, I knew I could not return to Bombay immediately. Instead, like the lost soul that I felt, I decided to return to Shimla, to my parents and to my roots. But en route to Shimla from Lucknow, I had an urge to meet my friend, Vijay Sehgal, in Delhi. I reached his house and knocked on the front door. He opened the door, saw me, assessed my condition in just a few seconds and asked: 'Did Meera also leave you?'

I replied: 'Vijay . . . I have realised that I am a mere common man. My training, my teaching, my acting . . . everything is meaningless. A total waste. I will not go back to Bombay. In that city for every successful individual, you find countless people living in the slums or on the streets. I am an ordinary, a faceless man . . . I am going back to Shimla. My street, my locality and my town . . . these are my boundaries. Let's face it, I am a nobody there . . . I am a nonentity, Vijay'.

Vijay put his hand around my shoulder, took me inside and said: 'No problem. Let's talk about your issues later. But first, let's eat something.' There it was: the non-patented Vijay Sehgal formula for solving all problems. Satiated by that simple gesture, I was ready for my next move.

Bidding goodbye to Vijay Sehgal, I went to Shimla to live with my mother and father with whom I had hardly spent any time over the past decade. We had a lot of catching up to do!

My daily routine changed completely. Every morning, I would take a stroll around the rejuvenating countryside, admiring the bounties of nature. I would walk up and down the hills for hours.

In the evening, I would watch the glorious sunset, ensconced on a bench in an isolated area of Summer Hill or Tara Devi or my favourite Forest Road. I would continue sitting till it became dark and cold. I would then find my way back home.

Although I appeared calm and composed externally, loneliness, frustration and uncertainty were gnawing at me. I was completely at sea, burning with insecurity.

One night, at home, I overheard my parents talking about me. My father asked my mother in a worried tone: 'What has happened to Bittu? Why is he always so quiet and pensive?' He continued: 'Earlier today, I met our neighbour Malhotra saab. He was mentioning that you need a different kind of body and face to become an actor. I know that Bittu tried his best but was not successful. Now, he should take up a job . . . There is a vacancy for the post of a clerk in the Forest Department. Should I suggest his name to the boss?'

My mother responded: 'What is the problem if our son wants to live with us? How many Kashmiri boys live with their parents? Almost every one of them leaves home to earn money elsewhere. We are lucky that our son is staying with us. Now if it is not written in his fate to become an actor, so be it!'

Overhearing this conversation was like a wakeup call for me. I felt that my parents had completely given up on me. They were already writing my fate as if all my efforts to become an actor had come to nought. I realised then that if I stayed on in Shimla, it wouldn't be long before I made the transition from *an unsuccessful young man* to *an unsuccessful old man*!

I was suddenly spurred on. I decided that if I tried once again to climb the ladder of success, I *may* face failure, but if I did not even attempt it, I would *ensure* it! I decided to go back to Bombay and informed my parents about it. They were positive about my decision and the very next day, they saw me off at the bus stop. For some strange reason, there was no worry in their eyes.

13

DESTINY TAKES OVER

After my tragic affair in Lucknow and the lonely sojourn at Shimla, I arrived by train in Bombay having survived a fairly long and tedious journey at the perpetually crowded Victoria Terminus Station—renamed Chhatrapati Shivaji Terminus.

On my earlier trips to Bombay, I had the opportunity of meeting Mahesh Bhatt (a bit of a maverick in the Hindi film industry) on a few occasions in the hope of landing a role, but in vain. He had developed the wacky habit of calling me duffer. Those were the days when my 'pilgrimage' around the city took me to almost all the production houses, which were nothing short of temples for me. I hauled my luggage with me to the nearest telephone booth and called Mahesh Bhatt.

'Hello, Bhatt saab,' I said. But in response, all I heard were crackling and hissing sounds over the line. 'Bhatt saab can you hear me? This is Anupam Kher . . . Anupam Kher speaking from VT Station. I have just reached Bombay from Shimla.'

In his characteristic manner, he responded: 'It's you . . . duffer! Where have you been . . . where had you disappeared to? You duffer, you are playing the main role in my next film as a director.'

I couldn't believe my ears! I had lost all hope of ever making it big in the film world. I rushed to meet Bhatt saab at our appointed time.

Here, let me digress a bit to recount a popular joke from my 'struggling' period, which is still doing the rounds among aspiring actors of today.

A wannabe actor goes to meet a famous film producer with his photographs. He offers one of them to a producer, who glances at it and comments: 'Nice photograph . . . Do one thing. Leave your phone number at the desk. I will call you later for an old man's role.'

'Sir, why an old man's role? I am still young!'

'Don't worry young fellow. By the time I call, you won't be young anymore!'

Jokes apart, something very similar was happening in real life with me as well. That actor may have got an old man's role in his twilight years, but in my case, Mahesh Bhatt wanted me *to portray an old man in my youth itself*. I was just twenty-eight years old then and the thought of playing a character more than twice that age was indeed daunting. Other upcoming actors (in my age group) such as Sunny (Ajay Singh) Deol, Jackie (Jai Kishan) Shroff and Anil Kapoor all of whom went on to make a distinct mark for themselves as a hero in the years to come were my role models to start my career with. I was convinced that, after playing an old man, I would be typecast in future films either as a father or a grandfather and many a death scene would seal my fate. This effectively meant that my career would be finished even before it started!

However, when Mahesh Bhatt brought alive, through his narration, the character of the retired teacher B. V. Pradhan for his forthcoming directorial venture *Saaransh*, I felt the role was ageless and timeless.

I was finally convinced that I had arrived and would make a huge impact and be finally noticed. The film was to be produced by the venerable Rajshri Productions, headed by the patriarch Tarachand Barjatya, known for depicting social and family-oriented dramas based on human values on celluloid such as *Aarti* (1962), *Dosti* (1964; an exceptional movie), *Taqdeer* (1967), *Uphaar* (1971), *Piya Ka Ghar* (1972), *Saudagar* (1973), *Geet Gaata Chal* (1975), *Chitchor* (1976) and *Dulhan Wahi Jo Piya Man Bhaaye* (1977). All these films were studded with fabulous songs, many of which are popular even today. What more could I ask for? I could almost taste success and sense fame around the corner.

I immediately put my nose to the grindstone and started preparing—methodically and diligently—for the role of the elderly B. V. Pradhan. I was then staying in a paying guest accommodation and leading a proverbial 'hand-to-mouth existence'. But I was determined to succeed. Every morning, dressed in a dhoti-kurta combination, I went to Shivaji Park (abutting the sea face in Central Bombay), in Dadar, a middle-class neighbourhood known for its leisurely lifestyle. Shivaji Park has been termed the 'nursery of Indian cricket' because several legends such as Sunil Gavaskar, Dilip Vengsarkar and Sachin Tendulkar cut their teeth in the vast maidans here. I was sure that on these very hallowed grounds now an actor too would be launched.

Saaransh, in essence, portrays on screen the poignant experiences of a highly principled schoolteacher who lives in the Shivaji Park area with his wife (played by Rohini Hattangadi[15]) who stoically copes with the death of his only son killed in New York in a mugging incident. He also takes on a local politician and his goons to save the life of a woman and the baby she is carrying. Like in most films, there are many dramatic situations and twists and turns in the movie presented realistically and credibly with each scene dovetailing seamlessly into the next.

In Shivaji Park, I would watch, for hours on end, the kids jumping all over the place, playing a variety of games, laughing gleefully and enjoying themselves in a carefree manner as only kids can. I would also carefully study the adults, especially the senior citizens—their mannerisms, their idiosyncrasies, their gaits and how they interacted with each other. I would trudge along like an infirm old man, using a walking stick. I continued with this routine for about six months. I was now thoroughly prepared for the role of B. V. Pradhan in *Saaransh*.

As always, I informed the whole world—well, at least all the persons whom I knew that my moment of reckoning was at hand! That I was going to be launched by a famous banner in a lead role!

And all of them were thrilled for me.

One day, as I was working on refining my character for *Saaransh* for the umpteenth time in my PG in Shastri Nagar, out of the blue, my friend from the National School of Drama, Suhas Khandke, came to meet me. He seemed a bit anxious. My first reaction upon his arrival was that he had come to retrieve his money from me. I was near broke at that time and was wondering how to wriggle out of an embarrassing situation. So, to divert his attention, I said: 'Sit, sit Suhas, sit. I am reading *Saaransh*'s script. I will perform a few scenes for you.'

He did not seem amused and said: 'Wait a minute. There's something important I have to tell you about *Saaransh*.'

'What is it? What has happened?' I asked.

'Yesterday, I happened to be at the Rajshri Productions office. I heard something there . . . I don't know if it's just a rumour or is it true, but you must know about it,' he answered.

'What rumour?'

'I heard that you are not going to play the role of B. V. Pradhan in *Saaransh*.'

'If I am not, then who is replacing me? Are you? Is Mahesh Bhatt himself playing the role?' I asked mockingly.

He said with an air of finality: 'No . . . Sanjeev Kumar[16] has been given that role.'

I rushed to a nearby grocery shop and telephoned Mahesh Bhatt: 'It's amazing how people spread weird rumours. Just now, a friend of mine from the National School of Drama told me that I am not doing the role of B. V. Pradhan in *Saaransh* and that Sanjeev Kumar is doing it.'

Mahesh Bhatt chose to remain silent. I continued: 'Hello . . . hello . . . is everything alright, Bhatt saab? Please do speak up.'

He responded: 'Yes, Anupam . . . everything is fine. It's just that Rajshri people don't want to invest their money on a newcomer and have decided to take Sanjeev Kumar for that main role. But you don't worry. You can play the other old man's role, which is equally good. Bye!' And he abruptly disconnected the line.

To say I was shocked by his cavalier attitude would be an understatement. I ran back to my room. I shoved all my worldly belongings into a suitcase and boarded a taxi. My first destination was Mahesh Bhatt's apartment on Pali Hill,[17] on the sixth floor of the building Green Acres.

After leaving behind my suitcase in the taxi and asking the driver to wait, I entered the building. It was my bad luck that the lift was not working. I have seen many ups and downs in my life, but this kind of an 'up' when feeling really 'down' was a first even for me.

The climb seemed unending, but I was not one to give up (à la Edmund Hillary and Tenzing Norgay, the first human beings to reach the Mount Everest summit in May 1953). When I eventually knocked on his door, puffing and panting, he opened it and said: 'Fantastic Anupam. I'm glad you are taking it so sportingly . . . This is the great sportsmanship spirit of theatre people. You see Sanjeev Kumar is from the world of theatre too and you are also from theatre. Both of you will create history. It's incredible! I am aware that the other old man's role is not as good as Sanjeev Kumar's. But don't worry, I will rework it. You must understand the concerns of the top people at Rajshri Productions. As I told you over the phone, they don't want to invest money in a newcomer and take unnecessary risks . . .'

I cut him short and said: 'One minute, Bhatt saab . . . just hold on. Please come here.' I took him to a window, from where the road was visible. I then told him in a loud voice: 'Do you see that taxi down there? My luggage is inside it. I have decided to quit Bombay. I will go anywhere . . . Delhi, Lucknow, Shimla, Timbuktu or even to hell. But I want to tell you one thing before leaving—Mahesh Bhatt, you are a fraud . . . number one fraud. You are also a cheat . . . a cheat of the worst kind. For the past six months, you have been telling me that I shall be playing B. V. Pradhan's role. Now, suddenly, you ask me to switch over to the other old man's role, which has a very limited scope! I have already told my entire family . . . and everyone I know that I shall be playing the main role in *Saaransh* and now I am being relegated to a side role.'

I had gained full momentum for having lost the role and there was nothing holding me back. Since I was not doing the film, the words of my grandfather, Pandit Amar Nath, sprang up like a bubble in my mind: 'If you want to be equal with anybody in this world, just don't expect anything from the person.' I continued relentlessly: 'You make such long speeches about theatre, cinema and commitment. You call yourself a film director. But you don't have enough courage to tell the bigwigs at Rajshri that *only* Anupam Kher can play this role for *only* he can do justice to it. And let me tell you one more thing . . . Sanjeev Kumar *cannot* perform this role better than me.'

I wound up by declaring: 'Before I leave, I am going to curse you . . . it is the curse of a Kashmiri Pandit . . . a Brahmin.' The curse of a Brahmin is believed to be very effective. I then walked out of his apartment and virtually ran down the stairs from the sixth floor.

As I was about to get into my waiting taxi, Mahesh Bhatt yelled from his lofty perch: 'Hey you . . . come up duffer!'

I shouted back: 'Sorry, I am leaving now.'

He again yelled: 'Come up *immediately* . . . I picked up my suitcase (which suddenly seemed very light) and, once again, walked up the stairs to the sixth floor. But this time, I reached his apartment in a jiffy.

Mahesh Bhatt studied me for a long time and then picked up the phone and called Rajshri studios and told them that the reaction he had seen that moment was exactly what he needed in his leading man. He convinced them to take me back in the film. My fiery response, my brimstone reaction and my heartfelt emotion touched a deep chord in Mahesh Bhatt and rescued my life. Looking back, I realise that we have to seize with both hands the opportunities that come our way, be greedy for the success we yearn for and dare to be worthy.

That day, Mahesh Bhatt paid the taxi fare (a goodwill gesture on his part).

14

THE MAGICAL METAMORPHOSIS

The shooting of *Saaransh* started on 1 January 1984. Some friends of the producers and Bhatt saab had gathered for the inaugural shot, as also Balwant Gargi. Without telling Bhatt saab, instead of merely colouring my hair grey, I had shaved off my hair, put on a hair patch instead and came dressed as an old man. I wanted to be fully in the character not just in the garb of the character. It would have not had the same impact. Many years earlier I had seen a photograph of an old Kashmiri man who was bald and had a patch on his head. I needed to look like him—not just a young man impersonating an old man. I added a walking stick also—the stick which I kept with me all the time. During the making of the film, I used to even sleep with it. That stick is still in my office, hanging on the wall as a precious memento. Amal Allana designed the costumes for the film.

Mahesh Bhatt was shocked to see me. So was Balwant Gargi. Half the unit did not recognise me and mistook me to be some old man visiting for the 'mahurat' of the film. When I bent down to touch Gargi's feet, he felt rather awkward and became very emotional. He was always a man of few words, but that day what he said was unusual as it was unique: 'No, don't touch my feet because today, it should be the other way around. You are the old man and your dignity shines through. I should be touching your feet.'

I was very moved. He was usually not very demonstrative but that day, his obvious pride shone bright and cast a glow over me. He looked over at Mahesh Bhatt and the expression on his face clearly showed his happiness as if saying: '*Kya bacha paida kiya hain maine*' (What a child I have produced). For me, all the memories of the past culminated into this moment of great pride—of the times that we had spent together during my struggling days, his unconditional encouragement, his every gesture be it offering me a drink or telling his man Friday, Kishori Lal: '*Anupam ke liye makhan daal kar kaali dal bana*' (Make kali dal with butter for Anupam), was a learning moment for an actor and not placating a hungry man. Everything he did, including discussing his personal domestic life, which was in complete shambles, was somehow an education for an actor. Strange, but true!

That day, my brother Raju was there, as were a couple of close friends like Suhas, but for me to have Gargi present for that epic moment, brought together the strands of time, the love and learning from the past, confidence of the present and complete trust and belief for my future. With such a brimming palate of emotions, I gave my first shot for *Saaransh* that day.

There was an off-screen incident during the shooting of *Saaransh*, which I can never forget. I was facing a lot of difficulties while performing a particular scene. It just wasn't working out and we had already shot for eight retakes. The atmosphere was becoming a bit tense.

Mahesh Bhatt then took me to a corner, out of the earshot of the others and whispered in my ear: 'Do you remember the aggression you showed when you came to my house and called me a fraud and a cheat when I told you that I was going to replace you with Sanjeev Kumar? Revisit the depth of that emotion, show me your promise, your inner conviction and truth . . . Come on, get going!' I reached into my creative innards and answered that calling.

Saaransh was like a diamond, honed to perfection—brilliant and multi-faceted. Wrought by life nuances, trials and tribulations that made the diamond shine even brighter. It was a blood diamond but what a precious unforgettable one. Offering glimpses of the truth at many levels. In those 41 days of its making, I ate, dreamt, slept, and romanced only *Saaransh*. It had become my junoon, consumed my entire consciousness. Even today, whenever I see it, I don't see myself in that role. I sincerely feel it's an old man . . . a sincere, honest, genuine old man, who is free from pretence or deceit. For me *Saaransh* is more than a film, it's a way of life. If I had done any other film in its place, I would not have been the person I am today.

I can relate to every character I have played in a film that includes Police Commissioner Prakash Rathod in Neeraj Pandey's *A Wednesday*, Kamal Kishore Khosla in Dibakar Banerjee's *Khosla ka Ghosla*, Gulshan Bakshi in Kundan Shah's *Kya Kehna*, Malhotra in Aditya Chopra's *Dilwale Dulhania Le Jayenge*, but *Saaransh*. The only other exception was the role of Dr Manmohan Singh in Vijay Ratnakar Gutte's *The Accidental Prime Minister*, because I don't think that's me. It felt like a ghost had entered my spirit and made me perform. But more about that later.

I was involved with *Saaransh* in a very intimate way and wanted to be associated with it at every stage, in every department. Mahesh Bhatt, I think, appreciated my passion for it, but wanted to keep me away lest I become a nuisance for others involved. For example, David Dhawan, the editor of the film had standing instructions not to let me enter the editing room. Once when I tried to suggest to David which is a good shot and which not, he just shouted and ordered me out of the room. For me, it was not a film anymore. It was my baby. My fixation. Even when the background music was being recorded, Ajit Verman would see me get demonstrative and cry. Yes, I would cry during the recording of background music, even in the scenes of violence. In fact, Ajit wanted me out of the recording room because my crying would make him emotional too. Mahesh Bhatt and I used to openly weep while watching many of the significant scenes.

There was a scene between me and Nilu Phule—that amazing Marathi legend—wherein I go to complain against his harassment to the police. And he is called to the police station. Like many others, I had great respect for Nilu Phule as an actor, for the kind of work that he had done. Before the scene was to be shot, Mahesh Bhatt, who as a director has the most unconventional way of directing his actors, came to me and said: 'Anupam, don't feel inferior to him. Remember, as a human being, as a person, you are superior to him. B. V. Pradhan is far superior to this politician, and the superiority comes out of your conviction about your beliefs. That's why status does not matter, does not count.

The entire experience was a strange mix of euphoria and madness. Though the compliments meant a great deal to me, I never felt triumphant. Perversely I used to feel tired and exhausted because my body, mind and heart had gone through this intense emotional upheaval for 41 days, at the end of which, the person who was doing that role was not me. It will never be. I can keep on getting offers for a remake of *Saaransh,* but I would like to say without sounding arrogant that nobody will be able to remake it. Neither Mahesh Bhatt nor Anupam Kher because such creative innovations cannot be remade, because of its mind, body and soul transformations. You cannot remake Martin Scorsese's *Raging Bull* or any of the great classics of the great masters. You just cannot.

Today, when I stand shoulder to shoulder with top performers whether in Indian cinema or in Hollywood, I am not in the least intimidated except by the demands of my character. I can also afford to take a stance on my social profile even if it means being unpopular because of my indelible convictions. Much of my thinking has been shaped by my unforgettable *Saaransh* experience. Mind you, it's not arrogance or a superiority complex; it's my foundation.

When *Saaransh* was ready, the Rajshri management organised daily previews of the film in their personal theatre. I think it was liberating for them too. *Saaransh* is a cathartic film which makes you believe in something good about life, even in the face of adversity.

So, all those who used to come to these previews, including actors and others from the film fraternity, were blown away by the unusual premise of the film and the young actor playing the old man while I was euphoric to see everyone's genuine reaction. The highpoint was when Sanjeev Kumar, whom I had replaced in the film, came to see the screening. He was alone in the auditorium. I was sitting in the projection room, from where I was shocked to see that Sanjeev Kumar was weeping throughout the film. Once the film got over, he took about 10 minutes to come out, where we were waiting for him. As soon as he came out, still misty-eyed, he walked up to me and said: 'This would have been a wrong film for me. Nobody could have done this film better than you.' This compliment from a man who was one of the finest actors was indeed a very special one. I will treasure it always and hold it close to my memory and mind.

The only person who thought that the casting of the film was wrong was actor Anil Kapoor. After seeing the preview, he called up Mahesh Bhatt and said: 'This time you have gone terribly wrong with your casting.'

Anil Kapoor is a close friend of mine. He, Satish Kaushik and I have been buddies for ages. I have interacted with Anil since many decades. In many ways, Anil, like me, has a very strong survival instinct and is extremely hard working. As a dear friend, I confide in him. I feel that in the film industry, I am perhaps, the closest to him. We have a similar kind of pungent, self-deprecating sense of humour. In fact, I would say he is undoubtedly the most hard-working actor I have seen in Hindi cinema. A very sincere, sophisticated, person, an immensely genuine actor, who has a great self-analytical quality. He knows where he stands, and he is brutally honest about it. No one can beat his sincerity. Even today, at 63, and with over 150 films and television serials to his credit and numerous national and international awards in his bag, he goes and rehearses every scene of a film till he gets the right note, the right expression, to capture the character that he is playing. Many feel that he is too much of a perfectionist because he is not happy till he does not get the right *sur*, the right frame that he is looking for.

For me, it's very difficult to judge him as an actor because he is my buddy. But look at his amazing array of films like K. Vishwanath's *Eeshwar*, S. Shankar's *Nayak-The Real Hero*, Subhash Ghai's *Ram Lakhan* and *Meri Jung*, Shekhar Kapur's *Mr. India*, Vidhu Vinod Chopra's *Parinda* and *1942: A Love Story*, Yash Chopra's *Lamhe* or Indra Kumar's *Beta* and you will notice that there is certainly a different quality that sets him apart. He was brilliant in Danny Boyle's Academy Award-winning film *Slumdog Millionaire*, which was his first international film. His performance in the eighth season of the action series *24* which generated rave reviews from the American press was unbelievable. It is very difficult to survive in this industry for 40 years, and he has not only done it but is also going strong. And still remains contemporary and relevant. That in itself speaks volumes for Anil.

I have done numerous films with him ranging from Satish Kaushik's *Roop Ki Rani Choron Ka Raja* to K. Bhagyaraj's *Mr. Bechara* to Subhash Ghai's *Ram Lakhan*, to Yash Chopra's *Lamhe*, to Rakesh Roshan's *Khel*, just to name a few. Together we have done some good films, some mediocre films, some indifferent films and even some botched-up films like K. Kodandarami's *Jamai Raja*. But that is normal in any creative field. Good, mediocre and bad productions all go hand in hand.

It was in 2007, that Anil Kapoor and I had a problem on the work front which strained our personal relationship for over two years. He was planning to produce a film *Gandhi, My Father* under his banner Anil Kapoor Films Company. The film, based on the book by Chandulal Dalal and Neelamben Parikh, explores the troubled relationship between Mahatma Gandhi and his son Harilal Gandhi. It was to be directed by Feroz Khan (Feroz Abbas Khan, not to be mixed with Feroz Khan, the actor). Feroz Khan, a reputed theatre director, had directed, in 1994, a play *Saalgirah* with both Kirron and myself in the lead roles. Later in 2005, he also directed my autobiographical play, a one-man, presentation—*Kucch Bhi Ho Sakta Hai.*

Anil Kapoor and Feroz had finalised me for the title role in *Gandhi, My Father* and had assured me that I would be given enough time to lose weight so as to look as skinny as Gandhi did. I had asked for four months. Then one day Anil informed that they were going to start shooting within two months and 'you're not in the film'. I was very hurt. Obviously, they had set their sights on somebody else. That certainly created a bump in our beautiful friendship. But, time, as they say, is a great healer. Two years later we were able to get past the hurdle and cement our friendship once again.

For me, Anil Kapoor is 'Chembur Ka Scamp'. And he affectionately calls me 'Shimle Ka Tramp'. For example, recently he called me in New York, where I have been shooting for many months for NBC serial *New Amsterdam*, and said: '*Arre, Shimle ke Tramp, wahan baitha aish kar raha hain . . . Robert De Niro ke saath.*' (You are enjoying there . . . sitting with Robert De Niro). Similarly, when he was in Germany, I would call him and say: '*Arre, Chembur ka Scamp, Germany mein baitha photo khichwa raha hain?*' (Are you getting yourself photographed in Germany?). We are totally open with each other and share our innermost feelings which, perhaps, we do not share with our wives also. Not secrets, mind you. But we speak freely about our feelings and emotional state of mind without any encumbrance. State of mind like 'I am feeling low, down and out' or 'I am finished'. It can also be 'I am feeling euphoric' or 'I am feeling bitchy'. And all these feelings do play an important role in our lives and we both are genuinely open with each other.

For a long time, Anil Kapoor did not tell me that he too had auditioned for David O. Russell's *Silver Linings Playbook* which had Robert De Niro, Bradley Cooper and Jennifer Lawrence in the main leads. I eventually bagged the role. Later he told me: 'I could not have done this role.' Similarly, for Anthony Maras' film *Hotel Mumbai* about the Mumbai attacks in 2008 on the Taj Mahal Hotel, based on Victoria Midwinter Pitt's *Surviving Mumbai*—he was to do the role of Hemant Oberoi, the chef, which is one of my recent roles. Recently, he was in London to meet a very famous casting director. Just as he was about to enter the room, I happened to call from New York. He said: '*Arre, Shimle ke Tramp*, your horoscope is at the top of the world as far as international cinema is concerned. I'm just getting into it . . . and you're calling me. Let me get at least some films . . . I will talk to you later.'

Usually in the Hindi film industry, personal-life friendships are also based where you are positioned professionally. For example, heroes become friends with directors and actors, and they treat them as equals. I have never operated like that. Just because I do character roles, does not mean that I am any lesser than them. Sometimes this attitude of mine does come across as 'arrogance'. Yet, that's what my survival instinct is all about. Today, these separations are even more delineated than they were way back in the 1980s and 1990s. At that time, we were fortunate that we all bonded on the sets as a cohesive film fraternity in the absence of the ubiquitous luxury mobile vans and appendage cell phones. The concept of managers, agents, press managers or social media managers did not exist. All communication was through verbal face to face conversations. We would all play games together, sit together in the evenings during outdoor shooting stints, share a drink, talk, exchange views or just gossip.

Anil and I talk regularly. It's like we are both going towards our sunset years together and to remain in touch is more important than anything else. During your younger years when you are at the top, you feel invincible and do not feel the need for people and the bonds they bring. But as you mature, one appreciates the need to maintain close friendships and have someone who is only a phone call away. I treasure friends. For me, friends are very important. And I call Satish Kaushik and Anil Kapoor as my friends, in the truest sense of the word.

Finally, *Saaransh* was released in Bombay's historic Metro Cinema on M. G. Road on Friday, 25 May 1984. That day, the Bhiwandi and Thane riots, which had started a week earlier, were at their peak. I was travelling with Mahesh Bhatt from Bandra when we saw buses burning through Shivaji Park and some other areas—a sequence somewhat similar to that in *Saaransh* when the riots take place and the old man gets stuck and robbed. The box office collections for the film got affected because most people dare not come out of their homes. As I stood outside the Metro Cinema for the 12-noon show, I saw that some people had ventured out to see the film. I watched from the stalls and realised that there was complete silence. I could not make out whether the film was being appreciated or being dubbed as boring and heavy. As the first show concluded, I went and stood outside hoping that people will come out and surround me to say: 'Oh my God, what an amazing performance.' But nobody recognised me, nobody was looking at me—neither those who were coming out nor those who were now going in for the matinee show. As I stood there, an old lady peered at me, walked up and then asked: 'You are the main actor, aren't you?'

'Yes,' I answered.

She immediately hugged me warmly with her frail arms and said: 'Can I have your autograph?' She took out a white handkerchief. I had a pen ready because I thought people would be mobbing me after this. But there were no mobs because people did not identify the young man waiting outside with the old man in the film. Just one autograph. While I signed her handkerchief, she said: '*Badi jaldi aapne autograph dena seekh liya*' (You have learnt to give autograph very fast).

I said: 'Ma'am, I have been practising it for the last 20 years.'

She looked at me, gave me a smile, and said: 'You will have a long career.'

For me that was worth more than a million autographs that day.

Later in 1985, when Anil Kapoor and I were going together to the Shanmukhananda Hall (Sri Shanmukhananda Chandrasekarendra Saraswathi Auditorium) in Sion for the 32nd Filmfare Awards Nite, he told me about his initial opinion about my casting.

For that special occasion, I was dressed in a new tuxedo, specially tailored for me because over the years I had seen pictures of actors in magazines wearing similar attire. That night, I won the Best Actor Award despite being pitted against Dilip Kumar (Yash Chopra's *Mashaal*), Amitabh Bachchan (Prakash Mehra's *Sharaabi*), Naseeruddin Shah (Sai Paranjpye's *Sparsh*) and Raj Babbar (Ravi Chopra's *Aaj ki Awaz*). Anil Kapoor got the Best Supporting Actor Award for his role in *Mashaal*.

It was my night of initiation into the film fraternity. *I have made it*, I thought. When I looked at the audience, I had an epiphany: They had chosen me, they were going to make me what I became. My life was a gift.

Kucch bhi ho sakhta hai!

15

THE SIGNING SPREE

After *Saaransh*, I was declared a 'happening person' in the film industry. I was inundated with congratulatory messages from friends, family and strangers. Although my fame reached dizzy new heights, my financial graph dipped abysmally. The public hears all kinds of rumours about a newly minted celebrity's wealth, but the reality of their financial status is often the best-guarded secret. In an industry where everything is magnified and often presented as larger than life, my new-found stardom also included empty pockets and no bank balance which often led to hilarious situations.

I was faced with the classic celebrity dilemma. I could not travel in public transport without being mobbed by enthusiastic fans that showered me with love and adulation. But I couldn't afford to purchase a new car. I was acutely aware that the film sororities were status conscious and susceptible to external appearances. Keeping up pretences was vital—if one was pedestrian enough to travel by bus or the local train, the remuneration offered would be equal to this. The impression would be entirely different if one showed up in a chauffeur-driven limousine; they will fork out a fortune.

Immediately after *Saaransh*, I was shooting for a low-budget film at Mehboob Studios in Bandra, which was a stone's throw from my place. Yet, I couldn't walk the distance as it would be embarrassing; the studio hands and the security staff would spread the word that the hero arrived on foot. And I couldn't get a taxi, as the drivers preferred to ply only long distances.

So, I hit upon an ingenious plan. I would hail a taxi from my old paying guest accommodation in Casa Maria on St Paul Road and tell the driver to take me to the Bandra (railway) station. On reaching there, I would say: 'I think I have forgotten something . . . take me to Mehboob Studios.' At the gate, in front of all those watching, I would step out of the taxi to create the right impression.

This routine from home to Bandra station and from there to Mehboob Studios was repeated frequently. One day, I actually wanted to go to Bandra station. As I was about to get down from the taxi, the driver asked me: 'Saheb, are you sure you haven't forgotten anything?'

I asked: 'Why?'

I then realised that I had travelled three times in that very same taxi.

Subsequently, in the mid-to-late 1980s, I became a full-fledged movie star and a celebrity in my own right. This status became quite apparent when, seemingly out of the thin air, a medley of people gravitated towards me and attempted to run my life.

One fine morning, while I was busy at a film shoot, a man approached me and said: 'Sir, I am P. R. Rane. I shall be your accountant.' H. D. Pathak came into my life as my chartered accountant and he keeps me honest. To this day, whenever I receive a phone call from him, I worry that he is going to admonish me for something because he is the epitome of honesty.

Another person asserted: 'Sir, I am Ashok Panjabi, I shall be your secretary . . . from now onwards, all your negotiations, your dates, your appointments, your schedules and all your tensions are for me to handle.' And so, it came to pass.

At this stage, a young boy came into my life when I was just about five to seven films old. It was in January 1985, while I was shooting for a film in a dockyard kind of a setting where there were no real

Clockwise:
With my mother Dulari Kher in 1955 when I was six months old. • My first passport size picture, 1967. • The suit I got for my first romantic interlude when I was in XI grade in 1971.

Facing page: (Clockwise) My first attempt at a portfolio picture, 1982. • As Mac the Knife from the play *The Threepenny Opera.* • A scene from the play *The Exception and the Rule* staged at the Panjab University campus in Chandigarh, September 1974. • My first attempt at bodybuilding in 1974 in Panjab University Chandigarh Hostel.

A scene from Nadira Babbar's play *Chandanpur ki Champabai,* 1982.
• As James Tyrone from the play *Long Day's Journey into Night.* • My audition picture for *Shankrabarnam* in 1983. The role finally went to Girish Karnad.

Facing page: (Clockwise) Marriage to Kirron on 26 August 1985.
L to R: My father Pushkar Nath Kher, brother Raju Kher and mother Dulari Kher. • With Kirron, Anil Kapoor and his wife Sunita. My first Best Actor Filmfare Award for *Saaransh* in 1985. Anil got the Best Supporting Actor Filmfare Award for *Mashaal*.

Dressed as Gandhi for a mini-series *Raj Se Swaraj*. • With my brother Raju in 1984. • With the legendary Dilip Kumar and the famous lyricist Anand Bakshi in 1986. • A still from the shooting of Indra Kumar's *Dil*, with Aamir Khan. • At the grand *mahurat* of *Karma* with Dilip Kumar, Jackie Shroff, Anil Kapoor and Naseeruddin Shah.

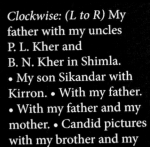

Clockwise: (L to R) My father with my uncles P. L. Kher and B. N. Kher in Shimla. • My son Sikandar with Kirron. • With my father. • With my father and my mother. • Candid pictures with my brother and my mother.

Facing page: With Kirron on the sets of Satyajit Ray.

Clockwise: With my childhood friends Vijay Sehgal and Satish Malhotra. • With my great buddies, Satish Kaushik and Anil Kapoor. • With Amitabh Bachchan who inaugurated my photo show in Mumbai. • With David Dhawan. • With Yash Chopra.

Facing page: With Sooraj Barjatya. • Three students of the National School of Drama; with Om Puri and Naseeruddin Shah. • Presenting a copy of my first book to Ruskin Bond. • A scene from my play *Kucch Bhi Ho Sakta Hai.* • Dressed as Prabhadevi for the April Fool issue of *Cine Blitz.* Photo by Gautam Rajadhyaksha, make-up by Mickey Contractor. • Paying for the blessings from Mahesh Bhatt.

Top: With Air Chief Marshal Birender Singh Dhanoa, Chief of the Naval Staff Admiral Sunil La[n]
and Chief of Army Staff General Bipin Rawat.
Bottom: Being awarded the Padma Bhushan by President Pranab Mukherjee in 2016.

(Facing page) Top: With Anna Hazare during the India Anti-corruption Movement, 2012.
Bottom: Presenting a copy of the sampler of my autobiography to Prime Minister Narendra Mo[di]

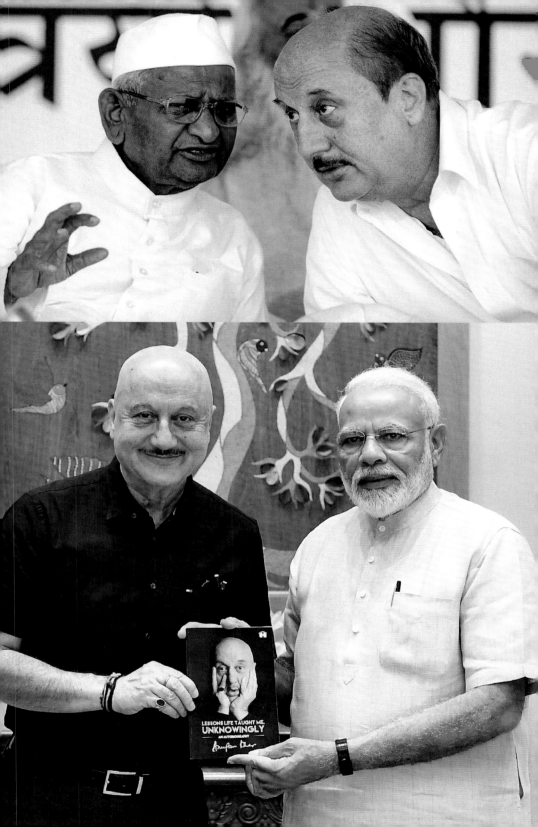

Dressed as Dr Manmohan Singh for the film *The Accidental Prime Minister.*

make-up rooms—which in any case were a rarity those days. I was sharing my make-shift make-up room with a senior actor, Suresh Oberoi. At that time, he was a successful actor who was shooting for at least ten films simultaneously, but I found him to be not only arrogant but also rather pompous. While getting ready, Suresh sat on a chair with his foot in the lap of a young boy who was trying to help him put on his shoe and tie its laces. By mistake, he tied the lace a bit too tight. That infuriated Suresh who gave the boy such a hard kick that he rolled over in pain. I could not resist and, as I helped the boy up, I told Suresh that what he had done was not the right thing to do. Suresh, the 'big actor' he thought he was, was appalled at the audacity of a junior actor and said in anger: 'What do you mean by that?'

'What you did was not the right thing to do. Why did you kick him?' I asked.

Suresh answered, 'This boy has been with me for six weeks and only I know how I have tolerated him, out of sheer pity. You won't tolerate him even for six days.'

'Okay . . . I will take him sir,' I replied.

That young boy is Dattu—Datta Sawant—my man Friday. He has been with me ever since—34 years. He looks after me and tends to my every comfort with utter commitment and single-mindedness. He is loyal. He is honest. He is dedicated. He is more than a family member. I shudder to think what my life would be without him!

Hindi film stories aren't the only ones that are clichéd; even Hindi film secretaries are. Ashok Panjabi belonged to that category. A few days after he entered my life, he told me: 'You are bald. You will have to wear a wig whenever you go out.'

I came up with a counter-question: 'Why do I need to wear a wig?'

He next queried: 'Have you ever seen a bald hero?'

Pat came my reply: 'Yes, I have.'

'Where?'

'In the film *Gandhi*!'

His persistence was commendable. He went on: 'In *Gandhi*, neither did the hero have a pretty heroine like Sharmila Tagore nor was he paired with the lovely Moushumi Chatterjee. Soon, you could be starring opposite these two leading ladies. On seeing you bald, they would call you 'uncle', although they are older than you!' (By the mid-1980s, both these highly talented women had built up a noteworthy oeuvre in Hindi and Bengali cinema. Even after that, they continued working in films, but less frequently.)

The hawkeyed Ashok Panjabi also had his ear to the ground in Bollywood. He knew virtually all the news about the goings-on in the industry and was up to date with the latest gossip and rumours with regard to the 'celestial beings'. The following *jumla* (line) fitted him to a T:

Hum zameen par hai, sitaron ki khabar rakhte hain
Hum bade woh hain badi tej nazar rakhte hain.[18]

I am on the ground, but I am well informed about the stars
I am one of those who has a sharp eye.

He was constantly nagging me to wear shades (sunglasses or goggles) when I went to parties, which were invariably held at night. I would then come up with the most obvious question: 'Ashok, why should I put on goggles at night-time parties?'

He gave me a look that implied that I was totally unaware of the party protocol of that period. He pointed out that that was the 'done thing'.

Of course, he was right. Apart from wearing goggles at parties, wearing white clothes, keeping the top few shirt buttons open and walking with a slight swagger were in vogue. I began following the trend.

Within one week, my self-appointed secretary, Ashok Panjabi, managed to bag a string of *fifty-seven films* for me (which must be a record of sorts). Very soon, I was now not only accepted but embraced as an insider in the film industry.

But before I proceed further, let me tell you an interesting little story of how Ashok got me my first signing amount for a film after *Saaransh*.

I can never forget the day I earned Rs 10,000. Yes, Rs 10,000! Not in a hundred years had anyone from my family seen such a large amount, let alone actually have it in their possession. The credit for getting me this princely sum goes entirely to Ashok Panjabi. Earlier, I had received a total of Rs 10,000 for my work in *Saaransh* and that too had come in dribs and drabs over a period of two or maybe three months. Right after the release of *Saaransh*, in May 1984, Ashok took me to meet producer-director Ramesh Behl in his office at the famous Linking Road, Bandra. It was 11 June 1984.

Ramesh Behl was a well-known producer-director and co-founder of Rose Movies, a banner known for big hits including *Kasme Vaade* (1978, starring Amitabh Bachchan, Rakhee, Randhir Kapoor and Neetu Singh) and *Pukar* (1983, starring Amitabh Bachchan, Zeenat Aman, Randhir Kapoor and Tina Munim). His children, Shristi and Goldie, too went on to make careers and a name for themselves in the film world.

While on Goldie, I must mention here about his wife, the vivacious Sonali Bendre, a bright and a very warm person and a well-known actress with whom I have done films like *Keemat* (1998), *Dhai Akshar Prem Ke* (2000), *Hamara Dil Aapke Paas Hai* (2000) and *Dil Hi Dil Mein* (2000). Today, in her early forties, she is battling cancer. We've met socially many times in Mumbai, but it was only in August 2018 and thereafter that I got the opportunity to spend some quality time with her in New York where she was undergoing treatment. I was immensely impressed by her determination and grit to overcome this scourge about which I also wrote warmly on Twitter. Now back in Mumbai since end-October, I can easily say that she is my HERO.

My morning prayers are for her!

But let me get back to my story about Ramesh Behl. Before entering his office, Ashok Panjabi had cautioned me: 'You have to just listen to the script and the role, don't say anything else. Don't utter a word. I will place my foot on your foot under the table. If I feel you are talking too much unnecessarily, I'll press your foot and you should stop speaking.'

At the outset, Ramesh Behl informed me that there were two roles in the film that he was planning titled *Jawaani*: one was 'opposite' Sharmila Tagore and the other one was 'opposite' Moushumi Chatterjee and I had to choose one. He then began narrating the script, but my mind started wandering.

I was thinking about whom I liked more—Sharmila Tagore or Moushumi Chatterjee? I realised I had seen more films of Sharmila Tagore—*Kashmir Ki Kali* (1964), *Anupama* (1966), *An Evening in Paris* (1967), *Aradhana, Satyakam* (both 1969), *Safar* (1970), *Amar Prem* (1972), *Daag, Aa Gale Lag Ja* (both 1973) and *Mausam* and *Chupke Chupke* (both 1975)—than those of Moushumi Chatterjee (such as *Anurag*, 1972, and *Roti, Kapda Aur Makan*, 1974). My apologies to the latter.

When he finished the narration, he asked me which role I would like to do. I was so caught up in my fantasy that I blurted: 'I will do Sharmila Tagore's role!'

Ashok pressed hard on my foot. In response, Behl merely laughed and pointed out: 'No, Sharmila will be doing *her* role . . . You mean to say that you will do the role opposite her?'

I nodded my head and said: 'Yes . . . yes . . . that is what I meant.'

Next, the crucial topic of money cropped up. Ashok made a few gestures with his hands, like a semaphore, whose meaning I could not quite decipher. Apparently, Ramesh Behl could. He began making faces as if to say: 'Oh! Oh! The amount you are asking for is too much!' To cut it short, I was given an envelope stuffed with Rs 10,000 in cash. I could not believe my eyes. Then, Ashok made a gesture that any dimwit would have understood. He was asking me to leave. When I came out of the office on to Linking Road, I felt as if all the people around were looking at me because they knew that I had a small fortune in my pocket!

I was extremely thrilled and bursting with excitement. I was very eager to inform my brother Raju (who was then working in a tin factory in Bombay) about the windfall because from getting approximately Rs 166 per day to amassing Rs 10,000 rupees in one shot was a quantum leap and a dream come true! The money was burning a hole in my pocket! On Linking Road was located the Khar Telephone Exchange and I rushed there to call Raju from a public booth. As I was waiting for the call to go through, I noticed a squat man with a bushy beard standing outside the booth.

My imagination began running wild. I thought the man knew that I had 10,000 rupees on me, and he was going to mug me! Meanwhile, my brother came on the line. Unfortunately, he could just about catch what I was saying as there was too much disturbance. Keeping a low voice and trying to speak in some kind of a code language, I kept telling Raju: '*Dus miley hain . . . dus miley hain*' (I have got ten).

A baffled Raju asked: '*Matlab kya hai dus ka?*' (What do you mean by ten?)

I replied: '*Baad mein bataunga sab kuch. Tum mujhe sham ko* Holiday Inn *mein milna*' (I'll tell everything later. Meet me in the evening at the Holiday Inn). And I specified the time.

I decided to blow up the 10,000 rupees with Raju and Deepak Sinha (our roommate who was an upcoming actor who was close to me). That evening I told my brother of the morning's meeting with Ramesh Behl . . . about the advance of Rs 10,000 in my pocket and that I was going to be paid a staggering Rs 75,000! Raju's was left with his mouth open for quite some time. It appeared to be an unreal entity—like a mirage—for a bloke who was struggling to eke out a living! Plus, as a bonanza, I would be working with Sharmila Tagore and Moushumi Chatterjee, not to mention the debonair Navin Nischol.[9] (The film *Jawaani* was released in late 1984 with newcomers Karan Shah and Neelam Kothari as the hero and heroine.)

I chose the ritzy Holiday Inn (near the international airport) because it was a 'very happening place'. That evening, we ordered chicken tandoori, naan, beer and a whole lot of other delicacies so that we could stuff ourselves to our heart and stomach's content. My only objective was to somehow spend the 10,000 rupees that day itself and I was very disappointed to learn that the bill came to just Rs 947 for everything we indulged in. I was under the impression that the total would be around Rs 8000 and the rest, I would pay as the tip to the waiter. The next day, Tuesday, 12 June 1984, I sent the handsome amount of 5000 rupees to my parents. I learnt later that my father was dumbfounded and my mother, with tears flowing down her cheeks just said: '*Mera Bittu!*' She put an offering of 500 rupees in the mandir that night.

Ever since I have earned a great deal of money, but even today when I think about it, I can honestly admit that I have never enjoyed as much as I did those first 10,000 rupees!

Let me try and explain why those 10,000 rupees were significant for me. I remembered the days, not too long ago, when I never had even two ten-rupee notes to rub against each other in my pocket. My father had never paid income tax because he never earned much. The only problem that we had about money was the lack of it. On the first of every month (salary day), I had to ward off all the creditors who would gather outside our house in Shimla by lying to them that my father was not at home. Sometimes, I used to see my father changing the normal pattern of his walk while passing the shop of one of the creditors. I asked him: 'Why do you walk as if you are limping?' His reply saddened me a great deal and left me disconsolate: 'Bittu, I don't want him to recognise me.'

My father's needs were few, but only according to him. He would regularly ask for Black Label Scotch, night suits and blades. Strangely enough, he would also regularly ask for extra money, besides the monthly allowance that I used to send. Every time our telephone would end with: 'Are you also listening to what I am not saying?' which usually meant some extra money. It would irritate me. Years later, I discovered the mystery behind the demand for extra money.

My father passed away on Sunday, 12 February 2012 at the age of 84, in Mumbai. It was least expected as he was mentally and physically all there till about September 2011, when he suddenly lost his appetite. The doctors failed to diagnose the actual cause of illness. For him, food had become 'sand' and water 'acid'. In fact, he literally starved to death in our very presence. For all around, it was a death of an ordinary man but for me, it was the passing away of an extraordinary person. My brother and I decided to 'celebrate' his life and not mourn his death. We consulted our mother and asked for permission to do so at the prayer meeting.

Yes, we 'celebrated' our father's death because he was one person who had lived a full life. He witnessed so many wonderful happenings during his life. He liked to spread happiness wherever he went. I'm sure, even today, he's making everyone laugh wherever he is. In fact, that morning I had left for Goa to attend my friend film producer-director David Dhawan's son Rohit's wedding when I got the news and had to return from the Goa airport. I'm sure if my father had his way, he would have urged me to attend the wedding instead of returning.

I recall that on the morning of my departure for Jaipur for the release of my book *The Best Thing about You Is YOU!* at the literature festival, I went to his room to wish goodbye to him and mentioned that my book is being released. He looked at me smiled, and then quipped, 'You have written a book?'

I nodded.

In the 'celebrations of his life', for the prayer meeting on Monday, 13 February, we asked all our friends 'to please not show up in the mournful black and white clothes. Come clothed in colours, please,' we requested. We were completely overwhelmed to see the number and kind of people who came ranging from the top-known film personalities to the spot boys and light men—with each of whom he had a personal link with. Coming to think of it, he had perhaps made more contacts off-camera than I had made 'on camera'.

For that is how my father lived his life—with lots of joy and positivity so I will forever associate colourful vitality with him. In my heart, I know he will find a way to connect with me, just like he did even in those days of bad STD phone connections between Shimla and Mumbai.

After his passing, one day, I enquired from my mother if she had any unfulfilled wish. She surprised me by saying, 'All my life I have lived in a rented house. Can I have a home of my own in Shimla where I can live happily . . . where my heart resides?' In March 2017, I bought a heritage building in Tutu, above Summer Hill, restored it and presented it to her.

She was thrilled to move in there as the owner . . . a 'landlady' after having lived in cramped rented houses all her life. I was overwhelmed when I saw the contentment and happiness that she was experiencing. The home is named as Dulari's Kherwadi.

16

PARTNERS FOR LIFE

I saw Kiron for the first time on 28 July 1974, in Chandigarh and was blown away on the very first glimpse of her. She was beautiful, with large eyes, deep dimples and long hair—a larger than life persona that one reads about in the papers. She was a year senior to me in the Department of Indian Theatre and I had heard a lot about her before I met her. A celebrity in our midst whose name regularly appeared in the *Tribune* newspaper. She was a well-known national badminton player, belonged to a sophisticated army family and in every way, a complete contrast to me.

Kiron (years later she changed the spelling of her name to Kirron) Thakar Singh, as she was known at that time, was a bright shining star, possessing a luminous quality much like Greta Garbo and Sophia Loren. In contrast, I was merely the lowly 'best actor from Himachal Pradesh University' and someone on the periphery of her glittering world. She flitted around, very bright and lively and came across as joyful and full of laughter, which endeared her to everyone. As I reminiscence about our relationship, I recall the striking black and white close up pictures of Kiron's face taken by Balwant Gargi which effectively captured her essence. It was the second day of my arrival in Chandigarh and Kirron was visiting the campus. When our paths crossed, I completely imagined our first 'hello' exchange not because she ignored me but because I was dazzled by her and she was so far removed from my firmament. But destiny made sure our paths continued to cross and soon after, we got a chance to collaborate together on the play titled, *Mirza Sahiba*—which along with *Heer Ranjha, Sassi Punnu* and *Sohni Mahiwal* is one of the four most popular tragic romances of Punjab—directed by Balwant Gargi. I played the part of Kammu Brahmin, a comic character and I was in my element. Kirron used to come to the rehearsals and laugh a lot at my comedy. We travelled together with the rest of the cast to a remote village in Punjab called Lahora Kutta. Giani Zail Singh who was the then chief minister of Punjab enjoyed the show and especially appreciated my performance and requested me to sit next to him afterwards. He would keep saying to me, '*Ek bar aur dialogue bol mere liye*' (Repeat the dialogue for me one more time) and I would sit next to him and perform again and again the lines of the play, full throttle, causing him to burst into a long, hearty laugh. I was having great fun, building my community and serving the audience with humour and charm.

Kirron and I remained in touch after I went to the National School of Drama in Delhi where I was growing both as a theatre actor and developing more confidence as a person. As we continued to see each other occasionally our friendship developed. She was warm and friendly but for me, a raw 18-19-year-old Kirron represented a distant dream.

She would stop by often and see our plays. Whenever we met, I would make her laugh a lot. The minute I would say, 'Let me tell you a joke,' she would instantly start laughing even before I could start, which made me feel very good. She was a good audience for a comic actor. Theatre was our common bond but soon we went our separate ways. I left for Lucknow. She moved to Bombay.

When I reached Bombay a few years later, I heard that she was married to Gautam Berry a businessman who was a friend and partner of Amitabh Bachchan. Nevertheless, I got in touch with her and she came to meet me where I was rehearsing for the play called *Kawa Chala Hans ki Chaal* (a translation of Molière's *The Bourgeois Gentleman)* at the magnificent Rang Bhavan open-air auditorium. She arrived in a chauffeur-driven white ambassador car, very vibrant, stylish and sophisticated. Greeting me warmly, she said:

'Anupam, you will become very big here.' At that stage, though I had taken the momentous step to come to Bombay, I was still finding my feet. Hearing her confident assertion gave me a big boost because at times, I would question myself, *I'm not conventional looking . . . I'm not a hero-looking kind of guy.*

Marriage and motherhood (Sikandar was very little then) had obviously not dimmed her passion for theatre. She proposed that we do a play together. 'I suggest that you come over to my house and we can discuss it further. And I will treat you to a good dinner.' On the appointed day, I along with Satish Kaushik went to her home. Balwant Gargi was also there and that evening, we decided to do Eugene O'Neill's *Desire under the Elms*—a play that had 'been inspired by the myth of Phaedra, Hippolytus, and Theseus and was O'Neill's attempt to adapt plot elements and themes of a Greek tragedy to a rural New England setting.'

Thereafter, Satish and I started going to her house regularly. We used to look forward to warm hospitality, good food and the bonus was fifty rupees for a cab ride to go back home which of course we couldn't bear to use because we used to stretch it as far as two starving actors could. At her home, I met her husband Gautam, who came across as a pleasant person but with a great sense of humour. In fact, he helped my brother Raju get a job since he had joined me in Bombay. Gautam also gave me my first wooden almirah (cupboard), which I really appreciated.

The play was extremely well received at Prithvi Theatre and thanks to Gautam, Kirron and Gargi, the crème de la crème of Bombay society graced the audience. Many came backstage to congratulate me and one of them was the renowned film-maker, Yash Chopra. He came to me and said: 'What an actor you are . . . Come and meet me tomorrow.'

Next day, I went and met him at his house. I remember he offered me a glass of lassi and said: 'I saw your play yesterday and was considering you for a small role in my film *Mashal*. But now I have changed my mind because you are made for bigger roles and not for the one I had in my mind for you.'

He was not aware of my dire financial situation and I said that I would do any role. 'No, no. This role is not meant for you. I will work with you next time. It will happen. But not this role. You are bigger than this', he said with great affection. I could make out that he meant it. He was being sincere and wasn't like so many others I had met earlier.

We did five shows of *Desire Under the Elms*. Kirron was fantastic in the play and I loved working with her. Over the years, we would go on to collaborate on many more projects.

But slowly and almost unknowingly, things were changing. One day during a play rehearsal, I watched Kirron and Nadira Babbar interacting from afar. From my vantage point, I could see that Kirron was nervous, and I felt that Nadira was being a little harsh to her. I could see the sweat trickling down Kirron's forehead out of nervousness, and it was the first time I felt possessive and protective about this strong and assertive person. I could sense her palpable vulnerability and felt like taking care of her and shielding her from the world and be her knight in shining armour. Even though it was not love at first sight and our relationship really blossomed from our friendship, in the final analysis, it was inevitable. We did a play in Calcutta and I made a pass at her and though she brushed it off, our physical chemistry was changing. On a parallel track, Kirron and Gautam, who were going through marital problems, were clearly drifting apart.

With the success of *Saaransh*, I had finally arrived and since I had changed my physical appearance, I started looking different too. I was shooting in Lodhi Gardens in Delhi when Kirron came to meet me. We went for a long walk and I finally acknowledged my feelings to her. By this time, she was living alone, since Gautam had moved in with someone else. I proposed to her.

Kirron, the elegant and glamorous woman who loved dressing in gorgeous saris and her most exquisite collection of jewels, who shared my passion for theatre, with whom I was travelling and performing, became my wife on Monday, 26 August 1985. It was very euphoric. For me, professional success and marriage happened at the same time. I was high on both.

Wanting to start a family, we strived to have a child but Kirron had trouble conceiving. We tried for a long time and I remember some very funny incidents around our efforts. We needed to be conscious of certain 'critical windows' for conceiving. I recall being busy shooting for the climax of Subhash Ghai's *Ram Lakhan's Ye Jee O Jee* (a popular song) with Satish Kaushik, when Kirron said to me, 'When I call, you better come at once'. Those days, of course, there were no mobile phones. In the middle of the afternoon, I got a call from her via the operator at Filmistan Studio. Mind you I was in my full costume—a dhoti, kurta and *shendi* (tonsure)—and she said, '*Aa jao*' (Come). I panicked. I was in the middle of the shot, for which a crowd of 400-500 people had been specially collected.

How am I going to get out of this?, I thought to myself. Finally, I went up to Subhash Ghai and with an expression and a tone full of sincerity, I pleaded: '*Sir, income tax ka raid ho gaya hai. Mujhe jaldi ghar jana padega*' (There has been an income tax raid. I have to go home immediately). In those days, income tax raids were pretty commonplace in the film industry and everyone felt sympathetic about it. I rushed home, in the same dhoti, kurta and shendi, with the deadline and agenda on my mind, instead of any thoughts of passion or romance and as soon as I rushed in through the door, Kirron took one look at me and laughed heartily. We both saw the comic side of this situation.

By the time I came back, I was like any fibber who had forgotten what he had fibbed about. Can you believe it, I forgot what excuse I had given to rush home. Only when Subhash Ghai enquired, 'What happened with the raid?' I answered, as an afterthought, '*Maine handle kar liya hai*' (I have handled it). Finally, Kirron did conceive and we were really looking forward to the birth of a baby but unfortunately, the foetus was not viable and Kirron had to have an abortion.

Ours is not a typical, traditional relationship and much of that stems from the fact that initially, we shared the closest of friendships. In fact, Kirron refers to me as her girlfriend *and* boyfriend and in turn, she knew everything about my love life—because inevitably I would turn to her. Between us, there is no

'Anupamji' or any such expression. But there is absolute respect. I've seen, at close quarters, other film people's lives, and because of their economic dependency, many are always 'yes-people' to their spouses. Kirron is her own person, totally unconventional and I never shy away from acknowledging that she is the far superior one in the relationship. Even though my parents were wondering about my choice when we got married, things worked out well. Kirron has always been very respectful towards my parents. She shares a warm, wonderful relationship with my brother Raju and his family. She is an amazing mother to Sikandar and has been a caring daughter to her parents.

She is never afraid to speak her mind. In fact, she is completely *moophat* (vocal, outspoken) and I am very happy about it even though there have been times when I have been hurt by her forthright comments. But when I have stepped back and thought about it, I have realised the truth in them. She is honest and I trust her completely. Our conversations at home are stimulating and she keeps me completely grounded.

When I look back at our relationship which one can only do after some time has passed, I feel that no love can translate to a romantic situation all through one's life. Over a period of time, at certain stages, I know I have disappointed her. When she had to have her uterus removed, I was not by her side. I did not realise the gravity of the situation for a woman and that hurt her deeply. After I tried to become a business tycoon and in the bargain, lost almost everything and came to the brink of bankruptcy. She was so upset that she said in anger, '*Yeh kya kiya? Tumne toh hame sadak pe la diya hai*' (What have you done? You have brought us to the streets) and I was very hurt. Her paranoia and her capacity to fast forward and imagine problems is what I find very tiring and irritating, while she in turn calls me 'passive aggressive'. For example, she will imagine that I will not switch off the light in the bathroom even as I am reaching for the switch to put it off! Yet, she is my biggest ally—my friend for life.

Here I must recount a hilarious episode which we had at an American airport during the security check post 9/11 when

Homeland Security was at its peak. I had unknowingly packed *dhoop* (incense stick) in my shaving kit and completely forgotten about it. Kirron had completed her security check and was waiting for me when I was stopped because the offending item was discovered and as the security officers demanded, 'What is this? Step aside and don't move.' Kirron, for whom nothing known as diplomacy, subtlety or underplay exists, started yelling loudly from across, '*Kya hai yeh? Charas leke ghoom rahe ho?*' (What is this? You are carrying weed?). Her exaggerated reaction confirmed for the security officers that they had caught a terrorist. My mind went blank and I couldn't remember what dhoop was called in English. Seeing Kirron's overblown reaction, I was telling myself that I was ready to divorce her if she didn't scale down herself to have a normal response. But she was unstoppable and continued to yell across the room, '*Pagal aadmi ho tum*' (You are a mad man), and here I was desperately trying to find the English word for dhoop and all I could manage to splutter was 'Stick, stick'. I was convinced that they were going to lay me down on the ground and put a bullet through me or else I would suffer a heart attack right there and then. Finally, I was able to explain to them that it was a prayer stick and requested them to find an Indian and convinced them to burn it, so that they could see that it was not a dangerous item. Nowadays, I travel everywhere with a small wooden temple which contains all my prayer items!

In sharing our life story and its intimacies, I would not like it to read merely like a cliché tribute to Kirron, my wife, but to the woman who has made a significant contribution to my life.

We share the same values, regarding corruption and righteousness, and she has stood by me through thick and thin. When she was declared the 27th in sincerity amongst 554 parliamentarians—which is a huge honour—I felt very proud of her.

When Kiron and I got married, Sikandar was just four years old. He was a naughty but a warm-hearted child. We share a close bond and though, initially, he used to call me Anupam, now he calls me dad. I pride myself for the father I have been to him. We share a close relationship and even today, whenever I am in Mumbai, before

I retire to bed, I go and spend some time with him in his bedroom, talking about the many things we share in common. Even though, sometimes, I have missed having my own child as an extension of myself, it is never a reflection of my close and affectionate relationship with Sikandar. He is affectionate, outgoing and emotional and is very respectful to my brother, his family and my mother.

I consider Sikandar one of the finest actors of the current generation but unfortunately, he has not got his due yet. I believe that he should have signed all the films that came his way initially because with work comes more work.

Gautam suddenly passed away on 1 February and we all felt his loss. He was a dignified person. Even after they separated, both he and Kirron handled the entire relationship with great poise and no one had to take sides.

My family completes me, and I am secure in the knowledge that I can return to them at the end of the day. Together we are the epitome of the modern family, each pursuing his or her own dreams—connected by our relationship but free to blossom and flourish.

17

A Victim of My Own Success

As I was a successful film actor, my days were like a revolving door through a slew of film studios, outdoor locations both near and far and countless parties in the company of the affluent and the influential. My career graph soared.

Achieving fame, fortune and a fabulous fan following through success in films catapults an individual—from leading a regular, invariably drab, tedious and routine-oriented life—to dazzling heights. Reaching this lofty perch, ideally one must strive to maintain a sense of perspective and balance and try not to be carried away by the glitz, glamour and razzle-dazzle of the celluloid world. Inhabiting that rarefied stratosphere, one should not look down upon the other inhabitants of planet earth.

In reality, such a sea change in circumstances often means one is bound to get disconnected from the ground realities. Unknowingly conceit rises to the fore. In my case, my fame greatly exceeded my emotional capacity to handle it with any modicum of equilibrium. At parties, it became my mission to be photographed with the elite crowds by the paparazzi.

In newspapers and magazines, instead of news articles, editorials and analysis on the state of the nation and the world, it became my mission to only search for my photographs. This was the era; TV was just beginning to make its presence felt in different parts of India and had not yet begun wielding its current phenomenal reach. I expected whoever I met to praise me in glowing terms and applaud my performances in diverse roles.

In a word, I was becoming a victim of my own success! In retrospect, I had the sense of candour and reality to realise that I too succumbed like so many others before me. What sets me apart is the fact that my humour rescues and elevates me and holds down my feet. And because of it, I have always emerged smiling and stronger for the insights.

After the phenomenal success of *Saaransh*, everyone thought that '*ek aur art film ka actor aa gaya hai*' (another art film actor has arrived) to add to the ranks of Naseeruddin Shah and Om Puri. But that was never my dream. I had the clarity of ambition that I wanted to work with commercial directors of the day like Yash Chopra, Manmohan Desai, T. Rama Rao, L. V. Prasad, Subhash Ghai, Prakash Mehra, because the wide-eyed boy from Shimla used to watch their films and dream big. Dilip Kumar, Raj Kapoor, Dev Anand, Manoj Kumar, Rajendra Kumar, Dharmendra, Amitabh Bachchan, Shashi Kapoor were my idols. I was not going to be an art film actor. I did not want to live in poverty. I wanted to own a house which I could call my home; I wanted to own a car. I wanted to be a star. There was never any doubt in my mind about this. I wanted to be written about in the media—small regional newspapers and magazines as well as the top prestigious ones like the *Times of India*, the *Hindustan Times*, *Indian Express*, *The Hindu*, *The Illustrated Weekly*, *India Today*, *Sunday*. I loved to be photographed, enjoyed giving out autographs, thrived on applause and was delighted when mobbed by people. I wouldn't mind travelling anywhere to attend a function, however small or insignificant it be.

I was on a signing spree and I don't even remember how many films I had signed. But I do recall that the first 'significant' film was Laxmi Productions' *Aakhree Raasta*. It was momentous because it had Amitabh Bachchan in a double role, along with Sridevi and Jaya Prada in the main cast. A. Purnachandra Rao was a very big producer from the south and K. Bhagyaraj was a well sought-after director. Another big name attached to it was T. Rama Rao, a well-known stalwart of the industry. Purnachandra Rao came to narrate the story to me and offered me the villain's role, which was ultimately played by Sadashiv Amrapurkar. He showed me the original Tamil film *Oru Kaidhiyan Diary*, on which the Hindi film was to be based. On seeing the film, I thought that the friend's role was more suited for me because of the comic elements. During my theatre days, I always performed comedy and it eventually became my hallmark. I used to enjoy comedy a great deal. But they did not see me as a comic actor and thought that I was more suited for a tragic role. I refused the offer. But they were really eager to cast me in the film since I had created this aura of an 'upcoming in-demand actor'.

After arriving at the studio on the first day of the shooting, I got worked up and irritated over trivial issues and started making unreasonable demands. Such behaviour had become my hallmark or 'signature tune' at that stage in my life.

The air conditioner in the make-up room was not working and I was literally getting hot under the collar. My signature tune began manifesting itself: 'What the hell is happening over here? Why isn't the AC working? Please call the production manager immediately.' When he turned up, with an apologetic expression on his face, I began verbally berating him: 'What the hell man, you told me that people in Madras are much more professional than those in Bombay. Is this a sign of your professionalism? You must understand I am a gold medallist from the National School of Drama, New Delhi, the nation's capital and *the* reputed actor from *Saaransh*. Without a functioning AC, my acting cannot be expected to be of a high standard and, if anything goes amiss, you have only yourself to blame.'

After calming down a bit, I asked: 'With whom is my first scene?'

He replied: 'With Mr Amitabh Bachchan sir.'

'Where is he now?'

'Sir, he came with his make-up at exactly 9 o'clock . . . you have arrived a bit late sir . . .'

I raised my voice again: 'Don't give me a lecture about punctuality. Just tell me, where is he?'

'He is on the set, sir.'

On the main set, where the lighting was being arranged for the shot and camera being installed in its position, I saw a man sitting on a chair in a corner. He looked old, had a grey beard, a moustache, long unruly hair and was casually attired in uncreased trousers, a crumpled shirt, an old jacket with a patch on it and a shawl wrapped around him, reading a book. In flesh and blood, I was in the presence of the one and only, Amitabh Bachchan, supporting a wig for his role. I shuffled across gawkily and said: 'Good . . . good morning sir . . . I am Anupam Kher, originally from Shimla sir . . . of *Saaransh* fame.'

In his renowned baritone, he spoke: 'Oh, yes, Anupam. I have seen your film *Saaransh* . . . You were very good . . . In fact, you were brilliant. Sit down, sit down.' And he pointed to a chair nearby.

'Sir, it is my good fortune that I have got a chance to be working with you . . .'

'Yes, I am also very happy to be working with you.'

In *Aakhree Raasta*, Amitabh Bachchan plays a double role of father David D'Coasta and son Vijay while I play the role of the father's close friend Mahesh, who brings up his son after David is framed and wrongly sentenced to a prison sentence for the murder of his wife Mary. After being released, he takes revenge, in a dramatic fashion, on the three perpetrators of the crime.

I couldn't believe that I was in the presence of an individual, who has been called 'a one-man film industry' and rewritten the history of Hindi cinema. Back in 1969, while watching Khwaja Ahmad Abbas' film *Saat Hindustani*, in which he had introduced Amitabh Bachchan, I was immediately struck by the brooding aura surrounding him. By underplaying his role, he was proving how effective it was to adopt the principle of less is more. With Prakash Mehra's *Zanjeer*, which gave Amitabh the 'angry young man' image, followed by Hrishikesh Mukerjee's two super hits—*Anand* and *Namak Haram*, both with the superstar of the times, Rajesh Khanna, he was able to consolidate and set himself apart. His persona and style of acting were different. The audiences lapped it all up. And the film fraternity was eating out of his hands. I recall Yash Chopra had once remarked that 'Amitabh is the only actor who can afford to choose his roles.'

For me what stood out about Amitabh Bachchan's performances was that he could perform the most ridiculous scenes with complete conviction. Remember that *Coolie* sequence where he is on a train, listening to the radio station to learn how to make an omelette and how to do yoga. Which other actor could have performed the way he did? He would never revert to a clichéd form of performance. He was unconventional and different, just look at his performance against stalwarts such as Dilip Kumar, Rakhee and Smita Patil as his co-stars in Ramesh Sippy's *Shakti*. In my opinion, Amitabh Bachchan brought an element of respect not only for himself as an actor but for the entire community.

In the process, he has dramatically changed the definition of the Indian film hero. His performances as 'the angry young man' fighting for justice have kept us spellbound. His characters reflected the mood of the nation, captured the essence of the restless youth, who were victims of unemployment and exploitation by a section of political and business class and industrial fraternity. When he was seriously injured during the shooting of Manmohan Desai's film *Coolie* in Bangalore (now Bengaluru) in late July 1982, people all over India and elsewhere—including me—prayed fervently for his quick recovery. He bounced back after several months of treatment and completed the film, which was released in late 1983. I was now sitting in front of the very same legend. And I was going to work with him. I thought: *Kucch bhi ho sakta hai.*

He was reading his book and the silence between us seemed very disconcerting. To break the silence, I said: 'Sir . . . the AC is not working. And with this beard, moustache, wig, shirt, coat and shawl wrapped around . . . aren't you feeling hot sir?'

He looked up from his book and said: *Anupam, garmi ke baare mein sochta hoon to lagti hai. Nahin sochta to nahi lagti'* (Anupam, if I *think* about the heat, I feel hot. If I *don't think* about it, I don't feel it).

Having delivered this weighty maxim most casually, he went back to reading his book. I was speechless. I was ashamed and completely bowled over. Since then I have emulated him and never complained about the weather or the surroundings in the studios.

My heart yearned to spend a little more time with him and get to know him better. I asked him, a bit hesitantly: 'Sir, will you please have dinner with me this evening?'

Once more, he looked up from his book: 'Anything special?'

'Sir, I will tell you during the course of dinner.'

'Oh! Got it . . . got it! The announcement of the National Awards is scheduled for later today . . . correct?'

'Yes sir. You are absolutely right!'

For my role in *Saaransh*, I had won the prestigious *Filmfare* best actor award plus a large number of other awards from all over the country. Later, in 2011, I would humorously declare in my autobiographical blockbuster play, *Kucch Bhi Ho Sakta Hai*:

Best actor at the Haridwar awards.
Best actor at the Malad (east) awards.
Best actor at the Malad (west) awards.
Best actor at the ladies' friends' club awards.
Best actor at the gymnasium awards.

Only one best actor award remained to be won by me and that was the National Award, which I believed was THE ONE that would compel everyone including my detractors to acknowledge: 'Anupam Kher, you are the "top notch" actor of them all.'

At the end of the long day's shooting. I went back to my suite at Taj Coromandel hotel in Chennai. The AC was working. I was in a great self-congratulatory mood. After a shower, I dressed up to the nines, poured myself a peg of the most expensive brand of scotch and said to myself: 'Make it large, Anupam, for you are a star now and this is going to be your day . . . your special extraordinary moment.' With the glass in my hand, I settled down to hear the news I had been waiting for.

I switched on the TV. On the Doordarshan channel, around 8.30 p.m., the well-known newsreader Salma Sultana intoned: 'And now for the National Awards. This year the best actor award goes to . . .'

I raised my glass with great expectations and said: 'Thank you, darling . . .'

'. . . to Naseeruddin Shah[20] for his role in the film *Paar*,' came the announcement. It left me stunned as if a bomb had exploded. I was shocked . . . nay, stunned. My glass stayed suspended in midair. It took me almost ten minutes to lower it. The high points and low points of my life flashed before my eyes. I was reminded of the school drama in which my classmate Nandu had lifted me and thrown me unceremoniously into the audience. I recalled vividly that night when my father was telling my mother in Kashmiri: 'Bittu is very weak, give him milk and almonds . . . they will make his body and mind strong.'

I called room service and said in a low dejected voice: 'Please cancel my earlier dinner order and just send a glass of milk and some almonds for me instead.'

That night, Amitabh Bachchan did not visit me, and my great lesson of that moment was: Never take success for granted.

Amitabh Bachchan is a man of few words. Even in his media interviews, you must have noticed, he speaks effectively but never loquaciously. There is an air of mystery about him. Being the son of the famous poet and writer Harivansh Rai Bachchan, Amitabh comes from an illustrious lineage.

Over the years, I have had some instances of close interaction with him. I recall once Pritish Nandy, who was then the editor of *The Illustrated Weekly of India* of the Times of India group, had published a cover story on him and titled it: FINISHED. It was immature and premature of Pritish to publish such a sensational story. All actors face rough patches, but they are rarely finished. But that was typical Pritish who had once called me a 'chameleon'.

Amitabh was very disturbed by that article and came to my house at midnight. Surprisingly my guard downstairs did not recognise him. Can you ever believe that? Then there was another instance of a story on the front page of *Indian Express* which claimed that Amitabh Bachchan had not paid the loan taken from the Bank of Baroda. It was very derogatory and when I asked him: 'How do you actually feel?'

He answered magnanimously: '*Zyada se zyada kya kar lengein. Toh maine apne aap se bhula diya hai . . .*' (What can they do maximum. I have dropped it from my mind). His reply showed me his inner strength on how to face adversity. Priceless lessons learnt along the way.

I recall that one afternoon as I was coming out after finishing my dubbing for a film at Ketnav, Vijay Anand's dubbing theatre on Pali Hill, I bumped into film actor Jeetendra, who was a favourite of the South Indian producers and directors who used to make films in Hindi too. He said: 'You are brilliant.'

'Thank you', I replied, thinking that he was referring to *Saaransh*.

He said: 'Yesterday, I saw the rushes of the scene between you and Amitabh from *Aakhree Raasta*. In fact, Poornachandra and Rama Rao showed it to me in the editing room with the comments: "This actor is fantastic. See what he has done". You need guts to be like that in front of Amitabh.'

'It is nothing to do with guts sir, it is all something to do with acting,' I replied.

'No, it's all about guts,' he insisted.

I don't know what he meant. Perhaps, that was his way of praising me.

After *Aakhree Raasta*, I did a number of films with Amitabh Bachchan including Tinnu Anand's *Mai Azad Hoon*, which was based on Frank Capra's film *Meet John Doe*, David Dhawan's *Bade Miya Chote Miya*, Satyanarayana's *Suryavansham*, etc.

Amitabh Bachchan has been encouraging, generous and kind towards me. He has always been there for me and for Kirron. He launched my previous book *The Best Thing about You Is YOU!* He has always been gracious whenever I have requested him for an appearance. He came to the inauguration of my acting school Actor Prepares, despite the fact that it was housed in a modest location. He came to see my play, *Kucch Bhi ho Sakta Hai*, on the inaugural night of 8 August 2005 and said: '*Aapka ye play ajooba hain*' (Your play is a marvel).

In spite of his dignified personality, something compels me to behave outrageously in his presence to see if I can glimpse a chink in his armour. For example, a couple of times, I have used a cuss word or a strong four-letter abuse in true Punjabi style in front of him. After his initial shock, he bursts into laughter. To me that represents the ultimate limit of 'breaking the barrier' since he commands a certain respect and such behaviour seems uncalled for. There is much to learn from him. I recall the most important thing that he once said to me. During the course of a conversation, I said: 'Since I did not go to an English-medium public school sir, I can't think in English . . . I think in Hindi. And if I have to speak in English, I translate my thoughts. But my thinking is all in Hindi.'

His reply was: 'But you do not realise that what you sometimes feel has been your minus point turns out to be an asset for you and the most important one. Imagine if your thinking was in English. In that case, you would not have been so effective in Hindi movies. It's because you think in Hindi that you are such a good actor. Half the job of an actor is being good with language.'

His answer was spot on because I frequently come across actors who think in English but venture into Hindi cinema. As I watch them work, I notice that it is rather difficult for them to fit into the right mode of acting.

Coming back to the National Award. Losing it soon became a distant memory. The razzmatazz of the film world seduced me once again into believing that I was invincible and unstoppable. There is an inexplicable force that grips almost everyone in showbiz. One can call it intense passion or obsession, craziness or even intoxication. For those in the film industry, life can, and does, change dramatically from one Friday—the day on which movies in India are normally released and the box-office collections shortly thereafter decide its fate—to the next. It is an eternal hope that always propels artistes forward. The big break, always, is just around the corner. It could be the next meeting, the next audition, the next role . . .

Whatever the reality, even though the National Award had slipped out of my grasp, with Ashok Panjabi managing my affairs, I believed in my own triumph. But I could not rest on my laurels. *Jeevan chalne ka naam*[21] (life had to move on).

Time was moving fast. So was my career. I was, as they say, ubiquitous—here, there and everywhere. During that period, the multi-talented Javed Akhtar—the famous shayar or poet, screenplay and dialogue writer—rolled into one came up with a memorable quote: 'You cannot make Hindi films without two things—film raw stock and Anupam Kher.'

My role and the character of Dr Dang in *Karma* were conceived by the genius of Subhash Ghai. He scaled the character magnificently with helicopters, jeeps, guns and coterie and topped it off with a massive bounty on my head. Only someone of his calibre could have created such a role.

Here, I must mention about the shooting of the helicopter scenes which were funny in more ways than one. It was the first time I was flying in one, but I did not want to let Subhash know how nervous I was. I also did not realise that the chopper took off vertically so instead of smiling as the shot required me to do, my face registered only my shock and surprise. The scene was to depict me staring down with pride and joy at my vast kingdom instead the expression on my face was just the opposite until a couple of takes later when I was able to summon up the villainous smile.

Subhas Ghai had the knack of presenting his characters lavishly but economically. After *Karma*, he cast me in the blockbusters, *Ram Lakhan* and *Saudagar*. I had moved into the 'A' list of the industry now. I was beholden to Subhash Ghai for it. But then came the dampener.

Sometime in March 1992, Kirron and I had gone to New York for the Natraj Awards event of my dear friend Kamal Dandona. Amitabh Bachchan and his family too were there and he had got six tickets, including two for us, for the premiere of the Paul Verhoeven's film *Basic Instinct* with Michael Douglas, Sharon Stone, George Dzundza and Jeanne Tripplehorn. For me, it was an honour to be going with

Amitabh Bachchan for the premier, and that too in his limousine, which was said to have a jacuzzi in it. It was decided that we would all meet at 3 o'clock in the lobby of the hotel.

That afternoon, as I was heading to my room, I saw Subhash Ghai sitting in the lobby with some 5-6 models of a fashion show that was also on in New York. I owe a lot to Subhash Ghai for having given me my stardom through those three amazingly popular films—*Karma*, *Ram Lakhan* and *Saudagar* with *Khalnayak* currently on the floor. I am very fond of him. He is indeed a wonderful person and I loved his larger-than-life showmanship. He used to invite us home and we used to meet often. That afternoon, he called me over and said: 'Anupam, come and sit down with us. We will have lunch together.'

I readily agreed thinking there was enough time to finish lunch and still get ready to join Amitabh Bachchan. Knowing about the unpleasant relations between the two owing to the shelved film project *Deva*, I did not mention anything about our plans with Amitabh. The lunch which I thought would get over in an hour or so, continued to drag on. Finally, at about 2.30 or so, I said that I had to go. But he would have none of it and said: 'Sit down and relax. Where do you have to go?'

At this stage, I had to tell him: 'Mr Bachchan has got tickets for the premiere of *Basic Instinct* and we have to go with him.'

Suddenly, he looked at me and said: 'So, you choose between me and Mr Bachchan.'

I was shell-shocked: 'What do you mean, choose between you and him? You're my friend and he is Mr Bachchan.'

Adopting a threatening tone, he said: '*Teri marzi . . . Dekh le phir, tu meri picture mein hai*' (Your wish . . . just remember you are in my film). You have to choose now—between me and Mr Bachchan.

I feel that he was being possessive and unreasonable, and I told him so. But he continued to become agitated and said: 'No, no you have to decide now . . . You don't know me, I'm a director, and you are an actor. Remember, I can do anything.'

This was the last straw. Whenever I am pushed into a corner like this, I think of the words enunciated by my grandfather, Pandit Amar Nath, which manifest in my mind: 'If you want to be equal with anybody in this world, just don't expect anything from the person.' In any case, I was feeling humiliated in front of those girls. Being backed into a corner, using strong Punjabi cuss words, I said quite angrily: 'If you want to be disloyal with my character in your film, it has nothing to do with me. You are destroying your own film. You're being dishonest and it doesn't matter to me. I am leaving.'

Not surprisingly, my role was chopped drastically from *Khalnayak*. Thereafter, we did not work together for many years, though I did work in a film that he produced in 2006 titled *Apna Sapna Money Money*, which was directed by Sangeeth Sivan. We did patch up a few years later and things are back to normal now.

In the film fraternity, nothing is permanent, be it friendships or enmities.

How I was chosen for the role of Dr Dang in the film is an interesting story. Those days, I used to attend all parties simply because I liked to be known. I still love to be photographed. Unlike most other film stars, I have never proclaimed that 'I don't like to be photographed' or 'don't take my pictures'. I always loved the attention and still love to be recognised. I had gone to the Sea Rock Hotel in Bandra for a party and as I was coming out at 11 o'clock, Subhash Ghai, who had several hit films to his credit by that stage, including *Karz* (1980), *Vidhaata* (1982), *Hero* (1983) and *Meri Jung* (1985), was going in. He saw me and said: 'What are you doing tomorrow?'

'Whatever you say,' I replied.

'Come to my office at 2 o'clock tomorrow afternoon', he replied.

I never hesitated to ask for work and never used to feel that since now I have arrived and won a Filmfare or other awards, I should shy away from telling people that I would want to work with them. The next afternoon, at the fixed time Subhash Ghai met me in his office. He briefed me about *Karma* and how he had already assembled and signed a huge cast. 'I need a villain for the film and you are that villain', he said with confidence and authority.

'Am I the villain of your film?' I shot back thrilled.

'Yes, you are,' he replied. 'Last evening, the way you walked towards me, I need that walk in my villain.'

'But I was walking normally,' I exclaimed.

'Yes,' he said. 'I want a normal man with a normal walk. Because it is I who will transform him into a villain . . . the way I have conceptualised him with great clarity.'

The 'mahurat' for the film was a lavish, grand affair, in typical Subhash Ghai style, hosted at Mehboob Studio, in Bandra. I was standing shoulder to shoulder next to the legendary Dilip Kumar, and we were supposed to raise our hands and loudly proclaim 'Karma' in sync with the background music. It was a special day for me . . . a joyous moment not only as an actor but also as a star. That day, my old friend, Satish Kaushik, came to meet me and as he gave me an emotional hug, he said: 'This moment is a miracle—you have made it.'

Karma became a huge success. A scene with Dilip saab, where he, Rana Vishwas Pratap Singh, the jailor, slaps Dr Dang and the dialogue that follows came to be much talked about. It was a very powerful scene of a young actor opposite a legend:

Dr Dang: *Rana Vishwa Pratap Singh, Dr Dang creates war. Dr Dang ko aaj pehli baar kisi ne thappad mara hain. First time. Iss thappad ki goonj suni tumne? Ab iss goonj ki goonj tumhe sunayi degi. Sunayi degi. Jabtak zinda rahoge, tabtak sunayi degi. Rana, mujhe tumhara ye thappad bhoolega nahi.*

(Rana Vishwa Pratap Singh, Dr Dang creates war. Dr Dang has been slapped by someone for the first time. First time. Did you hear the echo of this slap? Now, the echo of this echo will be heard by you. You will hear it till you are alive. Rana, I will never forget this slap of yours.)

Rana Vishwa Pratap Singh: *Bhoolna chahiye bhi nahi. Mujhe khushi hain ki tumhe Hindustani thappad ka andaza hogaya. Khayaal rahe, ye sirf ek haath tha. Baaki, tum khud kaafi samajhdaar aadmi ho.*

(You should not forget it. I am glad you have realised the value of an Indian slap. Keep in mind that this was just a hand. For the rest, you are an intelligent man yourself.)

Everyone in the cast gave a superb performance. The music too was good as was the photography, the choreography, the editing, and the backdrop settings. All in all, it was a well-conceived and executed film.

18

STRUTTING LIKE A PEACOCK

One of the major highlights of my life was working with the legend Dilip Kumar. Dilip Kumar has inspired generations of actors even before my time and will continue to be a beacon for future performers. Not surprisingly, he has many imitators, though none can match the original. I vividly recall having met him for the first time at a party organised by the *Screen* magazine. I had gatecrashed the party with the help of my film journalist friend Ali Peter John. As a newbie, I was totally star-stuck watching all the celebrities as they were being pointed out to me—Rajesh Khanna, Shabana Azmi, Amitabh Bachchan, Shashi Kapoor . . .

Soon I saw Dilip Kumar walk in. I quickly went up to him and greeted him; he thought I was an old acquaintance. He held my hand and asked: 'Where are you these days? I am seeing you after such a long time.'

I responded casually: 'I get around sir.'

Instead of trying to clear his misunderstanding and tell him that this was our first meeting, I relished the attention he bestowed on me.

Speaking about Ali Peter John, I must admit that I always had good relations with the media and most of them are still friends. We've had great times together. There was Bharathi Pradhan, Pammi Bakshi, Bhawana Somaaya, Jyothi Venkatesh, to name a few. Ali Peter John, who was always very generous in his praise for me and my work, is a good friend even today. Then there were the photographers Rakesh Shrestha and Gautam Rajadhyaksha. Those days the relationships between the press and the stars were completely personal.

Devyani Chaubal, a film 'gossip' journalist was 'among the first Indian film journalists to have a poison pen and insinuate' a great deal in her widely read column 'Frankly Speaking' published in the magazine *Star & Style*. Commonly known as the 'Queen of Mean', she was a star in her own right and everyone, who was anyone in the film world, wanted to be on her right side. After the release of *Saaransh*, she wrote a very appreciative review, in particular praising my performance as 'brilliant' and 'mesmerising'. As a gesture of 'thanks', I sent her flowers.

On 3 January 1985, I happened to meet her for the first time at the 10th International Film Festival of India (IFFI) in New Delhi, where *Saaransh* was also being screened and said, 'Thank you for your praise. I do hope you got the flowers I sent you.' She said nothing.

A couple of months later, in March 1985, when Mukul Anand's *Aitbaar* with Dimple Kapadia, Raj Babbar and Suresh Oberoi in the lead and me in a guest appearance was released, she wrote a very nasty piece because the flowers had not reached her, due to some mess up at the florist. I don't have that clipping on me today as it got destroyed in the Mumbai floods in 2015, but it went something like this: 'This wannabe actor Anupam Kher, whom I had praised in one of my previous columns sometime back, met me at the film festival in New Delhi and lied to me, that he had sent me flowers . . . and what a downfall. I saw his *Aitbaar* where his cheeks are shaking, his voice slurring etc. etc.' Obviously, she had written it with a lot of venom. I was horrified by this personal attack on me. I would always read her columns as good entertainment. But I could not swallow her attack on me, particularly when I had sent her flowers. I recall, it was 10 April 2015, when I decided to call her at the office. The minute she picked up the phone, I blurted out in an injured voice: 'I did send you the flower.'

'I don't want to talk to you,' she replied.

'Wait a minute,' I said, before she could bang down the phone on me. 'I just want to tell you, that till you are alive, I will send you flowers every month . . . on the 10th day,' I declared, before she hung up on me.

True to my word, after that day, I would send her a bouquet of flowers on the 10th day of every month. I did it for ten years, till she passed away on 13 July 1995, succumbing to an attack of paralysis. During her last days, she wrote in one of her columns: 'The only thing that I wait for now in my life is a bouquet of flowers on the 10th of the month from Anupam Kher.'

Ali Peter John informed me of Devi's death and the sad fact that she died alone. I rushed to help with the last rites, and the first thing that I saw in her room, next to her bed, was the bouquet I had sent her three days earlier.

At the time, I was due to begin working for *Karma* and I was also shooting for Rahul Rawail's *Arjun* which had Sunny Deol and Dimple Kapadia in the lead. This was the first film where I played a character close to my own age. It was no wonder that I was easily identified by the masses. In fact, people on the streets be it urchins, beggars, students or housewives, everyone recognised me easily and they all knew me as Chogle saab. This was an entirely novel and thrilling experience for me.

My first day shooting for *Karma* was at 7 o'clock in the morning, while the previous evening I was shooting for *Arjun*. I was very excited about *Karma* as I had been given the priceless opportunity to work with both Dilip Kumar and Nutan.

I requested Rahul to release me a little early in consideration since I was to give my first shot with Dilip saab the first thing next morning. It was a big mistake on my part for one doesn't ask Rahul for a favour of this kind as he was bound to do just the opposite. I like him as a director but as a person, in my experience, Rahul can sometimes be quite petty about such matters—all a question of ego, I suppose. Finally, he relieved me only at 5 o'clock in the morning for a 7 o'clock shift in a far-off location. He worked with me at night and for one scene, which was being shot at Palm Grove Hotel in Juhu, he made me give 27 retakes of a shot. Just when I was leaving, he quipped in a sarcastic tone, 'Now you are fresh for your shooting with Dilip Kumar.' It was his brand of humour. That morning, after having worked the whole night, I drove all the way to Esel Studio beyond Chembur, on Trombay Road in Sion, over an hour away. And barely made it in time for my shoot.

Though I had met Dilip Kumar during the mahurat of *Karma*, I did not know him at all, nor was I able to say anything. There were hordes around and everyone was in a celebration mood. Dilip saab, gave the shot and left. Hence, I was really looking forward to meeting him. During the drive to Esel Studio, flashbacks started, and I remembered scenes from Bimal Roy's big hits like *Devdas* and *Madhumati*, B. R. Chopra's *Naya Daur*, Nitin Bose's *Ganga Jumna* and so many other films. When A. Bhimsingh's *Gopi* was released, I was still in the tenth standard. In the ensuing stampede at the ticket window, I was kicked so hard by someone that I suffered a nosebleed. These and other thoughts were still swimming in my head when the car drove into Esel studio and I felt I had been woken up from my dream world.

Subhash Ghai had erected a giant set for the shooting that morning. He explained to me my scene and said: 'The biggest scene of this film . . . the most important dialogue of the film is the first shot and it is not Dilip saab's but yours.' I said to myself: *What is this? Why is he making me go through this? And that too my shot is with Dilip saab. He should have put a simple shot for this morning.* But who was I to question him? He was the master on the sets and perhaps, that was his way of creating confidence in me. I, as Dr Dang, got ready by 7.45 but there was no sign of Dilip Kumar anywhere around. *Perhaps he is in his make-up room getting ready for the shot,* I thought. He came around 10.30.

As he got out of his car and walked towards his make-up room, attired in his white trouser and white kurta, I could feel goosebumps on my arms. The great man . . . the Tragedy King, the actor credited with bringing realism to film acting . . . whom generations had followed and many had copied in their careers was before me in flesh and blood. I could feel his amazing aura. Everything about him was regal.

He said to Subhash Ghai: 'Lale, nashta karne ka dil hai' (I feel like having breakfast). Somebody introduced me to him and he shook my hand. It was a very firm handshake. He said to me: 'I've heard a lot about you. You're a good actor.' Somehow, he did not expect me to touch his feet and I thought that he might not like it if I did so. He seemed the kind of person who would shake hands and this made me respect him even more. In fact, to this day, as an actor, I have never touched anybody's feet, though it is a very prevalent tradition in the film industry.

The trend of touching feet in the film industry is quite amusing. As newcomers, they bend down fully to touch feet as if with great reverence to seek blessings to become successful. Once successful, they bow and bend down only as far as to touch the knees of a person. And once very successful, they just make a gesture of bending as a mere formality. It is an artful show in an industry where appearances count for a lot. From the very beginning, I have had the strength and fortitude to keep away from such formalities. Even in my acting school, I have forbidden students from touching my feet.

After breakfast, Dilip Kumar came out and asked Subhash Ghai: 'What's the scene?' He reviewed it and remarked to Subhash Ghai: 'Good, I don't have to say anything, only he has to speak. So, whenever you're ready, I'm ready.' Kamalarkar Rao, the cameraman, had set up a huge trolley along with a substitute one. The set was being prepared with the huge reflectors, lights, etc. By this time, it was 1.30 in the afternoon. The King said to Subhash Ghai: 'Lale, what is there for lunch?'

Lunch was served. The King was deciding what to eat. It was the first day of his shoot, wherein he was to play a jailer. Nutan too was there. During lunch, I was keenly observing Dilip saab, his nose, his eyebrows and other small things, like his hand gestures, how he moves, etc. Apparently, Subhash Ghai was observing me and later, took me to one side and said: 'You'll ruin my film man.

You are supposed to be the villain. Don't look at Dilip saab so admiringly.'

'Dr Dang is not looking at the jailer. Anupam Kher is looking at Dilip saab. I will know the difference once I am in front of the camera for my shot,' I replied.

After lunch, Dilip saab asked me: 'You remember the lines?'

'Yes, I do,' I replied and started narrating them thinking this is my one big opportunity to impress him and show how well prepared I was.

He said: 'No. No. Save your energy.' I realised that I was coming as being over enthusiastic. 'Are you from the theatre?' he enquired.

It was a big lesson for me that day—an actor needs to save his energy because the surroundings are not important. What he does before the camera, when he hears 'action', is all that matters.

It was now time for his afternoon siesta and he went off to sleep. Around 4 o'clock, he woke up, tried his costumes, called Subhash Ghai and said: 'Lale, I don't feel like shooting today.'

'Of course. If you don't feel like it, we'll not shoot,' Subhash Ghai replied and ordered 'pack up' for the day. Imagine, I was there since 7.30 in the morning with my full make-up and costumes, all ready for the shot. But my day had been made. I had spent time with the legend. I was happy—as happy as I could be.

So much has been written about Dilip Kumar that it is hard to add anything new, but I can say that I think that he is the only complete actor Hindi cinema has produced. With due respect to all the other actors, most of whom have tried to copy him over the years, he was also the first original actor. Watching his films over five decades, I realised that he is a grounded performer who has managed to remain commercially viable. He always retained his dignity not something many actors can claim, and he is in the same class as the top international actors. Even though not conventionally handsome, Dilip Kumar has a great persona. He can perform a romantic scene with unforgettable grace. Every opportunity I got to work with him, I used as one to imbibe something new from the Master.

One can engage in conversation about any subject with Dilip Kumar. He is exceptionally well versed in theatre, art, poetry and politics. Unfortunately, this is not the case with most actors who are mostly self-obsessed or snobbish, making communication impossible.

Once when we were shooting in Manali for *Saudagar*, I was very hungry. The morning schedule continued well after 2 o'clock with no lunch break was announced. Dilip saab, perhaps sensing my hunger pangs, started to describe to me how, back home in Peshawar, his family used to sell fruits. He then picked up an invisible apple and made an expressive gesture with his right hand and then said: 'The apple used to be so red that when you held it in your hand, you could feel its firmness, and when you put your teeth into it, the juice . . .'

The way he described, I actually felt that he was having a juicy apple. I was distracted enough by his 'succulent description'.

Let me recount another interesting interaction with the great thespian, which I consider a revelation. During the shooting of the movie *Saudagar* in late 1990, Dilip Kumar and I were stuck in a cave in Mahabaleshwar (a hill station in western Maharashtra) for around two hours due to very heavy rain. Imagine having Dilip saab all to myself for two hours!

After chatting about random topics, I said: 'Sir, may I ask you a question?'

He answered: 'For the past two hours, all you have been doing is asking me questions . . . go ahead, ask one more.'

From his manner, I thought that he was a bit upset with me. So, I said: 'Sorry, I won't ask.'

But he answered me in a soothing tone: 'Come on now . . . don't feel bad . . . ask me!'

I tentatively queried: 'Sir, in so many years, why have you done such few films?' (In a career spanning nearly six decades, Dilip Kumar has acted in just around sixty movies, *excluding* those that were announced but later shelved.)

He mulled over my question for a while with his eyes closed. After a long pause, he replied: 'As an actor and a performer, I am evolving and developing. I don't feel that I have fully grown or emerged, so I see room for growth.'

I was amazed and humbled by his perception and how he viewed himself.

We once talked about human possessiveness. I asked him: 'Why are human beings so possessive? How would you describe possessiveness?'

'Possessiveness is physical,' he replied. 'It has nothing to do with the mind. It's all about what you feel and what you touch, and it's not necessarily between a man and a woman. A child gets possessive when someone else touches his mother or his father. That's because it's physical. It all starts from there.'

'As an actor, have you ever felt insecure . . . because of the film not doing well … or because you were not sure about your role?' I asked.

'I am always insecure. It is insecurity that makes you do well. However, it's not necessary that everybody goes through these issues. Negative qualities are not negative until you start thinking about them as negative qualities.'

'Any actor who impressed you a lot . . . and influenced you?'

'Yes, the American actor Paul Muni. I would go to watch his movies like *The Last Angry Man*, *Angel on My Shoulder* and *A Song to Remember* at the Metro Theatre. At one stage, he was one of the most prestigious actors. He was a brilliant, realistic actor who I learnt would always do 'intense preparation for each role of his, often immersing himself in the study of the real character's traits and mannerisms'. 'Anupam, you did a 70-year-old man's role at 28, but do you know that Muni played the role of an 80-year-old at the age of just 12? I always wanted to be like Paul Muni. He did indeed impress me a lot. But I can't say he influenced my acting. No, he didn't,' he said.

Dilip Kumar used to always call me Anup—a shorter form of Anupam. 'Anup, *bada shaitan hain tu*' (Anup, you are very mischievous), he would say in a good way. What he meant was that I was very inquisitive, always eager to find out about him. I always had thousands of questions about food, cricket, Indian politics, American politics, world politics and he would answer them with great insight. Once I asked him: 'How did you do that famous step in *Naya Daur* while singing, *Nain lad jayi reh?*'

'*Lale, mere se dance wance nahi hota tha*' (I could not dance), he replied. 'I used to just enjoy the rhythm and do whatever I could.'

One day he asked me: 'Anup, can you tell me what method acting is? *Log mujhe bolte hain ki mai method actor hoon* (People say that I am a method actor). But I have no idea what it is.'

'I know you're trying to pull my leg. There is a method in acting and there is no method in acting. That's all. You have become the actor now,' I replied.

'No, no,' he laughed and said, 'No. I am always *aware* of the fact that I am Dilip Kumar.'

I recall his reply to my question as to how come he did comedy so easily: 'Because I look at life from a comic point of view.'

After watching my performance, Dilip Kumar told Subhash Ghai: 'My dear friend, a "dangerous" actor has arrived.'

And then he told me: 'You will go far.' I took his words as a blessing.

I thought that with none other than the legendary Dilip Kumar endorsing me, nothing in this world could now stop me from surging ahead. After *Karma*, I worked in three more films with Dilip saab—*Kanoon Apna Apna* (1989), *Izzatdaar* (1990) and *Saudagar* (1991). It was both a pleasure and a privilege to be associated with him. You will be surprised to know that I was even able to let my guard down and relax around the legend.

I also have great memories of working in Subhash Ghai's other multi-starrer, *Saudagar*, in 1991 and which was advertised as the 'Clash of the Titans' as it had Dilip Kumar with the so-called temperamental Raaj Kumar. They had acted 32 years earlier in S. S. Vasan's *Paigham* in 1959.

I was intrigued to make acquaintance with Raaj Kumar. There was a good deal of mystery surrounding him with any number of stories about his temperament, mood swings, whims and fancies and eccentricities.

It is not in my nature to judge people. That's not in my DNA. Working in cinema has taught me that everyone has two sides, the public image seen by all and the other which is kept very private. Only when one has a preview of both aspects does the total picture emerge.

Once we started shooting for *Saudagar*, I, realised that though he was a natural in his role of Rajeshwar Singh, the aristocrat landlord, it was his everyday personality I was drawn to. Like the others, I too noticed his quirks and eccentricities. Apparently, one of his conditions with Subhash Ghai was that during the making of the film, two large vehicles would follow him to the shooting locations carrying his complete wardrobe of costumes created for him for the entire film along with the other accessories like his footwear, walking sticks, wigs, bags containing his smoking pipes and all the paraphernalia that went with it including three briefcases containing the various spectacles he would use. Everything was under the charge of his own attendant. He would always travel alone in his car, without even his personal Jeeves, who would follow him in a separate one. Naturally, it amazed all of us in the unit and initially, whispers flew all around. Subhash Ghai dismissed it all 'stoically' and had 'given standing instructions to his assistants to see that the vehicles were ready each day and the clothes and accessories were transported exactly the way Raaj Kumar had wished.

I used to be quite disappointed that I had never heard him use the legendary word *jaani* on me. But I didn't have to wait for long. Once during a shoot in Manali for *Saudagar*, I said: '*Bhook lagi hain sir, bahut zyada. Aapko lagi hai?*' (Sir, I am feeling very hungry. Are you as well?)

His reply was: '*Jaani, hamesha to sirf jaanwaro ko bhook lagi hoti hain*' (Jaani, only animals are always hungry). That made my day. Finally, he had addressed me as 'jaani'—something I had been waiting for since long. I was amused. I could have felt hurt by what he said, but no . . . I was thrilled and went around telling everyone I met for the next couple of days or so about it. That makes all the difference. Nobody could ever say the word 'jaani' as Raaj Kumar said. Once we started working together, he liked me. He would normally say: 'Kashmiri pandit, I like you.' Born Kulbhushan Pandit, he, like me, too hailed from Kashmir. Larger than life, he had an inimitable style of walking and talking. He was an educated person and very well read but an introvert. He once said: 'I believe in things I do and I do things I believe in.'

Here, I must mention that I loved Nutan too, my all-time favourite actress, whose performances I had grown up on, whether it be Bimal Roy's *Bandini* and *Sujata*, Hrishikesh Mukherjee's *Anari*, Vijay Anand's *Tere Ghar Ke Saamne*, to name a few—each film better than the other. She was amazing, graceful and had immense substance, grace and dignity and I was fortunate to have the chance to work with her.

19

THE BEST OF TIMES,
THE WORST OF TIMES

In what seemed like a flash, a decade passed by in which I did over 200 or 250 films. I soon lost count. Leading a fast-paced life, three shifts a day, seven days a week, travelling and flying regularly far and near, was bound to have some effect on the body.

It did!

In early 1994, I underwent a traumatic experience which threatened to jeopardise my precious career. I became a victim of facial paralysis—Bell's palsy.

Maybe it was the pressure of the movie business or the stress induced by my professional life, or just because I was caught up in the mindless cycle of three shifts a day—a schedule that was very hectic (to put it mildly). One night, when I was dining at the house of my close friend, actor Anil Kapoor, his wife, Sunita, suddenly asked: 'Anupam, what is the matter with your left eye? Why is it not blinking?' I did not know the answer myself and casually attributed it to fatigue as a result of overworking.

But the next morning, when I was brushing my teeth, I noticed water dribbling down from my lower lip uncontrollably and I was unable to close my mouth fully. I was a bit worried now and sought the counsel of one of my dearest friends and guide, producer-director Yash Chopra. I told him: 'Yashji, since last night, my face is shifting a little too much to the left.'

He looked at me and thought that I was putting on an act. He told me: 'Don't joke, you idiot!' I assured him that I was dead serious.

He soon realised that I was not kidding and asked me to consult his friend, Dr B. S. Singhal, at the Bombay Hospital Institute of Medical Sciences. I wasted no time.

Dr Singhal, a highly respected professional, examined me and then advised: 'Mr Kher, drop everything for two months and start taking these life-saving steroids or cortisone.'

I still did not seem to grasp the seriousness of the illness. I proceeded to ask him: 'Should I confirm the morning or afternoon shooting shift with Rajshri Productions?'

I could see a flicker of irritation cross Dr Singhal's face as he cautioned me: 'Mr Kher, shift the focus from your films to your face. You have facial paralysis.'

Still, I persisted: 'Sir, I don't think you understand. Whatever I am today, it's because of Rajshri Productions . . . they gave me my big break in *Saaransh*. If I do not follow my shooting schedules, the producer, Mr Rajkumar Barjatya, will face a huge loss.'

Dr Singhal was not impressed. He again warned me: 'Mr Kher, I am not concerned with any producer. I am concerned with only my patient and that's you. Go home immediately. For two months, *don't do anything*. Just rest and take this medication.'

I responded: 'Okay, sir.'

When I was about to step out of the room, I realised I had forgotten to ask him a crucial question. I went back to him and queried: 'Dr Singhal, how will I know that I have become alright?'

He answered: 'Mr Kher, try to whistle.'

I felt I had not heard him correctly. Hence, I said: 'Sorry, but I did not hear you properly.'

'Try and whistle,' he repeated.

I said: 'No problem.' Following his instructions, I noticed that there was only air passing through my lips but there was no whistling sound. I was getting a little anxious now.

Dr Singhal then pointed out: 'The day you can whistle properly Mr Kher, you will be fine.'

In the hospital corridor, curious onlookers were smiling at my contorted face and thinking that I was working on some new comic character. But when I returned to my car and asked my man Friday,

Dattu, to get me a glass of water, I noted that he had put a straw in it so that I could sip the liquid without having to open my mouth fully.

It was then that I realised the true import of my condition. I had two options: First, go home and hide my face for two months, as advised; second, expose myself to the world with a twisted face. I chose the latter because sometimes in life, God puts you into situations like this so that you can discover your courage. The choice you make can distinguish between the ordinary and the extraordinary. I decided to reject the advice of Dr Singhal, however medically sound it may have been. While I wouldn't recommend anyone to act against a doctor's advice, I did the next best thing and opted for physiotherapy.

Despite my face being distorted, I reached Filmistan Studio in the Bombay suburb of Goregaon for the shooting of Sooraj Barjatya's *Hum Aapke Hain Koun..!* In this movie (which turned out to be a blockbuster after it hit the screen in early August 1994), I played the father of heroine Madhuri Dixit.

I requested all the unit members, including the director, the producers and the actors, to gather around me. I then informed them about my facial condition. And I noted that Madhuri Dixit was, for the first time, not laughing after hearing what I had to say. Normally, she would burst into her famous laughter whenever I opened my mouth. Everyone sympathised with me and went out of their way to devise ways to hide my facial paralysis on screen.

Sooraj wanted to cancel the shoot. I was not in favour of it and told him that I am okay with shooting if you are inclined towards it artistically. The shooting carried on and during that twenty-days schedule, I had a placard around my neck which said: 'Don't look at my face, look at my heart and hug me'. Those hugs healed me mentally.

As a villain, I have 'tortured' many actors in *reel* life. For instance: hanging people upside down and whipping them, threatening to throw people from the top of a mountain into a sea or pulling out their nails. Now, in *real* life, I was being subjected to torture. Every day, my physiotherapist would introduce electric pulses onto my face and, after every surge, I attempted to whistle.

The agonising process dragged on for a seemingly interminable period. In fact, it went on for months. Then one day, I *could* whistle. And I did whistle long and hard . . . over and over again . . . and again . . . and again. The relief I felt cannot be described in words. And since then, every morning when I wake up, the first thing I do is . . . whistle! Yes, whistle loudly as if to declare to the world that all is well. That's how I whistled my way out of a catastrophic and career threatening challenge.

Like me, don't forget to whistle every morning—it is the small things that give us the biggest reassurances in life.

Across the road from 403, Marina on Juhu Tara Road—the place where I lived—is a school for children with special needs—Dilkush Special School. Established in 1971 for students with disabilities by the Handmaids of the Sacred Heart of Jesus 'as part of their work in the field of formal and non-formal education and other developmental work'. Initially it started with 15 students and today, it has more than a hundred students. Before I could whistle again, every morning while waiting for the car in the patio of my block, I would notice a hundred odd children of different age groups laughing, playing and enjoying life. And as soon as the car came, I would get inside and drive off to my 'filmy' life with the children left somewhere behind in the recesses of my mind.

After I had recovered from my traumatic facial paralysis and things had returned to normal, I was still experiencing a vacuum in my life. Hence, one morning, I crossed the road and walked into Dilkush School, to meet Sister Maria Dolores, the principal. The middle-aged Spanish nun was soft-spoken, of medium height and gracefully dressed in her crisp, neatly ironed, grey coloured clothes. She was a reflection of my storytelling grandmother, Kalawati Kher.

'Sister Dolores', I said on meeting her, 'I would like to teach in this school.'

She saw the certificates which I had carried with me and said: 'Mr Kher, you are from the National School of Drama . . . and you want to teach in our school. That's very kind of you indeed. We would be very privileged. But there is one problem Mr Kher, we will not be able to pay you . . .'

'No sister, that's not the reason why I am here . . . I don't want any payment . . . I just want to teach . . . at least one hour every week . . .' I replied.

'That's fine then . . . We would be honoured. Would you like to meet the children in the class today?'

I said: 'Yes sister that will be great.'

She took me to the classroom to meet the children, who as soon as they saw me, started yelling and shouting in great excitement. They came to me . . . some hugged me . . . some held on to my legs . . . some wanted to shake hands. One of them said: 'Uncle, I have seen you on the TV', another said, 'I have seen you in films'. While one said, 'Uncle, please do not do bad man's role', yet another shouted excitedly, in a slow slurring voice, 'You do very good comedy.'

In the midst of the cacophony of excited voices, Sister Dolores stood in complete shock. Finally, she took me aside and asked: 'Mr Kher, are you by any chance some kind of an actor?'

'Yes sister,' I said with a trace of pride.

'And you have come here to learn how a mentally retarded person behaves . . . how he or she reacts? How he or she lives or learn about their day to day life? You have come here to prepare yourself for a mentally retarded person's role that you are doing in some film?'

'No . . . No . . . sister,' I replied but she cut me short.

'Mr Kher, before you, some other actors also came here. They spent time with us . . . and we all, particularly the children, got involved with them . . . then suddenly they went away, and we saw each of them doing a mentally retarded person's role on the screen in some film or the other. We don't want to be exploited . . . you can't imagine what that does to the young minds . . . emotionally . . . psychologically. Mr Kher, I am sorry, I am going to ask you to leave now.'

'No sister, believe me, I am sincere. . . I want to genuinely teach here,' I replied.

'I am sorry to speak to you like this. But you must realise our position . . . the condition of these children . . . These children are challenged and we don't want them to get hurt.'

I implored: 'Sister, please trust me. I am here to interact with them. Please let me.'

Perhaps she felt my sincerity . . . that I was not there to prepare for some film role and said: 'Alright Mr Kher, you can teach here. You said you will come here for one year?'

'Yes sister, every Wednesday for two hours. But there's one request.'

'What Mr Kher?'

'Please don't tell anyone that I am teaching here.'

'Why, Mr Kher?'

'Because people will think I am doing it for publicity.'

'Then don't instruct. Because out of 100 people, if 4 people believe you, then perhaps, those 4 people are very important.'

After that, for one year, whichever corner of the world I would be in, I worked out my travel schedules accordingly and made it a point to reach the school every Wednesday for two hours to teach those children speech therapy.

The innocence . . . the purity . . . the smile of those young children helped restore my mental balance and peace.

And here, before I proceed further, I would like to bow and with folded hands say: 'Thank you, Sister Dolores. I will always be beholden to you.'

There always have been legions of artistes out there who have attempted to use every trick in the book to claw their way to the summit of success. And when they get there, they completely lose their footing. They forget where they came from and what their struggle was. Success is sweet and distractions are many and the ego mushrooms very easily. It requires very little effort to fool yourself— that the world is at your feet and you are owed everything. I too lost my way. I too proved to be a mere human.

Wish I had kept in mind the apt sher by the noted Urdu poet, Wasim Barelvi:

Mili hawaaon mein udne ki woh sazaa yaaron
Ki main zameen ke rishton se kat gaya yaaron.

I paid the price for flying high my friends
I was cut off from links with the ground my friends.

But I didn't and the result was that one fateful day, I ended up in the dock at the Chief Metropolitan Magistrate's Court, Bombay, besides a bunch of petty criminals!

How did I land up in such a predicament? Let me elaborate.

In the last decade of the twentieth century, the entertainment business had begun to expand rapidly; in fact, too swiftly. This was the enchanting era when satellite television held most of India in thrall. From just two TV government-controlled channels—whose menu was mostly insipid and unappetising—suddenly, there was a proliferation of programmes that offered a variety of choices in diverse fields—entertainment (cinema and serials), news, sports, wildlife, yoga, religious programmes . . . and much more. Almost all over the country, people were glued to their TV sets, watching serials and programmes that had gripped the nation's imagination and became trendy topics of discussion.

I had begun to observe that whenever something major happens in India, Amitabh Bachchan is to be found in the epicentre of the event.

Funnily, I also noticed in my mind's eye that there were many similarities between me and him. Apart from the fact that our names start with the letter 'A', both of us were rejected by All India Radio. And, of course, to state the obvious: both of us were (and are) tall, dashing and handsome! Yes, don't laugh!

In 1995, Big B, as he is popularly known, set up Amitabh Bachchan Corporation Ltd, (ABCL), as the new media giant of India. ABCL churned out several movies and serials and also focused on event management; it even conducted an international beauty pageant. The same year, I produced a television serial *Imtihaan* directed by

Imtiaz Ali (along with a talented team), which was very successful. I believed that I too should follow in the footsteps of Big B and set up my own unit, to be named Anupam Kher Studio Ltd (AKSL).

Success had gone to my head. I started projecting as if my English had improved over the years as had my finances. I now decided that I should develop a state-of-the-art studio. But I felt, before that, I ought to throw a grand launch party and make a spectacular announcement. I chose Bombay's five-star hotel Leela Penta as the venue. It was a star-studded affair. My idol, my God, the great Dilip Kumar was the chief guest of the evening. He was captivated by the ambience of the evening and said to me: 'Lale, is there anything you cannot do?' Hand-picked guests from the film, corporate and political world were in attendance.

Can you believe it, at that stage, not even a single brick had been laid for the foundation and I had already declared myself as a 'TV tycoon'? I did not have the patience for the studio to take shape but was already celebrating its success.

I was apprehensive that if I dreamt small, I would remain stuck in a rut. Hence, I dreamt big. I felt that I should have two business addresses: one in Bollywood and the other in Hollywood! Instead of prose, I started imagining my future, in poetry:

A little bit of Julia in my life
A little bit of Spielberg on my side
A little bit of MGM is all I need
A little bit of Hollywood is all I see
A little bit of trophy in my hand
A little bit of Warner admires me
A little bit of De Niro, I might have been
A little bit of Oscar, oh you're mine!

Here, Julia refers to the famous actress Julia Roberts (of *Pretty Woman* fame) and Spielberg to Steven Spielberg, the internationally renowned film-maker. MGM (Metro-Goldwyn-Mayer) and Warner Bros are studios known the world over. De Niro is none other than the Robert De Niro, an all-time great, with whom I developed a close relationship but more on that later.

I had literally gone berserk in life.

I believed that my success would be unparallel, so my fantasy soared beyond all limits. I decided to go the whole hog into the burgeoning TV arena. I dreamt of my AKSL to be much bigger than ABCL. If Amitabh Bachchan offered one lakh rupees to his executive, I offered five.

Consequently, I was omnipresent in the media. I loved press conferences and needed no excuse to hold one and would shoot my mouth off and come up with what I thought were witticisms. For instance:

Question: Sir, why are you launching so many television channels?
Answer: That's an embarrassing question . . . but the more the merrier!

Q: Sir, how are you different from the others and what gives you the confidence to take the plunge into TV?
A: I am different from other people . . . I may be bald, but I am brainy . . . I may not be very tall, but the short point is that I know the medium of television (as an outsider) as well as the film industry (as an insider) inside out. Please understand that my National School of Drama education gives me a unique insight into the television world . . .

A few years after my various ventures had been launched, my chartered accountant, P. R. Rane, brought to my notice that my debt had assumed large proportions.

I asked him: 'How much? What are the figures in dollars? No . . . don't tell me in rupees.'

One million dollars?

How much in rupees?

'Four-and-a-half crore rupees,' he replied. (That was an enormous amount of money for those days.)

However, like a global tycoon, I observed: 'Oh, that's just about a million US dollars, right?'

'Right,' replied Rane.

My next question was: 'What is the position of the house and office?'

He answered in a sombre tone: 'Both are mortgaged.'

His answer shook me and finally, I was beginning to experience a reality check.

By this time (mid-1999), ABCL was also in the doldrums and struggling to stay afloat. My condition was similar—again one of the many similarities between him and me. I met Amitabh Bachchan and told him: 'Sir, even I am finished financially.'

He then wanted to know how much I was in the red. And I gave him the figure.

He remarked: 'You are a king compared to me!'

But this king was in dire straits for he was facing embarrassing and harrowing situations. Earlier, a crowd of eager aspirants used to gather outside my office looking for work. Now, they were replaced by a crowd of creditors—all fretful and angry.

A few days later, Rane shocked me by confessing to me: 'Sir, I have lied so much for you that I have confirmed my seat in hell for the next five births of mine.'

My situation was no better. I too had been telling so many untruths to my countless debtors that I could no longer keep my story straight. Finally, when lenders used to phone up or turn in person, my staff used to place me in different locations:

- He has gone to meet the chief minister.
- He has gone to meet the deputy chief minister.
- The Enforcement Directorate has called him to its office.
- When he was going to Mahabaleshwar, his car was involved in an accident and he is in a coma. When he recovers, he will certainly return your money.

If the lenders became more tenacious and aggressive, Rane would send me to meet the prime minister or the deputy prime minister. At that stage of my life, I was desperately clutching at straws, spending sleepless nights trying to figure out how I would free myself from the debt trap.

Can you believe it, it was Big B who once again, as in the past, provided a glimmer of hope.

With the advent of the new millennium, Amitabh Bachchan took on a brand-new avatar. On 3 July 2000, he began anchoring a TV show named *Kaun Banega Crorepati* (*KBC*) based on the British programme *Who Wants to be a Millionaire? KBC* turned out to be a mega success! Once again, the uncrowned king of showbiz raised the bar and conquered the entire nation. He locked it. From north to south and from east to west, millions of viewers waited with bated breath for each episode. As I had always believed, my thought was that whenever fortune smiled on Big B, luck would favour me as well. I tried to convince myself: 'Something good will definitely happen now for me too. Yes, it will happen cent per cent.'

And it did.

Three months later, on another TV channel, in October 2000, I too got the opportunity to host a game show titled *Sawaal Dus Crore Ka*. The prize money was ten times larger than the one crore offered by *KBC*. I felt I had gained a new lease of life and began gearing up for the show! I even took Amitabh Bachchan's blessings. I said: 'Sir, I too am going to fly high.'

The outcome of my efforts did not lead to any monetary benefits. To put it bluntly, it was a mega-flop show and was unceremoniously yanked off the air. I became the butt of many jokes.

The more serious issue I had to face related to one of my cheques bouncing due to 'insufficient funds' in my bank account. I could not evade the proverbial long arm of the law although I was a celebrity who was used to the company of my fraternity colleagues such as Shah Rukh Khan, Madhuri Dixit, Sridevi, Anil Kapoor, Dimple Kapadia, Boney Kapoor, Kajol and so many others. But in a noisy, chaotic and dingy Bandra sessions court (on the day when my case came up for hearing), my companions were a brood of self-confessed rapists, murderers, chain snatchers, pickpockets, thieves and their likes!

They asked my lawyer: 'What has your client done?'

'His cheque of seventy thousand rupees bounced,' he replied.

'Oh, that's too small an amount for him to be here,' was what they stated. Obviously, I was a small fry for them, and the case was not deemed very significant.

That was the second time in my life that I learnt the important lesson—*never* take success for granted. This time around, I heeded the moral and took cognizant of the situation.

The case finally fizzled out.

Apart from being pursued by creditors in 1993-94, I also became the target of malicious and salacious gossip. I have met with and interacted with people from all walks of life including innumerable heroines from the film industry during the course of my career. A film magazine with a large circulation published a story of my behaving inappropriately with a heroine's sister. As I have mentioned before, I have always enjoyed an extremely cordial relationship with the media, so I was really taken aback by the venomous personal attack which was completely based on falsehood. As rumours began to circulate thick and fast and my colleagues started to question me, I contacted Naresh Goyal, though this was before he founded Jet Airways. He put me in touch with Attorney Ghulam Vahanwati who filed an injunction on my behalf. But matters continued to get out of hand. I mustered and rallied the Actors Association to take out a *morcha* (a rally) to boycott the publication and its sister associations. It was a very lonely and troubling time for me. I soon learnt that everybody had their own agenda. I was literally backed into a corner. I ended up slapping a journalist—Troy Ribeiro—when he was visiting the sets of Yash Chopra's film, *Parampara*. Looking back, I should not have taken that extreme step, even though the slap was more of a symbolic gesture on my part because I was very frustrated and defenceless.

Today, Troy and I have a good working relationship. Ironically, we are also in discussions of doing a play together.

Before this incident, in Shimla, whenever anybody asked my father: 'Pushkar Nathji, what is Bittu doing nowadays in Mumbai?', my father would open his briefcase and show, with a flourish, all my press cuttings saved in his scrapbook. After this 'unsavoury' incident, he telephoned me from Shimla and asked: 'What is there for me to show now?' It was a typical small-town simple mentality reaction—'What is reported in the press, must be the truth.' I felt a tug in my heart for I never wanted to let down my father. But how could I possibly explain to him convincingly that the published material was untrue? But, I thought those who *really* knew me would have realised that this was 'fake news'! There was no social media in those days and no way to defend myself—I was being truly tested.

In Yash Chopra's 1975 iconic blockbuster, *Deewar*, there is the famous unparalleled temple scene where the protagonist, Amitabh Bachchan, renders his unforgettable soliloquy. But just before he goes to the temple, he says to his lady love in the film, Parveen Babi:

Maa hamesha kehti thi ki, jab koi raasta na ho, toh ek hi raasta hai. Aaj us rah par chal ke bhi dekhte hain.

Mother used to always say that when there is no road left, then there is only one road. Today let me try and walk on that path too.

That's true. In life, most of us remember God when all other doors are closed to us. I recalled that during my lean period, when I was struggling a great deal, I used to regularly visit a small temple by the road, adjacent to the famous Mahalaxmi temple, and pray: 'God, please give me some work in this city . . .' But ever since I had become successful, I hadn't even thanked God nor visited the temple and worshipped, even once. Which I interpreted to mean that my present troubled times were all due to God's ire.

That Sunday early morning, I gave the day off to my chauffeur and drove to the small temple to beg for forgiveness and pray in earnest like the old times.

At the temple, I took off my shoes, washed my hands and rang the temple ceiling bell—once slow but hard and then ten times continuously so as to add up to that auspicious number of eleven. I then stood in front of the idol of Lord Hanuman and said in an apologetic low voice: 'God . . . please Hanumanji, I am sorry . . . very sorry. Please forgive me for not visiting you earlier . . . Please take away all these clouds of despair and shower, once again, the flowers of happiness and prosperity.'

Generally, in Hindi films, when you pester God too much, He either gets fed up and smiles or drops a blessing in your hands in the form of a flower. But my God was in an indifferent mood. As I bent down to pay my obeisance, my token from God was out of this world. A thief stole and drove away with my brand new Maruti Suzuki 1000, purchased just a couple of weeks earlier. I shouted in desperation: 'Stop! Stop! . . . That thief has stolen my car . . . Somebody stop him.'

Seeing me run, the pedestrians around who recognised me, perhaps supposed that a shoot was on with a hidden camera. Little could anyone understand my predicament.

I rushed out, jumped into a taxi—Bombay's famous black and yellow Fiat cab—and told the 65-year-old driver to drive fast and follow my car. He certainly had a wicked sense of humour for he replied: 'Sir, your car is too fast.' I was reminded of the old saying: '*Uparwala jab bhi deta hai, chapar phaad ke deta hai*' (When God gives, He gives in abundance); but today I also learnt that: *Jab woh leta hai, to sab kuch phaad ke leta hai* (And when He takes, He takes in abundance too).

Eventually, God graced me with a blessing after a few weeks or so, He took pity on me for old time's sake. A door of opportunity opened.

Sometime in 2001, film producer, Vashu Bhagnani, gave me a film to direct. I named it after the God's hymn—*Om Jai Jagadish*.[22] I assembled a big star cast: Anil Kapoor, Abhishek Bachchan and Fardeen Khan with Mahima Chaudhry, Urmila Matondkar and the veteran Waheeda Rehman. I worked very hard on it and pinned great hopes on it. But the film was declared a dud at the box-office. Once again, I felt I had circled back to the very beginning. To quote the writer Salman Rushdie: 'Speaking from "a world behind the looking glass, where nonsense is the only available sense", I used to wonder whether I "will ever be able to climb back through the mirror again." As things stood then, and in the foreseeable future, it seemed unlikely . . .'

A few days later, my old friend, Vijay Sehgal, came to meet me. He said: 'Bittu, I saw your film *Om Jai Jagadish* . . . The whole family saw it, and everyone liked it too. It was a good family entertainer, but don't worry, sometimes even good films don't work. *Chal roti khate hain!*'

That evening, after many days, I ate wholeheartedly! Later that night, I slept peacefully after a long time.

And when I woke up next morning, Vijay handed me a piece of paper, before leaving. It was his old habit that whenever he read something good and meaningful, he would write and give it to me. It was an extract from a poem:

Lehron se dar kar nauka paar nahi hoti
Himmat karne waalon ki haar nahi hoti
Nanhi cheenti jab daana lekar chalti hai
Chadhti deewaron par sau baar fisalti hai
Mann ka vishwas ragon mein saahas banta hai
Chadh kar girna, gir kar chadhna na akharta hai
Akhir uski mehnat bekar nahi hoti
Koshish karne waalon ki haar nahi hoti.

Asafalta ek chunauti hai sweekar karo
Kya kami reh gayi dekho aur sudhaar karo
Jab tak na safal ho neend chain ki tyago tum
Sangharshon ka maidaan chhodh mat bhago tum
Kuch kiye bina he jai jai kaar nahi hoti
Himmat karne waalon ki haar nahi ho.

The boat that qualms the waves, never gets across
The one who tries never fails
The tiny ant, when it carries a grain
It climbs up the wall, slips and falls a hundred times
The determination of the mind fills your body with courage
Then falling down and getting up does not hurt
Ultimately, one's efforts never go waste
The one who tries never fails.

Failure is a challenge, accept it
Recognise your shortcomings and rectify them

Till you are successful, shun rest and sleep
Never run away from the battlefield of hard work
You cannot get praise without working for it
The one who tries never fails.

In the film industry, there is a rather thin line between the illusion and the reality. We are all caught up in the illusion that we alone are responsible for whatever we have achieved in life. We develop a false sense of grandeur believing that we are the true architects of our destiny. Nothing could be farther than the truth.

From the people I have met and the circumstances that have shaped me, I have learnt that failure is the one thing you should not fear in life. Better to experience it, face it, live it and thereby conquer, it by overcoming it.

Indeed, it is essential to fail before you succeed. The sentiment itself may seem paradoxical but it is not. Perhaps, the concept can be better grasped by recalling the memorable words of the disgraced US president, Richard Nixon, in his farewell speech on 8 August 1974 (when he was forced to step down halfway through his second term after the Watergate scandal): 'Only if you have been in the deepest valley, can you ever know how magnificent it is to be on the highest mountain.'

It is not just that success is sweeter when it comes after failure. It is about the whole process of failing which teaches you about many aspects of life: about humility, about inuring, about tenacity, about equanimity and much more. Currently, learning from failure has become a popular and lucrative trend worldwide, thanks to a range of luminaries in diverse spheres deciding to 'tell all'. Failure is an important juncture on the road to success. From the legendary Scottish king, Robert Bruce (1274 to 1329), to the more recent celebrities such as J. K. Rowling (of Harry Potter fame) and Michael Jordan (the famous US basketball player), their experiences and the vicissitudes of their life are the stuff of history. As far as I was concerned, I had realised the significance of attaining success through failure decades before it had become trendy.

Destiny plays with the lives of everyone on this earth. In my life too, I have been a victim of drastic reversals of fortune. I firmly believe and have also experienced, that everything can change in the blink of an eye. I wrote my autobiographical play, *Kucch Bhi Ho Sakta Hai,* to underscore this reality. *Kucch Bhi Ho Sakta Hai* premiered on 8 August 2005 and has since become more than a just a play; it has become a philosophy to which I am deeply dedicated. How did I decide to do this play? Sometime in 2004, a publisher had approached me for my autobiography. 'I am not a writer . . . I can't write,' I told them. 'Just record it and give it to us.' After days of recording, I realised that my life is a story that needed to be told. But I am an actor and thought that I should challenge myself and enact my life rather than penning it. I requested the comic Marathi writer, Ashok Patole, and approached Feroz Abbas Khan, one of the finest theatre director, to direct it. It was he who brought great pathos, dignity and humour to my life story. The play based on my failures and shortcomings liberated me from fear and made me feel the tallest man in the world.

This play is a tell-all life story which revealed the nuances of my life. I held back nothing. It describes the journey of a man who should have been a failure but who manipulated his destiny and forced it to become a success. At the zenith of my career and crossroads of my life, in this play, I paused to reflect and share my pain, joy, tears and laughter. My struggle seems like a shaky Hindi film finding some coherence by the sheer determination of the protagonist, played by me. The play is staged as a full production with me narrating and dramatising the important events in my life and tells the story of a small-town man making it big in the film industry. The audience could identify with me and find snatches of their lives being played on stage.

It has been a cathartic experience to perform more than 500 shows of my life story on the stage in front of a live audience, night after night, in different parts of the world. I came up with the concept of live audience interaction and in place of a traditional entrance on stage, I wander in through the audience rows, interacting at random with them, raising laughs, making connections and setting a tone for the evening. It was the beginning of a different theatre experience.

The play almost didn't see the light of day. The reaction to the rehearsals was not very encouraging and my director, Feroz Abbas Khan, was questioning if we should go ahead with the special preview the next day. We had invited all the top celebrities of Bollywood and resolutely believing that success comes from sacrifice, I remained steadfast. The next day as I waited alone in the green room, I was told Amitabh Bachchan sir has arrived, Dilip Kumar has come and the list continued. It was very lonely waiting in the green room when you are a cast of one. But history was made that day.

I even did a talk show on TV with the same title. The first season ran from July 2014 to September 2014 and the second season from August 2015 to November 2015. The show featured a host of celebrities such as Shah Rukh Khan, Anil Kapoor, Madhuri Dixit, Waheeda Rehman, Asha Parekh, Mahesh Bhatt and his daughter Alia Bhatt, Naseeruddin Shah, Om Puri, Akshay Kumar, Priyanka Chopra, Gulzar, Paresh Rawal, Boman Irani and Irrfan Khan.

When I was in the second year of the National School of Drama in Delhi, I recall an experience with my movement teacher, Rita Ganguly Kothari, who did not like me. In fact, she used to call me a lizard since I was not at all graceful and was not a good dancer. She worked hard on me and I thank her for her relentless criticism because it did improve my movements. For the final examinations, we were supposed to be in 'formation movement', but I was at the back of the class. I wanted to catch the attention of the five teachers in the front, so I slowly moved out of formation in such a way that they could notice me and get a chance to evaluate me. Rita Ganguly was mad with me for stepping out of line after two months of practise, but I was elated that I had made an effort to be noticed. It was yet another life lesson and that too a big one—always be noticed; never pass up an opportunity to turn the spotlight on you. This is my own personal handbook and one that I have always lived by. It has opened doors for me, afforded me myriad opportunities and rewarded me with friendships for life.

However, Rita Ganguly was strict with me. Years later, I realised that her movement classes made a great contribution to the actor in me.

20

COMMUNITY AMIDST COMPETITION

Salman Khan (named at birth Abdul Rashid Salim Salman Khan) and I have done a few notable films together, including Sooraj Barjatya's super-hit romantic-comedy musical, *Hum Aapke Hain Koun..!* (Who I am to You?) starring Madhuri Dixit and a galaxy of other stars. There was a phase during his early career years when Salman was quite an indisciplined actor, particularly during the making of Shirish Kunder's *Jaan-E-Mann*, in which I was playing the dwarf with Akshay Kumar and Preity Zinta in the lead. True, he was mired in his personal issues then, but he was very difficult to work with and totally unprofessional.

However, when I worked with him again in 2015 in Sooraj Barjatya's *Prem Ratan Dhan Payo*, I was pleased to see a completely transformed man in Salman. If Salman is so very successful today, it is by sheer design and inner motivation, because he's become much more responsible, completely motivated and more focused. He has also evolved into a better actor. His attitude and work ethic have also undergone a transformation. This change can be noticed in many of his recent films like Abhinav Kashyap's *Dabangg*, Anees Bazmee's *Ready*, Siddique's *Bodyguard*, Kabir Khan's *Ek Tha Tiger* and *Bajrangi Bhaijaan* and Ali Abbas Zafar's *Sultan* and *Tiger Zinda Hai*. He has always been very warm and respectful towards me.

Speaking about Salman, I must share an interesting story which Sooraj Barjatya told me during my interview conducted on Republic TV in 2017, on the show *Anupam Kher's People*. According to him, when he was planning his film, *Maine Pyar Kiya*, in 1988, he decided to cast Salman Khan opposite Bhagyashree. Though he felt that Salman was not that good an actor nor a great dancer, he was taken in by the fact that he was a very sincere person. In fact, Salman would frequently send other young upcoming actors to him with the words: 'I am sending a newcomer to you. Try him out for the same role, for he may be better than me.' Sooraj used to feel very odd about it as to how come a newcomer is suggesting other newcomers. And that too in a cut-throat, ruthless industry where everyone is trying to compete behind each other's back!

Then he decided to tell Salman that he was not in the film. As a courtesy, he wanted to personally inform Salman about his decision and went over to the location—Satish Bhalla's bungalow on Pali Hill—where the actor was shooting with Rekha and Farooq Shaikh for J. K. Bihari's *Biwi Ho To Aisi*—the only film that he had on hand at that stage. After hearing him out, Salman said: 'That's rather unfortunate because I was really looking forward to working with you. But why don't you try . . .' and suggested another newcomer without any malice.

Continued Sooraj: 'Once out of the meeting, I thought to myself, what an unusual and a unique person. He is, perhaps, the only person I know who can deal with this sort of a reversal the way he did—suggesting someone in his place. He is a genuine person and I was finally convinced that I had to make the film with him and him alone. That's how we cast him in *Maine Pyar Kiya*.' The rest is history.

In an industry where cut-throat competition is the norm, such behaviour is a rarity. Your honesty, your goodness, your sincerity always works in your favour. There exists a living proof. Another lesson I have learnt unknowingly in my interactions.

Over the years, I have enjoyed working with Shah Rukh Khan in various films. We have shared some great, fun times together. He is a very generous actor, brimming with enthusiasm and is very respectful. I played a very significant role in getting him into the

Yash Chopra films. It was sometime in December 1993, when Aamir Khan had quit Yash Chopra's film *Darr: A Violent Love Story*, at the last minute. Yash asked me if I could recommend someone to replace Aamir. At that time, I was doing a film with Ramesh Sippy, *Zamaana Deewana*, which had Shah Rukh and Raveena Tandon with Jeetendra and Shatrughan Sinha in the cast. Then, one day, when I was returning with Yash Chopra from a funeral, I told him: 'Yashji, you must talk to Shah Rukh.'

'But, will he do it at the last minute?' he enquired.

'The other role is an important one for an actor to play and I am sure he will do a good job for you,' I told him.

Yash Chopra signed him and did not regret it. Nor did Shah Rukh Khan. And there was no looking back for either of them. I have done quite a few films with him and I must admit that every film with him has been a delightful experience. He is the greatest example of a person who, without a single godfather in the film industry, has made it to the top. In fact, I give parallel examples of him and other actors like Akshay Kumar, who have reached the top through sheer hard work and immense determination. I love him greatly and feel very warmly towards him.

The best thing about Shah Rukh Khan is that he does not take himself too seriously. We all know that he is a very big star and yet, he always finds the time and is genuinely interested in the other people. When he engages with another person, he makes them feel important and actually listens. I really appreciate this quality about him. And of course, he is undoubtedly a dedicated actor with the most charming appeal because of which he is known as 'King Khan'. I feel that he was very good in Ashutosh Gowariker's *Swades* which had Gayatri Joshi and Kishori Ballal in leading roles, in Shimit Amin's *Chak De! India*, in Aditya Chopra's *Dilwale Dulhania Le Jayenge* (*DDLJ*) which had Kajol as his heroine, and of course, in Yash Chopra's *Veer-Zaara* which had Preity Zinta as his 'eponymous star-crossed' lover and Rani Mukerji as the Pakistani lawyer, with special appearances by Amitabh Bachchan and Hema Malini.

I recall that Shah Rukh was rather sceptical about the box-office result of *DDLJ* project. When Aditya (Aadi as he is commonly known), narrated the story of *DDLJ* to me I knew, it was going to be a blockbuster, simply because it was an unusual film where the hero Raj Malhotra, instead of eloping with the heroine Simran, says, first to Simran's mother Lajjo, played by Farida Jalal.

I was amazed by the thinking of a 24-year-old boy who was going to change the mindset of the coming generations and their attitude towards the new India. I am including a few important dialogues from the film for the readers to understand importance of the scenes without the visuals:

> . . . *Maaji, main bahut chota sa tha jab meri maa guzar gayi. Aaj main jaisa bhi hu, unhi ki wajah se hu. Woh hamesha mujhe ek baat kaha karti thi jo main aaj tak nahi bhoola. Woh kehti thi, 'Beta, zindagi ke har mor pe tumhe do raaste milengein. Ek sahi, ek galat. Galat raasta bahut aasaan hoga, tumhe apni taraf kheenchega. Aur sahi raasta bahut mushkil hoga, usmein bahut se museebatein, bahut si pareshaaniya hongi. Agar tum galat raaste par chaloge, toh ho sakta hain shuruwaat mein tumhe bahut kameyaabi mile, bahut khushiyaan mile, magar antt mein tumhari haar hogi. Aur agar sahi raaste par chaloge, to bhale hi shuruwaat mein tumhe kadam kadam par thokarein mile, museebaton ka saamna karna pare, pareshaaniya ho, magar antt mein humesha jeet hogi.' Ab aap hi bataeye maaji, mera raasta sahi hain ya galat?*
>
> *Tumhara raasta bilkul sahi hain bete, par tum mere pati ko nahi jaante.*
>
> *Aur maaji, aapke pati, mujhko nahi jaante. Agar mujhe Simran ko bhaga ke hi lejaana tha, toh ye main pehle bhi kar sakta tha. Lekin main Simran ko cheenna nahi, paana chahta hu. Main usse aankh chura kar nahi, aankh mila kar lejaana chahta hu. Main aaya hu, toh apni dulhaniya toh lekar hi jaaongo. Par jaaonga tabhi, jab bauji khud iska haath mere haath mein dengein.*

(Maaji, I was very young when I lost my mother. Whatever I am today is because of her. I have not forgotten what she used to always tell me. She would say: 'On every turn in your life, you will come across two paths—one correct, the other incorrect. The incorrect path will be a very easy one and it will pull you towards itself. The correct one will be very difficult; it will be full of misfortunes, full of problems. If you walk on the incorrect path, then perhaps, in the initial stages, you will find a great deal of success, a great deal of happiness, but the end result will be a failure. And if you walk on the correct path, then even if in the beginning you may get kicked around at every step, face difficulties, face problems, but at the end, you will be victorious.' Now tell me maaji, is my path correct or incorrect?

Your path is absolutely correct my son, but you don't know my husband.

And maaji, your husband doesn't know me. If I had to elope with Simran, then I could have done so earlier also. But I don't want to snatch Simran, I want to have her, possess her. I don't want to take her away from under someone's eyes but in front of them. Since I have come, I will take my bride with me, but I will go, only when Bauji himself will give her hand into mine.)

Absolutely brilliant. I loved the story. I loved the script. I loved the screenplay. It had so much heart and soul in it. And I told Aadi!

Even my scenes, some of which were improvised on the sets, depicting the father-son relationship where the father celebrates the failure of his son became a reference point for father-son relationship. The premiere of the film was attended by the who's who of the film industry. I recall, when the film got over, there was a stunned silence. I was next to Yash Chopra near the exit. He looked at me with fear in his eyes as if asking, '*Has the first film of my son gone wrong*?' And then the audience burst into a standing ovation. It's the magic of this cult film that it is still running at Maratha Mandir in Mumbai. A trivia about the film: for months, a title for the film could not be decided on. Then came Kirron's suggestion: 'Call it *Dilwale Dulhania Le Jayenge*.'

At the 43rd National Film Awards, it won the 'National Film Award for Best Popular Film Providing Wholesome Entertainment'. And, at the 41st Filmfare Awards, can you believe it that it bagged 10 awards for Best Film, Best Director, Best Actor, Best Actress, Best Supporting Actress, Best Lyricist, Best Screenplay, Best Dialogue and Best Playback Singer. I bagged the Award for Best Performance in a Comic Role, which was an eighth Filmfare award for me.

Aamir Khan is another actor in whose initial career, I played a key role, particularly when we worked in Indra Kumar's *Dil* which had Madhuri Dixit in the female lead and then Mahesh Bhatt's *Dil Hai Ke Manta Nahin* with Pooja Bhatt as the heroine. There was also Yash Chopra's *Parampara* which had a massive star-cast led by Sunil Dutt, Vinod Khanna, Saif Ali Khan, Raveena Tandon, Neelam Kothari, and so many others.

Success does a lot of things to a lot of people. And Aamir Khan was no exception. I think that in the initial stages of his career, Aamir Khan was more real. Gradually, after having attained a significant foothold, he started cultivating a social persona. There is no harm in that. In fact, it is fantastic. But in his case, it diminished the spontaneity of his personality. Undoubtedly, a very fine actor and a very hard-working one, but his personal interpretation took more precedence above all else. We had a major problem during *Dil Hai Ke Manta Nahi* as he was very unhappy with my interpretation of Pooja Bhatt's father's character. He made it clear to Mahesh Bhatt that this was not the way the father's role should be enacted. When Mahesh Bhatt told me about it, I was upset and wondered why he was stepping on my creative toes. In turn, I turned to Bhatt saab and asked: 'Do you have faith in me or not? My brief is that anybody who, at the end of the film, tells his daughter that "I am the biggest idiot on earth", who tells his daughter to run away from the wedding, has to be slightly eccentric . . . he has to be little different.'

He agreed. I told Mahesh Bhatt: 'Please tell Aamir that I may not be the "hero" of the film but I am far more educated and learned in the field of acting. I know what I am doing.'

Mahesh Bhatt being Mahesh Bhatt went to Aamir and repeated exactly the same words.

When the film released on 12 July 1991, my character became extremely popular. The audience and critics went overboard with their praise.

When you start together in a profession, the relationships are on the same keel. However, if over the next ten or twenty years, one becomes a bigger star, it doesn't follow that the other person is lesser than you.

In our film world, when people become successful and earn a name, they collect 'yes-men' around themselves of whom there is no dearth of in the industry. I think the same has happened to Aamir. He likes to give the impression of being an independent, aloof person, who lives in his own world, and depicts how magnanimous he is. But in reality, he is no different. He too like most successful stars, has surrounded himself with people who say 'wow' to everything and anything he says or does. He is guided, and misguided, by them. We started our careers together, have seen successful days together, but I am different. I don't like to behave like him. I don't work like him. I don't live like him. He wants to follow the Indian cinema's classification of actors—the hero, the character actor, the villain, the comedian, etc. For him, I am a character-actor. He is a hero. I have my own place in the industry, my own standing. He has his. I have not worked with him for over 20 years now. I applaud him as an actor who has raised the bar high by sheer hard work and his choice of films.

I own my views and vocalise them, and I am earnest in my belief that my interpretation matters and bears substance on my life and those in my stratosphere. By the same token, I don't see the need to blindly follow others or adopt their views. Unfortunately, relations between us further plummeted in November 2015, when in a conversation with Anant Goenka, Wholetime Director & Head, New Media, *The Indian Express*, at the eighth edition of the Ramnath Goenka Excellence in Journalism Awards, Aamir said that a sense of 'insecurity' and 'fear' had seeped deep within the society, even in his family. He said: 'Kiran and I have lived all our lives in India. For the first time, she raised the question, "Should we move out of India?" That's a disastrous and big statement for Kiran to make to me. She fears for her child. She fears about the atmosphere that will be around us. She feels scared to open the newspapers every day. That does indicate that there is a sense of growing disquiet.'

I would have not reacted to his statement, had it not come to me the way it did. I was in Toronto shooting with Gerard Butler for *A Family Man*. On an off day, I was travelling to a mall and my cab driver was an elderly Muslim who had family in India. He recognised me, told me he was my fan and said: 'Sir I like your films.' I thanked him. During our conversation, he said something that jolted me: 'Yesterday Aamir Khan has made a statement in India that his wife is scared to live in India . . . Saab, if such a big star with security around him is scared, then shouldn't ordinary people like us be concerned too?'

His words devastated me . . . made me angry. I felt in my heart that it was not true. And Aamir, who was ironically the brand ambassador of 'Incredible India' was joining the bandwagon of the intolerant brigade. I felt the need to respond because I have never been 'afraid of taking a stand when it comes to matters that plague the nation'. Those who have been following my Twitter feed know that well. And for those who don't, I would say, just open it and see how it is 'full of opinions about the goings on in the country'. The whole debate on intolerance and the 'resulting comments on it had piqued' my interest. With my tweets on Aamir's statement, things deteriorated between us.

Back in the hotel, on 23 November 2015, my first tweet went out at 11.37 p.m. (IST):

> Dear @aamir_khan. Did you ask Kiran which country would she like to move out to? Did you tell her that this country has made you AAMIR KHAN.

At 11.41 p.m., I said:

> Dear @aamir_khan. Did you tell Kiran that you have lived through more worse times in this country but you never thought of moving out.

At 12.24 a.m., I tweeted:

> Dear @aamir_khan. When did 'Incredible India' become 'Intolerant India' for you? Only in the last 7-8 months? #AtithiDevoBhavah

At 12.31 a.m.:

> Dear @ aamir_khan Presumed country has become #Intolerant. Wat do u suggest 2 millions of Indians? Leave India? Or wait till regime changes?

At 12.58 a.m.:

Dear @aamir_khan. #SatyamevaJayate u talked about evil practices but gave Hope. So even in 'Intolerant' times u need 2 spread Hope not Fear.

I know the liberals, like many other people, did not like my views. But for me, it was a genuine issue and I reacted in the way that came naturally to me. It was heartfelt and I was deeply invested in it since I felt strongly about it. I meant every word since it came from deep within and I still stand firmly behind them. Above all, I felt no qualms about expressing myself.

I have nothing against Aamir Khan or those of his ilk who think and speak in that tone with those views. Aamir is a wonderful person. He is a great force to reckon with in today's time. But, I feel, that to suit the 'agenda' of a group of people or some political party, you don't run down your country. That's why I asked him as to which other country would Kiran Rao want to stay in where she would not feel insecure?

The problem is that in the film industry, people don't like to confront people's courage. They don't like individuality. They want everything, all views of theirs, to be accepted without question.

As mentioned earlier also, at such times that thought bubble of my grandfather has always helped me: 'If you want to be equal with anybody in the world, just don't expect anything.' And I don't. I have gone through bankruptcy. I almost lost everything I owned in business. I may not be the richest man on earth, but I'm doing okay. I have survived against all odds and stared down every challenge and I am more the stronger for it. I am much more resilient, self-reliant, self-aware and successful in my mind than others around me. Today, I am working on some of the most prestigious international film and television projects. I am deeply invested in the enterprise of education. I am taking it forward through my acting school, Actor Prepares, where every year, youngsters graduate to do amazing work in the world. It's true that not everybody has become a Deepika Padukone, a Hrithik Roshan or Abhishek Bachchan, all of whom have graduated from my acting school, but all the others are doing phenomenal work on television, in theatre and in the world of advertising. I feel very happy because for me education is a very significant contribution. I feel unique and empowered to have written a self-help book which has become a number one bestseller and has remained so for many years and has been translated into numerous languages. How many others can claim to have done an autobiographical one-man show and staged it around the world? And presently, I am working on this—my autobiography. I am obsessing over every detail as I commit thought and memory to pen and paper every day. I do count myself as a star in my firmament, an author in my space and a teacher with a voice. I have become a multidimensional avatar and have preserved onwards through life's interesting journeys and I am proud of how far I have come and there is no stopping me.

In an industry surrounded by the likes of Aamir Khan, Naseeruddin Shah, Akshay Kumar, Ajay Devgn and others, Govinda is an epitome of a 'complete actor'. I have worked with him in many films and can say without any hesitation that he is one actor who can do any role and every role, and in one film itself, do various roles. He is an expert dancer and is great in tragedy and brilliant in comedy. Working with him in *Shola Aur Shabnam* and *Haseena Maan Jayegi* helped me improve my comic timing. His timing is just incomparable. He is ahead of all others. Nobody can improvise as he does. What Govinda can do, not many people can do. But what everybody else can do, Govinda too can do. His and David Dhawan's team will always remain one of the finest combinations, comparable to that of Amitabh Bachchan with Prakash Mehra or Manmohan Desai.

However, Govinda's biggest bane is that he had no respect for time simply because he became too busy to be on time anywhere. His late-coming on the sets is what became his undoing. Moreover, unfortunately for him, he too surrounded himself with 'yes-men' who did not guide him properly and he got enticed by them and carried away by his success. Very sad indeed because he is capable of giving so much which was shortchanged by his own behaviour.

Naseeruddin Shah, who is not only my senior but also a friend, is undoubtedly one of the finest actors. His films like Shekhar Kapur's *Masoom* and Sai Paranjpye's *Sparsh*, where he played a blind man, were brilliant. He is an intelligent actor . . . who came in more as an alternate hero of the parallel cinema. He and Om Puri provided life to every actor from theatre schools. He was the Amitabh Bachchan of alternate cinema which is often called art cinema. Sometimes, I feel that he is not happy with the circumstances that he finds himself in. In the back of his mind, he always wanted to be a popular actor . . . a commercial star. And mind you, he did try with films like Rajiv Rai's *Tridev* and a super-hit song like *Oye Oye* written by Anand Bakshi and composed by Kalyanji-Anandji, but he could not adapt himself completely to it—a typical grammar of Hindi cinema which is larger than life and which has its own language and grammar. It's not possible for everybody to fit into it. It's very difficult. In my opinion, Naseeruddin Shah never made the transition and always fell between the two stools of alternate and commercial cinema.

I don't meet Sunny Deol very often, but we have very fond memories of the times spent together on the films we have done together. With Rishi Kapoor, I have worked least with him—Yash Chopra's *Chandani* and *Vijay*, David Dhawan's *Eena Meena Deeka*, Rajeev Kapoor's *Prem Granth* and one or two more films. Rishi was the most successful and much sought-after actor much before I got into films. I became close to him when he came to New York for his treatment. He is the most straightforward person in the industry and sometimes, uncomfortably so.

Jackie Shroff and I got along famously because we both tasted success at the same time. I did a lot of films with Jackie Shroff and we are good friends, perhaps because, sometimes middle-class bonds closely together. Hunger, humiliation and lack of dignity makes for an implacable connection. He loves my childhood stories. He is one person who has never projected his personal tragedies and represents what being 'cool' is all about. Every time we meet, he hums *The Good, the Bad, the Ugly* tune—his way of telling me that he remembers my stories.

I was once asked that which movie would I count as my worst film. That got me thinking and for quite some time, I could not answer the question. Finally, my answer was: 'I don't think that I should have not done any film.' The fact is, as also mentioned earlier, I signed every film because I wanted to do each one of them. I never wanted to be without work, the dreadful experience I had in my earlier days. Moreover, I was also witnessing, or knew about, the terrible fate of some of the most popular actors and actresses, even the one-time top heroes and heroines, the singers, the musicians, not to talk of the extras or those who work hard in the background. So many of them died in penury without anybody to pay their medical bills, and in the case of one most popular heroine of her times, there was nobody to clear the hospital bills and take her body for a decent burial—not her estranged husband nor the stepchildren nor her own family.

I was enjoying every film. Each was an experience for me in its own way. However, some were very rewarding.

One such film was Dasari Narayana Rao's *Wafadar* which had Rajinikanth, Padmini Kolhapure and Vijeta Pandit in a love triangle. That was my first film with Rajinikanth. And what an unforgettable experience it was. Four years later, in 1989, I did another film with him Pankaj Parashar's *ChaalBaaz* with Sunny Deol and Sridevi in a double role. It is one of my favourite films for I experienced first-hand the magic of Rajinikanth. While shooting for *ChaalBaaz* at the famous AVM Studios in Madras (now Chennai), in one sequence, I fell down on a table and the glass pierced my thigh. As the producer A. Purnachandra Rao, with whom I had earlier done *Aakhree Raasta*, tried to call the doctor, Rajinikanth said: 'It is peak hours and the doctor will take a long time to come. I think I will take him to the hospital.'

Rajinikanth, who was driving himself, helped me into his shinning white Premier Padmini car, which had the number 400. As we drove out of the studio, I realised how bad the evening peak-hour traffic of 5 o'clock was. There was no way we could have reached the hospital in a rush. And then I saw the magic of Rajinikanth. He got out of the car, just looked around and did not even utter a word, and you will never believe this, within a maximum of one minute, the entire road got cleared. In India, it doesn't happen that fast even for an ambulance or a fire engine, but for Rajinikanth, it did happen. I would have never believed it had I not witnessed it myself.

Another incident with Rajinikanth was when Kirron and I were on our way to Tirupati for a visit to the famous Sri Venkateswara temple. He and his charming wife, Latha, insisted that we stay with them. Their hospitality was overwhelming. They were extraordinarily magnanimous. They vacated their own bedroom for us saying: 'Guest room is for the guests. You are family and you have to stay in the best room in this house and that is ours. We will sleep in the children's room. We are quite used to it.' This was my first, and only, experience where the hosts put up the guests in their own bedroom.

God bless Rajinikanth and Latha!

You may wonder how come I have not written a word about the actors like Vinod Khanna, Manoj Kumar, Dharmendra, Jeetendra, Sanjeev Kumar and others of that era. They were all my seniors. Later, when I joined the industry, I did work with some of them, but I can't say that they were my contemporaries or that I shared a close relationship with them. I had grown up watching their films. They were all larger-than-life heroes. True heroes. Real men. In comparison, today we have boys. Very hard-working, professional and responsible boys. But, for me, still boys!

Of the older generation, one actor I regret not having met is Balraj Sahni. He was, according to me, the most realistic actor that we ever had. Even today, I remember very vividly, scene by scene, frame by frame and song by song, some of his movies, most of which I have seen numerous times. How can one ever forget his role in Khwaja Ahmad Abbas's *Dharti Ke Lal*, which was called 'a gritty realistic drama' by *The New York Times*, as Shambu Maheto in Bimal Roy's *Do Bigha Zamin*, as Abdul Rehman Khan in Hemen Gupta's *Kabuliwala*, and as Salim Mirza in M. S. Sathyu's *Garam Hawa*. Then there are those two classic songs: One, from Amiya Chakrabarty's *Seema*, in which Balraj Sahni, as Ashok 'Babu', renders that beauty composed by Shankar-Jaikishan and written and sung by Manna Dey: '*Tu pyaar ka sagar hai, teri ik boond ke pyaase hum . . .*'; Second, that incomparable gem, '*Aye meri zohra jabeen, tujhe maloom nahin, tu abhi tak hai haseen aur main jawan . . .*' composed by Afghan singer and compositor maestro, Abdul Ghafoor Breshna, with Ravi to the lyrics by Sahir Ludhianvi, where Balraj Sahni as Lala Kedarnath in Yash Chopra's multi-starrer *Waqt* sings to his wife, played by Achala Sachdev—a song that even today 'endears listeners across generations with excitement and sentimentality'.

My other big regret is not having been able to spend some time with Sanjeev Kumar. He too went away too soon. A pity indeed!

One important lesson the film industry teaches one and all is never to take any role for 'granted'. Much changes between the planning, the signing and the announcement of a film project and its release. Roles are offered and then suddenly withdrawn, rarely with an apology and mostly without any explanation. Roles are also rejected on valid or vague reasons. The industry is full of numerous examples. Remember, when Danny Denzongpa was offered a meaty role (as the dreaded dacoit Gabbar Singh) in the Ramesh Sippy-directed *Sholay* (released in August 1975, which turned out to be a great blockbuster and is popular even today)? He declined the offer due to the inevitable 'prior commitments' and 'lack of dates'. Danny was then an upcoming actor and had done a variety of roles, including that of a villain. Finally, it was a relatively unknown actor called Amjad Khan who went on to depict Gabbar Singh on screen with rare panache. Amjad Khan stole the limelight despite a formidable cast made up of the veteran Dharmendra, the versatile Sanjeev Kumar and the towering Amitabh Bachchan.

After seeing *Sholay*, Danny apparently admitted that he could not have pulled off the role as superbly as Amjad Khan had. Similarly, as I have mentioned above, after watching *Saaransh*, Sanjeev Kumar too conceded that he could not have performed as well as I had.

Years later, when in the mid-1980s, film producer, Boney Kapoor, decided to make an Indian science fiction thriller film titled, *Mr. India*, to be directed by Shekhar Kapur, with a screenplay written by Salim-Javed, I was considered for the role of the villain—Mogambo. Anil Kapoor and Sridevi were to be in the lead with Ashok Kumar, Satish Kaushik, Ajit Vachani, Sharat Saxena and others in supporting roles. The film had already been delayed due to casting issues. Originally, the lead role was first offered to Rajesh Khanna, the superstar of the era, and then to Amitabh Bachchan, both of whom refused as neither could 'relate with the invisible hero' of the film. That's how Boney's younger brother, Anil Kapoor, a well-established actor with many successes to his credit, came in. With Anil coming in, I was thrown out, removed as the villain, and that too at the advice of my very dear friend, Anil Kapoor, himself. Amrish Puri was signed. I felt let down . . . disheartened . . . and immensely hurt.

Amrish Puri was phenomenal. He was a very fine actor—both in theatre and cinema—along with being a very fine person too—a thorough gentleman the likes of which they don't make anymore. I think he did not get his due just because he was not marketing savvy. He worked with notable playwrights of the time like Satyadev Dubey, Vijay Tendulkar and Girish Karnad and perhaps with every prominent and not so prominent film director. Having acted in over 400 films, he played some of 'the iconic villainous roles in Indian and international cinema' and I don't think there was anybody like him in terms of not only the negative roles that he did but all the character roles that he played. Imagine that he was the main villain—Mola Ram—in a Steven Spielberg Hollywood film way back in 1984—*Indiana Jones and the Temple of Doom*. An honour he carried so lightly on his sleeves. He was fantastic from every point of view. A very disciplined person and most hard-working. He was an innocent, simple man *aur jo unke man mein hota tha wahi bolte the* (He spoke whatever was on his mind).

Mr. India, which was released in May 1987, went on to become the second highest-grossing Indian film of the year, and remains, to this day, 'a cult classic' in Indian cinema. While the film became famous for several of its dialogues and songs, including Sridevi's 'Miss Hawa Hawaii' performance, it was Amrish Puri's superb performance, particularly his oft-repeated quote, '*Mogambo khush hua*' (Mogambo is pleased), which became one of the most famous quotes of Bollywood and is, even today, synonymous with Amrish saab. My interpretation would have been different. But what he did was impossible to perform.

Today, I can honestly say that it was Amrish saab who made the Mogambo character as one of the best villains in Bollywood history. I also admit that I could have never played Mogambo and made it a cult figure the way Amrish Puri did. What a performance!

I shared a very straightforward and simple relationship with him. I used to joke a lot with him and at times, he would get tired of me. And see how the industry has forgotten him. Our memories of him are left in his films. I recall his autobiography—*The Act of Life: An Autobiography of Amrish Puri*, which he had done with Jyoti Sabharwal, which did not do justice to either the man or his life. But then he was not in an era of social media. Amrish saab, wherever you be today, I salute you for being what you were—an outstanding actor and a great human being. I miss you!

Pran saab too was a very fine actor—the finest villain of his times for a long, long time to the point that 'so powerful and fearful was his performance on screen and its impact that no parent ever named their son as Pran, close to 50 years.' However, unfortunately in Hindi films, character actors, who were much better actors than many heroes of the day, did not get their due. Fortunately, the scene has changed, the cinema has changed, the language of cinema has changed, the feel of cinema has changed, because of which whether it's Irrfan Khan or Nawazuddin Siddiqui or Naseeruddin Shah or me, we have all been given our dues and are able to stand shoulder to shoulder with other principle leads in a film.

Just to mention that all the 'bad' guys of Hindi cinema with a 'golden' heart are from Shimla—Pran, Prem Chopra, Amrish Puri and of course, yours truly Dr Dang.

If there was one actress I always admired since my childhood days, it was Waheeda Rehman. And there was no way I would miss any film of hers. Some of them like Guru Dutt's *Kagaz Ke Phool* and *Pyaasa*, Vijay Anand's *Guide*, Mohammed Sadiq's *Chaudhvin Ka Chand* or Biren Nag's *Bees Saal Baad*, I watched again and again and again. In 1991, I finally got the opportunity to work with her in Yash Chopra's film *Lamhe*. That was when I told her: 'Waheedaji, whenever I direct my first film, I would be honoured if you would work in it.'

'I promise, I will,' she had replied then. And she kept her word.

So, she played Anil Kapoor, Fardeen Khan and Abhishek Bachchan's mother's role in 2002, when I made *Om Jai Jagadish*. Three years later, in 2005, I decided to produce *Maine Gandhi Ko Nahi Mara* which was directed by Jahnu Barua. There was a very small sequence, literally two small scenes for which I thought that she was the right person to play it. I approached her and she agreed. I was overwhelmed and very touched. There was always a great amount of grace in her.

Rohini Hattangadi was my senior from the National School of Drama in Delhi. She had played Kasturba opposite Ben Kingsley in Richard Attenborough's *Gandhi* and was fantastic in that role. As far as the casting of Mahesh Bhatt's *Saaransh* was concerned, it couldn't have been better. Both of us were from the NSD and I couldn't have given that performance without her support. Hence, I owe a lot to her for making my role what it became, for providing that chemistry in front of the camera, for being there in the frame and for giving so much as an actor, as a co-star. I was too hungry to do something different . . . something real and she provided that support that an actor needs. I couldn't have done that role of B. V. Pradhan if Rohini Hattangadi had not played my wife. I still can't think of any other actor who could have played that role to perfection as she did. As a person, she understood what was required.

In certain ways, *Saaransh* was like a full-length play. Even though it had the format of a film, it was basically like a play between two people. The film's ambience reflected a lot of theatre because all those in the main cast came from a theatre background. Suhas Bhalekar, who had played the old man Vishwanath, was from theatre, Madan

Jain as Vilas Chitra, Nilu Phule as Ganganan Chitre and Soni Razdan as Sujata Suman were all from the theatre. Each one of them contributed to the film and to my performance. When people talk about *Saaransh,* the first thing they talk about is my performance. It's not really as simple as that. That performance would not have been possible without Soni playing that character of the tenant and Madan Jain being her boyfriend. The cast created the atmosphere of a family. True, everyone performs well for the particular character he or she is playing but when the entire cast joins together and wants you to do well, it adds an extraordinary dimension which is a bonus to the entire production. I cannot say it enough that Rohini Hattangadi was extremely generous with her performance. She would rehearse with me all the time so as to give a perfect shot in front of the camera. She would put her head on my shoulder . . . her back shot . . . she would give the same amount of emotional comfort and support to me. She is one of my best leading ladies. She will always remain so!

In Ramesh Behl's *Jawaani,* I worked with Sharmila Tagore and Moushumi Chatterjee. But I have always had a softer spot for Sharmila, perhaps because I had seen innumerable films of hers during my growing up years. My all-time favourites included Shakti Samanta's *Kashmir Ki Kali* where she acted with Shammi Kapoor, Gulzar's *Mausam* with Sanjeev Kumar and the gem of a role of Pushpa that she played in Shakti Samanta's other 1972 super hit, *Amar Prem,* opposite Rajesh Khanna. However, as far as my interaction and work with them are concerned, I enjoyed working with both, who are unbelievably pleasant and charming. Moushumi was the innocently mischievous one, full of little pranks, light-hearted jokes and a bewitching laughter. Once, years back, she happened to meet my mother but to this day, she remembers that meeting and asks me about her and if the picture taken with her is still in the house!

Smita Patil left us a bit too early. Perhaps, the gods needed her more than we did. From all points of view, she was a very fine human being. A wonderful actor with exceptional talent and I have the greatest regard for her. I remember when shooting for Mahesh Bhatt's film, *Thikana,* in 1986-87, even after a late-night shoot, my work didn't finish. The next day, I had to leave. Hence, the only way I could finish my schedule was by reporting very early in the morning again. 'But you don't have to come,' I suggested. She was a big star after all. But she was very adjustable and said: 'Not to worry. I will come in the morning and shoot with you to finish the scene. What time should we meet?'

Her death was a big tragedy. I still remember her outstanding performance in Shyam Benegal's *Bhumika* in 1977, wherein she had Amol Palekar, Anant Nag and Naseeruddin Shah in the main cast. And she was incredible in Mahesh Bhatt's *Arth* in which, even though Shabana Azmi had the author-backed role, she did steal many a scene. A wonderful film which I was doing with her was Amit Khanna's *Unth* which unfortunately was shelved.

Hema Malini was the first actress whom I ever saw from close quarters in my life. It was during the picturisation of the song, *Hume tumse pyar kitna*, for Chetan Anand's star-studded film, *Kudrat*, at Sankat Mochan, near Tara Devi in Shimla. I was spellbound. Thereafter, I saw a lot of her films including my favourites like Ramesh Sippy's *Sita Aur Geeta* in which she played a double role with Dharmendra and Sanjeev Kumar as her co-stars, Pramod Chakravorty's *Dream Girl* with Ashok Kumar and Dharmendra, F. C. Mehra's *Lal Patthar* with Raaj Kumar and of course, how can one ever forget the Basanti in Ramesh Sippy's *Sholay*? I have acted with her in quite a few films, with the first one being Yash Chopra's *Vijay* which had a large star-cast in it. One day, when we were shooting the film in Hyderabad, a group of people came to take a photograph with her. She made a face. Then some more people came, and she made a similar face. I was quite inquisitive to know as to why she did that, so I asked her: 'Hemaji, why do you make a face when they want to take a picture with you. Are you tired or what?'

'You see,' she replied rather innocently, 'they will put up this picture in their homes and I don't want them to think that Hema Malini is very happy to take a picture with them. It is they who are very happy to take a picture with me.'

This gave me a great insight into the working of her mind.

I must say that she's the most emancipated and dignified woman who has lived life on her own terms. She, by her mere presence, has commanded respect. There are no rumours, no behind-the-back loose talk, at least not to my knowledge. I think, even today, there is no other actress as regal as her—very graceful and still stunningly beautiful. Just see her in Ravi Chopra's *Baghban* opposite Amitabh Bachchan and you will know for yourself. For me, she is still the ultimate 'Dream Girl'!

I did a film with Asha Parekh called *Jeevan Sandhya* which was directed by Pravin Bhatt, Vikram Bhatt's father and Mahesh Bhatt's cameraman. It was a great experience to work with her.

Over the last 35 years of my life in films, I have worked with almost all the actresses of their times. You name them and I am sure to have worked with them. However, I have done the maximum number of films with Madhuri Dixit and, perhaps more than that, with Sridevi—the person who made a major impact on me as an actor.

I had seen her give two superb performances—first in Balu Mahendra's *Sadma* opposite Kamal Haasan in 1983 and then in Shekhar Kapur's *Mr. India* with Anil Kapoor, in 1987. My first film with her, if I remember correctly, was Yash Chopra's *Chandni*, in 1989, in which she was opposite Rishi Kapoor. But it was only after I worked in Pankaj Parashar's *ChaalBaaz* in 1989, in which she had a double role opposite Rajinikanth and Sunny Deol, then Yash Chopra's *Lamhe* in 1991, in which she was paired with Anil Kapoor, and finally, Mahesh Bhatt's *Gumrah* in 1993, with Sanjay Dutt, when I realised that here was an actress who can be compared to any actor, anywhere in the world. She was stunningly electrifying in front of the cameras. In her day to day life, she was always very normal, down to earth with no airs or make-up, just like a regular person next door. Once we met her in a restaurant, where she sat like any other person, without any make-up or flashy, expensive, designer clothes. She engaged in regular conversation and discussed food.

We had a great time doing *Lamhe* and that parody that we did together, was phenomenal. During the making of *ChaalBaaz*, where I was playing a villain, we would interact a great deal. She was not a trained actress and yet, her acting instinct was absolutely perfect and completely spot on. She never wavered between the first and the tenth take. Normally, her first take in itself was okayed but then she would play around with the takes. She had a great sense of timing for comedy.

A few days before, she passed away in Dubai where she had gone for a family function. I had last met her at a Maharashtra police function in Mumbai. She looked happy. I asked her: 'Madam, (that's how I used to address her), are you happy?'

'I am always happy,' she replied with her charming smile.

Because conversations were short and few, it was easier to come to the point. I used to meet her at her brother-in-law Anil Kapoor's house or at some function or the other. Interacting with her was always very stimulating.

I think during the last few years, she was very anxious about her daughter Jhanvi's career. You could see that the mother in her had taken over the heroine or the actress that she was. That she was literally worshipped by the masses was clear from the reactions to the news of her death, the love that she got from them on the streets of Mumbai where hundreds and thousands lined on both sides of the road, for the entire route, to pay their last respects to the 'first female superstar' that India had. In her career which spanned over five decades, starting from the age of four, she performed all the range from slapstick comedy to epic dramas. She indeed epitomised a rare untutored textbook in acting.

In 1984, when I was dubbing for Mahesh Bhatt's *Saaransh* at the Sea Rock Dubbing Theatre, I saw a young girl of just about 17 years old or so, wearing a light blue salwar-kameez, coming out, after finishing dubbing for her first film Hiren Nag's *Abodh*. Both the films were being produced by Rajshri Productions. She was an unbelievably pretty girl with a real dream smile, accompanied by bewitching laughter. She was also absolutely stunning. Her name: Madhuri Dixit. She was to become a famous and popular actress during the 1990s and much sought after with six Filmfare awards and 14 nominations in her kitty.

Over the years, I did many films with her—Sooraj Barjatya's *Hum Aapke Hain Koun..!* with Salman Khan, Rakesh Roshan's *Khel* with Anil Kapoor, Prakash Mehra's *Zindagi Ek Juaa* with Anil Kapoor,

Lawrence D'Souza's *Dil Tera Aashiq* with Salman and N. Chandra's *Tezaab* with Anil Kapoor, to name a few. In fact, it is difficult to remember how many films we did together. Like Sridevi, she too is great when it comes to amazing one-liners. And like Sridevi, Madhuri is the ideal person to tell a joke to. Before I could even start, she would start laughing. Basically, she is always ready to be happy. And what a phenomenal storehouse of acting. She has superb spontaneity. She was a great learner and adapted over a period of time. She blossomed with every film.

Another prodigious co-star who is also a very successful actor is Jaya Prada. With her, I did quite a few films not only in Hindi but in other South Indian languages and one in English too—R. Sarath's *The Desire*. The first film with her was Vijay Reddy's *Main Tera Dushman*, with Sunny Deol, Jackie Shroff and Sridevi, though K. Bhagyaraj's *Aakhree Raasta* with Amitabh Bachchan and Sridevi was released earlier. However, the most amazing film that I did with Jaya was Blessy's romantic drama, *Pranayam*, in Malayalam. It was a love triangle of three elderly people—Mohanlal, me and her. It won numerous awards. I find Jaya Prada to be a very graceful actor.

And how can one not write about Juhi Chawla, with whom I must have done a dozen films or so, comprising Hrishikesh Mukherjee's *Jhooth Bole Kauwa Kaate* with Anil Kapoor, David Dhawan's *Deewana Mastana* with Anil Kapoor and then *Eena Meena Deeka* with Vinod Khanna and Rishi Kapoor, Yash Chopra's *Darr* with Sunny Deol and Shah Rukh Khan and Ashutosh Gowariker *Izzat Ki Roti* with Rishi Kapoor and Sunny Deol, to name a few. A wonderful actress, Juhi is very affectionate and warm, full of humour and laughter. Always with a ready smile on her face.

With Rakhee, I did half-a-dozen films, the first being Vishwamitra's *Mere Baad* and the most notable being Subhash Ghai's *Ram Lakhan*. It was, once again, a great experience to work with her. And what a great cook she is? She would occasionally cook on the sets. That reminds me that she is a very slow joke-teller. On average, each joke of hers would take about ten minutes or so to narrate, during which one had to keep on laughing. Her jokes would not end, because she would interrupt them herself by asking someone or the other: 'Have you eaten? Is the food good?' Just shows how caring and affectionate a person she is.

All these leading ladies had bewitching smiles. Even today, whenever I get the time, I switch on some film or the other just to see their smiles. I was never able to work with Madhubala or Meena Kumari, but even today, I watch their films just to see their smiles.

The two other actresses that I enjoyed working with are Kajol and Mahima Chaudhry. With Kajol, I did three important films— Satish Kaushik's *Hum Aapke Dil Mein Rehte Hain* with Anil Kapoor, Aditya Chopra's *Dilwale Dulhania Le Jayenge* with Shah Rukh Khan and Karan Johar's *Kuch Kuch Hota Hai* with Shah Rukh Khan, Rani Mukerji and Salman Khan. Kajol is a brilliant actress who is very spontaneous. She is bright and fascinating, with a lot of spunk and someone we can be really proud of. She comes from a great pedigree and has aced her vast potential.

When I was casting for my directorial debut, *Om Jai Jagadish*, I had taken Mahima Chaudhry to pair with Anil Kapoor and she did a good job. Since then, I did work with her in a few films. The last being Manoj Bhatnagar's *Chess* in 2012.

Of the Hollywood actresses, the one I really enjoyed working with was Jennifer Lawrence in David O. Russell's *Silver Linings Playbook*. Her performance as a depressed and bipolar widow, for which she picked up the Academy Award for Best Actress, was a great heap of talent and it was fascinating to watch. Here was a 20-year-old, working with the likes of veterans like Robert De Niro and Anupam Kher—I am thrilled to be able to write this in the same sentence—who have an enormous amount of work to their credit, she was always calm, cool and totally confident. She knew what she had to do. Most of the time, one would see her reading a book on the sets. But the moment the shot was announced, she would transform herself for the role, as if magically.

In films, most of the relationships are need-based. When you work with people in a film, you become friends with them. Once the film is over, you move on and attach yourself to another set of people to work with who become friends. However, some people remain constantly in your lives and you share warmth, affection and love with them like Madhuri and Juhi. I think there was something very special about the people one worked with in the 1980s and 1990s. The main reason being that there was no social media to indulge through, there were no managers who handled life for you, there were no media advisers who kept you briefed about what to do and what not to, there were no personal vans to retreat into after every shot and there were no mobiles to be stuck to all the time and become oblivious to the world. Hence, those of my generation were lucky that we had a great bonding with our colleagues and friends, whom we met regularly. We had a one-to-one communication, face-to-face relationships. We were also less competitive. Gone are the days of the silver jubilees and golden jubilees being celebrated. Today, the primary question and the main subject is which and whose films are making 100-crores and in how much time and who has a million followers on Facebook or Twitter or Instagram. I am lucky to have seen both the eras—the one gone by and the one that we are experiencing—full of great social media skills, of FaceTime and Facebook, where one has more friends who are faceless than friends who have a face.

Part–IV

THE MASTERS

———◆◇ ❦ ❀ ❦ ◇◆———

I accept all interpretations of my films.
The only reality is before the camera.
Each film I make is kind of a return to poetry for me,
or at least an attempt to create a poem.

—Bernardo Bertolucci

21

MAHESH BHATT—MY FATHER IN CINEMA

*T*wo film directors who had a great emotional and professional impact on me were Mahesh Bhatt and Yash Chopra.

After eight years, during which he made five films, Mahesh Bhatt finally tasted success with *Arth* (with Shabana Azmi, Smita Patil, Kulbhushan Kharbanda and Raj Kiran) which was released in December 1982. It brought him various accolades. With it, he came to terms with the kind of cinema that he wanted to make. When I saw his fourth film, *Lahu Ke Do Rang*, in 1979, which had Vinod Khanna, Shabana Azmi and Danny Denzongpa with Helen in the main cast, I thought what a stylish and amazing film it was.

As already mentioned earlier, in 1983, I was at my wits' end and desperately looking for work, going from studio to studio and from one director's office to another, without any success. Then someone suggested: '*Mahesh Bhatt ko milo. Woh achi tarah milta hai*' (Meet Mahesh Bhatt. He is accessible). I called him up from a ration shop from Bandra Linking Road. His first question was: 'Where have you come from?'

'From the National School of Drama, in New Delhi, sir,' I replied. He gave me an appointment for the following day.

Next day, when I reached his sixth-floor apartment in Green Acres building on Pali Hill, he opened the door and said: 'Anupam, from the National School of Drama? Right?'

I was impressed that Mahesh Bhatt remembered my name because in the sea of anonymity of Bombay, being recognised by one's name was like being given back your identity. Otherwise, you are an unknown face in a city, lost forever. When I was led inside to the sitting room, I was introduced to actor Marc Zuber and the screenplay and dialogue writer Sujit Sen who had worked on *Arth* and was working on the script of *Saaransh* with Mahesh Bhatt and Amit Khanna.

I had carried with me some press reviews of my plays and a write up by my journalist-friend, Ali Peter John, for the *Screen* newspaper which said that here 'was somebody to look forward to as an actor'. The write-up also carried a photograph of mine in a straw hat. Sujit Sen looked at it and said, somewhat, 'Oh, you are ashamed of your baldness? Is that why you are wearing a hat?'

'No, that was the only picture I had, and I gave it to *Screen*,' I replied.

In this social group, it was quite the norm to speak frankly and shock each other—this was seen as attractive and being quite 'with it'. Soon, I too was drawn into this habit. As we were talking, Mahesh Bhatt's wife, Kiran, came in for something and when she went away a few moments later, Mahesh Bhatt, in order to shock me, said: 'Are you attracted to her?'

I was taken aback, and I did not know what to say. Raised in a small town with a somewhat traditional mentality, when you go to somebody's house, you don't look at anybody from that angle. And even if you do, it's not something you proclaim out aloud. *Was Mahesh Bhat trying to shock me? How could he say such a thing about his wife . . . Pooja Bhatt's mother?* I thought to myself. Later, much later, I realised that this was quite usual for Mahesh Bhatt . . . it was his way of dealing with many ongoing issues in his life. He would say something very scandalous, or something very shocking, straight to your face.

Meanwhile, that afternoon, Sujit Sen was trying his best to provoke me. I am sure, like me, innumerable actors must have gone to meet Mahesh Bhatt in hopes of getting a chance for acting in his film. I was a little tired of telling people that I was different. Suddenly, Mahesh Bhatt said: 'I have heard you are quite good.'

'You have heard it wrong, sir. I am not good. I am brilliant,' I shot back at him, adopting his and Sujit Sen's blasé attitude. I had uttered these words out of desperation because I didn't want to carry on with trite words.

'You will get a role from me in my film for this answer,' he replied.

'I know . . . for this answer and for others also, I will be able to deliver whatever you give me in whatever you make,' I responded.

I had learnt to reply in a language that suited him and his friends.

I can never forget that one particular evening with my dear friend, Pritish Nandy, who at that time was editing the *Illustrated Weekly of India*, the flagship magazine of the Times of India group. This was around the time Mahesh Bhatt was on an alcoholic binge, drinking every night. Pritish and I would join him frequently, in spite of the fact that I hardly drank. Pritish was with me in the lift when he told me: 'You are a boring man . . . too goody-goody.'

'I don't have to be nasty for you to like me,' I replied. I had started enjoying answering them back in this fashion which echoed their method—even though it was not in my nature or culture to do so.

'I feel like punching you,' Pritish said.

'I will punch you back and so hard that you won't say that again,' I replied. He knew I meant it.

And that's how we became friends. The evenings would be laced with the most stimulating and amazing conversations about real issues. We would have forthright and dynamic discussions sparing no one on a wide range of subjects. The world was ours for the taking. 'I have the journalistic power,' Pritish would say. 'I have the brains, the ideas,' Mahesh Bhatt would chip in.

I was very impressed by Mahesh Bhatt. Every conversation of his, each thought, idea, quote of his, stayed with me and I would ponder over them for a long time. He became a kind of a 'guru' for me . . . a teacher for my mind. Earlier, I would count Balwant Gargi and Amal Allana as my guides. But then, Mahesh Bhatt became the dominating force, the main influence in my thought process. I knew a bit about life and now he gave me an approach towards it. In his inimitable style, he transcended it to another level. That came easily to him. As I was grounded in my middle-class mentality, I found it hard to keep up. But he taught me the valuable lesson of candour with the words: '*Jo dil mein hai woh bolo*' (Say what's in your heart). Forthrightness is very important because it's paramount to tell people what you feel, because, in any case, you cannot always be popular with people for they will discard you when it doesn't suit them.

Mahesh Bhatt was close to the philosopher U. G. Krishnamurti (UG) who questioned the 'state of enlightenment'. He was his guru. Whatever he was learning from UG, he would share with me. His entire being was obsessed with UG.

My mind was filled with images of my grandfather, Pandit Amar Nath. His simple teachings and the home-grown wisdom he had imparted to me in my childhood and growing up years is what truly formed the core of my being. For me it was an amazing combination. In fact, I internally dedicated *Saaransh* to him. Before every shot for the film, I would say to myself: 'This is for you Babuji'. All the important films that I have done in my career, I have done for the important people in my life—my family members, my friends, my colleagues. This is my way of giving them a silent tribute.

Saaransh, I knew from day one, I would do for my grandfather because he was the kind of person I wanted to emulate. He was a grounded person, solid in his values, without airs but one that I could emulate. Few of his iconic sayings have become more as 'quotable quotes' to me. For example: '*Bheega hua aadmi barish se nahi darta*' (A man who is drenched is not afraid of the rain). Another quote which is even more valuable in today's world is 'Don't go through a problem twice, once by thinking about it and then by going through it.'

Me centring my character on my grandfather and Mahesh Bhatt drawing inspiration from U. G. Krishnamurti added a multi-dimensional layer to the character of B. V. Pradhan. After the phenomenal success of *Saaransh*, Mahesh Bhatt started including me in his other films too.

I recall that before we started shooting *Saaransh*, Mahesh Bhatt took me to the superstar Rajesh Khanna's house for a party. It was the first film party I was attending. All the big stars, producers, directors, distributors and socialites were there. I was sitting, in one corner, on a garden swing, when Mahesh Bhatt came to me and said: 'Remember Anupam, you are a far bigger person than all these people here. So be a superior person. Sit tall on this *jhoola* (swing) and watch people . . . observe them because by this time next year, you will be ruling the city.'

I followed his instructions to the T and observed and absorbed the scene as well as the surroundings like a sponge.

If I had not signed *Saaransh* and had Mahesh Bhatt not come into my life, this would be a different tale altogether. It was he who initiated the consciousness and awareness. He nurtured me to think and present myself differently so I would be noticed. I also realised that success has no time for anybody. It only acknowledges successful people. It is impatient with potential talent. It has no time for that. But failure does. It notices everything. And, if you succumb to self-pity on the way then you are finished—written off before you have even begun the journey.

But I remember that party very well. I felt like an outsider, a stranger at the party. As I sat there engrossed in my own thoughts, Rajesh Khanna walked up to me and asked: 'Not drinking anything man?' I felt thrilled. *Today, the superstar had noticed and spoken to me*, I thought. *Wonder what tomorrow will bring?*

Once, Mahesh Bhatt finished the film, he presented me with the following introduction: 'He is the future best actor.' In his own manner, he was very proud of his 'discovery'. Every director, when he discovers someone who comes through with flying colours, he becomes possessive and that person becomes his personal property. With Mahesh Bhatt, one film followed another: *Janam* with Kumar Gaurav, Shernaz Patel and Kitu Gidwani, *Kaash* with Jackie Shroff and Dimple Kapadia, *Awaargi* with Anil Kapoor, Govinda and Meenakshi Seshadri, *Swayam* which had Waheeda Rehman in it with Sadashiv Amrapurkar and Soni Razdan, *Maarg* with Vinod Khanna, Hema Malini and Dimple Kapadia, *Gumrah* with Sanjay Dutt and Sridevi and so many others.

Kaash was about a couple with a son who had cancer. Though it was a very depressing film, it was well made. A film which I was eagerly looking forward to was the ever helpful Johny Bakshi's *Zamin* with Hema Malini and Kabir Bedi. It had a very interesting story, and for the first time, I was in the lead role, playing Hema Malini's husband. I took it to be my film as I was the hero, for all practical purposes. It was a film centring on jealousy, where Hema Malini falls in love with Kabir Bedi, and her husband just asks: 'Choose, who is better? Him or me?' Being a Mahesh Bhatt film, shooting was on at full speed and after a long shooting stint at the Ashok Hotel in Delhi, we had finished over 80 per cent of the film. One day while shooting at Satish Bhalla's bungalow in Bombay, I remember that we were shooting a scene between Hema and me, when two workers came and picked up the sofa and walked away. And this was when the camera was still on. *What is happening?* I thought. Just a few minutes later, they returned and picked the table. This time the furniture contractor, who was accompanying them said: '*Inki aisi ki taisi . . . Paise dete nahin hai aur film banane chale hain*' (To hell with them . . . they don't pay money and want to make a film). The producers ran out of finances and the film got shelved. Very sad for all of us but for me, it was a personal loss.

Hence, with all these films Mahesh Bhatt was adding to my knowledge in cinema and shaping my mind and psyche further. In *Kaash*, which like most of Mahesh Bhatt's films 'contained serious and realistic content', I played Dimple's lover, who is a sophisticated businessman, and Jackie Shroff, who was once a big star turned alcoholic due to a serious crisis after bankruptcy. Their marriage falls apart. After the film got completed, Mahesh Bhatt told me: '*Tera role kafi kat gaya hain . . .* (Your role has been edited quite a bit) and has become rather small because when we saw the film, we discovered that the father, mother and the son's bonding, should not get polluted because of the third person coming into their lives.'

'But that precisely is the main . . . the central theme of the story . . . and the reason why you are different from other people,' I replied, somewhat taken aback.

'No, no. You must understand that sometimes we have to listen to the distributors and the producers. I have to sell the film to them and they have to release it,' he replied.

By now, Mahesh Bhatt had created a monster within me by teaching me to be straightforward and always speak the truth. So, in great anger, I said: 'That means you are ready to compromise, that today, Mahesh Bhatt lacks conviction about his own creation, that he is no different from other directors who sort of listen to their producers and their distributors.'

I could say all this to him because he had given me the authority, the right to do so. It was he who had fashioned this man, it was he who had given me the courage to express my true feelings. There is a beautiful line in his film *Daddy*: '*Sach ko sach banane ke liye, do logon ki zaroorat hoti hain. Ek jo sach bol sake, doosra jo sach sun sake*' (To make the truth come alive, you need two persons—one who can speak the truth, and the other who can listen to the truth).

Then, with the passage of time, my novelty started wearing off for him which was bound to happen. I was like any other actor now as I had started working in any and every film which was offered to me. While I was busy from morning to night, he started making films without me.

Yet, I carried on my personal ritual of giving him Rs 500 to start with and then more, at times with some gift or the other, as my 'guru dakshina' for every film I signed. I can't calculate how much I must have given him till date, but I am sure the amount runs into a few lakhs. Whenever he comes to my school to deliver a lecture, we give him Rs 20,000. He doesn't need it for he will certainly grace us with his presence without the payment but the expression of glee when he shows that money to the world is to be seen to be believed. He publicly says: '*Pehle, mere paise do*' (Give me my money first). For me, it is a tradition, a solemn ceremony, which makes me feel closer to him. I don't have to, but it is just a reflection of my upbringing.

There is one notable incident, I recall after the release of *Saaransh* and its success at the box office. My mother came down to Bombay. I took her to meet Mahesh Bhatt at his house. In his incomparable way, he said to her: 'Look, I have made your son a big star.'

Without any hesitation, my mother replied: 'Well, there must be something in him that you could do that. I'm sure you can't do that with everybody else.'

Mahesh Bhatt was stunned. I was not. Even though she came from a small town, this was typical of my mother. People like her epitomise the simple, honest, straightforward and uncomplicated, and are capable of speaking their mind. Once, I told my father to please write a letter to Mahesh Bhatt, thanking him for giving me the biggest break of my life. My father could not write very well. So he requested my grandfather, Pandit Amar Nath, who was known for writing well, to compose the letter as Pandit Pushkar Nath. It was a very poignant letter—straight from the heart. Unfortunately, all the letters of my grandfather were destroyed in the 2005 floods of Mumbai.

My biggest regret was that my grandfather did not live to see *Saaransh*. I was very keen for him to see it which is evident from the fact that in every interview with the media, I would say that my portrayal was based on my grandfather. And my grandfather, who by then had moved back to Srinagar in Kashmir to live in the ancestral home, would devour every word, every line, of those interviews. He would look at my photographs repeatedly and show them to all in the family. On 17 September 1984, he was to fly to Bombay to see the film. I had sent him business class tickets of Air India—Srinagar to Delhi and Delhi to Bombay. He was very excited and in one of his letters, he had asked me: 'What should I wear?'

'We will go to see the film in a cinema hall,' I replied. 'You wear your normal jacket with your *safa* (turban).'

He bought a new turban and got a new jacket stitched and was waiting to don it and proudly accompany me to the movies. I too was looking forward to the day I would take him to see me on the big screen in a theatre where hundreds of people would surround me, shake hands with me, congratulate me and seek my autographs during the intermission and after the show. How proud he would feel, I thought. I was eager to see that expression on his face—on the face of the man, who had guided me to the goalposts through his homespun lessons and whose hand has sheltered and blessed me. But it was not to be! Just the night before he was supposed to travel, he told the family members: 'My time has come. Help me get out of this bed and lay me on the floor.' A few hours later, he was no more. I couldn't believe it. I was broken, devastated. The only consolation I had was that he had seen at least one scene from the movie—the famous TV scene—which was televised frequently. The scene: *Main TV lene nahi aaya hu. Main apne mare hue bete ki asthiya lene aaya hu . . .*

Mahesh Bhatt and I drifted apart from each other, I think, when I took a political stand, about eight years back. He was disappointed with me. I joined the '2011 Indian Anti-Corruption Movement' led by Anna Hazare and later, started talking about the present government and the policies and programmes of Prime Minister Narendra Modi. I was rather vocal about all the major political issues. Then, one day, he had a major altercation with me and categorically said: 'Your thought process is absolutely wrong. You have totally changed. You are no longer what you were . . . no longer the person I knew all along but a different person.'

'That's what evolution is all about . . . I have to be, because today, I don't feel what I felt earlier on certain issues, which are now important to me and I feel strongly about them,' I replied.

He was upset enough and said one day: '*Woh line jo tunhe mere baare mein apne drama mei daali hui hai, usey nikal de. Nikal de use jahan tu kehta hai: "Agar zindagi Kurukshetra ka yudh hai, toh main Arjun hoon aur Mahesh Bhatt Krishna hai"*' (Delete that dialogue which you have on me in your play. Take it out where you say: "If life is a battlefield of Kurukshetra, and me the questioning Arjun, then Mahesh Bhatt is my Krishna"').

'No, that will remain . . . remain as it is because that's the truth. It is from the heart,' I replied. 'I will not remove it under any circumstances.'

Our views were different. Our opinions clashed. On all issues such as corruption, Hindus, Muslims, Modi, Congress, he took a firm stand. So, did I. It led to friction. Suddenly, we drifted apart.

My answering back must have shocked him because he was not very happy about it. But I must clarify here, that it had nothing to do with my respect for him. I have always thought of him as my guru, my guide, my father in cinema. He will remain one. Then in June 2017, I was commissioned by Republic TV for a series of interviews for the show: *Anupam Kher's People*. Being one of the most evolved persons in the film industry, I did interview him for one episode on 1 August 2017. That brought our relationship back to an even keel. We talked of old times, of how I had once read his palm—the art of palmistry having been taught to me by my grandfather—and had predicted: 'Bhatt saab, one day you will quit making films.' And he had done just that for all these years. Today, he is making one . . . only a daughter could have made him come back. That day, as we sat over a cup of tea after the shoot was over, he became very emotional. And so did I. I found myself becoming teary-eyed. He hugged me, held my hand and started singing, the following lyrics from the song of the singer Jagjit Singh:

> *Log zaalim hain, har ik baat ka taana dengey*
> *Baaton baaton mein mera zair bhi le aingey*
> *Unki baaton ka zara sab hi asar mat lena*
> *Warna chehre ke taassur se samaj jaingey.*

In fact, Mahesh Bhatt is my *habib*, my *hafeez*, my *humkadam*, my *rehnuma*, my elder brother, my father figure, my mentor, my financier, my guide, my . . . I can carry on and on.

Excuse my digression, but here I must talk about Khwaja Ahmad Abbas, with whom I shared a very special relationship. K. A. Abbas was the author of the column 'Last Page' for 40 long years, first for *The Bombay Chronicle* and then for the *Blitz*. He also made and directed films and wrote novels and screenplays. I had first met him in Chandigarh, when he had come to see Bertolt Brecht's play *The Threepenny Opera* (directed by Amal Allana) in which I was the lead actor. He reviewed it in his column in glowing terms. One day, he invited me to his apartment in Juhu which was close by my place and said that he wanted me in his new film, *Ek Aadmi*. I had great respect for him. His house was filled with books. He was wonderful, kind-hearted and a big literary person. He said: 'It's my last film and I would like you to portray me.'

'Abbas saab,' I deferred, 'I would love to do it but I have no time as I am already heavily committed and doing three to four shifts a day and at times, I even have to sleep in the studios.'

'You just give me one hour, twice or thrice a week, in the mornings. There is only one outdoor stint to be done in Shimla, your hometown and that too for just three days. That will be a big help as this film means a lot to me,' he pleaded.

I just couldn't say no to him. Shooting started and somehow, we managed to finish the film. But when I saw the rushes, I was horrified. The film had no beginning or end. It was just a jumbled mess. I was really saddened to see his life's work reduced to this. Once finished, no distributor was ready to buy it. Even Doordarshan—an autonomous public service broadcaster founded by the Government of India—did not want anything to do with it. I have no idea whether anybody ever saw it or not.

Then on 1 June 1987, I got the news that he had passed away. I went to his apartment and saw that as per the ritual his body was lying on the floor with a white sheet covering it. He looked peaceful. There were flies flitting around his face. I was very upset and went to the other room to call someone from the family who could watch over the body and protect it from the flies. But no one, it seemed, wanted to take that responsibility. And then, I was shocked to see that all his books, a rather large and valuable collection had disappeared overnight. All stolen or taken away.

Previously when Abbas saab was in the hospital, I went to visit him one day. He handed me a hand-written note which read: 'Will you finish the dubbing of my film? I'm dying now. At least, finish the dubbing.' The same day, I cancelled my shooting schedules and went straight to the dubbing theatre. That evening, I met him again, and after taking his hand in mine, I said: 'I have finished it.' He became misty-eyed.

It was around the same time that Mahesh Bhatt offered me *Daddy*—his daughter Pooja's launch film. It was about a failed, alcoholic father, who is desperately seeking to transform himself into a success to redeem himself in his daughter's eyes. I consider it as one of my top performances for which I was recognised with my first National Award. Throughout the film, I used a corduroy brown coat, brown trousers and a black shirt. As mentioned earlier, I had seen Balwant Gargi, always dressed in a brown corduroy jacket and the famous Greek American director, Elia Kazan, too donned a similar brown corduroy jacket when he came to India for the sixth International Film Festival in January 1977. Naturally, I had come to associate the corduroys with success.

Since I was shooting with Abbas saab in the mornings, I would report for *Daddy* about two-three hours late. My senior from the National School of Drama, Manohar Singh, one of the greatest stage actors that we had who also hailed from Shimla, too was in the film and would get very impatient and upset with me, as he would have to wait for me to report. Manohar bhai, as we called him from the NSD days, was a brilliant actor and very professional. I recall, when he would look back in anger in the Feroz Shah Road auditorium on the third floor of the NSD, it was electrifying. I, like many other students, would never miss his plays come what may. One morning, I learnt that Manohar bhai's father had passed away and he had a performance that evening. I went to see the play. It was unbelievable to see him on the stage. There was no difference. In fact, he was even better that evening.

At every phase, I have been very fortunate that certain people have come into my life and imparted a great deal of knowledge. Without them, my life would have been so much poorer. Many of them have been older than me and much wiser but I was able to form a great connection with them. Looking back at the previous generations, I see that they lived their life to the fullest and were generous to share their experiences and resources. They were true and real and not cosmetic or pretentious just for the sake of appearances.

My relationship with the larger than life actor-producer-director Feroz Khan bears a narration as well.

In 1997-98, Feroz Khan had decided to make a film, *Prem Aggan*, which he had written and was going to produce and direct himself so as to launch his son Fardeen and Rita Kothari's daughter, Meghna. He offered me a role. I went over to his impressive house. It was a very dramatic start to our meeting. I was led in with great respect. He came in a few minutes later, dressed in a green colour lungi-kurta and made me sit across the table. As he sat down, he took out a revolver and put it on the table and he said: '*Kya piyoge?*' (What will you drink?)

As I mentioned at the beginning of this book, I look at life from a comic point of view. *Is he trying to scare me?* I thought. On the contrary, in reality, I was amused, for nobody had shown me a revolver to discuss a role for a film.

I was still in my thoughts when he said: 'I am going to give you the most stylish role of your life. In my next film, you are the girl's father—Jai Kumar. It is Fardeen's film. Brother, you have to decide.'

'I am doing the film. Simple,' I answered. I was still looking at the revolver.

'Oh, sorry.' he said and took the gun away. 'Now decide.'

'It has nothing to do with the gun. I am doing the film,' I replied, wanting to make it clear, in my own way that I had agreed not because of any pressure . . . not because I was scared of his revolver. Little did he know that in any case, I was not saying no to any film those days. Moreover, Feroz was certainly a very stylish director and it was every big star's dream to work with him. He was the original cowboy of the Indian film industry. He liked to be a phenomenon and wanted the world to look at him as such.

Shooting started. Watching him on the set, I felt that he was grand and stylish, which at times came across as very comical. He would lose his temper without any reason. Anyone could become his target. For example, one day, I got delayed because my costume designer did not get my trousers. After having waited for me for some time, I think he ran out of patience and came to my dressing room. I was in my underwear, tie and shirt, waiting for the trousers to arrive. Seeing me he said: 'Why are you not on the sets brother? What the hell is going on?'

'My clothes are not ready. I can't come out like this,' I said.

'I don't care. Be on the sets.'

I said: 'Sir, I can't come without a trouser.' How I controlled my laughter in comparison to his anger, I don't know. He vented out his anger by calling some assistant and firing him mercilessly.

A part of the film was to be shot in Sydney, Australia. Kirron accompanied me. Feroz was with his girlfriend. One day, we had an outdoor shoot by a roadside. Kirron had gone out shopping. Feroz was doing a sequence with Fardeen and Meghna. I was sitting across the road reading John Grisham' Cold Harbour. Feroz's girlfriend came and sat next to me and asked softly: 'What are you reading?' Since the shot was on and complete silence was to be maintained, I showed her the cover of the book.

'Is it good?' she enquired.

I made a gesture with my right thumb and forefinger to say: 'Very good.'

After the shot was over, he came to me and sort of stood on top of me and said: 'You were talking.'

I said: 'Yes.'

'Why?' he asked.

'Your girlfriend asked me a question about this book and I answered,' I replied.

'Don't give me this bullshit,' he screamed at the top of his voice. Everyone in the unit was stunned into silence, including some Australians who had been gathered for a crowd scene. But Feroz was not satisfied and the drama was getting uglier. He then turned to me again and said: 'This is what they teach you in drama schools? No professionalism? This is what Alkazi taught you? Don't you realise that I am paying you 70 grand?' His reference to my acting guru Alkazi, was the last straw for me.

By now, I had had enough of his crap: 'Yes, you are giving me 70 grand because you are required to give me that, not because you are doing me a favour. Feroz Khan, to hell with your film. I quit,' I said and cursed some more in Punjabi and walked off the set.

He was shocked and so was his unit. No one could believe the fact that I had answered back. Perhaps nobody had done that to him before, so he was not used to it.

Back at the hotel, I told Kirron about the incident and said we are leaving . . . going back tomorrow itself. Then, I called up my manager, Shetty, in Bombay. I knew it was well past midnight back home and he must be fast asleep. 'Mr Shetty, I have quit Feroz Khan's film.'

Without even asking me why or what happened, he said: 'Sir, only two-three days work is left. Why don't you finish it and come back.'

That was all. The moment he said that, all my anger disappeared at the practicality of his thought, and I said to Kirron: 'The chap has no idea . . . doesn't even know what all has happened here and he just says, "Complete the work and return". Little did I know that he already knew what had transpired.

The next day, I reported for shooting in my usual frame of mind. While everyone was looking at me, with some surprise and amazement, Feroz came to me and said: 'Brother, some *sher da puttar* (son of a lion) you are. A lion stood up to a lion. This is what I love about you.' Then he hugged me.

We were friends again. We finished the film and came back.

Even today I feel that Feroz Khan was a humane person. A great guy, whom I liked and in spite of that incident, I was very fond of him. Many years later, when I directed my first film, *Om Jai Jagadish*, one of the reasons of taking Fardeen was that in my heart of hearts, I felt that I should not have answered him back that day in Sydney. I remember and appreciate the fact that in the entire altercation, Fardeen did not interfere. Then one day, when we were shooting *Om Jai Jagadish* in New Zealand, I said to Fardeen: 'I want to thank you for something which is very important for me.'

He asked: 'For what?'

'That day, when your father and I had a fight in Sydney during the shooting, you never intervened. If you had, I would have really felt weaker and smaller. So, I want to thank you for keeping out of it.'

He laughed and said: 'My father had taught me to be professional on a film set. The altercation was between the actor and director. Not between any guy and my father.'

Feroz Khan passed away on 27 April 2009 in Bangalore. I felt sad. As I have said earlier, he and Vinod Khanna—who passed away on 27 April 2017—were great personalities and larger than life. There is nobody like them today. I do miss them!

I think an actor's most important job is to focus . . . to concentrate. And then any work done with passion and sincerity, has its own energy, its own intoxication. It will naturally create excellent work. During those years, I was loaded with films and doing all kinds of different work—work which I did not enjoy. But I was doing it and signing every film I got so that I would never be without work. But I would regain my creative sanity when I would put on that beard on the sets of Mahesh Bhatt's film, *Daddy*. In the movie, I had to play the role of an alcoholic father when I was just 32 years and hardly touched liquor in real life. Looking back, I don't know how I did those roles. Coming to think of it, I have played father to everybody. I can't think of any actor or actress of those days to whom I did not play father to. That must be a record in itself.

I think this was because B. V. Pradhan in *Saaransh* happened when I was just about 28 or so, and before that when I did plays with Amal Allana, I was mostly playing the older man's roles. For example, when I was acting in Eugene O'Neill's *Long Day's Journey into Night*, I was playing James Tyrone Sr, a 65-year-old man. I think my theatre background enriched my understanding of age, layered it and textured it with such a depth of emotions that I have lived my life to the fullest. I am also spurred on to reach higher because I have an equal fascination for dreaming. Whether it can be attributed to the actor in me or the person in me, I do not know. Both coexist in the same frame.

22

YASH CHOPRA—MY ADDICTION

I vividly remember when I first laid my eyes on Yash Chopra for the first time. It was in 1972 when I was in still a college student in Shimla. We found out that a film shooting was in full swing on the railway tracks beyond Kiarighat, about 25 km from Shimla. It was the shooting of *Daag: A Poem of Love* which was Yash Chopra's first film under his own banner—Yash Raj Films. He had parted ways with his elder brother, B. R. Chopra, after making five lavishly mounted films under the BR Films banner. Those five were: *Dhool Ka Phool* which had Rajendra Kumar, Mala Sinha, Nanda, Ashok Kumar and Manmohan Krishan in the main cast, *Dharamputra* with Shashi Kapoor, Mala Sinha, Rehman and Ashok Kumar, the multi-starrer *Waqt* with Sunil Dutt, Raaj Kumar, Shashi Kapoor, Sadhana, Sharmila Tagore, Rehman and Balraj Sahni, *Aadmi Aur Insaan* which had Dharmendra, Saira Banu, Feroz Khan and Mumtaz in stellar roles and *Ittefaq* with Rajesh Khanna and Nanda.

The *Daag* unit was scouting for young boys and girls for a student's crowd scene with Sharmila Tagore for picturisation of the song: 'Hawa chale kaise, Naa tu jaane, Naa mai jaanu, Jaane wohi jaane. . .' (How does the breeze blow, I know not, nor do you. Only He does). My brother Raju was selected. I was not. I noticed that Yash Chopra, attired in a jacket and his hallmark polo golf cap, was the most energetic person on the sets, running from one place to another while doing multiple jobs at the same time—holding the microphone, giving instructions to the spot boys, discussing the scene with Sharmila Tagore, briefing the cameraman Kay Gee, etc.

We also heard that the next day, the unit would be shooting another song in the grounds of Chail Palace Hotel, about 45 km from Shimla. We landed at that location where the song, *Ni main yaar manana ni, chahe log boliyan bole* . . . (I have to win a friend, even if others talk) was being picturised with Padma Khanna against the backdrop of a group. Along with all the bystanders, I myself was in the crowd, watching the shooting. Years later, after I too had become a film actor, I showed Yash Chopra a frozen shot of mine from that song, which marked my film debut. It just so happened that because of the round trolley shot, the crowd was included, and I happened to be in the frame. My presence in that shot made me a part of the historic Yash Raj Films.

I have already mentioned earlier about my initial meeting with Yash Chopra and his promise to sign me when there was an important role befitting me. Hence, when he started work on *Vijay* sometime in 1977 or so, which featured an ensemble star cast comprising Rajesh Khanna, Hema Malini, Rishi Kapoor, Anil Kapoor, Meenakshi Seshadri, Raj Babbar, Moushumi Chatterjee and others, he called me and said: 'I had promised to give you something big. In my new film *Vijay*, there is a very important role which was to be done by Dilip Kumar, but for some personal reasons, he is not doing it. Now, I want you to do that role—play Hema Malini's father and grandfather to Rishi Kapoor and Anil Kapoor.' *God, what a challenge*, I thought to myself. But this role was a significant milestone for me on two accounts. First, I got to step into Dilip saab's shoes. And second, Yash Chopra, who, during the making of *Mashaal*, had not given me a role, thinking it was too insignificant and not befitting me, had now thought of giving me such an important one.

This movie was the start of a great friendship between me and him. He was undoubtedly a typical larger-than-life, large-hearted, Punjabi, who loved life. A brilliant film-maker—affectionate, warm and loving—and for me, he was to soon become an addiction.

Vijay was shot in Hyderabad's Krishna Oberoi, a part of which was under construction then. It was here that I faced a life-threatening situation when I got stuck in a lift for nearly 40 minutes.

While the unit members went around looking for me, I was banging the steel lift which was not yet equipped with an alarm. The more I banged, the more everyone thought that it was the construction noise. Mercifully, an assistant director who was looking for me, . . . and had the door open. It was great working with Yash Chopra and for my role as Yodh Raj Bhatia, I won the Filmfare Award for Best Supporting Actor. Thereafter, I was in every film that Yash Chopra made—*Chandni, Lamhe, Parampara, Darr, Veer-Zaara* and his last film, *Jab Tak Hai Jaan*, which was released in 2012.

On the sets, while making a film, Yash Chopra was like a king who would treat every actor royally. In fact, the king made everyone feel like a king. His organisation and arrangements would be top class—the best hotels, the best cars, the best food. Everybody would eat together like one large family. While shooting, he would be like a man possessed. He would shoot every scene with complete passion. If it was not with passion, it was not there. He had an amazing sense of story. For every shot, he would say: '*Jaan daal de*' (Put your life into it). I don't think his films were technically more brilliant than some of the top films of their times, but each one had more heart and soul in them. With his boundless energy and zest, he created an aura that brought out the best in the actors on the set. Just look at *Chandni* or *Lamhe* (which was a little ahead of its time) or even his earlier films like *Dhool Ka Phool, Waqt, Deewar, Kabhi Kabhie, or Trishul*. All these films are legendary. Each one is more beautiful than the other and it is evident that each one has been made with so much love, passion and sincerity. Unbelievable!

I love people. I thrive in the company of others. This is cinema's greatest legacy. It creates links, a web of associations that feeds and fuels mutually and builds great sustainability. Ingmar Bergman used to travel with his actors and his unit for the whole year and in that space, he would make the film. Yash Chopra was somewhat like that.

But more than being in his films, the greatest joy was being with him at his home, which for me became a second home. Our weekly ritual was that every Sunday, Kirron and I used to have brunch with him and his wife, Pam. It was like a weekly family get-together—

intimate, cosy and relaxed. We would play games, particularly cricket, or listen to music, particularly *DDLJ* music, which the more we listened to the more we enjoyed. We saw both the boys, Aditya and Uday, grow up and watched Aadi write his first film. Every now and then, we enjoyed evenings of live performances organised by him and Pam. I met and listened to Ustad Nusrat Fateh Ali Khan, Ustad Fateh Ali Khan, Shiv-Hari and so many others at his house. The *mehfils* were outstanding. And Pam is still the best hostess whose circle one can have the privilege to be part of.

Soon after he built the YRF Studio and after Aadi successfully directed *DDLJ*, Yash Chopra was able to relax and had plenty of spare time. So, I would visit him almost every other day, if not every morning, and we would have breakfast together. He would communicate freely with me and openly share what he had on his mind. He would tell me things like 'I am depressed today', 'I am feeling very low' and 'I don't like meeting anyone'. There were even times when he would stop talking to people and just go and sleep. I think, unknowingly, I had adopted the role of a psychiatrist for he would tell me anything that weighed on him or was bothering him about those close to him—his family and his near and dear ones. He granted me that position as well. He showed me by his actions that he felt a deep sense of confidence in me.

One day when I was at his home, I teased Aadi and said: '*Aadi, tu itni filmein bana raha hain lekin mereko koi film mein nahi leta*' (Aadi, you are making so many films, but you don't take me in any).

I will never forget how Aadi replied. He said: 'You know what AK, the problem with you is that you are in every film that is being made. And if we also take you in our film, my film will look jaded.'

I was very upset with Aadi for saying that. Later, I thought that *Aadi loves me very much, but he is a practical person. Perhaps, I was not ready to hear the truth that was spoken to me so blatantly to my face.* More than me, Yash Chopra was upset: 'What does he mean by saying that?' he asked. 'Jack Nicholson has done so much work. Do his films look jaded? Or Al Pacino? Rubbish. Nonsense. This is a new style of telling people no.'

Then, in 2011-12, when I got the role of Dr Cliff Patel in David O. Russel's prestigious film, *Silver Linings Playbook*, I called up Yash Chopra from Toronto to give him the good news. He congratulated me. He was very happy, and suddenly said in his typical Punjabi (a language we always conversed in): '*Ek mint hold kar*' (Hold for a minute). He dialled Aadi's number from the other phone and said: 'Oye, Anupam Kher has got *Silver Linings Playbook* with Robert De Niro.' He kept the phone and said to me: '*Dus dita behen de takey nu*'—his special sentence for endearment. The film was a great commercial and critical success. It received eight Academy Award and four Golden Globe Award nominations. I received much critical appreciation and was noticed in a big way. I have written about the making of this film and my role in it, in detail, later in this volume.

The worst part of being in this profession is that sooner or later, one becomes redundant at some stage of their career. The fall from grace can be sudden and dramatic and only few can adjust to the changed circumstances. The history of cinema is full of such stories. This can happen because of a number of reasons—either because your time is over or age has caught up with you or because your ideas don't resonate with the current generation. Or simply, it could be a matter of running out of luck. The only way out *perhaps*— yes *perhaps*—is to reinvent yourself and evolve constantly to keep up with change, since change is the only certainty and accepting it is the best way to make peace with it. This maturity and vision lead one to a better YOU, a new YOU, that most beautiful you in YOU. Though possible, it is easier said than done! Many have done it. Many more will do it. The survivors, the fighters are the true winners.

Yash Chopra was one such example. A highly thoughtful and inspired person who was active even at 80. He was encouraging like a father—always extending himself. I recall calling him from London once, where I was shooting for a film, when he said: '*Halli, bahut kaam karna hain yaar* . . . Jab Tak Hai Jaan *da naya gana wi shoot karna hai*' (Have still got to do a lot of work . . . have to still shoot a song of *Jab Tak Hai Jaan*). It was his last film which he was directing after a gap of eight years or so, to coincide with the 50th anniversary of his career in films. He was still to add some scenes from the Swiss Alps to the title song, but that never came to pass as he was diagnosed with dengue on 13 October 2012. I had spoken to him a couple of days earlier and he had said: 'You just come back soon now. I miss you.'

'Yes, as soon as this shooting schedule is over, I will be back with you,' I promised.

But I was not destined to meet him for a week later, he passed away. I couldn't accept it.

At his *Terawi*—the 13th day ritual of prayers—I was asked by the family to pay my respects to him. I was the only one besides Shah Rukh Khan and two other people from the family. Everyone was aware of my relations with him and thought that I would have the maximum to say about him. But because of my deep and acute sense of loss, I became very emotional and made a complete fool of myself. What should have been my eulogy was a total disaster. I couldn't sort out my thoughts to pay tribute to the man who meant so much to me. My words could not convey what I had lost. No words will ever suffice.

Unfortunately, besides Yash Chopra, three other important people left me and this world around the same time—my secretary Bhaskar Shetty, my father, Pandit Pushkar Nath Kher, and Sister Dolores, the Spanish nun who was the principal at the Dilkush Special School. Each one of them in their own ways were my anchors, my reference points of life. Suddenly I was bereft. To lose four people so dear to me in a span of just one year was more than I could handle.

Every time I had a problem, I would go to Sister Dolores (whose rosary I loved) and say: 'Sister, I am feeling rather restless and uneasy.'

Her usual response would be: 'Anupan (which she thought was my name), I have prayed for you to Jesus. You will be fine. Don't worry.'

In her will, she left her rosary to me!

If I had any issue, I would call my father in Shimla. His voice would comfort me. It was the soothing balm I needed at that moment.

Bhaskar Shetty was my secretary for six years and was a wonderful human being. Actually, I never considered him my secretary because he was not like other film secretaries. He was more of an educated manager. He was family. And one night when I was busy shooting for *Jab Tak Hai Jaan* in London, I got a call from Shetty's number. I answered the phone and asked: 'Why are you calling me so late. It's 2.30 in the morning there?'

'This is his son Varun. Papa is no more. He was watching a film on the television and he passed away,' came the sad answer.

Four people went away from my life, in quick succession. This took a heavy toll on me and I slipped into a depression.

In early 2015, I divulged to the media about my battle with depression and how I overcame it. My main objective was to spread awareness among the public about mental health issues.

I was grappling with depression and anxiety. I did not want to cope with this under cover of darkness. In my opinion, I feel that celebrities and people in positions of power should be trendsetters, not just in fashion but also in significant social and personal causes. We should not only handle our own problems with honesty but also aid others who have doubts in their mind regarding mental illnesses by being open and upfront about such issues. Unfortunately, too often people think that successful people are not supposed to have any issues or problems. This is not true at all. Just because they have a fleet of cars, live in air-conditioned houses and are affluent does not mean they do not endure trauma or undergo bouts of depression. For me, it all started with sleeplessness. Since I was unable to get sound sleep for a month, I went to get my eyes checked and that was when the eye-specialist, Dr Ryan D'souza said to me that I should consult a psychiatrist. 'Your problem is not related to eyes . . . you are suffering from depression . . . you . . .'

I interrupted pompously: A pschiatrist? Why should I go to a psychiatrist? . . . I am the most positive thinking and optimist person . . . I have also written a life-coaching bestseller. I deliver lectures on positivity.'

He still almost pleaded to meet his psychiatrist friend, Dr Vishal Sawant.

Dr Sawant's clinic comprised different departments—Eyes, ENT, Dentistry, etc. As soon as I entered the clinic lobby, patients and/ or their attendants recognised me and each was curious to know what was I there for. 'I am going to meet the psychiatrist,' I answered. Some were baffled as I looked quite healthy to them. On meeting Dr Sawant I presented him a copy of my book and before he could ask me anything, I said: 'Dr, before you ask me anything about my problems, I would like to ask you about yours. He took me seriously and spoke to me patiently, listing his numerous problems, for nearly an hour. I talked to him and seemingly solved each one of them. I even left my mobile number with him to contact me in case need be.

As I was leaving after my soliloquy about life and living, I noticed that he was not paying attention to me and was scribbling something on a notepad. I enquired, 'what are you writing doc?'

His brief answer was: 'Your medication . . . you have manic depression . . . you push things away and want to move on without addressing issues.

I followed that advice and the diagnosis revealed that I was suffering frm hidden depression. A lot of people, who could be suffering from any kind of mental ailment, are often unaware of it. Many of us have internal issues, but in India, this is a taboo subject because of the stigma attached to any form of mental issues, be it anxiety, depression or something more severe like schizophrenia or split personality disorder. In India, moving towards a nuclear family set-up has played a major role in giving rise to such problems. Earlier, we used to live in joint families and talk to our family members about the problems that bothered us. We also used to speak to our milkman and newspaper delivery boy and many others and could freely discuss matters that affected us. Now, we hardly interact one on one with each other.

I envisage a clear role for the government to step in more actively, especially in spreading awareness and tackling the problem at the root. I see a therapist once a month and over time, I have suggested several friends of mine to seek professional help if necessary. We now live in a world where people pretend to be brave. Unfortunately, the human mind is very fragile. We do get hurt at times and if we don't tend to it, it may lead to bigger problems. When faced with a problem, any problem, talk about it to loved ones, family and friends. Share it with your parents because they are the people who will never judge you. My sincere advice is to not bottle it up in your heart. I have constantly encouraged people to overcome depression and not shy away from coming out in the open about the issue. I am happy to say that people have been reacting positively to my message.

I have also observed that the excessive use of technology and social media has led to people becoming insensitive to each other's thoughts and feelings. I declared: 'Loneliness is not attractive if it is affecting your mind. We are all dealing with a lot of machines these days. There are mobiles and the Internet. The human touch is missing.'

As mentioned earlier, we used to live in a small house in Shimla and we used to frequently bump into each other. My grandfather would say that whenever you are about to bang into someone, then just hug each other. But nowadays, the situation has drastically changed. People want to be left alone with their modern-day gizmos. Even in crowded places, everyone seems to be obsessed with his or her smartphone.

Sadly, in today's world, a beautiful scenery is not just to be seen and enjoyed. It is meant to be captured for Instagram. The youngsters are stressed because their pictures on Facebook do not have enough likes.

From time to time, I have also prepared special scripts and shot small duration videos with special messages which I feel are important to convey encouragement and support to people. I can't say it's my mission to do so nor do I want to use any such term, but I just feel like reaching out and spreading the message.

For example, I produced this two-minute video on depression, only as an attempt to create awareness about the most silent and perhaps, the biggest disease that is spreading at an alarming speed all over the world today. With it, I also sent out a message to all those who watched it, to forward the same to as many friends, family members and other people as possible, so as to create a ripple effect with ever-widening circles.

I hope it helped some. My message was simple:

When you live under the burden of pretence for long, it is difficult to identify the real essence of life. We are all born equal and in the first few years, we radiate life's energy, passionately. We are filled with light and love. Children up to the age of five or so laugh, cry, love, fight from the heart. There is nothing fake about them. They express exactly what they feel! And then as we grow, we learn to hide our emotions and fake them. And how effortlessly we train ourselves to do that. On broken relationships, on lost companionships, we often say, 'It's okay! I have moved on.' Exam grades, the shape of your body, salary figures, all these are top priorities in our lives. Instead of learning from these and emerging stronger, loneliness pushes us into an endless abyss of hopelessness and extinguishes all positivity within us. I have experienced the darkness of depression closely. And can assure you that if this feeling is shared with a loved one, you will develop the courage to fight the depression within you.

If you are unable to fake an emotion, don't fake it. If you are suffocated by loneliness, speak to someone; reach out to a loved one. You don't need to fit in! You are not alone. Together, we will find the hope we need. All we must do is offer and receive a helping hand!

Love life, live life!

I wanted to open up about the various issues mentioned above . . . about coping with life and living. Let people, who know me as an actor . . . as an artiste . . . who think that my life is all glamour and glitz, know the truth—the *real* me behind the *reel* me. I wanted to share with them my experiences of meeting and learning from the many people I encountered over the years. Perhaps my opening up may help someone somewhere, I thought. I spoke about it to my friend Ashok Chopra, who by then had created quite a name for himself in the publishing world and published the who's who in the field of arts, literature, politics, finance, sports and what not. He just said: 'Let's do the book. And do it fast!' His instigation and guidance were what made the book *The Best Thing about You Is YOU!* The rest is history.

Published in January 2012 and released by Amitabh Bachchan in Mumbai and then launched at the Jaipur Literature Festival, the book has been a huge success and is still selling. It has gone into 22 reprints and has been translated into numerous languages. Among the celebrities, Oprah Winfrey, the renowned talk show host and philanthropist from the USA, wrote: 'What a powerful title. I believe it.'

For writing it, I did not consult any books. In fact, I have not read any self-help book or books about how to be successful and happy. I only know that the best thing about you is YOU because I strongly feel that there is a power in each one of us that can actually drive us to success. I have been fond of reading books since childhood; the first book I read was *Mother* by Maxim Gorky and since then, it has become an obsessive habit. As an actor, I have used my craft over a period of time but at least, in this book, I have used nothing but the experiences of my life.

I have been as open and honest in baring myself, in telling my life's story without deliberately hurting anyone. By sharing my experiences and revealing the nuances that have shaped and transformed my personality, I open a window to my world to initiate a dialogue.

23

DAVID DHAWAN—THE KING OF COMEDY

$\mathcal{D}$avid Dhawan was the editor of *Saaransh*. We have been friends since those early days. I would often visit him at his residence on Carter Road. Our bonding happened because we were more or less in the same category—we were both trying to make it. When he became a director in 1988-89 with *Taaqatwar* which had Sanjay Dutt, Govinda, Anita Raj and Neelam Kothari in the main cast, he gave me the role of the municipal officer, Sharma, who was known as the 'demolition man'. The film was not a great success at the box office, but I liked working with him. He always had a very jovial, happy nature. He's one person who lives without any stress and is always positive about all situations in life. It was at this stage that his friendship with Govinda started and the two went on to make a string of very successful films.

Three years later, in 1992, and with five films in his kitty, he started shooting *Shola Aur Shabnam*, a romantic comedy with Govinda and Divya Bharti in the lead. I played the role of Major Inder Mohan Lathi. It was one of the funniest films I have acted in and as was expected, it became David's first super hit. This success was followed by more success and he made another 35 films, with *Judwa 2* being the latest one, released two years back. I have been in almost all of them.

What I love about David is that he loves me. And when people love you back, they become your favourite people. That naturally makes it easy to work with them. Also, being a born optimist, he is very encouraging. There are very few people who can recognise the inner self of another person and can genuinely appreciate and feel proud of the achievements of a friend. For example, from a certain point of view, I do come across as an arrogant man because sometimes, when you speak your mind to people, they mistake it for arrogance. Initially, I would get surprised when people would say: '*Yaar, humne suna hai tum bade arrogant ho. Tumse dar lagta hain*' (We learn that you are very arrogant. It scares us). That's because my perception about myself is that I am a very kind, nice and happy-go-lucky person. But I also saw their point of view and realised they were right. On the other side is David, who has seen me not only as a friend but also as a professional. He once said to me: 'You are the best. You have left everybody . . . all of us behind. Look, where you have reached. You need guts to do what you have done . . . the risks you have taken. Normally, people are frightened and they take very careful steps. You have always reinvented yourself and now you are sitting in New York doing international films and television serials.' Both views are important for me. They show me the mirror and tell me what I am, where I stand, what I am doing wrong and what I am doing right.

Professionally, having known him for over three decades, I know that I can work with David anytime and anywhere. Personally, I have the same relationship with him as I had with Yash Chopra—going to have breakfast at his home, talking and discussing various issues and subjects and being open about so many aspects of life. People don't realise that bonding over food is so very important. It gives us an opportunity to meet up regularly, exchange views, discuss personal matters or just have a *gup-shup*. We also don't carry the burden of always having intellectual conversations. In any case, this can't be planned. They just happen organically. It is very artificial to decide to engage in an intellectual conversation. It's not possible. In any case, what is the definition of an 'intellectual discussion'? Just because David makes typical masala films that doesn't mean that my conversations with him are not intellectual. Intellectualism does not mean discussing existentialism or abstract art. To me, intellectualism means anything that touches your heart. It can be anything and everything which is real and engaging. Those who pretend and behave like someone else don't like themselves. That's why they want to be somebody else.

David is the same person who used to get very impatient with me and throw me out of the editing room during the making of *Saaransh*. And he is the same David who would then sit with me patiently and narrate a story which he wanted to shoot. The same David who once said: 'I will not make a film without you.' And he has stuck to his word. I do know that there are times when a producer tells David: 'Don't take Anupam. He is too expensive. We can have the same role done by another actor for a lower fee.' He always says a categorical 'No'.

I have a feeling, rightly or wrongly, that David also feels emotionally stronger with me on the sets.

Because he is a professional editor, and I would say a very capable one, he can edit a film while shooting and has a great sense of what works and what does not. He does not make pedantic, boring stuff but rather creates the sort of cinema where you can leave your brains and logic behind at home and just go and enjoy his films. I have often been asked as to why is he so successful? My reply is candid: 'Because there must be some essence in his films.' His success also comes from the fact that he is very impatient with wasting footage. While making a film, he constantly says: 'Don't drag it! Don't drag it! It will not work!' He is a ruthless editor and cuts major chunks. I recall a sequence in *Shola Aur Shabnam*, where I, as Major Lathi, was having a conversation with my father which was also played by me. I thought it was a fantastic comic scene, but David cut out the entire bit from the film. Naturally, I was very upset and questioned him. His reply was simple: 'It was not working in the story.' He has this firmness intermingled with politeness. He knows that as the director, he is the captain of the ship. He gets what he wants, but without ruffling any feathers.

However, of late, particularly during the making of *Main Tera Hero*, which had Nargis Fakhri, Varun Dhawan and Ileana D'Cruz in the lead, I noticed that he has developed a habit of getting impatient on the sets. And then, when *Judwaa 2* was being made in 2017, with Varun Dhawan in a double role and with Jacqueline Fernandez and

Tapsee Pannu as his heroines, he had become even more impatient.

Sometimes I feel that this is because of over directing his son. He does not want to wrong him. David should relax. Varun will be a star for a long time.

24

SOORAJ BARJATYA—GOD'S OWN CHILD

Grandfather: Tarachand Barjatya.
Father: Rajkumar Barjatya.
The Empire: 71-year-old Rajshri Productions, makers of
43 films in the first 42 years itself.

A pedigreed lineage can become a liability but Sooraj Barjatya, like Aditya Chopra in Yash Raj Films, has carried forward his legacy with great aplomb into the twentieth century and beyond.

At the age of just 20, Sooraj was an assistant on Mahesh Bhatt's *Saaransh*. The first job that was given to him as an assistant was by me. On the first day of the shoot, I saw him standing in a corner and realised that being the son of the film's producer, nobody was giving him work. So, I said: '*Sooraj idhar aao. Mere dialogue ki file upar table par reh gayi hai. Please usey mere liye le aao*' (Sooraj come here. I have left my dialogue's file upstairs in my make-up room. Please bring it for me).

To this day, 35 years later, he still remembers it and says: 'That day, I felt important.'

He is a soft-spoken and an unusually quiet man and in many ways, an introvert, I would say. But who knew then that one day, this young producer's son would not only take over the reins of the Rajshri empire but expand it beyond limits and give one of the biggest hits in the history of the Hindi cinema—*Hum Aapke Hain Koun..!*

Sooraj writes his own scripts and once he was ready with *Hum Aapke Hain Koun..!*, he called me for a narration. Those days, I was immensely busy with back-to-back shootings, so I asked him: 'Sooraj, how much time do you need?'

'About 4 to 5 hours,' he replied.

I was shocked by that reply. What is wrong with him, I thought to myself. Why is he asking for 4 to 5 hours just for the narration of a story he has written for his next film? There is no way I can give that time.

In the film industry, we actors, are all used to narrations which last for about 15 to 20 minutes or a maximum of half an hour. The director comes with the writer and says that in the film this and this happens, this is your role and when you come in, there is music, a song here, who are in the main lead, etc. etc. At the best of times, there is no script. Dialogues are given on the spot. Of the over 530 films that I have done so far, I don't think I got scripts for more than say 30 or maybe, for a maximum of 35 films. We sign merely on narrations.

Sooraj narrated the script for four hours, covering every single detail that included my role in it, every close up, every long shot, every trolley shot, every song that was going to be picturised, which he sang himself for me so that I could get a feel of the entire project. By the end of it, I was mesmerised. Though I am a rather impatient person with somewhat limited attention span, the way he narrated the story made me lose the sense of time. Also, I completely forgot about the shoot I had to go for. I had never come across a director who had done so much detailing on a script before the shoot itself. And, mind you, *Hum Aapke Hain Koun..!* is not a thriller! It's not an event-oriented film. It's a treatment-oriented film. He had created scenes of weddings, of family togetherness through a unique treatment and punctuated them with the most beautiful song and dance compositions. The fact is that I saw the entire film on the day he narrated it to me.

Sooraj Barjatya is God's child. Yes, he is 'God's Own Child'. He dons his mantle lightly. He is like the Buddha—very genuine, pure, humble, courteous, completely sorted out and focused. There is nothing artificial or superficial about him. And that too in an industry where courtesies are drenched in pretentiousness, where humility and humbleness are just a facade. When pushed, he does crack a 'joke', once in a while, but rather dry ones, most of which are humourless. In fact, it's more of an apology of a joke. Hence, I have taken it upon myself to crack a dirty joke in his presence or litter a sentence purposely with a rustic and an earthy four-letter Punjabi word. That's when he responds, though still feeling shy. That's my way of lightening the atmosphere on the sets and as mentioned earlier, I have done that with Amitabh Bachchan and even with Dilip Kumar. I wish I could have done that with Raaj Kumar too! For me, one-to-one relationships have been, and still are, very important. On the sets, Sooraj is absolutely in command and at the helm of affairs. He knows exactly what he wants and where and when—the pauses, the music, the stresses, the colours. Everything has been worked out in detail in black and white so that nobody has any doubts of any kind.

The trial-run and special screening feedbacks of the completed *Hum Aapke Hain Koun..!* (*HAHK*) were not very encouraging. Everyone, who was anyone, felt that it seemed to be more a video of marriage songs than a feature film. Perhaps, I can claim, that I was one of the very few who told Sooraj's father, Raj Babu: '*Bahut crowd hoga. Police bulani padegi*' (There will be massive crowds. Police will have to be called in). It happened and in certain places in the country, like Jaipur, police had to resort to lathicharge. The rest is history. Sooraj's film took the nation by storm. It completely changed the mindset when it came to any kind of family celebration, especially the culture of wedding festivities in India. Even other family celebratory occasions today are basically a replica of what happened in *HAHK*.

That apart, Sooraj became a phenomenon whom other film-makers wanted to emulate. Even, the young and highly successful Aadi Chopra and Karan Johar once told me that they wanted to be like Sooraj. What a compliment!

After *HAHK*, Sooraj did not take me in his next film, *Hum Saath Saath Hain*, but I worked with him in the romantic drama, *Vivah*, which had Shahid Kapoor and Amrita Rao in the lead, as also in his 2015 release, *Prem Ratan Dhan Payo*, which had in its cast, once again, Salman Khan with Sonam Kapoor and Neil Nitin Mukesh. Salman is like a good, innocent and disciplined boy when he is working with Sooraj. He is at his best behaviour. I think it is because of his respect for Sooraj.

The Barjatyas don't ask for respect. You just want to give it to them. The whole Barjatya family is like a temple where you just bow out of reverence. Sooraj's son, Avnish, the fourth generation I know, who is now planning to make a film on his own, is also growing up in the typical family tradition. I have often wondered how they produce generations of such fine stock. What do they eat? What do they drink? What do they do so that every child grows up to be intelligent and immensely gifted in the art of film making while also being kind, humble and respectful? How come everyone is blessed in the same manner? And yet, they are modern forward-thinking people, not conventional or orthodox in any way.

For me, working with Sooraj is like getting purified. It's like meditation which always gives me a great sense of calm, purity and an amazing bliss.

25

THE GIFTED FILM-MAKERS

*R*ahul Rawail has been a creator of many stars. A bankable film-maker who is not just adept at his job but also an expert in it. He is precise, always on point, insightful and has a feel of the pulse of the audience. There was a time when the big stars of the industry like Rajendra Kumar, Dharmendra, Tanuja and her husband, Shomu Mukherjee, and even Sunil Dutt would depend on Rahul to launch the careers of their children. For example, he is responsible for launching Kumar Gaurav and Vijeta Pandit in *Love Story*, Sunny Deol and Amrita Singh in *Betaab*, Kajol in *Bekhudi* and Aishwarya Rai in *Aur Pyaar Ho Gaya*. In fact, even Sanjay Dutt was launched by him in *Rocky* in 1981, but due to certain differences with Sunil Dutt, he left the project midway and Sunil Dutt completed it. Each one of these films was a super hit and he made stars out of these young newcomers. He is truly a great director to work with.

He is also very fond of the trolley shot which he sets up at a certain point and then as the dialogue gets over, he comes closer to it. Once I asked him: 'Why do you take so many trolley shots?'

'That's the joy of using a camera,' he explained. 'In theatre, the actor has to reach out to the audience. In cinema, the audience can reach out to the actor.' I found this sentiment and vision very profound and realised that he was able to capture the essential difference between cinema and theatre.

I have worked with Rahul Rawail in six films—*Arjun* in 1985 with Sunny Deol and Dimple Kapadia in the main lead, *Samundar* in 1986 with Sunny Deol and Poonam Dhillon, *Jeevan Ek Sanghursh* in 1990 with Rakhee, Anil Kapoor and Madhuri Dixit, *Mast Kalandar* in 1991 with Dharmendra, *Aur Pyaar Ho Gaya* in 1997 with Bobby Deol, Aishwarya Rai and Shammi Kapoor and *Buddha Mar Gaya* in 2007. Like his father, H. S. Rawail, who gave many memorable films in the 1960s and 1970s like *Mere Mehboob, Sunghursh, Mehboob Ki Mehndi* and *Laila Majnu*, his films unfurl like a beautiful tapestry.

Vidhu Vinod Chopra is a film-maker who touches the minds. See—if you haven't already—his films like *Parinda* or *1942: A Love Story* and you will realise what I mean. When he was planning *Parinda*, in 1988-89, he had come to me for the role of Anna, the gangster. He narrated it to me and I was very excited. But suddenly, after a few days, he told me that he had decided to give that role to somebody else because 'you don't have enough venom in you' is how he put it. 'Instead I will give you inspector Prakash's role which is . . .' Naturally, I was very upset but I enjoyed working with him because he is one of the most methodical film-makers that we have. Anna's role was finally played by Nana Patekar.

I am a professional actor and at the end of the day, I like to work with professional directors—directors who know their job, unlike the majority of the directors in the industry. Vinod is a hard-working and thoroughly professional director.

Around 1992-93, he decided to make a patriotic romance film, *1942: A Love Story*. He offered me the role of Raghuvir Pathak, father to Manisha Koirala as Rajeshwari 'Rajjo'. We were to shoot in Dalhousie which was an added bonus for me for my father used to be posted there at one stage and I was looking forward to revisiting the scenic hill station in Himachal Pradesh. As luck would have it, I was detected with paratyphoid. But I was determined to continue my work in the film since I was very taken in by Vinod's passionate work ethic. I am so glad that I did the film.

During the couple of days which I got off in my shooting schedule, I went trekking with my friend Satish Malhotra from Dharamshala. While exploring the area during the trek, we saw some young boys sitting next to a highly dilapidated mud structure. We walked down into the valley and discovered that it was a school. The dilapidated structure, without any doors or windows or roof, or toilet facilities, was an apology for a school building. There were no classrooms, no chairs, no blackboards. And in there sat a cluster of young girls and boys and one young man who was their tutor. I can't recall his full name but, if my memory serves me right, his first name was Dinesh. I asked him: 'How does this school function?'

He answered: 'The day it rains, we don't function. The day the weather is clear, they come. They know that the day it doesn't rain, they have to come . . . There are no benches or any chairs. This used to be an old house, perhaps deserted by someone. Nobody was around, so I started teaching here.'

I enquired further: 'Why do you teach here? What do you get out of educating them?'

His reply was most fascinating: 'I don't educate them. I give them the possibility of dreaming a better life. And for that, I don't need a building.'

I was stunned to hear this enlightened message in these verdant woods in such a remote setting. With these simple but powerful words, the first seed was sown in my mind for wanting to do something for underprivileged children. I came back and wrote to both the chief minister of Himachal Pradesh, Shanta Kumar and his education minister, Kishori Lal. I don't know what happened to those letters of mine. On my part, I sent a lot of chairs from Dalhousie to Dinesh.

My relentless work schedule began to take a heavy toll on my physical and mental consciousness. A deep fatigue set in as a result of working, shooting, dubbing and travelling for 25 years without a break. I was burnt out.

For a long time, I had genuinely enjoyed my work and looked forward to the daily routine of getting out of the house, sitting in the car, going to the studios or outdoors stints and working day and night. I had done films in all regional languages—Tamil, Telugu, Malayalam, Punjabi—except Gujarati. Through the years, I had hundreds of films to my credits, countless awards and accolades and built a community within the industry. But unknowingly and insidiously, I began to lose interest. Work seemed to be getting very monotonous. In short, I was no longer excited about being a star. I was working mechanically, functioning like a robot, just because I was an actor. I had plateaued and reached a saturation point. I was bored and this boredom led to a feeling of constant irritation. I became short-tempered which was unusual for me because I always used to be cheerful and viewed the optimist side of life. I could not feel the surge of excitement that always elevated my work and my being. Everything seemed grey and plain. No interesting scripts were forthcoming. The roles being offered were the same old ones that of the dadaji (grandfather), chachaji (uncle), mamaji (maternal uncle), cruel seth saab (rich landlord), village head, rich man with a golden heart, or the other way around, each one of which I had played numerous times earlier in various films and in all forms and styles and mannerisms possible.

Life carried on as did work—film after film after film. Yet, I was not excited. Monotony had set in. I was feeling jaded. To me, each film was just another number in my filmography.

Then came an interesting turn in the road sometime in late 2004 or early 2005. The famous Assamese National Award-winning director, Jahnu Barua, came to me with the script of a proposed film, *Maine Gandhi Ko Nahi Mara*, which was to be financed by the National Film and Development Corporation (NFDC). I found it to be a very unusual and interesting script. It was about a retired Hindi professor, Uttam Chaudhary, who is suffering from dementia. Because of it, he feels that it was he who actually killed Gandhi, because on 30 January 1948, when he was an eight-year-old boy, he was playing with his toy gun and shot at a balloon, which had a photograph of Gandhi. This happened around 5 o'clock—the time Gandhi was assassinated. His father had casually remarked: '*Tune mara hain Gandhi ko*' (You have killed Gandhi) or words to that effect. This comes back to haunt him in his sunset years.

Then all of a sudden, NFDC refused to finance the film. Since I liked the script and my role in it, I told Jahnu that I would produce it. I went to Yash and Aadi Chopra and asked if they would like to 'finance the film with me as the producer'. They agreed and I started working on my role as Professor Uttam Chaudhary. I had no clue about Alzheimer's and how a person afflicted with it would behave in his day to day life. The only thing I knew was that I needed to push my creative limits and not be complacent. Then, one night, while reading a book, I came across an interesting sentence which went something like this: 'When you are competent, you can never be brilliant. Either you go into the degradation of complete creative bankruptcy or you stop being competent.' This thought fitted the current state of my mind. It was just the impetus I needed to propel me out of my fog.

I started preparing in earnest for the role. I didn't want to depend on cinematic liberties. I met a lot of Alzheimer's patients. I also spoke to many competent doctors and research scholars. I also did independent research and read up books and looked up information on the internet. One predominant thing I discovered was that Alzheimer's patient's eyes are very vacant. Now, I am a very expressive actor and anything I do has expressions. *How to make my eyes expressionless so that they are dead?*, I started thinking. I started practising, day and night, but somehow, I was not succeeding. Being the producer, I was conscious that the shooting dates were fast approaching. We had already settled on the rest of the cast for this father-daughter story. Initially, I had thought of Mahima Chaudhry who had acted with Shah Rukh in Subhash Ghai's *Pardes* and had also worked for me in *Om Jai Jagadish*. However, finally Urmila Matondkar agreed. I kept practising my role but to no avail. I would go to the beach early mornings, well before dawn to practise my expressions, so that nobody could see me and I would have no interruptions. The main idea was that even I should not know who I am. That was my daily exercise. But then the question that disturbed me most was, 'How will I act if I don't know who I am?'

One morning, with just a week left for the shooting schedule to commence, I started walking towards the sea at 5 o'clock and said to myself, I don't know swimming so let me reach a situation where I do not know who I am. When I was half immersed into the water, practising in my mind to completely go dead, then suddenly the feeling came—for a second or two, I did not know who I was. I was able to connect with the vacant emotion and then I threw up. How devastatingly self-destructive actors can be? But that is precisely what the joy of acting is all about. Based on that feel, based on that experience, based on that memory, which was just about a two-three second memory, I did that entire role in *Maine Gandhi Ko Nahi Mara*. It got me a lot of appreciation and recognition, some international awards and at home, a special mention at the National Film Awards.

It was during this phase that I heard about two Delhi based ad film-makers, Jaideep Sahni and Dibakar Banerjee. They wanted to meet me to discuss a film project—*Khosla Ka Ghosla*. I was feeling ennui—a creative low and non-productive phase. After one month of being chased around, I finally met them in my old Andheri office. At the scheduled time, two young, smart and charming boys walked in. Jaideep Sahni was the writer. Dibakar wanted to direct the film. He said: 'We can narrate some scenes or, if you want, we can tell you the story in a nutshell.'

'If it's good, I will be able to make out within the first five minutes but, first tell me, why do you want me in it?' I responded.

'Because only you can do this role . . . nobody else can,' he replied. I wearily thought to myself, *I have heard this sentence a million times before.*

'And, who is the producer?' I asked.

'That has still to be worked out,' Jaideep replied, a bit hesitatingly.

Dibakar started narrating the script with Jaideep pitching in wherever necessary. Having initially allotted them about 20 minutes or so, we were together for nearly six hours. The script was mind-blowing and had a magical quality about it. In my mind, I had already decided that I would play the role of Khosla which I based on Vijay Sehgal's father—one of the millions of anonymous middle-class retired people who lead a routine life hemmed in by their day to day pressures. I agreed to do the film.

Though Savita Raj Hiremath came in as the producer, I was aware of the fact that finances were limited. Shooting started in June in Delhi, with the summer season at its peak. Because of budgetary restraints, the unit stayed in some hotel while I stayed at ITC's Maurya, courtesy my friend, Nakul Anand, the chief executive of the Hotels Division at ITC, who gave me a good deal. The shooting was very real and fascinating and Dibakar was completely on point. Though irritatingly stubborn, he was brilliant and knew what he was doing. The solid cast comprised of Boman Irani, Parvin Dabas, Vinay Pathak, Kiran Ramesh Sippy and Ranvir Shorey, amongst others, all backed by their theatre background. However, all along during the making of the film, the problem of finances was ubiquitous. There were times when the actors were thrown out of the hotel and there were times when there was no vehicle to transport them. I knew that if shooting stopped, the film would never be completed. I did my best to keep up the morale of the cast and crew by engaging them in games, taking them out for dinners and letting them stay at my place. I did my best to keep things moving along and the morale high.

I don't blame Savita Raj, the producer, but making a film of this nature is not easy. Just when we all thought that the film is now complete with only a day's work left, things came to a standstill. At this stage, the man who pioneered cable television, Ronnie Screwvala, labelled as the 'Jack Warner of India' by *Newsweek*, came into the picture and his company took over. And yet, it still took another year to get the entire cast together again. Finally, three years later, the film was released. In the world of commercially driven Indian cinema, *Khosla Ka Ghosla* came as a breath of fresh air that everyone could identify with. My role as Khosla saab (Kamal Kishore Khosla) was very well received and the film was a great success at the box office and also won the National Award for Best Feature Film in 2006. Kudos to Jaideep and Dibakar!

For me personally, it was one of my five best performances. I had to put in so much of everyday life and the slices of regular normalcy into it, not only as an actor but emotionally as well, to help put the whole project together. I know for certain that if I was not the lead actor, *Khosla Ka Ghosla* would have never been made. It was because of my efforts, my spirit of camaraderie, which made the entire cast stay together in spite of the difficult financial situation. And today, I can very honestly say that Dibakar owes the making of this film to me.

By 2006, Dibakar announced his next film, *Oye Lucky! Lucky Oye*, with Abhay Deol and Neetu Chandra in the lead, and he came to me: '*Ek father ka role hai* (there is a father's role) and I want you to do that.' However, in my next meeting, he told me: 'There are three roles of three fathers now. You choose whichever role you think is best for you. The other role I will offer to Paresh Rawal.'

I agreed, because I felt I had emotionally invested in his earlier film. It was all confirmed.

Then suddenly one day, I found out that Dibakar, without even having the courtesy of informing me, had given all the three roles of the three fathers to Paresh. I was very disappointed and hurt. The man had changed. I felt used. However, as is my nature, I put it behind me and moved on with my life.

Since then Dibakar has made six films—*Love Sex Aur Dhokha, Shanghai, Bombay Talkies, Detective Byomkesh Bakshy!, Lust Stories* and *Sandeep Aur Pinky Faraar*—some average, mostly 'bad'. A pity indeed that such a brilliant director, who could have given 'good' cinema, has just kept on deteriorating. A sheer case of brilliance gone indifferent!

Around the same time as *Khosla Ka Ghosla* came to me, I got a call from B. L. Gautam at Zee TV, saying that there was a good script which he would like me to look at and that its writer would like to meet me. The script was titled *A Wednesday*. The writer-director was Neeraj Pandey and the producer, the amiable Shital Bhatia—two rank newcomers.

'Okay, just tell him to leave the script at my office,' I replied.

He did, but with a rider: 'I want you to act the role of the police commissioner in this film. But sir, we don't have enough money. Hence, whatever you charge, we will give you half of that.'

What the hell, I thought to myself. *What an arrogant man? He is asking me to read the script; he is keen for me to act in it but at only half my fee.* A few days later during a Mumbai-Delhi flight, I started reading it and by the time I reached Palam airport, I decided to call him immediately, lest he gives the role to someone else. The script was super and my role was excellent and exactly what I was looking for to challenge myself. The possibilities were immense. I called Gautam and said: 'I am doing the film and I agree to do it at just half the amount I charge . . . I would like to meet the director as soon as I get back to Mumbai.'

This veteran actor who has done over 500 films asks to meet this director—a newcomer. I am doing him a favour. Aacha idhar aa. Ab main batata hoon ki mere kya suggestions hain (Okay, now come. I will brief you as to what my suggestions are), I thought to myself.

Neeraj Pandey came to see me in my office. 'Good script,' I told him. And then continued to say, 'But you must keep in mind that the script is the film. Now let me give you my point of view on certain scenes.' Then I talked to him about the various suggestions I had for the script and my genuine concerns regarding it.

After listening to each point of mine with great patience for 1 hour and 45 minutes and without interrupting me even once, he said very calmly: 'What you say is right, the script is the film. And because my script is the film, I am not going to change a single scene, not a single shot, not a single line, not a single word. If the script interests you and you want to do this film, do it. Or let me know.'

So, *ek khoon ka ghoot pee ke maine kaha* (After consuming a bitter pill), I said: 'Yes, yes, of course. I am doing the film.'

That was the beginning of a joyful association with Neeraj and his films. He was so clear and precise—every detail had been worked out to its minutest detail and every shooting schedule had been elaborated in precise terms. He had told me that he would 'finish the entire shoot within 28 days, perhaps half-a-day less, but not a day more'. He finished the film within 27 days. It's a different matter that the film remained 'in the cans' for three years before it got released on 5 September 2008.

In those days, it was difficult to sell a film with Naseeruddin Shah (who played the common man) and Anupam Kher in the main lead. Today, the entire system of marketing films has changed and it's easy to sell such films also. It was a 'sleeper hit' at the box office. Recently, I was honoured to hear Prime Minister Narendra Modi mention in an interview with Akshay Kumar that the last film he watched was *A Wednesday*. I was both humbled and elated to know this and feel that it is a testimony both to the remarkable prime minister as well as the trailblazing script and path-breaking movie that we created. It was remade in Tamil and Telegu and then in 2012-13, Sri Lankan film-maker Chandran Rutnam made it in English and was titled *A Common Man* which had Ben Kingsley and Ben Cross in the role of the two protagonists. This American-Sri Lankan film, which was a commercial success, won numerous international awards.

I think *Khosla Ka Ghosla* and *A Wednesday* were the forerunners in this distinct type of cinema and prepared the future audiences of coming generations in this country to films with a different perspective. Thereafter, Neeraj directed four more films of the nine that he produced—*Special 26, Baby, M. S. Dhoni: The Untold Story* and *Aiyaary*. I was in all four.

In my opinion, Neeraj is a sincere man and genius as a film director. He devotes a great deal of time to his screenplay and his meticulousness and unique approach on the sets, all create a completely different kind of cinema. He works wonders with the camera to get the right composition for every shot because he is a thinking man, a creative man, who has a clear vision of what he wants. On a personal level too, relationships are very important to him and he goes to great lengths and makes an effort to maintain them. In the film world, what you earn, besides the role you play, are also great relationships. I think I share a great relationship with Neeraj as a person. I like him on the sets as a film-maker, and more so off the sets as a human being. I feel I am his elder brother who can talk to him on a one-to-one basis. For example, I did not agree with him on his choice regarding *Aiyaary* for I felt there was a problem with the script and told him so. It was my personal opinion and I felt duty-bound to express it. I wish I had the same relationship with Dibakar Banerjee because I had invested a great deal in it. I loved him and I still like him very much.

Recently I went to Friday Filmworks—their production house. It was huge. Both Neeraj and Shital are the current tycoons of Indian cinema.

26

The Accidental Prime Minister

I have mentioned this earlier but it bears repeating that during the first two decades of my career, my focus was never to be without work. I had encountered the empty hours of having no work and did not want to face an uncertain future ever again. I had been seduced by success and enchanted by the world of glamour and did not want to forfeit it at any cost. Consequently, I signed films one after the other and was working seven days a week, three shifts a day. I reached a stage where I was doing a medley of films, some of great consequence, most films of little consequence and many films of no consequence. Work became security. I did not exercise choice and just treated films as work and kept my days chock-a-block. The reality is that no actor, no artiste, no painter, no poet, no composer, has done only 'good' work. Everybody has done mediocre work and indifferent work. In some cases, 'very bad' work too. Name anybody and you will see the truth for yourself. It's just that people are remembered only by their brilliant work. I too am no different!

In the last few years, with the exception of a few films like Dibakar Banerjee's *Khosla ka Ghosla* or Neeraj Pandey's *A Wednesday* or *Special 26* and some films in Hollywood like David O'Russell's *Silver Linings Playbook*, I was discontent on my work front. I was apprehensive that even after working in over 500 films, winning innumerable awards and honours and spanning my 35-year career as an actor in roles ranging from comedy to tragedy, suspense thrillers to romances, low budgets to lavish productions, aged man to young person, villain to angel, Bollywood to Hollywood, there were goals still to be conquered. Something continued to exasperate me at the back of my mind—I wanted to challenge myself further . . . push the barriers. I had indulged in a lot of gimmickry and audiences loved it. The producers were happy, the directors were happy, my co-stars were happy. But I was not. I knew there was much more to be done.

When you send out a message to the universe, it often comes back and finds you. Even so, when *The Accidental Prime Minister* film project came up, initially, I was taken aback. I had been a vocal critic of Dr Manmohan Singh and the Congress Party. I had followed that by praising Prime Minister Narendra Modi. Because I was criticising Dr Manmohan Singh and praising Narendra Modi, I was labelled a BJP (Bharatiya Janata Party) 'spokesman' and it is quite natural for people to come to this conclusion. When the producer, Sunil Bohra, came with Ashok Pandit and the film script, I was rather sceptical: 'Why do you want me to do this film? Are you trying to create controversy?' I asked.

Then the director, Vijay Ratnakar Gutte, also came to meet me. But I had made up my mind that I was not going to do the film and put it out of my mind. The film was based on the book—*The Accidental Prime Minister: The Making and Unmaking of Manmohan Singh* by Sanjaya Baru, the one-time media advisor and chief spokesperson (May 2004 to August 2008) to Dr Manmohan Singh. It became a number one bestseller when released by the publishers Penguin Random House India in April 2014.

Then, one evening, as I sat at home watching the news, I saw Dr Manmohan Singh as the Leader of the Opposition in the Rajya Sabha (India's upper house), talking about demonetisation in Parliament. At that particular moment, watching him for the first time from the perspective of an actor, I thought to myself, *it would have been so difficult to portray him because there is nothing tangible about him. His body language is not solid, his voice is not substantial and his expressions are not real. There is nothing in his manner that suggests he is a politician. He's not interested in impressing anybody. He does not adopt any particular tone and the pitch of his speech does not fluctuate high or low. He just reads his speech and that too in a flat, monotonous and bland manner. It must be so tedious and boring for a listener. There is nothing extraordinary about him except for the words that he writes on a piece of paper. My God, what an unbelievably difficult person he would be to portray as an actor!*

I thought about it the whole night and the next morning, I called up Sunil Bohra and told him that I would like to give it a try. 'Send me the script,' I instructed him. The first scene of the script is Dr Manmohan Singh walking to take *shappat* (oath) of office of the prime minister of India. I got up from my office chair and tried to walk in a similar manner just to see how well I would fit in his shoes, if at all. Even in my own eyes, I was a complete disaster.

Completely intrigued, I began doing extensive research on the prime minister's actual walking stance. I rehearsed exhaustively for ten long days and still could not get the hang of it. The more it eluded me, the more of a challenge it became. I thought that if I do this role the way it should be done, to perfection, it would be my *Saaransh* after 35 years . . . a reinvention, a rediscovery!

That is when I confirmed my commitment to the producers. The big difference being that when Anupam Kher did *Saaransh*, he was a novice. In making *The Accidental Prime Minister*, I had to bear the burden of more than 515 national and international films. In *Saaransh*, B. V. Pradhan was doing everything; Anupam Kher had nothing to do with it, from the people's point of view. There was great freedom in that fact. But here Dr Manmohan Singh was not on trial, it is me, Anupam Kher, who had to make people believe that the person on the screen is Dr Manmohan Singh and not Anupam Kher the actor. I realised that if I achieved that, it would be a significant accomplishment, a spectacular success, my personal creative fulfilment as an actor not just in India, but the world over.

The producers wanted to start shooting in August but I was not ready. I informed them that I would need three months to prepare for the role. Finally, I took six months. The preparation for *Saaransh* involved emotional upheavals aided by life struggles and personal turmoils I had undergone. Dr Manmohan Singh's emotional upheavals were not my issue because as a politician, as a bureaucrat, he hid them and hid them well. I could not find a single clip where he showed, even minutely, when he was hurt or upset or angry. His emotions were quite static. And yet, I was able to catch glimpses of defiance, anger, hurt and even smiles. I asked myself: *How do I dramatise all this? How do I capture all that?* A big test for me was to capture his vocal essence and it was not going to be easy at all. When you see the final product on the screen, it seems effortless. All those who complimented me by saying things like 'Fabulous', 'Arre yaar, very good', 'Fantastic performance man' and 'Well done!' have no idea how much I invested in it and how much it consumed me.

I had to internalise the entire role and the person as a whole. I decided to go inwards rather than the other way around. I had a conversation with Kirron about it. When I told her over the phone in Chandigarh that I had accepted the role and was going to do the film, she advised: 'Good, I am glad. Just be the person. Don't try . . . don't pretend to be the person.' Sound advice indeed but it was easier said than done. Her words: 'Be the person' became my cue.

I began with meditation, something I had never done before in my life. However, I took to it since I knew it was necessary to both internalise as well as distil everything to reach the point of saturation and feel that I have culminated at zero, emotionally. During the four months of preparation, I was not just mimicking Dr Manmohan Singh, but evolving into him in every minute detail. Watch closely and you will realise that he is not coordinated in his movements. His dexterity is not like regular people. Just see his body language and his speech . . . he says something and then he moves, then he gestures. His hand gestures are minimal.

I had to study him and his personality in great depth. There is a sequence in the film in flashback where Dr Manmohan Singh's chacha (father's younger brother) takes him, a ten-year-old boy, for admission to a school. The principal says: '*Kee naam hai?*' (What's his name?).

'Manmohan Singh.'

'Date of birth *ki hai?*' (What's his date of birth?)

The uncle answered: '*Tussi jo marzi likh deyo. Anne keda koi prime minister banna hai'* (Write whatever you want to. He is not going to become the prime minister).

That small scene describes that he himself was never important for anybody. But my toughest challenge was his voice. I have a very bass voice . . . a theatre voice. On the other hand, Dr Manmohan Singh's voice and tone are very different. He has a voice where the breath and air go out together while he is talking. Then, his Punjabi *lehja* is not the typical Delhi-Punjabi. It is very different. It took me two months of working on it and still it was not correct because I kept reverting to being Anupam Kher. But in the end, I mastered it.

Once we were shooting in a remote little place in England, where there was no distraction . . . there were no outsiders. Just the unit. It was the loneliest place in the world. On the sets, outside my make-up room was written Anupam Kher. I said: 'Change it to Prime Minister Dr Manmohan Singh. And whenever I come out of the make-up room, please don't refer to me as Anupam Kher or sir or anything. Just show the respect that you will show to the prime minister.' And that's exactly what they did. I became the *man* he was.

I very strongly feel that my biggest achievement as an actor, manifold more than being B. V. Pradhan in *Saaransh*, is becoming Dr Manmohan Singh in *The Accidental Prime Minister*. A role that was an antithesis to every experience I have faced in my life and everyone who has left an impact on me. By sheer force of my will, I was able to bring alive to the screen the bland, opaque character of the man known as Dr Manmohan Singh.

Part–V

BEING POLITICALLY [IN]CORRECT

. . . it only takes one voice, at the right pitch, to start an avalanche.

—Dianna Hardy, *Return Of The Wolf*

27

THE WATERSHED MOMENT

In almost every individual's life, inevitably, there comes a watershed moment, like it did in mine. I view the early years of my career as two segments. The pre-*Saaransh* period and the post-*Saaransh* one. Many of us spend the better part of our lives trying to achieve fame or wealth or both. We doggedly work day and night; we cope with failure and setbacks; we bear affronts and insults with stoicism . . . all in the hope that our endeavours will one day catapult us from the ranks of the mundane to the envied heights of the rich and famous.

Even though most of us may learn to come to terms with *failure*, very few of us can really cope with *success*. I too have been cut from the same cloth. Sometimes we are tested not just for what we do but who we are as a person. A litmus trial that reveals and shakes us to our core.

I have often asked myself: *What does one do in stressful times . . . when one is wrongly charged with a trespass that one did not commit?*

Seven days in April 2011 were remarkable, with me being on a swing between one end of the spectrum to the other, in terms of activism. What started as my participation in a non-violent crusade, ended up with me being the target of violence. The period was also perhaps, the stormiest I have ever witnessed in decades.

It all began very peacefully on 5 April 2011, when I visited Jantar Mantar in New Delhi, joining the ranks of supporters of the respected social activist, Anna Hazare, who was known for his 'movements to promote rural development, increase government transparency and investigate and punish corruption in public life. In addition to organising and encouraging grassroots movements, Hazare frequently undertook a series of fasts—a tactic reminiscent, to many, of the work of the Father of the Nation, Mohandas K. Gandhi'—to protest against the widespread corruption (highlighted by several scams) that was ruining the Indian economy and causing great agony and distress to the poor and downtrodden, including farmers.

At the rally, I was interviewed by several television channels. Some politically mischievous elements in Mumbai misrepresented my comments about the Constitution and later said that I had stated that it (the Constitution) should be thrown out or something to that effect.

My alleged comments raised the hackles of legislators in the Maharashtra Legislative Assembly and the speaker passed a privilege motion against me, calling for an investigation. No amount of replaying of my quote by the channel—in which it was clear that I had never stated anything even remotely resembling what my detractors were trying to allege—could pacify the politicians that the channel interviewed.

My acting school in Mumbai—Actor Prepares—was the scene of demonstrations that afternoon and later in the evening, my 2nd floor apartment in Juhu was stoned. The next day, my effigies were burnt in some parts of the city. All this happened because of something that I had never said. It was evident that the situation was being exploited by people with an ulterior motive.

I resolved not to react as it would cause matters to spiral out of control. But more importantly, I did not respond as I did not feel compelled to reply. I retained my equilibrium and sense of calm even though I was incessantly badgered by the media for comments and sound bites for several hours.

In retrospect, I am happy with the way I reacted to these tumultuous events. It is very easy to be on the sidelines and give expert advice, but the true test comes when one is facing the heat. The next morning, I went to see the gentle nun who had initiated me into the world of differently abled children a decade ago, Sister Maria Dolores.

To me, she has always embodied spiritualism. After a quiet chat, she left me with a moving message:

> Remember Anupam, your fight is against corruption . . . and not against the corrupt. Do not confuse one for the other. Forgive those who threw stones at your house; they do not understand what they have done. In your peace will lay your strength.

I saluted her maturity.

In his Nobel lecture delivered in Stockholm on 7 December 2017, the eminent author, Kazuo Ishiguro, raised a few pertinent questions: 'Does a nation remember and forget in much the same way as an individual does? Or are there important differences? What exactly are the memories of a nation? Where are they kept? How are they shaped and controlled? Are there times when forgetting is the only way . . .?'[23]

On 5 April 2011, Anna Hazare started a hunger strike in Delhi 'to exert pressure on the Dr Manmohan Singh led UPA government, to enact a stringent anti-corruption law and for the institution of an ombudsman with the power to deal with corruption in public places'.

For my part, I decided to root for Anna Hazare. My support stemmed not only from my convictions but also from personal experiences.

As mentioned earlier, my grandfather, Pandit Amar Nath, was a man imbued with Gandhian ideals and principles and I have always remembered his sagacious counsel during my different periods of crises. Many years back, when I was going through a rough patch, I wrote a letter to him stating that I was tired and felt totally dejected in life . . . that I would now like to return to Shimla as there was nothing for me to explore and search for in Bombay. His brief reply concluded with the following words, which, since then, have given me great strength in my difficult days:

Bheega hua aadmi baarish se nahin darta.
A man who is drenched in not afraid of the rain.

We, the privileged ones, were shirking from our social responsibilities and were letting down millions of our poor, uneducated and underprivileged compatriots by not standing up for a clean, transparent and effective system of governance.

We had forgotten that Mahatma Gandhi could have led a life of ease in South Africa as he was a successful barrister. But faced with injustice, he gave it all up and returned to his homeland to fight for rights—one man against the mightiest empire in history. If we have largely forgotten history, we shall be condemned to repeat the mistakes of the past.

I did not wish to forget history. For me, it was more important to live respectfully than by compromise. I run an acting institution and if my students, or my son, Sikandar, would ask me: 'Why did you not raise your voice against corruption?' I would tell them that I did! Years later when my grandchildren ask me: 'Where were you in the days of Anna Hazare's crusade against corruption?' I would tell them that *I was there by his side!*

We have definitely progressed a great deal since attaining independence in August 1947, but corruption has proved to be a major drag on the economy. It was affecting every section of society. Whether it was in providing good roads or quality education or safe drinking water, our very existence was in jeopardy because of the corrupt bureaucrat-politician nexus. Money was just being siphoned off from all welfare schemes and there was no accountability. It was not Anna Hazare but former Prime Minister Rajiv Gandhi who, in 1985, had said that of every rupee spent on development, only 17 paise reached its intended target. Where did the other 83 paise per rupee of funds go? Just imagine what economic wonders and miraculous rates of growth could be achieved if we could plug the missing 83 per cent.

I was convinced that if I wanted to make people believe that corruption was evil, I needed to speak out myself. When you raise your voice, you discover your strengths because you are on the side of the truth. Anna Hazare's movement against corruption was a historical moment for our country. We needed someone to become a symbol of strength and hope for the masses. Fortunately, in Anna there was the personification of a man who was completely non-corrupt. He lived in a temple in the small town, Ralegan Siddhi, in Maharashtra, had just two sets of clothes and didn't get married because he wanted to live for a cause. He listened to his conscience. We too could hear our conscience, but we did not act because of fear.

I was clear that we could not cleanse the land of corruption in one sweep. It would take a long time just as the road to independence took nine decades after the first rebellion in 1857. But the journey had to . . . and it must . . . begin somewhere and with someone. The citizens of the country had a right to expect a clean system of administration.

The most heartening thing was that the cause had attracted and galvanised the youth of this country. Wherever I went, I was astounded to see that it was the youth who were fuelling the cause and wanted to clean up the system. Under these circumstances, it was time for the people of my generation, and my seniors, to move on too. We owed the youth of India . . . the future generations . . . the inheritors of this great land, to do right by their aspirations. And the time had come.

As was to be expected, many people questioned my motives in this campaign. And my detractors taunted me by saying that *filmon mein kaam nahi hai, toh netagiri mein aa gaya hai* (He has no work in films, so he is trying to become a political leader). Many well-wishers advised me to keep quiet, or else life and living could get difficult. *Let them say what they want to*, I said to myself. I too could have stayed in the shadows, away from the media glare like many from my fraternity. I have not done this for publicity; there are easier ways to get it! I did not do it because there is no other way for me if I have to live up to my grandfather's ideals.

I did not want to wrestle with my conscience. I wanted to live with it.

Eventually, Anna Hazare's mass movement yielded some positive results. The Lokpal (equivalent to an ombudsman) Bill was tabled by the UPA government in the Lok Sabha on 22 December 2011 and was passed five days later as the Lokpal and Lokayuktas Bill, 2011. It was subsequently introduced in the Rajya Sabha on 29 December 2011. Despite a prolonged debate there, voting could not take place due to lack of time. On 21 May 2012, the bill was referred to a select committee of the Rajya Sabha for further consideration. It was finally passed in the Rajya Sabha on 17 December 2013, after making certain amendments to the earlier bill and in the Lok Sabha, the next day.

The bill was signed by President Pranab Mukherjee on Wednesday, 1 January 2014 and came into force fifteen days later as an Act of Parliament. Five years later, on 23 March 2019, retired Supreme Court judge, Pinaki Chandra Ghose, was appointed as the first Lokpal of India by a committee comprising Prime Minister Narendra Modi, Chief Justice of India Ranjan Gogoi and Lok Sabha Speaker, Sumitra Mahajan. Four days later, on 27 March 2019, eight members—four of them judicial and four non-judicial—were appointed.

Soon thereafter, sadly somewhere along the line, Anna Hazare himself lost sight of his goal and the movement became a footnote in the history of the country.

28

The Big Let-down

As mentioned in the previous chapter, with the dawn of 2011, came the promise of a positive change in our country from a political and administrative point of view. Like many others, I too believed in that promise only to be heavily let down by its makers. India Against Corruption movement started in 2011 with Anna Hazare, a social activist from Ralegan Siddhi, leading the cry with a hunger strike in Jantar Mantar, New Delhi. The main objective of the movement was to weed out corruption in the system and the establishment of an independent body to investigate such cases through the institution of the Jan Lokpal Bill.

Being a person originating from humble means and having lived through the life a common man before I became a known actor, I felt strongly drawn towards this movement. There seemed to be something organically truthful about it. But I was an outsider to it all. Then, one day, while I was shooting in Pune for my Marathi film, *Kashala Udyachi Baat*, I received a call from Manish Sisodia, at present the deputy chief minister of Delhi, that he, Anna Hazare and Arvind Kejriwal need support from like-minded people to create more awareness to their cause. I was charged with the vision of being involved in this momentous movement and landed in Delhi to pledge my support.

Over a period of time, I got actively involved in the cause and would attend their meetings too. When I met Arvind Kejriwal, he came across as a person who was sincere, honest and someone who resonated the views of Anna Hazare. There were also retired police officer and social activist Kiran Bedi, the poet Kumar Vishwas, eminent lawyer Prashant Bhushan and social activist Mayank Gandhi amongst many others. I sincerely believed that everybody, together, would bind India and unite against the seeds of corruption. I had never seen our youth participating, at least since independence, and being galvanised in such massive numbers. I made emotional speeches, pleading to the people of our country to lend their support. I did all this, fully aware that such a stand would directly affect my popularity as an actor and, more so, my work. My life till then was on a somewhat smooth track. My ups and downs were related to my work which kept me busy, and my professional achievements as an actor kept me happy. I did not have to stick my neck out for this cause, which was slowly becoming a major movement. I could have taken the easier route of being diplomatic about it from the stands like many others did. But then, that wouldn't be me. All my life, I have tried to stand up for what is righteous, without any fear. A clean conscience is more important to me than an easy life. I could not not be involved in this historical movement. Kirron and I would frequently inquire about Arvind's health, due to the week-long hunger strike he had maintained. We were genuinely concerned. She would often get worried for him and ask me, 'Will he be alright?' Such were our emotions towards these, then seemingly, brave men.

Then, a few days hence, in the early hours of the morning, around 2 a.m., I got a call from Salman Khurshid, a cabinet minister in the UPA government, that he appreciates my good work in promoting awareness about the India Against Corruption movement. In my mind, I questioned the intention of the call, especially since the movement was against his government. Another surprising proceeding was an e-mail from Prashant Bhushan calling for a meeting the next day to announce that the members of the India Against Corruption movement would be forming an official political party and he wanted me to make this important announcement to the media and the gathered people.

I reached Delhi. In the meeting, I was seated amongst Anna Hazare, Kiran Bedi, Prashant Bhushan, Shanti Bhushan and Manish Sisodia. My seat was next to Anna Hazare. It was only then that I discovered that Anna Hazare strongly opposed the establishment of a political party. In fact, he was very angry and hurt about it. I did try reasoning out the matter with him, but he was firm. He said, and I quote him: 'Nahi nahi yeh galat baat hai. Yeh party banni nahi chahiye. Pura iska purpose khatam ho jaayega' (No, this is wrong. This party should not be formed. The whole purpose will be defeated). Despite his disapproval, and with the belief that an official establishment would be the ideal way to deal with corruption, I went on stage and announced the formation of the party which was later christened as Aam Aadmi Party (The Common Man's Party— AAP). Since the official formation of the party, which gained large momentum, my job was done. I respectfully stepped aside from any active involvement as I was clear about not wanting to be associated officially with any political party. Even now, I am able to express my opinions on politics or current affairs, fearlessly, only because I have the power of a common man within me, without any allegiances. An official affiliation would need me to restrict my words and manipulate the truth, if needed, in support of the association. Although, I was always ready to support the cause, not the party, with any assistance needed of me.

Then came the volte-face! Elections began and I was called to campaign for the Aam Aadmi Party. I refused, stating that I would not want to campaign for any political party. Their anti-corruption sloganeering during the elections won the trust of the common man and they won the elections with a huge margin. It was a historical moment! Deep down I still hoped, now that they are within the system, they will reciprocate the faith put in them by the common man and move against corruption. My first disappointment came the same evening. During the oath-taking ceremony, I discovered that the AAP had joined hands with the Congress Party to form the government—a party they were strongly fighting against all along.

After the victory announcement during a media interaction, a journalist questioned Kejriwal on the steps he intends to take against

Sheila Dikshit, the former chief minister of Delhi. His response was: '*Aap le aayiye saboot aur hum unn par case kar denge*' (You bring the evidence and we will bring in a legal care against her). I was aghast. Personally, I had nothing against Sheila Dikshit. She was doing good work and was always very warm towards me. But in the India Against Corruption movement, I was looking at the bigger picture. The movement was against the establishment and Sheila Dikshit was merely a part of that. So how could Arvind Kejriwal give this response? Wasn't he, till the time of victory, constantly accusing Sheila Dikshit of various corruption crimes and promising to bring her to justice should his party win the election? Here, he is victorious on the aspirations of millions of faithful people, and instead of going for the kill, he was sidelining the issue by claiming that he doesn't have proof and wants the media to procure it so as to be able to take any action.

I then realised that Arvind Kejriwal was no longer his former honest self. It was all a mask. He had become a politician, similar to the many others already present in the system. Maybe even worse! This hit me like a jolt of lighting. I then started to think: 'Why did I become a part of this?' The very people he was fighting in retrospect, he now vied for their support. There are many instances of him prior to this of swearing his commitment to the purpose of rooting out corruption: '*Main bacchon ki kasam kha ke kehta hoon ki mujhe raajneeti main koi ruchi nahi hai*' (I swear by my children that I have no interest in politics), and here he was doing just the opposite).

Then, 44 days later, they left the government. *Where is all this going . . . ? What is the objective of this all?* were the thoughts ringing in my head. Since, at its inception, I was a prominent face in the campaign, post victory, there were people coming to me asking numerous questions and saying: '*Ji yeh toh galat hogaya hamare saath*' (They have wronged us). They reached out to me: '*Aap inko samjhaaayi, yeh aisa kaise kar sakte hain? Jab se yeh chief minister baney hain, humari sunte nahi. Jo AAP ka main maksad tha woh toh ho hi nahi raha hai ji*' (Why don't you make him understand? Ever since he has become the chief minister, he doesn't listen to us. The main goal of AAP has been defeated). I had no answer for them. I, like them, felt completely deceived and let down.

Soon, I saw, one by one, almost every founding member leaving AAP—dejected, disillusioned. I also spoke about it in a couple of media interviews or so. I couldn't change what had already happened. From there to what happened subsequently is well known. I personally had placed a lot of hope in Arvind Kejriwal. Arvind Kejriwal will remain my biggest disappointment and the disappointment of millions of Indians all over the country who believed in him.

Then came Narendra Modi! I would hear people talk about a political leader who, as the chief minister of Gujarat, had reinvented the state. He was very successful in that mission. Sometime in mid-2008, I sought an appointment with him in Gujarat, requesting him to see Neeraj Pandey's *A Wednesday*—a film in which I was performing the role of Prakash Rathod, a retired police commissioner. When I met him, I observed that he did not talk like a regular politician and only spoke about his vision for India. He spoke about how he transformed Gujarat. He broke the cliché of a typical politician and instilled hope. My past experiences with the AAP could have easily diminished my enthusiasm and could have turned me into a cynic. However, being an eternal optimist, I sought refuge in Narendra Modi's vision and wished that he becomes the prime minister of this country. Six years down the line, on 26 May 2014, he was sworn in as the 14th prime minister of India. The majority with which he has been re-elected for the second term in May 2019 establishes that people find, in him, the leader they deserve. India has the ability of becoming a world superpower under his leadership.

29

EXILED IN OUR OWN LAND

Exile . . . is the unbelievable rift forced between a human being and a native place, between the self and its true home; its essential sadness can never be healed.' And this applies to more or less all exiles—those who are exiled by others and those who impose exile on themselves.

Being 'exiled' is a subject that has somehow always fascinated me. I recall Erich Fromm's *Those without Roots* and George Steiner's *The Extraterritorial*—two classic studies on the condition and concerns of those in exile. Then there is another volume—incidentally my favourite—*The Oxford Book of Exile* edited by John Simpson which acknowledges many literary voices and focuses on the real experiences of those who have been forced into or have chosen exile.

The thing that is of great value in this volume is the fact that Simpson selected writings from several centuries and included poetry, fiction, memoirs, letters, news reports and general historical writings to illustrate the widest possible definition of the term 'exile'. He included not only the story from Genesis of Adam's and Eve's expulsion from Paradise, but also the Chinese poet Liu Shang's song (c. A.D. 770) of the abduction of Lady Wen-Chi, kidnapped from the region of modern Honan and taken to Mongolia. Other accounts include the plight of the Africans taken as slaves as well as that of the Kurds in the Middle East, the imprisonment of the great Russian master, Fyodor Dostoevsky, in Siberia as well as that of Nelson

Mandela in South Africa and of Chinese families during the Cultural Revolution and the laments of the Palestinians in Israel as well as the stories of the Jewish survivors of the genocide.

Simpson emphasises political events and external facts; the courtroom scene when Nelson Mandela is sentenced to life imprisonment (1964), the military degradation of Alfred Dreyfus (1895), the efforts of Napoleon III to find a new home after the defeat of his army in 1870, the details of Ayatollah's business in France during his exile from Iran in 1978, the efforts of an Argentine mother to get the newspapers to help her find her daughter, one of the many who 'disappeared' during the late 1970s and the arrest of Soviet physician Dr Andrei Sakharov in 1980.

To these, I add the story of the exile of my people—the Kashmiri Pandits from their homes, their land, their *watan*: Kashmir. The same Kashmir which the generations of their ancestors helped build over centuries . . . the same Kashmir to whom writers and poets wrote numerous odes . . . the same Kashmir whose beauty was captured by numerous artistes on canvas and craftsmen on cloth . . . the same Kashmir about whom the fourth Mughal Emperor, Mirza Nur-ud-din Muhammad Salim, known by his imperial name, Jahangir: the conqueror of the world, had said:

Agar Firdaws ba roy-i zamin ast,
Hamin ast-u, hamin ast-u, hamin ast.

If there is a paradise on earth,
It is this, it is this, it is this.

Over the years, I have addressed audiences in different parts of the globe and have highlighted in various fora (including the print, electronic and social media) the plight of my fellow Kashmiri Pandits, who have been reduced to refugees in their own land. As is well known, the large-scale exodus of Pandits from the Kashmir Valley began in January 1990. They were forced to flee their homeland as they were asked by the terrorists (who were, and are, a law unto themselves) to convert to Islam or be slaughtered. Most of them wound up in the Hindu-majority areas of Jammu (in refugee camps) and the rest sought their fortunes elsewhere in India or abroad.

I have been described by a section of the media as 'the most vocal supporter' of Kashmiri Pandits in recent times who 'has used his status as a celebrity to speak about the community'. However, not all, including my own brethren—the Kashmiri Pandits—have appreciated my contributions. In early 2014, I was labelled as 'a clown with political ambitions'. But such a barb did not, and does not, deter me in the least and I did not slacken, in any way, my efforts to help them.

In 2014, I went to Jammu where I addressed a rally organised by a newly formed political outfit and clearly pointed out that I was not representing any political party but was there 'because my soul was in Kashmir'. I emphasised that nothing much had changed in Kashmir in the past 65 years while other states have witnessed growth and development and also that only politicians have prospered in Kashmir and thus, highlighting the fact that the dynastic politics in Jammu and Kashmir should end.[24] I stressed that change was absolutely necessary to ensure a brighter future of Kashmir, especially for the youth for whom the business opportunities, infrastructure, administration and quality of life should improve. I exhorted the youth to take destiny in their own hands and become the agents of change. Then I struck an optimistic note with the words: 'The day isn't far when a smile will be back on the faces of Kashmiris.'

Time rolled on. As 2015 drew to a close, I again visited Jammu and on 25 December, went to the Jagti township (13 km away) which housed thousands of the displaced Kashmiri Pandits in less-than-ideal conditions. Most, if not all, families were struggling to survive there, but they did not lose hope. I was deeply moved by their never-say-die attitude and their perseverance and determination to meet all challenges. The fact that not one of them had taken up weapons or resorted to any form of violence only increased my respect and admiration for my fellow compatriots.

While interacting with them, I tried to motivate them to fight for their rights, especially for their rehabilitation in the Kashmir Valley (from where they had been uprooted). I also counselled the elders to teach the young ones the Kashmiri language (so that it did not become extinct) and explain to them the remarkable features of Kashmiri culture and civilisation, which had survived for millennia despite numerous attempts to obliterate them.

To mark the twenty-sixth death anniversary of the respected lawyer, Prem Nath Bhat, a victim of terrorist brutality, I declared forcefully that nobody could stop the journey of progress of Kashmiri Pandits. I asserted that while we should keep our wounds and pain alive, we should also find the path to achieve the goal of our return to and rehabilitation of the Kashmir Valley. I pointed out that we did not have to resort to begging bowls; instead, we should demand our rights as we were fighting a war for freedom. I assured that we would emerge victorious and added that we were heroes because we were not expressing our tragedy publicly but were carrying it in our hearts and that we possessed the capability of laughing even in difficult times. I concluded by stating: 'The moot question is that we should keep the sustenance for our fight alive. We are now settled. It was important to settle in life and have jobs. But we should not forget the fight and the struggle. We should not only remember some specific dates but should also ensure the fight for our existence throughout the year.

Every time I go to Jammu and meet the displaced Kashmiri Pandit community, I am struck by two aspects—their staunch patriotism and their sanguinity. Here is a community that was driven out from their homes, torn out of the state and forced to abandon their moorings and yet, they are able to hold on to such qualities.

From 1990 onwards, most of them have been living in highly squalid places. Meanwhile, a new generation has been born, raised and educated in the most deprived conditions. Despite facing tremendous setbacks, many youngsters have gone on to get jobs all over India and overseas. A generation that should have been bitter and resentful and may have even turned to violence, has instead chosen the path of light. It is working towards the betterment of their own lives, of their families, and ultimately, of the nation.

People talk easily about tolerance. I would like to proudly assert that this is what tolerance truly emulates.

I was also struck by their idealisation. There they were, attired in their best, about 7000 of them, talking, laughing and singing. And yet, when we were remembering the ones who have fallen and the graphic descriptions of what had been done to their near and dear ones, the atmosphere became sombre. Some of them described the way their relatives had been killed, which made a shiver run down down my spine.

One of those done to death was a pujari (priest). He was offered protection from the militants by a Muslim constable who had asked him to convert to Islam every day. When the pujari refused to do so, he was killed with a rifle butt. The details of the murder were excruciating to listen to.

Another incident included a 23-year-old Hindu constable who had come home on leave to spend time with his mother. He had gone out to run some errands. At a nearby shop, he was engaged in a conversation with the shopkeeper, who, he thought, was an old friend. The constable was held up with the talks long enough till the militants could come and pump some bullets into him. The wounds were not fatal, which was intentional. His hands and feet were tied, and he was dangled from a bridge where he was left to bleed, even as a crowd collected and watched him die in agony. His wife was there listening to these ghastly details but with composure.

I asked the organisers why this horror had to be recounted in such detail. They told me it was important to keep the wounds and the pain alive.

Yet, the leaders of the Kashmiri Pandit community have not become separatists, who, as their name suggests, separate people on the basis of religion. Yet, the separatists walk freely in democratic India even though they have raped, killed and maimed many Kashmiri Pandits.

Even after all this, the displaced Pandits have endured and not become terrorists. Instead, they have gone on with their lives, even though the world seems to have forgotten them.

One government after the other has come and gone in the past three decades. Promises have been made by politicians of all hues only to be broken. But then Kashmiri Pandits are not a vote bank. There is no one to weep for their wounds.

In January 2016, I made a small documentary which was telecast on the Times Now TV channel. It was in black and white and went as follows:

I am a Kashmiri Pandit. I am citizen of this country who truly believes in Indianness. I am also peaceful, non-violent, secular, law-abiding and patriotic.

On this day, 26 years ago, I was thrown out of my house. This is my story. As the winter of 1989 set in, Kashmir was dominated by terrorists. The state government had abdicated all its responsibilities and there was no administration whatsoever. The diktats of the terrorists held Kashmir in their grip. It seemed as if being an Indian was a curse. The terrorists were busy preparing a hit list. All those who were supporters of India were branded as 'informers'. Killing them was jihad (holy war, according to Islam) and a virtuous act.

First, important Kashmiri Pandits were being targeted and killed. In Srinagar, the social worker, Tika Lal Taploo, was killed in broad daylight in public. Neelkanth Ganjoo was killed in Karan Nagar (a locality in Srinagar) and his body lay on the streets for many hours. The advocate, Prem Nath Bhat, was mercilessly killed in south Kashmir's Anantnag area. Numerous unknown Pandits were ruthlessly killed. The message was clear—leave the Valley or convert to Islam.

On 5 January 1990, in the *Aaftab* newspaper, the Hizbul Mujahideen's press statement asked all Hindus to leave the Kashmir Valley. The same statement was printed in another newspaper named *Alsafa*. Soon, the same notice was stuck on the doors of the Kashmiri Pandits' homes.

On the tragic night of 19 January 1990, Kashmir was in the grip of an eclipse and it seemed that darkness had swallowed all the light. From every nook and corner of Kashmir, from every street, from every bazaar and from every village there rose such a loud voice that sent a message of death to the Pandits. In the streets of Kashmir, crowds made up of lakhs were shouting provocative slogans (against the Pandits). Such scenes had never been seen before and such slogans had never been heard earlier. All over Kashmir, there were announcements being made in masjids (mosques) that 'Kashmir will become Pakistan'. Mujahids (holy warriors) were being eulogised all over Kashmir. Also, guns were being flaunted by some members of the crowds.

Wake up, wake up; dawn is here. Russia has lost the game (referring to the Soviet troops being driven out of Afghanistan), India is trembling. It's now Kashmir's turn (to gain independence).

This song was being played again and again in masjids across Kashmir. The terrorists declared that those (Hindus) who wanted to stay in Kashmir had to say: Allahu Akbar (Allah is great).

The terrorists also announced (targeting the Hindus): 'O cruel ones, O infidels, leave our Kashmir.' The series of slogans seemed unending. If one stopped, another started. Among these slogans was one that proclaimed: 'Kashmir will become Pakistan! Without the Pandit males but with the Pandit females!' This slogan was repeated over and over again. Our fear now took on a new form. The Pandit families hid the women in storerooms. There is no need to say that if a mob attacked them, they would immolate themselves. The fear generated that night was unparalleled. The state of gloom seemed endless. The message (to the Pandits from the terrorists) was sharp and clear: 'Either join us or die or run away.' There was no village, locality, street or place where the din of this slogan was not heard. Most of the Kashmiri Pandits, under these adverse circumstances, collected whatever household goods they could and fled to save their lives and their honour. They hid under tarpaulin sheets in trucks or else boarded buses or hired taxis to take them out of the Kashmir Valley. The large-scale exodus had started. The conscience of the government, the intelligentsia and the secularist nation had gone to sleep. Nobody was ready to talk about the Pandits.

In the days following 19 January 1990, Kashmiri Pandits (who were left behind) began being massacred. The atrocities committed on them reached their limit. In Bandipora (about 65 km north of Srinagar), a lady teacher named Giriraj Tikoo was gangraped and then murdered. Such incidents became commonplace. An entire book can be written on how the Pandits were abused and how the government remained a mute spectator to the brutalities unleashed on them.

By 1991, a majority of the Pandits had left the Kashmir Valley and they were taken to an inaccessible area in Jammu and kept in places filled with dust and thorny shrubs. Around 6000 families fled and were sent to camps that did not have the basic necessities such as toilets. Each family was allotted one tent and, at times, ten members had to live and sleep there. There was a total lack of hygiene. In these camps, people in large numbers perished due to disease. Many deaths occurred as a result of snake bites and excessive heat. Kashmiri Pandits were left to die.

Thousands of houses and hundreds of temples of the Kashmiri Pandits were set ablaze. All this was happening in a multicultural and secular India. The small number of Pandits who were left in the Kashmir Valley were slaughtered by terrorists; they did not even spare young innocent children.

Entire villages once inhabited by Pandits were wiped out. Till today, not one person has been convicted. Punishment for the murder and massacre of thousands of Pandits has not been questioned; no one has even expressed concern over the exodus and the killings. Our houses are desolate, and our temples have been desecrated and are on the verge of collapsing. Even after 28 years, the Kashmiri Pandits are living as refugees in camps on the outskirts of Jammu. They are not getting much help there. Although people are today coming closer through the social media and almost everything is available at one's fingertips, the plight of the Kashmiri Pandits still remains unchanged. They have been abandoned as they are. Despite all this, I am hopeful that justice will prevail for us.

Jai Hind!

I had visited Jammu and its surrounding areas several times, but now I felt that I must go to Srinagar, the home of my ancestors.

My last significant 'Kucch bhi ho sakta hai' moment happened in Srinagar, the capital of Jammu and Kashmir, on 10 April 2016.

It was just another morning when I boarded the Indigo flight 6E 653 from Delhi to Srinagar. It was ready for departure eight minutes before its scheduled time of 1005 hours. The doors of the Airbus 320 were shut, one of the two engines was switched on to power the air-conditioning system, the aerobridge had been withdrawn and the cabin crew members were walking down the aisle doing the final headcount. Soon, the pilot switched on the second engine so that the plane could now taxi on to the runway under its own power.

I was seated in the first row and the air hostess, who was about to start the routine safety demonstration to passengers, smiled at me. I bet she, like most other hostesses on all flights around the world, meant to convey: 'Here we go again. No one really pays attention to these safety demos.'

I was returning to my native Srinagar—the city that my parents had left in 1953 (two years before I was born) and moved to Shimla. Though we had moved to Shimla, every holiday season for two to three months, we would go to Kashmir, where I was admitted as a temporary student for that period. During this period, we would travel, visit various temples and mosques to pay our reverence. Those three months were the most joyous for me for I was not only breathing fresh, cold, crisp air but I also lived a real life. For me, Shimla was where I stayed. Kashmir where my home was. Where my heart was! The 1950s, the 1960s, the 1970s and most of the 1980s were by and large peaceful in Jammu and Kashmir. But from 1989-90 onwards till date, violence and militancy have dominated its history. I shall not go into the details on the catastrophic events of the past few decades, which are only too well known and have been recorded in numerous books, documentaries, articles and news reports (both in the print and electronic media). All I would like to say is that there should be an immediate end to so much tension, conflict, violence and bloodshed and the leaders should ensure that peace and prosperity return to J&K.

Since the beginning of 2016, the separatists have been routinely ratcheting up tension with cries of *azaadi* (freedom) and infiltrators have been engaged in gun battles with the security forces. In the first week of April 2016, students of the National Institute of Technology (NIT) in Srinagar were embroiled in an ugly fracas, which was assuming national dimensions. It all began when India lost the semi-final of the T20 championship (cricket) to the West Indies on 31 March in Mumbai. As it often happens in the Kashmir Valley, whenever India plays another country in cricket or hockey, the locals are vociferously anti-Indian in their sentiment. They raucously cheer the opponents which is very galling to many diehard Indian fans, especially if India loses the match. The same situation occurred on 31 March, when the local students jeered the losing Indian cricket team and applauded the West Indians.

The next day, the non-Kashmiri students of the NIT lodged a complaint with the authorities and took out a morcha (an organised march or rally) against the supporters of the West Indies, waved the tricolour (Indian flag) and burnt the Pakistani flag. In volatile Srinagar, such acts were considered 'hostile' in several quarters. Fearing that matters would get out of hand, the institute authorities closed the campus for the weekend and asked the students to vacate the hostels. When studies resumed on 4 April, the non-Kashmiri students boycotted classes and took out a rally keeping up the tension while the local students attended the lectures. The following day, the agitating non-Kashmiris took out another rally demanding, among other things, the shifting of the institute from Srinagar as they felt the attitude of the Kashmiri students was hostile towards them. There was a scuffle with the Jammu and Kashmir police and the latter cracked down hard on the protesting non-Kashmiri students. Nationwide protests against the police action followed and the matter was taken up by the Union Ministry of Home Affairs, which immediately sent a fact-finding mission to Srinagar.

While the matter was soon painted to be a central government versus state government issue, things were not so clear-cut since the Mehbooba Mufti led coalition government had been sworn in barely a day earlier on 4 April 2016. (Mehbooba Mufti's People's Democratic Party or the PDP and the Bharatiya Janata Party or BJP had formed the coalition.)

I was mulling over these developments as the Airbus moved on to runway 11/29, which was India's longest (4430 metres). Clearance for take-off came through and at 1005 hours, the aircraft began rolling and in next twenty seconds, it would become airborne.

Twenty seconds is a long time when thoughts are racing through your mind. I remembered Srinagar as the capital of an Indian state that had faced trouble celebrating India's Republic Day (26 January) for decades. The tricolour was hoisted with great difficulty at a public function at Lal Chowk, the city centre, access to which was mostly restricted to government servants. Elsewhere in the city (which seemed to be particularly embattled on such days), instead of raising the Indian flag, political parties with separatist agenda held gatherings where people stamped on the Indian flag, urinated on it and finally, burnt it. For me, who was increasingly feeling the flame of patriotism surfacing from deep within, such memories were disturbing. I wondered why they indulged in such nefarious activities.

My agenda in Srinagar was clear. I would go to the National Institute of Technology and wave the tricolour there, after a fervent appeal to national pride.

The wheels of the Airbus lifted off from the sun-drenched tarmac. Flight 6E 653 was now airborne and heading towards Srinagar. I was homeward bound, or so I thought.

During the flight, my mind was recapturing the events of the past few weeks.

On 9 February 2016, a group of students of Jawaharlal Nehru University (JNU) in Delhi organised an event on the campus to protest against the hanging of Afzal Guru. The event was held despite the university withdrawing permission and witnessed clashes between various student groups. Anti-India slogans were also raised which were castigated by several political leaders and some students of JNU.

A few weeks before undertaking the trip to Srinagar, on 18 March 2016, I had visited the Jawaharlal Nehru University campus—known for its leftist tilt—in Delhi to screen Vivek Agnihotri's *Buddha in a Traffic Jam* (a political film in which I played a key role). I took this opportunity to address the students there. During my speech, I pointed out: 'Someone who has come out on bail is not an Olympic hero.' I was referring to the bail granted by the court a few hours earlier to JNU students Umar Khalid and Anirban Bhattacharya who had been arrested in March for their involvement in a controversial event in support of the terrorist Afzal Guru (who was hanged to death on 9 February 2013, in Delhi's Tihar Jail). For his participation in that event, JNU Students' Union President, Kanhaiya Kumar, also had been arrested and granted bail. My speech at JNU had been widely reported in the media as 'a nationalistic show of the flag in a leftist bastion'.

On 6 March 2016, an event was held in Kolkata, organised by the *Telegraph*, a widely circulated newspaper of the Anandabazar Patrika group. The panel was made up of Justice Asok Kumar Ganguly (a retired Supreme Court judge), Barkha Dutt (a noted senior TV journalist) and Randeep Surjewala (politician and a spokesperson of the Indian National Congress) on one side, while the famous actor Kajol, the 'TV pundit' and author Suhel Seth and me were on the other. The topic was: 'Tolerance Is the New Intolerance'. In his speech, Justice Ganguly raised doubts regarding the execution (hanging to death) of the 13 December 2001 Parliament attack convict, Afzal Guru, on 9 February 2013 in Delhi's Tihar Jail. (Afzal Guru had been given the death sentence by the Supreme Court.) When my turn came, I decided not to mince my words. I discarded my prepared speech and spoke extempore about what I felt. When I spoke, I did so with total conviction. Here are the relevant excerpts:

> I seek your forgiveness as I would like to speak in Hindi because I think in that language. In between, if I slip into English, it would be your good fortune. (I did speak in English too, but not much.) Before coming here, I had thought a lot about what I should say, that I will not make my speech personal. I will not make it pro-BJP. I will not make a list of people (and their wrongs).
>
> However, I am shocked and ashamed and saddened by what you said Justice Ganguly . . . It's so sad that you're calling the verdict of the Supreme Court wrong, being a judge yourself. It's a matter of complete disgrace that you were hounded by the press and you were intolerant of them when there was a case against you. (He had been accused of sexually harassing an intern; the charges were later dropped.) And today, you say what happened at JNU[25] was right. It's absolutely unpardonable that instead of condemning the protests taking place at JNU, you are saying the Supreme Court was wrong.
>
> Let me ask you one question. We are totally forgetting (our soldiers) and making a hero out of one guy (I was referring to

Kanhaiya Kumar) who was a participant in the night of 9 February 2016 and what were the slogans that were (being shouted) there?

- *Destruction to India!*
- *India, you shall be broken into pieces! Insha Allah . . . Insha Allah* (God willing).
- *Afzal Guru, we are ashamed that your 'murderers' are still alive.*

Who were his 'murderers'? Were the Supreme Court judges (who awarded the death sentence) his 'murderers'?

This is the crux of the matter. Instead of condemning it (the slogan), you are saying that the Supreme Court was wrong, and that the Afzal Guru judgment was wrong (are) absolutely unpardonable your honour! (Justice Ganguly then tried to interrupt to say something). No, no, you can't speak in between, sir. Let me finish. I'm sorry. It's my turn now . . .

Surjewalaji, you talked about and prepared a full list about what the BJP (has ostensibly done to encourage intolerance). You forgot that the Emergency was declared by Indira Gandhi (on 25 June 1975, when the people's Fundamental Rights, as guaranteed by the Constitution, were abrogated and coercive sterilisation was carried out on a large scale) . . . That was the biggest intolerance in the country, ever. All those people (mostly journalists) who spoke against the (government) were jailed . . . there were whisper campaigns (against them) . . . my grandfather (was put behind bars) . . . Do you know who I think are the most tolerant people in this country? It is the Congress (members). They are tolerating a person (Rahul Gandhi) who they want to project as the prime minister of this country and can't even say to each other that we are wrong. We are so sorry this is our prime ministerial candidate. They must be (telling) each other we are stuck with this (person) . . . Show the same tolerance once in Parliament and let the Parliament function. (The Congress was then stalling proceedings in the Parliament.) If you can tolerate that person then you can tolerate anything in the world.

Eight months ago, had any of you heard tolerance (versus) intolerance (debate)? I am sure not. This has been 'marketed'. Yes! This has been marketed by the opposition whose failure has turned into a defeat. Their entire thinking is: 'How to avenge this defeat?' The prime minister (Narendra Modi) has won with a majority of 282 seats in the Lok Sabha in the 2014 general elections).

A tea seller has become the prime minister . . . I am not advocating (his cause); I am just speaking as a citizen of this country. People say you are talking about Mr Modi because your wife is in the BJP. I have been married to Kirron for the last 30 years. I don't have to prove my loyalty to her by talking about BJP.

You (meaning those opposed to the BJP) cannot tolerate the fact that Mr Modi goes abroad (and has become very popular there). You tolerated a prime minister who kept quiet for ten years. (Dr Manmohan Singh, a Congressman, was prime minister from May 2004 to May 2014. He hardly ever spoke in public except for the Independence Day address from the Lal Qila or Red Fort.)

The present prime minister is very dynamic not because he speaks well but because he talks about the idea of India. He has not taken a single holiday in two years and his Diwali is always spent in Kashmir; he is the only prime minister who has visited Kashmir twice on Diwali ...

For the past two years (from May 2016 onwards), has there any mention of corruption? And for ten years (May 2004 to May 2016), only corruption prevailed: 2G, 3G, this G and that G! Oh G! Since the Modi Government was not involved in corruption, a new word needed to be used to describe Modi. Thus, we got the word 'intolerant'. Spread this word all around so much so that dada (elder brother; i.e. Justice Ganguly) has to talk about intolerance in this Kolkata event. This is no debate sir. People are tolerant. Do you know who is talking about intolerance? The intellectuals, the rich and the famous who travel with twenty bodyguards ...

If you ask a man on the street, about intolerance, he would find it difficult to even pronounce the word! 'All I want is two square meals a day. If that happens, I am not concerned about intolerance. I just do my work.' Those who go to five-star hotels and follow that culture and those who wear diamond studs and say that I don't hold (any grudge) against them, sip champagne and say (in their clipped English accent or American slang): 'India has become such an intolerant country.'

Whether you are talking in India or America, it does not matter. We have the presidential candidate in America (Donald

Trump) who says that Muslims should be thrown out of the country. That is frightening . . . that is intolerance.

If you heard the speech of the prime minister recently, he said: 'Parties will come and parties will go, but the country is important.' The prime minister talks about the country. And you (those opposed to him) have made him an outsider. He is also your prime minister who has been elected by the people. He has not begged you to make him the prime minister. Those who campaigned that Narendra Modi should not be given a visa by the USA have seen the change. The USA gave him a red-carpet welcome (in 2015) and President Barack Obama and he even embraced each other!

You have trouble with that? You have trouble with me? 'Whosoever speaks in the prime minister's favour, let us make him 'in-credible'; i.e., finish off his credibility. If Anupam Kher organises a march to protect India's freedom, brand him a *chamcha* (sycophant) of the prime minister. If Anupam Kher is awarded the Padma Bhushan, he got it because he is a chamcha.'

Articles and editorials are written about me. I never knew that I was such an important person . . .

A forty-six-year-old has been projected as a 'youth icon' (by the Congress). I did not want to mention the name of Rahul Gandhi (the Congress vice-president) but it is necessary for me to do so. The day Rahul Gandhi attains even one-tenth of Narendra Modi's status, I will vote for him.

Please give the Modi Government five years to work for the nation. After five years, it can be voted out. We do not want an intolerant government . . .

All those should be arrested who have been behaving arrogantly (ranting against the minorities, mainly the Muslims), whether a *sadhvi* (saintly woman) or a yogi. There are some members in the BJP who speak nonsense. They should be reprimanded and expelled from the party. But those who claim that there is a lot of intolerance are playing with the destiny of the country. Now, here is tolerance. The audience members are showing tolerance by listening to you (i.e., Justice Ganguly) and not hooting! I have seen you on television sir. When the camera was focusing closely on your face, you were getting intolerant. Don't become like that.

My friends, this is a great country. Let us tolerate the intolerance of these people.

Thank you very much.

My speech was widely appreciated as 'nationalist' in nature. It went viral within just a few seconds.

The Airbus touched down at Srinagar's Sheikh ul-Alam airport, on time, at 1140 hours and I was among the first to step out of the aircraft. A posse of senior police officers of the J&K Police, some in civilian attire, met me and spoke to me warmly in Kashmiri. There were some non-Kashmiris too among them and they broke into Hindi. I presumed that it was a gesture on the part of the state government to welcome home a Kashmiri celebrity.

They escorted me to the VIP lounge at the terminal and one of them went to fetch my luggage. They continued to treat me cordially and said they wanted to make me feel at home. I felt strange that they had to spell it out because I was at home in 'my Kashmir'. But as the minutes passed, I realised that they were not allowing me to leave the terminal. Initially, I thought it was a joke. But later, it dawned on me that the situation was turning serious. I also saw their growing discomfort at restraining me. Obviously, they had got their orders from their political masters.

I surmised that the policemen might want me to refrain from going to the National Institute of Technology campus. Perhaps they feared that I might make a bold speech and stir up sentiments. But I wondered how they had come to know of my plans. When I asked them, they merely smiled . . . as if to say: 'We have our sources.'

In a flashback, I realised that though I had been publicly silent about my Srinagar trip, the newly inducted coalition government had tried to get in touch with me. I had telephoned M. K. Dhar, the personal secretary to the chief minister (Mehbooba Mufti), to keep her informed about my visit. I had also sent him several messages on 7 and 8 April. In one of them, I had stated: '. . . I may come to

Srinagar on 10ᵗʰ [April] morning and I want to meet the honourable chief minister sahiba. Please let me know if it can be organised.' There was no reply to any of my messages.

I then assured the policemen that I would not go to the NIT as I realised that my visit might create some problems. From the airport lounge, I rang up a high political figure in Delhi who assured me that he would talk to the concerned officials and things would be sorted out very soon. But nothing happened. I was then informed by the policemen that my return ticket to Delhi had been booked on a flight, which was to take off after four hours. So, I told them that rather than stay at the airport, I would like to visit my cousin's house at Karan Nagar, where she ran a school. The policemen said they would organise the visit but as time ticked away, nothing of that sort happened.

By this time, I had resigned myself to my fate. Nevertheless, I requested them to allow me to step out of the airport just to breathe the air of Kashmir. But they turned down my request peremptorily. Very soon, their smiles disappeared, and they became firmer in their stand about not permitting me to leave the airport. It then dawned on me that I was actually under house arrest or rather 'airport arrest'. This time it was the authorities who were preventing me from entering my home state. I realised that most, if not all, of my relatives were forced to flee their homeland in 1990 (as victims of inhumane terrorism) and I, a Kashmiri, who has constantly been protesting against their exodus, was now being prevented by those in power from entering Srinagar.

At the Srinagar airport, I felt isolated, friendless and cut off from all help from a distant administration. I could have called up someone in the media and vented my frustration or anger. Or I could have tweeted. But I did not do so. It was only when I was gathering my thoughts for this book, I realised that, deep down, I was extremely hurt by this incident. But I have accepted it as another 'Kucch bhi ho sakta hai' moment in my life.

I have regularly introspected about the vagaries of my life and its ups and downs. And I believe that whatever happens, it is for my good and so was the case with the Srinagar incident. I feel that, in a larger context, nothing much has changed for the displaced Kashmiris in the past (nearly) three decades. We are all children of a lost land which include those who are in the Jagti township near Jammu and elsewhere as well as the Padma Bhushan Anupam Kher.

Part–VI

SPREADING THE WINGS

——◆◇ ⟐ ◇◆——

Inside of all the makeup and the character and makeup, it's you, and I think that's what the audience is really interested in . . . you, how you are going to cope with a situation, the obstacles, the troubles that the writer put in front of you.

—Gregory Peck

30

WESTWARD BOUND

*C*rossing the so-called 'divide' from Eastern to Western cinema has taught me some valuable lessons. I must start with professing that it is a complete myth that 'Bollywood' actors can act only in 'Bollywood' films as they are familiar only with a certain kind and style of acting. I remember the initial reaction when I inaugurated my school, Actor Prepares, in London after its great success in India. The stigma that surrounds Indian cinema became apparent when a prominent BBC anchor asked me during the course of an interview: 'So you will teach Bollywood acting in your school here?'

'I don't understand. What is Bollywood acting? What do you mean by that?' I enquired.

'Oh, where you go singing and dancing around the trees. Where you sing songs every now and then,' he answered.

I thought for a few moments about my response and then said: 'I implore you to look at our cinema in a different way. Instead of looking down upon what we do, it's important to recognise that you need a lot of guts to do these kinds of movies . . . our performance comes from an immense amount of courage.

'We, as people, as a country, are larger than life. We have 28 official languages in the country and more than 3000 dialects. Every 1000 km or so, an entire culture morphs from one to another—different food, different dialect, different language and even different attire. It goes to show that when an Indian Hindi film actor has to reach out to Telegu or Tamil or Bengali audience, he has to exaggerate, because it's not one English or French or German language that everyone would understand. It takes a highly accomplished Indian actor to be able to do things which he himself is not convinced about. And yet, he convinces 1.3 billion people.

'Let me pose this question to you: can you imagine a Tom Cruise or a Brad Pitt or anybody else in Hollywood doing what our Indian actors do? Can they do what Shah Rukh Khan or Akshay Kumar does in film after film consistently? Can they act in the same manner and sway the audiences? If it were a level playing field to the same kind of money, the same given circumstances, the same amount of professionalism, Indian actors can do what a Tom Cruise does, what a Brad Pitt does. I don't think we should run down Indian cinema just because of songs or running around trees. Music and songs are all a part of our everyday life.'

I don't know whether the anchor or those watching the interview were convinced with my reply, but I want to point out here that it was the British who coined the word Bollywood. Why don't they call the cinema from China as Chinawood? Or French cinema as Frenchwood? We are fools for accepting the term Bollywood and the stigma that goes with it, which in turn, stems from a need for acceptance.

In Indian cinema, be it in any language, a great deal of conviction is required to portray any scene, any sequence and any storyline. For example, those of you who have seen Indra Kumar's *Dil*, where I, in the role of Hazari Prasad, am an extremely miserly person to the extent that in one scene, I literally take a fly out of the teacup and suck it—a purposeful reference to a *makhi choos*. The goal was to portray the height of being a miser. I had to gather all my acting skills to make the scene convincing . . . so that it would look believable . . . so that the audience would react to it. For every film, for every role, a conviction is needed and each one of them requires an enormous amount of acting talent. Look at Mahesh Bhatt's *Dil Hai Ki Manta Nahin* or Subhash Ghai's *Ram Lakhan* where I had to act as Girdhar Shastri, the bania. Again, it was all about conviction. Of course, that conviction also stems from the fact that I am a trained actor. The films we make in Indian cinema are no less than any other in any part of the world and I have lived through these films to be able to make that statement. Tuning of performance is necessary of course, but the art, craft, energy and commitment it takes to perform are universal.

It was sometime in the summer of 2000 during a shooting schedule for a Hindi film in the US, that I got a call from a friend of mine—Deepak Nayar. He informed me that a group of British companies like the Film Council, Future Film Financing, Kintop Pictures and some others were collaborating to make a film, *Bend It Like Beckham*, which was to be directed by Gurinder Chadha. As casting was being finalised, they wanted me to *read* a role. At this stage, I was strutting around like a peacock as I was being sought after by every other Indian film director. I had become very arrogant and pompous. 'How can they ask me . . . Anupam Kher, without whom no blockbuster is being made in India, to *read* for a role? Where do I have the time to read a role?' I asked Deepak. I was, in hindsight, totally ignorant of the casting systems in place in the West.

Deepak was, at one time, an assistant to producer-director-actor O. P. Ralhan, who way back in the 1960s, 1970s and 1980s had made some big hits of the time like *Gehra Daag* with Rajendra Kumar and Mala Sinha, *Phool Aur Pathar* with Meena Kumari and Dharmendra and *Talaash* with Rajendra Kumar, Sharmila Tagore and Balraj Sahni. Deepak is today a successful producer in his own right in Hollywood and has produced some amazing films like *Lost Highway, Vampire Academy* and *Partition 1947*.

He said: 'Okay, don't read it but can you come and meet Gurinder Chadha in London on your way back from America?'

I agreed.

I had seen Gurinder Chadha's *Bhaji on the Beach* and had liked it very much. We arranged to meet at the St James Court Hotel. She told me about the film and briefed me of the role she had in mind for me. I liked the story of this Indian family settled in England and how they want their daughter, whose passion in life is football, to hang her football boots, learn to cook and run a house, find a boy and settle down to a 'happy' life of domesticity. But the girl bends the rule—and how—to reach her goal in professional soccer. Coupled with that was the fact that it would give me an opportunity to work in an English language film. She was also frank enough to tell me that they had also approached Amitabh Bachchan for the same role.

A few days later, I got a call from Deepak who said: 'Gurinder really liked you and wants you to be on board.' The kind of money that they offered was paltry but for me, it was a great opportunity to be part of this British project.

The first day that I went for the reading, the entire cast was there—Keira Knightley, Jonathan Rhys Meyers, Parminder Nagra, Shaznay Lewis, Archie Panjabi and Frank Harper. It was Keira Knightley's first film. That day I realised that in comparison to others, my role was a very small one on the script with a few lines. Also, I had this baggage of being a so-called Bollywood actor. Gurinder kept on reminding me: 'Don't do extra acting! Don't do Bollywood acting please.'

Once the shooting started, I realised what Gurinder meant when she said: 'Don't do extra acting' which I was then in the habit of doing. For example, if there was a scene in which I had to get the expression of being 'angry', I would exaggerate it and do much more than was necessary. Gradually, I adapted myself to what she wanted. That's where my training as an actor came in handy. When we shot the required scenes, Gurinder was happy, but more than that, I felt very strongly about my work.

The other thing was that everybody was very professional in their respective jobs and at times, irritatingly so. Unlike the culture I was used to, this meant 'every morning at sharp 7 o'clock the car will pick you up from the hotel. They will *not* call you up in your room. You have to be in the lobby at 5 minutes to 7 a.m. sharp.'

No such routine is followed in India. Instead, what we have is: '*Saheb aa rahe hain* (Sir is coming). *Saheb car mein baith geyein hain*' (He is in the car now). None of the nonsense is here. Here, you have to get in the car at 7. Dot 7. You reach the set and go straight for your make-up.' The wardrobe lady, the make-up man and the assistant would be waiting for me early in the morning, all ready. No gup-shup, just get on with the job. Not a minute was being wasted. Since, I was used to chatting a little and exchanging pleasantries over a cup of tea on reaching the studio, it was a little difficult to adjust to this 'new' system of work. I am not running down anything or anyone. I love the way we work in India because I love what's created there. In many ways, we have a much more one to one interaction at that level. I get down from my car, meet my producer, who is waiting for me, and have a chat with him. I'll chat with the light man or the cameraman or whoever is there. Then I will ask: 'Aaj, nashte mein kya hain?' (What's there for breakfast today), in that order. And when the assistant comes and asks: 'Are you ready sir?', I will say: 'Hold on na . . . I am just coming na.'

Of course, this was the culture and the habitat at the time—over 15 years back. That's how we functioned. How we made films. But here in England, it felt almost like the system was not giving me any time to even breathe. You have to be ready on the dot, every day, so as to be able to report whenever required for a shot. At home, it's common to get ready just before your shot. For example, for a 2 o'clock shot, you can get ready anytime, perhaps in afternoon or so. On this new set, I would be dressed and ready with complete make-up and costumes every morning, regardless of when my scenes were to be shot.

While shooting for *Bend It Like Beckham*, I also discovered that I was primarily thinking in Hindi with the result that whenever I had a long dialogue, I would find it difficult to memorise it. I would first translate it in my mind from Hindi to English or English to Hindi, then understand the feelings to speak my dialogues. In comparison, everybody else in the unit was speaking fluent English. I was the only outsider. The only import from India.

Despite the differences and the newness of the situation, I thoroughly enjoyed my work and my time with Gurinder. I must say she was fantastic! I loved the process of being disciplined, of having no distraction whatsoever during work. Each individual concentrated and together, everybody was working to complete the mission. Also, unlike in India, the equality of people was amazing. Even the light man could sit down and have dinner with the producer or director or a lead actor or lead actress.

Deepak became a friend and I realised that behind that thick exterior as a very strict Hollywood producer, he is just a typical, relatable Punjabi guy. He just takes a little time to open up. People may not like him sometimes, because he is very cut and dry, but if you scratch the surface, the real Deepak emerges—the same O. P. Ralhan assistant from Delhi who has grown to become famous in life, but at heart, is still the same. Much later he told me that he was afraid that I would be a typical obnoxious Bollywood actor who would need to be indulged due to an over-bloated ego. He was pleasantly surprised to find that I turned out to be a regular guy who would engage with everyone and make him and others around us laugh. I did not display any airs and had no whims and fancy.

I recall a very interesting and humorous incident during the making of *Bend It Like Beckham*—my first and last *drag*. Gurinder was shooting the scene of my daughter's wedding. I had stepped out of the set for some fresh air and went to stand next to Jonathan Meyers and some others who were smoking. It was cold and I asked: 'Can I also have a puff?'

'Are you sure?'

I thought he is asking because I normally don't smoke. Or because he had never seen me smoke. I had just asked for it because he was blowing smoke and I too felt like taking a puff in the cold. 'Okay, but only one drag,' he said. 'Just one.'

A very strange man. Why is being so possessive about his cigarette? I thought to myself. How was I to know then that a 'drag' meant one puff of a loaded 'joint'? I don't think even Gurinder knew that all this was going on in her unit. Anyway, in my ignorance, I took one drag and gave it back. Soon after, I was called in for the dance sequence of my daughter's wedding. I didn't have any dialogue to speak but had to dance and take part in the festivities that were being filmed. Precisely then, the 'drag' hit me. In my mind, I was dancing like Michael Jackson, in frenzy, but in reality, I was just moving one finger and making it dance in some silly dancing posture! Gurinder kept on telling me: 'Anupam, it's your eldest daughter's wedding. You are supposed to be enjoying it and you are supposed to do a little more.'

'More than this?' I asked her.

'Yes, you are not doing anything. Come on dance . . . lift your leg . . . Can you smile, be happy? It's a wedding scene . . . be happy . . . laugh!' she replied.

But in my head, I thought I was smiling too much, while she kept on insisting to smile a bit more...? *What is wrong with her?* I thought. *She's asking me to smile when I'm almost bursting. My teeth can fall out, my eyes can pop out and I am dancing like nobody's business.* How I finished the shooting of that sequence and that too, to Gurinder's satisfaction, I still don't know, because the effect of the drag lasted for over three hours. Thank God I had no dialogue, otherwise, I really would have been in a complete mess.

The film became a super-duper hit at the box office. It got superb reviews also. The whole cast was brilliant. Every one of them. Back home, the much-awarded director-cinematographer Govind Nihlani called me and said: 'Anupam, you are outstanding in the film.'

'But I have not done much. There is no dramatic scene in the entire film. There's just one scene where I tell my daughter, "You know when I used to play for Tanzania . . . ," only four lines. Otherwise, I haven't done much.'

He said: 'You are outstanding. And look at the great reviews.'

True, the response was phenomenal. The reviews were mind-boggling, not only in the British but in the American press too. The film did a business of nearly a hundred million dollars. Keira Knightley became an overnight star. For me, it was a wonderful career move too since it paved my way into the British cinema. Thereafter, I did a lot of episodes of *Spooks* (also known as *MI-5* series in some countries)—a British television drama series aired on BBC One. Immediately after this, in 2002, I was signed by Channel Four for the blockbuster *Second Generation*, a drama adaptation of William Shakespeare's tragic hero King Lear which also had Om Puri and Roshan Seth. It was while working on this project that I noticed how effortlessly Om Puri would render his English dialogues. In fact, I think, his problem also was his effortlessness! He, along with Saeed Jaffrey, was the first Indian actor to work in international cinema in a big way—both British and American. He did amazing work right from his first project in 1984, the British TV series, *The Jewel in the Crown*, based on Paul Scott's *The Raj Quartet* to Roland Joffe's *City of Joy*, adapted from Dominique Lapierre's famous book by the same name, to Damien O'Donnell's *East is East* which became a super hit at the box office in 1999, through to Gurinder Chadha's *Viceroy's House* released in 2017. He was undoubtedly a versatile actor with a great range who could play anything and everything with great competence. Another one like him is difficult to find. Unfortunately, like Amrish Puri, Om too did not know how to 'market' himself. He was a simple man. And yet, look at the number of British and American films and the TV serials he worked for in 33 years—23. Phenomenal indeed!

I was working with Roshan Seth—the man to whom I had lost the role of Pandit Jawaharlal Nehru in Richard Attenborough's *Gandhi*—for the first time. For some indescribable reason, he had a bit of a chip on his shoulder. He seemed to be a restless type of a person. Too fastidious about everything, a direct contrast to Om Puri and the other cast. Instead of a hotel, where we all stayed, Om Puri wanted to stay in an apartment by himself. 'I like being in an apartment because then I can regularly go shopping in the supermarket, which I love doing. I like doing grocery shopping because I want to cook,' he would say. He would invite me to his apartment for dinner and would cook a very sumptuous meal and serve it with style too. It was one of his many hidden talents, which few knew about.

I would like to add a note here about what I mean when I use the term 'market' himself. I feel that it's very important for actors to freely share how they achieved what they did. Acting is an actor's job and in today's world, an actor must advertise it. It's like a man with a monkey. Unless the man plays that little *dug-dugi* (small drums), nobody will come and stand around to see the monkey's antics. In the business of entertainment, it is essential for an actor to be like that. You need to tell people and take charge of your own destiny. Gone are the days of subtlety that my work will speak for itself. Today, when the choices are unlimited, the work may not speak for itself. You have to get promoted, marketed and retailed in the marketplace of cinema. This is something I am constantly aware of and consciously do. I never lose sight of the work because only quality work begets more work. Instead, it is essential to continue to grow your brand and connect with your audience. Just recently, I was speaking with a young Indian actor in New York, and I gave him this advice as he continues to build his way up: 'If you make space for everyone else, you'll never make space for yourself.'

At this stage, I decided to hire an agent for myself to promote and market me in the West. Somebody recommended me to Ruth Young, a very well-known senior agent at United Agents—a highly respectable agency. In the first meeting itself, she was gracious enough to accept me. She is one of the finest agents that I could have asked for. Many years later, by which time I was doing more international projects, some friends, including Ashok Amritraj—a former professional tennis player who had, after retirement, gone into film production and was CEO of National Geographic Films, after which he set up his own production company, Hyde Park Entertainment Films—told me that I should have an agent in Los Angeles. I spoke about it to Ruth: 'Ruth, I think I need an agent in LA.'

'No,' she said, 'I can handle it from here.'

'But many friends in the business, including Ashok Amritraj, are recommending it very seriously. It makes a great difference they say. I think I would like to do so.'

'Okay, I leave the decision up to you,' she replied. 'If you would like me to fix up your meetings with all the top agencies, I can do that,' she suggested.

I went to LA where she had fixed up my meetings with seven or eight top agencies. Soon I discovered that even though I met eight different people, I was meeting the same person again and again, with a different face. They are all trained to talk to you in a certain manner. Their questions and answers are the same. Also, most of them said: 'We are looking for a younger person who will be easier for us to present.' A couple of them said that there is 'very limited scope for a person like me'.

'Limited scope?' I asked. 'I'm not looking for a life-changing experience for myself.'

Back in London, I told Ruth: 'You are my agent.'

She laughed and said: 'I told you. Anupam, I know you now. I know what kind of a person you are. You like to be you. You like to go beyond a hello, beyond the normal conversation of how you are.'

I agreed: 'Yes Ruth, you are right. For me, a human interaction is imperative.'

The greatest quality of Ruth, who has been my agent for the last 15 years and represents some of the biggest names in the profession, is that she has retained the human touch. She is as real as one can be. She is strong, straightforward and my biggest strength.

After the phenomenal success of *Bend It Like Beckham*, Deepak came back with an offer to work in *Bride and Prejudice*, a 'Bollywood' style adaptation of Jane Austen's classic, *Pride and Prejudice*. It was, once again, to be directed by Gurinder Chadha who had also written it along with Paul Mayeda Berges. By now, we were friends and could talk frankly. He said to me: 'Anupam, since now we know each other well, I thought I will talk to you directly, instead of going through your agent Ruth. Let's talk directly.'

It is important to describe what I did next as these are lessons I have learnt about not just being able to 'market' myself, but to be honest about my work and my value system.

'Deepak, I appreciate that and do understand your thought process, but in all fairness, you will have to discuss it through my agent Ruth. That's the system here and I would like to stick to it. I don't want to do anything that is unethical . . . I don't want to do anything behind Ruth's back and hurt her,' I replied, thinking the matter was over.

Later, Ruth told me that Deepak was offering me the role in

Gurinder's next movie, but just like last time, for very little money. I was confused. Here was *Bend It Like Beckham,* an international monster hit, and here's the follow-up film by the same team, with a much longer role that will require me for 40 days on set. 'Deepak says he will look after you well,' Ruth tried to explain. *What's the alternative? An actor at my level should be looked after well regardless of the project,* I thought. Ruth advised me to ask for more money and I agreed. The message was clear: no compromises and fair duty!

Deepak invited me for breakfast at the Marriott Hotel in Mumbai. I knew, as friends, I could take the liberty of conversing with him the way I wanted to. Over breakfast, I came straight to the point: 'Why are you giving me so little money for the film?'

'Anupam, there are too many expenses. It's a very expensive film this time,' he replied.

I said: 'You again went to Mr Amitabh Bachchan *pehle se na sunane ke liye* (to get no as an answer). And now you want me to agree to such a small amount.'

Then I did something that shocked him. I stood up on a chair in the crowded Marriott dining room at breakfast time and said: 'Ladies and gentlemen, may I have your attention please?'

Suddenly, there was pin-drop silence and all eyes were on us. 'Anupam what's wrong with you? Are you mad or what . . .? Please sit down,' Deepak said in a loud whisper.

'Friends, this is Deepak Nayar, the producer of my film, *Bend It Like Beckham* and he is now planning to produce another film, *Bride and Prejudice.* But he is not giving me the money that I deserve. Do you think I should do the film? Please tell me. Don't you think he should raise my money . . . give me what I deserve?'

Everyone, as if in one voice, said: 'Yes . . . yes . . . yes.'

I looked at Deepak and asked: 'Are you giving me more money . . . what I really deserve?'

'Yes! Yes!' he replied hurriedly as everyone clapped.

That was indeed a dramatic moment and I signed *Bride and Prejudice.* And yes, I got what I deserved. What I wanted. I was happy and so was Ruth. By now Gurinder Chadha, who had become successful with *Bend It Like Beckham*, was a big name in the world of cinema. She had assembled a big star-cast. There was Aishwarya Rai, Martin Handerson and Daniel Gilles in the main cast along with Nadira Babbar, Namrata Shirodkar and Sonali Kulkarni. We all had a great time during the making of the film. We were put up in a good hotel and of course, Deepak looked after us very well.

This is my personal opinion, but I do feel that when you are trying to make it big and you don't have the security of being a big name, there's certain sincerity in your film-making. It's like the old saying: 'You never forget your first...' As soon as you become big, become a name, then you want to become bigger and an element of artificiality, of external reward, starts to come in. It's like the Anupam Kher in *Saaransh* and the Anupam in *Karma*. If I do not look at my life from a zero point of view ... from Shimla point of view, I will play the role from a different viewpoint. But once I know my job, it will be different. I think that is precisely what happened with Gurinder. I felt her films started to become somewhat indifferent. Not in talent but in the thought process. Don't get me wrong, Gurinder is a wonderful director and a very nice, warm person, but I think film projects become big not because you plan to make them big, but because there's an element of sincerity in them. There is an element where the audience relates to what you're making. There is an element of truth in what is being made.

For example, if I do *Saaransh* today, I don't think I will be able to capture that same magic that happened in 1984, because I was raw and a nobody then. Today, I will try to bring in those emotions but will not be able to do so. How can I? I have already felt them. It's like diminishing marginal utility. I remember that our economics teacher, Professor Ramesh Chander, would come to the class at 1 o'clock, after having had his lunch. It was a time when our hunger pangs would be at their peak. Whereas, he would be completely satisfied after a hearty meal. To make matters worse, he would describe diminishing marginal utility using examples of food! 'In diminishing marginal utility, for example, you take this nice cold *rasgulla* and put it in your mouth. The minute you bite into it, the sweet juice flows down your throat and when you chew it, you can feel the real joy of having the rasgulla. But when you pick up another rasgulla from the same pot, the syrup doesn't taste the same nor does the rasgulla.'

It's similar with emotions. What you have already experienced the first time cannot be the same the second time around. You simply cannot hold on to the past. My personal feeling is that's what changed with Gurinder's movies. After *Bend It Like Beckham* and then *Bride and Prejudice*, they offered me a role in *It's a Wonderful Afterlife*. I had to express my regrets for it. It didn't do well.

Gurinder also produced a musical *Bend It Like Beckham* which had its West End and world premiere at the Phoenix Theatre in May 2015. I saw it and felt that it could have been much better. But I am not here to pass judgement on Gurinder Chadha's work. I am merely expressing what I think could have gone wrong. And it's a very personal opinion. What I must express though, is I'm forever grateful to Deepak and Gurinder for opening the doors for me to a new culture of work and cinema—a move that has opened my eyes to many more opportunities and a wide variety of roles that I've been able to sink into ever since. It's been a lesson for me to continue to foray into unknown territories, to never be afraid of being an outsider and to unite my fans regardless of which part of the world they reside in.

Ruth Young, my agent, started getting me more offers. But before I really made it to the big league, I had to go through numerous auditions with every casting director for every film. Initially, I was reluctant to do so and told Ruth: 'Why should I audition? They can check any film of mine . . . there are over 400 films. They can check any to see the range of my work.'

'Anupam, first of all, you must understand that an audition is not questioning your talent. It is whether you are suitable for the role or not. And, if you don't get a role, it doesn't mean that they have rejected you,' she explained.

I said: 'But it raises my expectations.'

'Yes, but you will have to go through it. Everybody in the world of international cinema auditions for a role.'

Ruth sent me to the casting director of an untitled film that was to have Orlando Bloom in the lead, who had risen to great fame as Legolas in the *Lord of the Rings* trilogy. It was on the life of a mountaineer and I was to audition for the role of a guide in Nepal. I worked on the audition from 15 different angles simply because to this day, there is a small-town person in me. I have still not understood that why, even after doing hundreds of films, should I be held back? On the contrary, I should portray myself in a little more—pious poise. Poise or dignity should be there. I worked on this audition. The casting director said: 'Okay, so you know the lines?'

I said: 'Yes, backwards.'

For some strange reason, she gave me an odd look as if to ask: 'What do you mean by backwards?' It became abundantly clear to me that during work hours and in the process of auditioning, a sense of humour was not always appropriate.

I was ready for the audition. The lines were normal and not difficult or long ones. I had asked myself the normal questions to prepare myself: Should I walk up a little? Should I take a small breath or collect my breathing or do some breathing exercises to show that we are climbing the mountain? I decided on the latter and even added two words from my side: '*Sahebji. Sahebji.*' (Sir. Sir), in a typical Nepalese Gurkha tone while breathing heavily as if we were climbing the mountain.

Needless to say, the casting director was horrified and thought that I was some sort of a madman who was performing with the aim of expecting an Oscar immediately from the casting director: 'Mr Kher, Mr Kher, please stop. Can you please cut down a little on the performance part of it?' Years later, I was told the same thing by some other people as well.

I said: 'Okay, this is not working? Is it too much? What percent do you want me to cut down?'

From the other side of the glass, she said: '99 per cent.'

'Basically, you don't want me to act?'

She said: 'No. I don't want you to act. Just be normal. Act normal . . . just with your voice and expressions. That's what I want.'

That was when I understood that you don't do 'extra' in auditions. I never heard from them again which meant I was not selected.

While more and more work came to me at home, nothing substantial followed at the international level. I think it was sometime in 2005, when Danny Boyle, the British director who had films like *Shallow Grave*, *The Beach* and *28 Days Later* to his credit, came to India to make his ambitious film, *Slumdog Millionaire*, which was loosely based on Vikas Swarup's novel *Q & A*. I was very sure of bagging a role in it. We met up. He was wonderfully warm but at the end, he just said: 'There is not much for you in it.' He did not even audition me.

Around the same time, Shirish Kunder called me one day and said: 'Ang Lee is making a film *Lust, Caution*.' I had seen *Crouching Tiger, Hidden Dragon* (2000) and had been mesmerised. Shirish Kunder used to work along with Imtiaz Ali in my media entertainment company. He was an editor there while Imtiaz Ali was writing and directing television shows including the episodes of *Imtihaan*. Both of them, like many others who used to work in my office at some stage or the other, have done well for themselves and made it big.

Based on the novella of the same name by the Chinese author Eileen Chang, it was an 'erotic espionage period thriller film' about an attractive young woman who lays a honey trap for a high-ranking special agent. I had read somewhere that they had auditioned nearly 10,000 girls before they chose Tang Wei for the role. It also had one of my favourite Cantonese actor, Tony Leung Chiu-Wai. I was selected to play the role of a jeweller—Hali Salahuddin. Shooting for the film started in Shanghai where I met the famous Mexican cinematographer Rodrigo Prieto known for 'the unconventional use of the camera that is often combined with strong moody lighting'. Having worked with some of the biggest contemporary directors and won numerous international awards, he had earlier worked with Ang Lee on *Brokeback Mountain* also.

Though my schedule required me to be there for eight days, I decided to readjust my other commitments here and spend two extra days in Shanghai, which I'm really glad that I did. Meeting Ang Lee was like being with Sooraj Barjatya—a kind and most simple man. With numerous awards to his credit including two Academy Awards for Best Direction—*Brokeback Mountain* (2005) and *Life of Pi* (2012)—his work is 'known for its emotional charge which is believed to be responsible for his success in offsetting cultural barriers and achieving international recognition'. He is a person who understands the Asian psyche and feels it within himself. I learnt that he has a great belief in meditation. Besides spending as much time with him as possible, I would do yoga with him every morning followed by a massage for a few minutes. He was very interested in Ayurveda, hot water therapy and the mystics of India. Being with Ang Lee for those ten days was like a spiritual cleansing for me.

Working with Ang Lee was an experience within the experience of living in Shanghai, China. The way in which Ang Lee would brief us, the manner in which he would explain a scene to the cast members, the way he would set up his camera, the way he would discuss a shot with Roderigo, have remained with me ever since. My first scene was with Tang Wei and Tony Leung—an amazing, brooding actor who reminded me of the cigar-smoking American actor, Humphrey Bogart. Because of the whole atmosphere on location and on the sets, it was very easy to shoot with Tang and Tony Leung who always had his three women assistants with him. He was a very present, non-fussy actor who would perform in a relaxed and calm manner, whatever his scene was, whatever his role demanded. I would have long conversations with him and also with Roderigo. There was so much to learn from each one of them.

These experiences showed me the value of auditioning and trying for new types of films. If I hadn't gone through auditioning, I may have never had the chance to work on *Lust, Caution*. There is a special product that comes from putting together talent from different parts of Asia all into one film, and I wouldn't trade that experience for anything. Little did I know that these landmarks were setting me up for my next big career frontier.

31

THE HOLLYWOOD DREAM COMES TRUE

It was sometime in late 2009 or early 2010 when my agent Ruth Young called me and said: 'There is a film already under production. It is Woody Allen's film, *You Will Meet a Tall Dark Stranger.* There is father's role . . . Freida Pintos' father's role. It's only two days' work and possibly only two scenes, and they are offering very little money.'

But those facts didn't dampen my excitement one bit. I couldn't believe it and replied immediately: 'Woody Allen? Woody Allen will ask me to stand in the street scene . . . ? Ruth, I don't want any money. I just want to be in this film, whatever the role is.'

She said: 'You will have to take the money.'

'I have done so many films in India without taking any money. This is my tribute to Woody Allen . . . a dream come true for me.'

Ruth replied: 'It does not work like this. You will have to take the money; whatever amount is offered.'

'This is a very strange system,' I said. 'A system that forces you to take money.'

'That's the system. For your name to be on the credits, you have to be paid,' she told me on a serious note, but I was hardly paying full attention because my head was already in the clouds dreaming of what our work together would be like.

I said: 'Okay. I am all set. Please go ahead.'

That night, I couldn't sleep. I couldn't believe that I would be in a Woody Allen film. In my time at drama school, I had read all his books and seen all his films. He was an inspiration, a genius. Woody Allen, Michael Jackson, Clint Eastwood; these were no ordinary names let alone commonplace personalities. They were rare species of legends and I don't use that word lightly. For me, this was another landmark and my true entry into the Hollywood sphere, a chance to fuse together my artistry with a special talent that influenced my youth and my upbringing.

Woody Allen has a completely different approach towards cinema. His dialogues, his writings, his thought process are all products of a genius. How else can one explain the way he conceives his scenes? I recall a scene from a film of his, where Woody's character is escaping from a prison. I can't recall the film's name . . . but the scene is still vividly implanted in my mind's eye. In it, he makes a gun out of soap and while he is holding it and crossing the courtyard of a jail, it starts raining . . . and the soap starts frothing! It was hilarious! This and other memories flashed before my eyes in great excitement. In that state of mind, I asked myself: *Will I be in a frame where Woody Allen says action and I will act?* The film had great actors like Anthony Hopkins, Lucy Punch, Josh Brolin and Gemma Jones along with Freida Pinto, Naomi Watts, Roger Ashton-Griffiths and many others.

I was to report in London for the shoot. *Why does Woody Allen always come to London to shoot?* I wondered. I got the answer soon. While all the directors shooting in England or Europe wait for the sun to come out so that they can commence shooting, Woody Allen does not like shooting in the sun. He likes cloudy weather. And where can you get better clouds than in England? Amazing!

The moment I got down at Heathrow, I had to go for the trial of my costumes. I was like an eager child. I was dying to meet my hero. *How would I address him: Mr Allen or Mr Woody Allen or Mr Woody or just Woody?* I asked myself. I always get confused about these matters. *Oh, no I can't address him as Woody. That's not done. He is so much elder to me . . . so much senior. I will call him Mr Woody Allen,* I answered my own question. After the costume trials were over, I asked one of the assistants: 'I want to meet Mr Woody Allen.'

He looked at me with a surprise and asked: 'You want to meet Woody?'

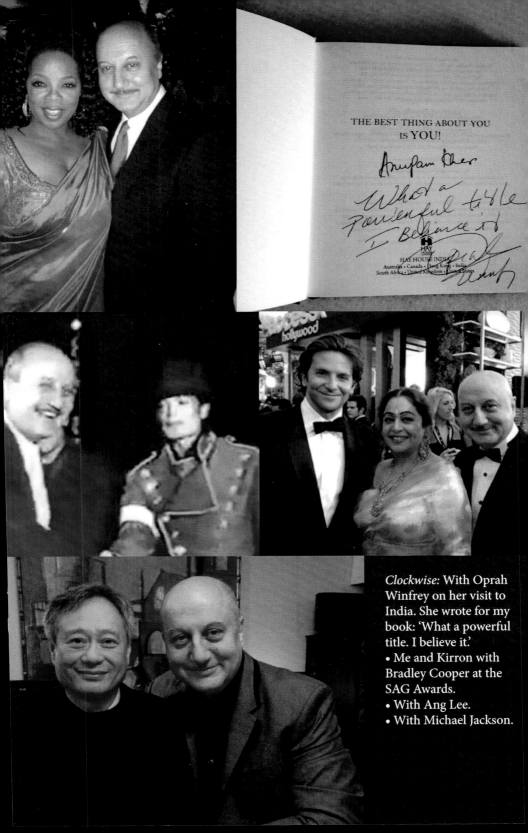

THE BEST THING ABOUT YOU
IS YOU!

Clockwise: With Oprah Winfrey on her visit to India. She wrote for my book: 'What a powerful title. I believe it.'
• Me and Kirron with Bradley Cooper at the SAG Awards.
• With Ang Lee.
• With Michael Jackson.

With Sidney Poitier . . .

Bruce Willis

Gerard Butler

Jennifer Lawrence

Hugh Grant

John Travolta

atrick Stewart

Leonardo DiCaprio

Clockwise: Being directed b[y]
Woody Allen for the film *Y[ou]*
Will Meet a Tall Dark Stra[nger],
2010. • With Robert De Ni[ro at]
my office in Mumbai, 2013[.]
• With the cast of the NBC[TV]
series *New Amsterdam*, Ne[w]
York, 2018. • With Robert [De]
Niro, David O. Russell and
Martin Scorsese.

I shook my head in affirmative. 'No, he can't meet you today. You will meet him tomorrow directly at the location . . . when you come for your scenes.'

I was somewhat hurt and thought to myself: *Here I am, having travelled all the way from India, doing this film for so little money and he can't even meet me? Why does it matter to him? I just want to stand behind and watch him? Why are they so adamant? After all, I am an also an actor . . . a well-known star from India. Surely, he respects another actor.*

I insisted: 'No, I want to meet him today.'

He replied, somewhat politely but firmly: 'Mr Kher, he will not meet you today. You go to your hotel now. Your trial for your costumes is done and tomorrow, I will keep them ready, well in time for your shoot.'

But I was equally adamant. I had to meet him. I was able to find out where he was shooting. It was in a street quite close by to my hotel. I went there, did a recce of the street and discovered that there was a Bangladeshi restaurant, very close to where Woody Allen was shooting. I went into the restaurant. The moment the staff and some guests saw me, they all surrounded me saying: 'Dada, dada, one picture please ... Mr Kher, one autograph please.'

I said: 'Now, all of you hold on. You all get together . . . in fact, collect everyone you can, your friends, your relatives, your customers, everyone you can. I will go and stand in that corner there. All of you come there and ask for autographs or your pictures with me. I will do so there, with each one of you. You can take as many pictures as you want. But do collect some more people.'

I could make out that they were surprised, animated and excited. I went and stood at a particular spot, very close to where the shooting was in progress. Within just about ten minutes or so, about 15 or 20 or 30 people had collected, mostly Bangladeshis. They started creating a ruckus . . . all wanting a photograph while standing next to me, as close as possible. Soon, the word spread that an Indian actor was there and a crowd had surrounded him. The noise must have disturbed the shooting because soon, two of the production managers came. One of them recognised me and said: 'Mr Kher? You are here?'

I said: 'Yes. Came to have a bite here at this restaurant. I am in the film but I'm shooting tomorrow.'

'Okay. Okay. Why don't you come and sit with us?' he said.

They made me sit next to Woody Allen. I was happy, as happy as I could be. Pictures were taken and everyone in the crowd was happy too!

Though I was sitting right next to Woody Allen, he did not look at me. He was looking at the monitor for the shot going on between Freida Pinto and the well-known American actor, Josh Brolin. I discovered that he was of much fairer complexion than I had seen in his movies. But Woody Allen had no time for me. Not that I had anything in particular to say to him. But for me, this was a moment of truth. I knew that one day, perhaps years later, I would be writing about this day of my life in my autobiography. I was creating a moment with him. An instant that would be an essential part of my autobiography. Don't forget what I had mentioned at the beginning of this volume: 'I have always looked at my life from an autobiographical point of view.'

After the shot, as Woody Allen turned, we were face to face with each other. I said: 'Hi.'

Now, he was forced to reply to me: 'Hi. I am told you have done a lot of movies.'

I said: 'Yes, 418.'

He paused, looked around and asked: 'In how many lives?'

That was it. I got my Woody Allen moment! My unforgettable anecdote.

The next day, I had to shoot. It was a party scene and the cameraman, Vilmos Zsigmond, a Hungarian-American, came and stood next to me. Woody Allen then came and briefed me: 'The camera will go from this place to that man smoking a cigar, to that lady reading a magazine to somebody else scratching his head . . . to a dialogue over there and then another dialogue over there. It will then go to a wine glass . . .'

Strangely, Woody Allen reminded me of Balwant Gargi. There was the same awkwardness in his communication as he explained to Vilmos what all to capture, how to capture and from which angle to capture: '. . . take the camera from the magazine to those faces, to the wine glass, to Anupam, to Josh, to Freida and then you should come back to the man smoking a cigar.' After a couple of rehearsals, the first take was announced. When the shot was over, Woody Allen said: 'Okay, next.'

The cameraman, Vilmos, went running to him and said: 'No Woody. We will have to do it again. I missed a few things.'

Woody Allen looked at him and said: 'That's what I loved about it. I love chaos.'

That was another Woody Allen moment that I was able to capture for posterity. Then we did another one scene where you can only see and recognise me because of the back of my head. In the final scene, the camera captures me from the front. That was all.

But I had acted in a Woody Allen film. He had directed me. I was thrilled. My life seemed complete and I was filled with joy at the memories I was creating.

Released on 23 September 2010, the film did not do well at the box office. It had just an average run in comparison to the other films in the series that he had made.

Here I must mention another incident connected with Woody Allen. I was on a visit to New York and on the recommendation of Anil Kapoor, I stayed at the legendary Carlyle—A Rosewood Hotel on 76th Street. While at the hotel, I learnt that every Monday evening, Woody Allen played the clarinet with Eddy Davis New Orleans Jazz Band at the Café Carlyle, situated on the ground floor of the hotel. 'It's very difficult to get a seat as everything gets booked days in advance,' I was told.

'Please... help get me a ticket. I am ready to pay anything for a front row seat,' I literally begged Sonal, the Indian girl at the front office. The front row seats are known as the VIP seats and of course, they are very expensive. Sonal, who had to jump through various hoops, finally did manage a seat—not in the first row but in the second row. It meant sitting just about two feet away from where Woody Allen would sit. The first row was almost like squatting on his lap. And I had to pay a hefty amount for it—not that I was complaining. Those who have been to Café Carlyle know how classy it is with its walls covered with painted murals which were borrowed heavily from the works of artistes such as Pablo Picasso and the French artiste, Henri Matisse. It's a very informal but beautiful atmosphere in this limited seat café.

I was led to my seat and suddenly, after a few minutes, I saw Woody Allen walk in carrying a small leather briefcase. He sat down, opened his briefcase, took out his clarinet and started to assemble it. For me, sitting there was an extremely surreal scene. While playing, he did not look up at all, just played with his eyes shut. There was no eye contact. It seemed like a scene directly out of one of his films. But I was dying during that one-hour performance for an eye contact; an eye contact that conveys to him that I have worked with you my friend and that this is a historical moment, not only for me, but for you as well. I really wanted him to know that your actor is here, especially to watch and admire your performance and that too after going through extraordinary lengths to secure a seat.

After the performance was over, he emerged from his 'stupor'. He then gathered his instrument, packed it and got up to leave. I stood very close to him and said: 'Sir, sir, I worked with you in *You Will Meet a Tall Dark Stranger*. I am your actor, sir.'

He turned and without even looking at me, he said: 'Good for you,' and just walked away.

I was ecstatic. His words 'good for you' were for me yet another Woody Allen instant. It was an experience of mystical proportions.

I had no knowledge on Western music. I must admit, coming from a Hindi-medium background, I was not familiar with English songs and Western music culture. Michael Jackson was my only reference point for pop music, country or anything associated with English music, and the reason was the magical quality of his dance. 'Beat It' was the only words I understood or the sound 'Ouuuuu' he produced. His moonwalk I would practice as an actor, not to see whether I can dance but to see how it is humanly possible. For me, Michael Jackson was a myth and a phenomenon. So, when in October-November 1996, the Wizcraft team comprising Andre Timmins, Sabbas Joseph and Viraf Sarkari, along with Raj Thackeray, decided to host the Michael Jackson concert in Mumbai, I had to meet him. History had to be created between me and him and not just by me being a part of the audience while he was performing on stage. That would have been hysteria instead.

A day before the concert, I was invited to The Oberoi hotel as a part of a group of twenty-five people or so comprising of industrialists, socialites, top bureaucrats, and politicians. The area of our meeting was barricaded heavily, and Michael Jackson was surrounded by his bouncers. How can I not have a picture with him, I thought to myself? This is my only chance . . . my autobiographical moment. Breaking the security cordon, I crossed the barricades and jumped on to the stage. The bouncers nearly caught hold of me but, suddenly, they heard the famous film producer and financier Bharat Shah shout in panic, 'He is India's best actor, the topmost!' Bharat Shah's idea was to save me from a possible assault by the guards. The bouncers stepped back, and I was right in front of the miracle—Michael Jackson. Time stood still. For me, it was just the two of us, everything else was blurred and in slow motion. He then bowed to me, and I froze. I saw my right hand in his right hand, in a handshake. I screamed in my heart loudly, wishing for someone to click a picture. History was being made here, not for Michael Jackson, but for me, Anupam Kher from Shimla. This was my Michael Jackson moment, preserved for my autobiography. Truly in life, kucch bhi ho sakta hai!

I cannot not mention another element of kucch bhi ho sakta hai here. Our own Indian Michael Jackson and now a very successful director, Prabhu Deva, had done me a favour two years prior to the Michael Jackson show in Mumbai by hosting the New Year eve show in Chennai for Doordarshan—organised by my event company along with Sonali Bendre—for free. Impressed by this humble gesture, I had offered to fulfil any one wish he had. Little did I know, two years later, he would ask for something impossible. He called and said, 'Michael Jackson is in Mumbai. I hope you remember your promise to me. Can you get me to meet my idol, Michael Jackson?' Yours faithfully managed to do so. How? I hope Prabhu Deva details it in his own biography.

After working with the likes of Gurinder Chadha, Woody Allen and Ang Lee, my profile got enhanced in the sense that I was working with the top people on the top projects in the world of international cinema. In addition, I did a couple of British television appearances and worked in some Indian-American films like Girja Shankar's *Banana Brothers*, Ajmal Zaheer Ahmad's *Perfect Mismatch*, Varun Khanna's *American Blend* and Tanuja Chandra's *Hope and a Little Sugar* which was shot over 25 days in New York.

Then, sometime in 2010-11, I started to work on Samir Karnik's Hindi romantic comedy film, *Chaar Din Ki Chandani*, which also had Tusshar Kapoor, Kulraj Randhawa, Anita Raj and Om Puri in the main cast. During a shooting schedule conducted in an old palace of a village over 100-kilometre away from Jodhpur, I received a mail from my agent Ruth informing me that the American film director and producer David O. Russell is making a film called *Silver Linings Playbook* which had in its cast names like Robert De Niro, Bradley Cooper, Chris Duicker and Jennifer Lawrence amongst others. 'There is a role of an Indian doctor, a psychiatrist, Dr Patel, for which he would like to consider you. It's a major role . . . a parallel role . . . For it, David would like to Skype with you.' The date and time were given to me for it.

David O. Russell wants to Skype with me? In this village? I don't even know how to Skype . . . I have never skyped in my life before. I don't even know how it's done, were the questions that flashed through my mind like a tempest. There was great excitement and panic running simultaneously within me. Even today, the feeling is indescribable.

A couple of weeks earlier, I had watched David Russell's *The Fighter*—an American sports drama film which had Mark Wahlberg, Christian Bale, Amy Adams, Melissa Leo and Jack McGee in the main cast. It was a mesmerising movie and was nominated for various awards, including six Academy Awards out of which it bagged two—Best Supporting Actor Award for Christian Bale and Best Supporting Actress Award for Melissa Leo.

This was a great opportunity for me and I just could not afford to lose it under any circumstances. I called up my manager, Shetty, in

Mumbai: 'We have to organise a Skype in this place.'

'But there is a connectivity problem there. We can't do it,' he replied.

'I don't care. This is the most important move for my career. Do you realise that my all-time idols are going to be in this film, including the god of acting, Robert De Niro? I have a chance to feature with this dream cast and you are telling me that Skype can't be done. I just don't care. Just work it out,' I said agitatedly.

Finally, we got some sort of connection from Jodhpur and a laptop was bought specially for the purpose. In those 24 hours, Skype acquired the proportions of a folklore in the village where we were shooting. 'Skype is coming . . . Skype is coming' was what everyone seemed to be talking about. Much later, I told David Russell and some others about the whole excitement in the village, much to their amusement.

On the fixed time and date—when it was early morning in Los Angeles and late evening here—David called. I sat with all my dialogues on one side of the laptop. Behind me sat half the village—because the Skype was coming—in pin-drop silence as they had been instructed before. I saw David on the monitor of my laptop. The problem was that there was no sound and I could make out that he was getting irritated. He was impatient because, according to him, he had given me enough time. His office too had confirmed that I was prepared. Ruth had also checked with me if all was okay to speak with him. But what Ruth, or for that matter David, didn't know was that where in the interior of Rajasthan I was shooting and how spotty the connection was at this location. He could see my face and I could see his, but the audio just refused to cooperate. No one could help. In any case, there was nobody around with any technical abilities to sort the problem. Then, I could see David writing something on a piece of paper and holding it up for me to see: 'Next time, be more prepared.'

I too wrote a message back: 'Google search me.'

Ruth was very upset about this whole affair and said: 'This is not done. You were given enough time and you should have been more prepared.'

A few days later, I had to rush to Canada to attend the Toronto Film Festival where my Canadian sports comedy, *Breakaway*, was to be screened. It was directed by Robert Lieberman and featured Russell Peters, Rob Lowe, Camilla Belle and a new boy, Vinay Virmani. It turned to be the biggest grosser of the year 2011. Once again, a date and time were fixed for the interview through Skype with Russell. *Nothing should go wrong this time*, I told myself. I was staying at the Four Seasons Hotel on Yorkville Avenue. The laptop had been arranged and the hotel technicians set it all up for me in my suite. *Yes, nothing will go wrong this time*, I assured myself in a superfluous outburst of optimism. And I also assured Ruth in great confidence. I even placed the sheet containing my dialogues next to the laptop, just in case I had to read out anything because of my tension, which seemed to be setting in gradually.

My room service attendant—provided by the hotel—was a young smart man from Bangladesh named Jamil. He was overjoyed to see me and couldn't believe that he had been selected to be my butler. The first thing he told me when he came to my room was: 'I am a big fan of yours, dada.' For him, I was Robert De Niro, Al Pacino and Jack Nicholson all rolled into one. He had also made me speak to almost every member of his family. He was making tea for me when suddenly, the call came. I rushed to the other room, telling Jamil to not make any noise and just keep my tea ready and wait for me. The Skype session started and David Russell appeared on the laptop. I did too. But, once again, the audio played truant. This time David Russell got really pissed and he disconnected the line with a bang. I couldn't believe it. *Yes, it could happen in a remote village of Rajasthan. But this was Toronto . . . Four Seasons Hotel. How could it go wrong?* I asked myself.

I had these questions on mind when Ruth called: 'What is wrong with you, Anupam? Why has this happened again?'

I explained but she was upset and perhaps, like me, frustrated as well. She later came back with an update and informed me: 'He says, now you should send a clip of your audition to the casting directors Lindsay Graham and Mary Vernieu by tomorrow evening at any cost.'

I came out of the room rather dejected. Seeing me, Jamil asked in Bengali: '*Ki holo dada?*' (What happened dada?)

We Indians have a habit of telling our problems to everybody. So, I sat down with him and said: 'Jamil, I have a problem. I was going to get a role in a big Hollywood film but there was a problem with Skype. For some reason, it didn't receive any audio in it. I have to send them a clip now. I don't know how to send it . . . nor do I have any such facility here.'

'Dada, I have an iPhone 4. I can record the clip for you on it and send you the link so that you can forward that,' he suggested.

'Really? Will that work? Will you do it?' I asked in great excitement.

He said: 'Yes dada, it should work. Anything for you, dada!'

Jamil went and soon came back with his iPhone. He was now my director and my cameraman and my room service attendant. We got ready for the shoot. I told him: 'Jamil, when I make a gesture with my hand to start, then you say "action". And when I make another gesture, a different gesture, you say "cut". Are you ready?'

'I am ready.'

I could make out Jamil was very excited with his new role. 'Jamil, don't move much and don't shake the camera. Just stay where you are. I will come closer to the camera; I will go back. You just stay there and keep the camera stable.'

We both were ready—me to perform and he to record. I made a gesture with my hand and he said: 'Action, dada.' Getting my clue, I started and completed the entire sequence with my dialogue, after which I made my second gesture and he said: 'Cut, dada.'

After about half-an-hour, Jamil sent me the link which I sent to my casting directors. That evening, Lindsay called me to say she had got the clip. 'And by the way, what is that "dada" with which the clip starts and ends?'

I explained her what it was and how it came to be in the clip. That is how my casting for the film *Silver Linings Playbook* was evaluated. That's how I was selected to play Dr Patel in my biggest Hollywood film.

A week or so later, I received my dialogues and my shooting schedules and all the necessary details about the making of the film. I was to shoot in Philadelphia in September 2011, if I'm not mistaken, and they asked me to come for 15 days. I decided to stay for some more days.

The moment I land in a new city, the first thing I do is check all I can about Indian restaurants. I checked into the Rittenhouse Hotel on West Rittenhouse Square. There, in my suite, I found some pamphlets for Indian restaurants. I looked up the information and shortlisted one known as Tashan Restaurant and Lounge advertised with the line—'a bustling, buzzy vibe resides at this upscale spot serving non-traditional Indian fare'. Though it was a little past lunchtime, I got ready and went to Tashan for lunch. By the time I reached there, they had shut it. The manager—a lady—said: 'Sorry sir, we are closed today for lunch as the entire restaurant has been booked by a private party for brunch.'

'Can you tell me who the owner is?' I enquired.

'Mr Munish Narula,' she answered.

'Is he there?'

She said: 'Yes.'

I said: 'Okay, give him my name, Anupam Kher and tell him that I am waiting outside.'

'I am sorry Mr . . .'

'Okay, let me write it down for you. Just give this to him and tell him that I am waiting at the entrance,' I said handing her the visitors slip with my name on it.

She hesitated for a moment or two and then went inside. A few minutes later, Munish came running out and touched my feet in the traditional Indian form of respect to get blessings from an elder family member.

'What are you doing here? Please come in,' he said.

For the next 24 days, I ate there the most delicious food I have had in a restaurant, at times with Munish, but all free of cost. He would just refuse to take money. Munish's hospitality, warmth and respects were overwhelming. In return, I can only say: 'God bless you Munish and keep it up. I am proud of you.'

The day I landed in Philadelphia, David Russell invited me to his apartment in the evening and said: 'I am going to call up Bradley Cooper. You pretend that you don't know English at all. Let's see what happens.'

Bradley Cooper came with Jonathan Gordon, one of the three producers of the film. He was informed by David: 'We have a problem on our hands because this Indian actor does not know English at all. He is saying that he will try. All along he thought that his role was in Hindi—his Indian language.'

At this point, I started saying in Hindi: 'What can I do? How was I to know about this . . .?'

Bradley Cooper interrupted here and said very deliberately, as if talking to a slow learner: 'No, no, no. You have to speak in English.'

I said: 'No English. No English. Only Hindi, Hindi.'

The three of them looked at each other. Bradley said: 'We are fucked man. We have got this fucking actor who doesn't know English. And we are shooting the day after tomorrow. What the hell. What do we do now?'

Pretending that I have not followed any of their conversation, I said: 'No homework done before to know Indian actor. I can't do any dialogue in English. But any dialogue which is written, I can improvise.'

'Okay, improvise,' Bradley said. Deliberately, I did an awful improvisation and at one stage, I got a little aggressive with David Russell to which Bradley said: 'Hey, hey, man. You better watch out. Don't talk to my director like this.'

'Hey! You don't talk to me like this,' I answered back, as if, in great anger.

At this moment, David gave it all away and started laughing. Everyone realised what the game was and joined in the laughter. They were relieved. It was David's way of getting Bradley and me familiar with each other before the shoot could start.

The shooting started on schedule. My first scene was with Bradley Cooper. I had worked out each and every detail of my scene and was fully prepared with every dialogue of mine. I had worked out the pauses—this is when I am going to look down . . . this is where I am going to look up. In my mind, I was an American actor and I constantly thought how would he do this scene? I was very fascinated by English films where the characters look around rather than looking at the person. After the entire rehearsal of the scene, David came to me and said: 'Dude. I already have De Niro in the film. I don't need another one.' I found that funny and remembered a line I had read somewhere: 'When the original exists, who wants imitations.'

'Okay,' I said.

He said: 'Just look into his eyes and speak your dialogue to him with compassion. There is no need to act.' The word compassion reminded me of Mahesh Bhatt and how he had asked me to do the same during the making of *Saaransh*.

'How much per cent?' I asked David.

'No percentage. Acting is fine. But don't look around. I want you to look at him.'

The scene was shot pretty fast. Then I heard David Russell's voice: 'That was fine. We have the time, so let's do all the three scenes now.'

Now, I had prepared only one scene because that was what was scheduled for the first day. 'But I have not learnt my lines because the other two scenes were not scheduled for today.'

David overruled me and slated two more scenes for the same day. I did manage to do the other two scenes too. It was then that I realised that the shadow of fear is longer than the fear itself.

Having canned those scenes, I was waiting for my moment with the one and only, Robert De Niro. *When would the day come?* I thought to myself and was getting impatient about it.

Finally, the day arrived!

But before I write about that, let me mention here that before coming to Philadelphia, I had carried out a competition on Twitter. On it, I had announced: 'I am going to work with Mr Robert De Niro. Which are your favourite films of his?' I had five million followers at that time and a very large number of people replied, each listing his or her own favourite film of De Niro.

On this particular day, the entire cast was going to assemble for a scene in which we all are coming back after seeing a game of the Philadelphia Eagles. Also in the scene, Patrizio 'Pat' Solitano Jr played by Bradley Cooper is drunk and I, Dr Patel, Pat's therapist, is also drunk. It was a very dramatic scene in which I had only three lines out of 12 pages of script, but I was an important part of the entire sequence where Patrizio Sr, played by Robert De Niro, gets very angry with his son and in walks Tiffany Maxwell (Jennifer Lawrence) etc. etc.

Before the whole cast could collect for the shooting, I was told that Robert De Niro had arrived. I went to his assistant and said: 'I want to meet Mr De Niro before the shooting starts.'

'Oh, no. You can't meet him. He will meet you straight on the sets,' he replied.

'Listen,' I said very calmly, 'I have got this ruby Ganapati Ganesha for him all the way from India. It's been specially blessed for him and I have to give it to him,' I pestered him.

'Sorry, Bob doesn't meet anybody like this. Only on the sets,' he stuck to his reply.

'Please do understand,' I begged him now. 'Look, it's important for me to meet him. And meet him before he comes on the set. I have to give him this Ganapati Ganesha. He is one of the most important, best-known, deities in our religion.'

He seemed quite bewildered. He looked at me and then went away shrugging his shoulders. I have a feeling that he just got fed up of me and out of sheer desperation must have gone and told Robert De Niro about this Indian actor. A few minutes later, I was called into his long trailer. Finally, my moment had come and I was in front of THE Robert De Niro—my God, my King of Kings of the acting world. My immediate feeling was that in person, he looked smaller than what he appeared on-screen. Face to face, I was so overwhelmed that I just didn't know what to say to him. Moreover, as explained earlier also, my problem is that when I have to speak in English to an English-speaking person, I have to translate my thoughts from Hindi to English and then say what I feel. So, when I presented him the Ganesha, I don't know why but I got emotional. He saw tears in my eyes and asked: 'What is it?'

I wanted to say that this is a great moment for me in my life that I am meeting you, but what came out of my mouth was: 'Today, I am very moved by my story, sir.'

'What do you mean?' he asked.

'I am a person from a very small town in India . . . What a rising graph for me, sir. Here I am meeting you today, fulfiling my dream.'

He should have been quite used to hearing such words but I have a feeling that he was a bit embarrassed because he said awkwardly: 'Good . . . good, good!'

'I have done a contest on Twitter sir, asking my followers as to which of your films is their favourite?' I boasted.

Now actors are actors—no matter who you are or where you reside. Suddenly, his interest was piqued and he asked: 'So which of my movies are people talking about?'

'*The Godfather II, Raging Bull, Cape Fear. . .*'

'What about *Awakenings*?' he interrupted.

I said: 'I think some have mentioned that too.'

I clicked some pictures with him—my great 'Robert De Niro' moment—for posterity and recording purposes for my autobiography. I was elated.

At 4 o'clock that afternoon, I was on the set, as was everybody else—the entire cast, crew, director David Russell and producer Bruce L. Cohen who had produced films like Gus Van Sant's *Milk* and Sam Mendes' *American Beauty* which got him the Academy Award for Best Picture.

Then Robert De Niro arrived. My God, I couldn't believe it. He WAS a completely different man. From Robert De Niro he had become Patrizio Solitanio Sr. This transformation was magical. He was what he was supposed to be in the film—angry. It was vintage De Niro. I was mesmerised.

Just when the rehearsal was about to start, Robert De Niro looked at me and said to David Russell: 'David, why the fuck will I tolerate this Indian doctor in my house? I personally feel that nobody utters the word 'fuck' like Robert De Niro on-screen.'

But in this instance, I was shocked. *What is he saying?* I thought to myself.

David asked: 'I didn't understand. Bob, what do you mean by that?'

He replied: 'Why the fuck will I tolerate this Indian doctor in my house. It is because of this quack that Pat went to the Eagles' game . . . and he could have gone to the police station, in which case, he would have gone back to the mental asylum. So, why will I tolerate him in this house? I don't like this quack.'

'So what would you like to do?' David enquired.

'Fucking hell. I would throw him out!'

What's going on, I thought to myself. *I just gave him a ruby Ganesha and now he is throwing me out of the house. What is he saying?*

David said: 'Okay, let's rehearse.'

Before I could say my first line, Robert De Niro caught hold of my arm and threw me out of the house and bolted the door from inside. The scene was going on inside and I, bald, half-naked, half-green faced with an 'S' written on my chest, was standing outside in the month of September in chilly Philadelphia, waiting for them to open the door. After about half an hour, the door opened and David said, 'Working well . . . but the character has been in my mind for a long time . . . I will need one more rehearsal.'

One more rehearsal meant wasting another 45 minutes or so. Before I could say anything, I heard once again: 'What the fuck? This doctor . . . ,' and he shut the door and bolted it from inside again. And here I was still standing outside saying to myself: *An actor who has eight Filmfare awards, two National Awards, Padma Shri and is chairman of Actor Prepares has been pushed off the set to stand outside in this cold. What the hell is going on man? Here is my moment, my magic moment with Robert De Niro and he has thrown me out. I have a dialogue on the first page, the eighth page and eleventh page. But before I could say a single one, I, the Indian doctor, has got evicted.*

In life, when you are humiliated in front of people, it's a separate issue. But when you are humiliated in front of your own self, in your own eyes, it's a bigger issue. But God has always been very kind to me. As I mentioned earlier also, I have always looked at the humorous angle in every situation. I also don't give in easily to humiliation. I was still caught up in the whirlwind of thoughts when the door opened and David said: 'Come in . . . I think it's working very well. Okay, so Bob will throw you out Anupam . . .'

I heard myself say loudly: 'Hold on . . . one second.'

I could see the irritation on people's faces. They don't want to waste more time as time is big money for them. I said: 'There are eight characters in the scene.' At that crucial moment when I wanted to enunciate my thoughts due to my translation problem, something else emerged: 'And of these eight characters in the scene, why are we listening to only one interpretation?'

Suddenly, there was pin-drop silence and all eyes were on me. A few long moments followed before David asked: 'What do you mean?'

I said: 'The interpretation of Dr Patel is also important.'

I knew immediately that the next question would be: 'What is your interpretation?'

Frankly speaking, I didn't want the conversation to go in the direction it was going. But then the thought bubble of my grandfather's lesson rescued me yet again: 'If you want to be equal with anybody in the world, just don't expect anything.' So, I thought to myself, *what is the worst that can happen? At the maximum, they will throw me out . . . the word will spread around . . . I won't get work in Hollywood again. So be it. But I must tell them my interpretation. What I feel about the scene.* Then I finally said: 'My interpretation of the role is to tell Mr De Niro's character that it's because of you . . . the kind of father you have been, that your son had to be sent to a mental asylum, and today, it is thanks to this Indian doctor that he has become better. And the second thing I must tell all of you very frankly is that I signed this film for this particular scene. And, come what may, I am not getting out of it.'

Having stated my piece with conviction after getting over my initial hesitation, I sat down on the chair. All eyes were now focussed on Robert De Niro. He gave the matter some thought and then agreed. The shooting carried on and now he did not throw me out on the street. Later, David commented to me: 'Oh, dude, you fought for your life.'

Yes, I did because I sincerely believed in what I had said—with utmost passion and as a reflection of my inner faith in my ability. And, in those moments, Robert De Niro too saw me come into my own.

The next morning, I happened to show him a bound copy of the manuscript of my forthcoming book, *The Best Thing about You Is YOU!* He said: 'Sign it and give it to me. I will preserve it in my library.' It still resides there today. When circumstances test us, how we react is what sets us apart. Facing everyone in that moment, especially my idol Robert De Niro was my ultimate trial and one I did not back down from. My training and the lessons I had unknowingly absorbed along the way came to the fore. My personal victory was my personal vindication. I now consider the great Robert De Niro as one of my dear friends! He insists that I call him Bob, 'Anupam, call me Bob everybody else does . . . All my assistants call me Bob.' But I cannot. I am in awe of him always; to me, he is the one and only Mr Robert De Niro.

Working on *Silver Linings Playbook* was certainly one of the most exceptional and unforgettable experiences of my life. Upon completion of the film, I hosted a party for the entire cast at Munish Narula's restaurant, Tashan. And Munish went out of his way to make it a novel experience for everyone.

The film was nominated for eight Oscars and for the Best Ensemble Cast for the Screen Actors Guild Award for Outstanding Performance by an Ensemble. It was a huge commercial success too. Jennifer Lawrence got the Oscar for the Best Actress.

While on the Oscars, I must mention a remarkable experience I had. Since the film had been nominated in eight categories, I was keen to attend the Academy Awards ceremony. Befitting the special occasion, I had a Burberry suit tailored through the South Indian actor, Siddharth Suryanarayan, who had played my 'son' in Rakeysh Omprakash Mehra's *Rang De Basanti*. His brother-in-law, a senior official in Burberry, got the suit ready for me. I had presumed that I too will get a pass. But it was not to happen. I was disappointed for I was keen to be there at the event and send pictures back home. So, I did the next best thing. There is an event organised for those who don't get a ticket. In it, a hotel space is arranged and the red carpet is rolled out where people can stand and be photographed. I took my own pictures and I sent out the photograph with the caption: 'Oscar night on the red carpet'. A lie? No, not really! Think of it as if I was on the red carpet, and it was Oscar night.

Life has its own indelible instants and during the making of *Silver Linings Playbook*, I had my incredible moments too. The film was the budding start to many friendships with amazing people—a truly great team. Today, I consider David Russell amongst my close friends and feel that I have been bestowed the sweetest gift from God in my close association and friendship with Robert De Niro. During his visit to India in November 2013, he came to my school, Actor Prepares, for about four hours. I had called the entire film fraternity—Anil Kapoor, Ranbir Kapoor, Varun Dhawan, Dia Mirza, Ayan Mukherjee, Aditya Roy Kapur, Rohit Dhawan and many others. Ranbir came and touched his feet in the traditional *guru-shishya* tradition and sat at his feet. In my school, I made him sit in my chair and then tweeted: 'Making Robert De Niro sit in my chair in my off @actorprepares will always be the greatest joy of my life.' That evening, I again tweeted: 'All dreams can come true. But Robert De Niro coming to our school @actorprepares was a fantasy comes true.'

On 17 August 2013, Robert De Niro invited me to his house on his 70th birthday. It was a very personal affair for just about 20 people or so, mostly his family . . . his inner circle. I felt honoured to be included in it. Here, I met George Lucas, the creator of *Star Wars* and the *Indiana Jones* franchises. It was a great evening. Then on 7 March 2018, my 63rd birthday, when I happened to be in New York for a shoot, he organised a surprise party for me at his residence and actually sang 'Happy Birthday Anupam'. Cherished memories for me. Memorable moments—all great treasures of life!

On 17 August 2018, Robert De Niro turned seventy-five. I too was there for the celebrations. A toast was proposed by those present. When my turn came, I recited the Mahamrityunjay Mantra[26] for De Niro (believed to ensure good health and longevity) and gifted him a Ganesh idol and a hardback copy of the Bhagavad Gita.

On 7th March 2019, my 64th birday, it was my turn to reciprocate. I invited him and his wife along with David Russell and his wife, Holly, and De Niro's billionaire philanthropist friend, Barry Rosenstein, the famous cardiologist, Dr Siddhartha Mukherjee, and his wife Sarah, for dinner to Rohit Khattar's Indian restaurant— Indian Accent in New York. They loved the food there and relished each dish. We spent nearly two hours together and had a wonderful time.

In between all these films, I did quite a few other projects including Mark William's *A Family Man*, Michael Showalter's *The Big Sick*, James Dodson's *The Other End of the Line* and Paul Mayeda Berges's *The Mistress of Spices*, which was based on the novel by Chitra Banerjee Divakaruni. It had Aishwarya Rai, Dylan McDermott, Toby Marlow and Padma Lakshmi in the cast.

Quite recently, I think it was just a couple of years back or so, a distant cousin of mine, Priyanka Matto, called me up out of the blue. She said: 'Anupam, there is a film being made by Judd Apatow called *The Big Sick* which will be directed by a relative newcomer, Michael Showalter, who has done one film earlier. It's based on the life of the Pakistani-American stand-up comedian Kumail Nanjiani and his girlfriend, Emily V. Gordon. Kumail will be playing himself and Zoe Kazan, the famous film-maker Elia Kazan's granddaughter, will play Emily. In addition, there is also Ray Romano and Holly Hunter. In the film, there is Kumail's father's role. He is a Pakistani and lives there itself. His wish is that you should play him in the film.'

I said: 'Okay. Tell him to call me.'

Judd Apatow, I knew, is a very fine producer who has done some amazing films like *Get Him to the Greek*, *Bridesmaid*, *The Cable Guy*,

Wanderlust—all romantic, well-made films which earned at the box office and also collected many awards.

About Michael Showalter, I learnt that he had done some TV serials and one film, *The Baxter*. However, the idea of a father wanting to be played by me was an emotional matter rather than a professional one. Kumail explained to me the story and reiterated how his father wished that I portray him in the film. 'Okay, I will do the film,' I told him. 'For me, I think it's more of an emotional matter.'

He was shocked: 'Without reading the script?' he asked.

'If I read the script, I might say no to you. However, promise me that you will make the necessary changes in the script, as per my suggestions, if need be.'

'Don't worry about that,' he assured me. 'I will take down your suggestions and we will pass them on to our writers who will incorporate them.'

When he sent me the script, I realised it had a very weak role for me. I felt that the girl's parents' roles were played by Ray Romano and Holly Hunter very good and well defined. However, Kumail's father's and mother's roles were very clichéd and that too without much depth. I sent him my suggestions and I must acknowledge that they did incorporate most of them.

For the shooting, I flew to New York. However, a problem arose— my work permit had not come in and without it, I couldn't start the film. Ruth Young too warned: 'Please don't shoot the film without the work permit.' Sitting in the Carlyle Hotel in Manhattan, paying half the money from my pocket because the unit did not have much money to pay me, I had no alternative but to wait. They were trying their best and had even tried to use some influence through a senator. I too went with them to the immigration office but all to no purpose. They had started shooting the scenes where I was not needed. Finally, they finished it and now had no work without me. We had a meeting one night and it was decided, very reluctantly, that if the work permit does not come in by tomorrow 2 o'clock, they would have to look for a substitute. I agreed. I wanted to be a part of the film and I had already spent 10 days and even told people back in India about it. *But perhaps, I am not destined to play the role in it,* I thought.

Nothing happened! At 11.30, I started packing my bags and called the concierge to fetch them. Just when the attendant came to fetch my bags, the phone rang with the message: 'The work permit has been issued.'

When released on 14 July 2014, *The Big Sick* was a big hit. Produced at a budget of $5 million, it earned a whopping $56 million. It got many awards and was also nominated for Academy Award for Best Original Screenplay. It had the nomination for the Screen Actors Guild Award for Outstanding Performance by an Ensemble. My performance was highly appreciated.

Besides that, on a personal level, *The Big Sick* was a landmark film—my 500th. Robert De Niro created a small video for me: 'Congratulations Anupam on your 500 films'. Immensely touching!

Just when I was wondering as to which will be the 501st film of my career, I was approached by the Australian film director, Anthony Maras, who was planning *Hotel Mumbai* based on the 2008 Mumbai attacks at the Taj Mahal Palace Hotel. I was to play the role of Chef Hemant Oberoi. Everything was finalised when suddenly, after a few days, I discovered that I had been replaced by Anil Kapoor. Naturally, I was most disappointed. However, about six months later, for whatever reasons, they came back to me wanting me once again to do the role. Instead of asking any questions like what happened? Why had you dropped me? Why are you back again? I raised my fee substantially from what I had quoted earlier. They agreed to it. I am very happy that I did the film. It's certainly the best film made on the 26/11 Mumbai attacks. Here a question comes to my mind: Why is it that it takes someone from abroad to come and make a great film on an Indian subject? Look at that epic historical drama *Gandhi* by Richard Attenborough. I don't think anybody here could have made that film the way he did. And those who see *Hotel Mumbai* will realise what I am talking about.

Working with the unit not only gave me an opportunity to be part of the most important film of our times dealing with terrorism, but it also gave me friends for life—director Anthony Maras, producers Joe Thomas, Mike Gabrawy and actors Dev Patel, Armir Hammer, Nazanin Boniadi and Jason Isaacs. *Hotel Mumbai* premiered at the Toronto International Film Festival on 7 September 2018 and got some amazing reviews. It released on 29 March 2019 in the US. For me, it was a fabulous opportunity to work in this film simply because it not only resonated with me but also because the tragedy of 26/11 is etched in every Indian's mind. What happened during those three days is what the film captures. It's not just about the terrorists' attacks but also about the spirit of the people who work at the Taj, how the Taj group produces a culture for its staff, how each one reacts in a situation that they faced then, how they saved the lives of so many of their guests that day and how for them, each guest is like a God.

The film was shot in Adelaide in Australia and Mumbai. I was there for 35 days and each day was a new experience, not only for me but for the rest of the cast too. There are a lot of Indian taxi drivers in Australia. Every night when I would step out for dinner with any of my co-stars, they would be very surprised to note that no Indian taxi driver would charge any money. They would drop me anywhere and everywhere I wanted to go but never take the money for it. This also happens in New York where most of the Indian and even sometimes Pakistani drivers don't let me pay. Whenever I force the issue, they place it back into my pockets saying: 'How can we charge you?'

As I look back on these recent experiences, I'm struck by this duality in nature. Having done 501 films, I'm known to an entire constituency of people, but at the same time still feel like a new, fresh-off-the-boat actor in some circles of Hollywood. The industry as a whole is so vast and broad yet interconnected at the same time and somewhere amidst it, I have found a path to call my own. In the rising tides of my life, there are very few moments left behind and so many twists and turns that not a day goes by without me being grateful for the opportunities that continue to come my way. I feel as if I'm being reborn and dancing with the ups and downs of life and awakening parts of me that have been evolving year after year, decade after decade.

32

BEST OF BOTH THE WORLDS

As an actor dedicated to searching the truth in make-believe characters, I feel I still have much more to contribute to the cinema and arts. However, whichever way I turned, I was already being called 'a thespian', 'a veteran' and 'an icon'. In fact, once I read an article in a popular English newspaper in which I had been termed 'legendary'. This did not flatter me. It disturbed me—it sounded like they were ready to write me off . . . send me off into the sunset. Judging by the traditions of our film industry, anyone who has worked for about two decades or more gets categorised as a 'veteran' or a 'thespian'. It does not matter what quality of work they have produced, how they feel about their career graph, how much more they have to contribute. According to me, Dilip Kumar is a thespian, Lata Mangeshkar is a legend, Amitabh Bachchan is an icon and Waheeda Rehman and Hema Malini are veterans but speaking for myself, I am still far removed from such titles and certainly do not see myself as legendary. No, not at all!

I am self-aware and know that I have done some good work (and a lot of bad work too) and have been amply rewarded and appreciated by my audiences as well as penalised by the powers that be. But by labelling me, I felt boxed in and was not ready to be displayed on the shelves with my many trophies.

I also feel that my pro-Modi stance and my expose of the 'intolerance brigade' over the last few years has cost me in terms of my work. Suddenly, I was not popular with certain groups of people in the industry. I was being talked about: 'Arey yaar Anupam is a fantastic actor but he is dabbling a little too much in politics.' It did disturb me to a certain extent but I refused to get paranoid about it. I was still secure in the knowledge of many who extend me work and would continue to do so. If this paradigm shift had occurred some 10 years back, maybe I might not have taken this stance. But on second thoughts, let me clarify that these were issues I really believed in. I have no regrets about them. Given another opportunity, I will still stand by my actions.

As I was mulling my options and seeking new outlets, the universe came to my rescue yet again. As the time-tested saying goes: 'When one door closes, many others open.' And that's precisely what happened to yours truly. His innate optimism conjured up a thrilling new world of possibilities.

Once the doors opened, it became the best of times. Presently, I am straddling two worlds. One foot remains entrenched in cinema and the other has forayed into Television—American television to be precise. How mind-blowing and exciting is this world. Unlike the world of every-man-for-himself climate, I am involved in a collaborative engagement that is fulfiling on a personal level as well in the macrocosm of the culture and production that it represents and sustains.

To name a few thrilling projects on Netflix, I must mention *The Indian Detective* with Russell Peters and *Sense Eight* by the Wachowskis. Another project that I am proud to be part of was *Mrs Wilson* of BBC One which was nominated for four BAFTA (British Academy Film Awards) awards.

The project on which I had to do a lot of creative heavy lifting was Lynsey Miller's *The Boy with the Topknot* produced by Nisha Parti which is based on Sathnam Sanghera's bestselling memoir with the same name. It is about Sathnam, a young man from a traditional Punjabi family who tries to gather the courage to introduce his English girlfriend to his parents who live in a small place in Wolverhampton, on the outskirts of London. Just as he works up enough courage to break the news to them, he discovers that his aged father is suffering from Alzheimer's. It was a very gripping, depressing story, which also forces the audiences to search their souls. The script had first been offered to my wife, Kirron, for the lead role but she had just joined politics and was immensely busy with her parliamentary duties and could not make the time. Then they approached me for the father's role. Though it did not have as much footage as the mother's lead role, I saw great potential for a nuanced performance. I could envisage the stamina and technique required of me including the fact that it was based on a true story. Since Sathnam's father was still alive, I had access to information from which I could get a true picture of him. Moreover, the cast was excellent. The role of my wife was played by Deepti Naval.

But I faced multiple challenges and travelled an even tougher road during the filming of this project. A few months earlier, in order to lose more than 10 kg, I had taken to brisk walking as a part of my daily routine. I developed a problem with my right leg. It was perhaps, because of my over-enthusiasm, I overdid it and as a result, I tore some muscles. I was in constant pain and even routine walking became a challenge. Added to this was the fact that I was going through a phase of depression as I mentioned earlier.

To make matters worse, as the filming location was in Birmingham, I spent a lot of time there. Adding to my woes was the weather with its overcast skies, heavy, dark clouds and constant rain. I was staying on the fourteenth floor in a cramped room. Whenever I would look out of the window, it was raining and gloomy. It was one of the low periods of my life. And, on top of that, I was playing a man who had lost his memory and was suffering from Alzheimer's.

If there was a silver lining to it all, it came in the shape of Gora (yes that was his name)—the hairdresser from India who owned the Gora Hair & Beauty Salon on Templefield Square on Wheeley's Road and whom I had met by chance. He would take Deepti and me out for dinner frequently. There was also our transport manager—a wonderful, courteous sardar, Charanjeet Singh, with a rustic, earthy sense of humour. His family would send me lunch regularly. In his large-hearted manner, he would ask if there was anything special that could be cooked for me. That's how I survived. I translated my depressive state of mind to portray Sathnam's father.

I recall the shooting of my first scene for the film. I was in the foreground, whereas my son Sathnam, played by that fine young actor Sasha Dhawan, and my wife (Deepti) are in the background, and engaged in a conversation. During this entire scene between the mother and son, the father is sitting in the foreground. I focused and reached the peak of my concentration. And to maintain it, in my mind, I had visualised an invisible ant, walking around in circles. This became my reference for my performance. After the shot was completed, Lynsey Miller, a fully committed first-time director came to me and said: 'Mr Kher, can we do it once more?' And there I was the experienced pitted against the novice.

'Are you not happy with this?' I enquired. 'My God, I was totally immersed in the scene!'

She said: 'True, but I feel that you should do a little less.'

I asked my ubiquitous question: 'How much per cent less?'

She said: '99 per cent.'

I should have expected that. Once again, the same old question. Once again, the same old answer.

Lynsey proved to be a brilliant director with immense capacity to draw out the best from the cast. I used both my physical and mental tribulations effectively in the portrayal of my role and Lynsey capitalised them as a director. The film released to superb critical acclaim and was a great hit. I personally came in for great praise for my performance. On Wednesday, 4 April 2018, Ruth Young, my agent, rang me to say: 'Anupam, congrats. You have been nominated for BAFTA (British Academy Film Awards) in the category of Best Supporting Actor Award—the second Indian actor to be so honoured. The other being my colleague Rohini Hattangadi for her work in the film *Gandhi* by Richard Attenborough.'

She won that award. I did not. But just to be nominated for such a prestigious international award was a great feeling in itself, particularly when all four nominated performances were equally brilliant. One thing I greatly admired at the ceremony was that every selected performer, in each category, attends the awards event and applauds the winner. It is a very different scenario to the awards ceremonies in India where the winner knows that he or she has bagged it and as a result, hardly any of the other nominated actors attend the event. That aside, I felt proud of my great moment of achievement. It taught me a lesson that sometimes, if you turn a challenging situation into an affirmative circumstance, it can greatly enhance an actor's performance. It certainly did, in my case!

During the making of David Russell's *Silver Linings Playbook*, I had the good fortune to meet the wonderful and warm Lisa Wright of Link Entertainment in Los Angeles, who became my manager to form a dynamic team with Ruth Young. I had just about started shooting for my 512th film, Jeremy Alter's *Singh in the Rain,* in January 2018 in the picturesque locales of Malibu in Los Angeles when Lisa informed me: 'The producers of *New Amsterdam*, an American drama, based on the book *Twelve Patients: Life and Death at Bellevue Hospital* by Eric Manheimer, are planning a television series and want to meet you. They want to cast you in a pilot which is to be made by the NBC (National Broadcasting Company). Meanwhile, CBS (Columbia Broadcasting System), also wants to cast you for a pilot.'

'Lisa, what about the audition and such requirements?' I enquired.

'These are confirmed offers. There is no audition or anything,' she told me.

I met the producers of both the projects. The CBS pilot—*Pandas in New York*—was about a family of Indian doctors. It had an interesting script but somehow it did not resonate with me. The CBS studio was very gracious with my decision.

On the other hand, *New Amsterdam*, created by David Schulner was about a medical director, Dr Max Goodwin (played by Ryan Eggold) who takes charge of one of the country's oldest public hospitals with the endeavour to reform 'the neglected facility by tearing up its bureaucracy in order to provide exceptionable care to the patients'.

The main reason for saying yes to *New Amsterdam* was because I was looking forward to working in an American series with an international cast and not a 'transplanted' series with a majority of Indian star cast where I would once again be a 'veteran'. In fact, when I shot the pilot of *New Amsterdam,* I told the producers David, Peter Horton and pilot director the brilliant Kate Dennis that I was very confident that it would be picked up. And it was!

In the US, a lot of the TV pilots are shot during the months of February and March for submissions. Only a few, say just about 10 per cent, get confirmed. My co-stars are Ryan Eggold, Freema Agyeman, Janet Montgomery, Jocko Sims and Tyler Labine. I play the role of a neurosurgeon named Dr Vijay Kapoor. There are many attributes to his character which make it quite demanding and fun and gives it a true East meets West quality. I had to memorise, once again, reams of dialogues in English and this time, it comprised of complex medical terms as well. I needed a reference point for Dr Kapoor and I found one—Dr Samin Sharma, head of cardiology in Mount Sinai, New York, a boy from Jaipur who makes it big in New York.

With *New Amsterdam* I got a tremendous opportunity to integrate into mainstream American TV which has taken me into the homes of countless millions . . . in numerous countries around the world . . . What more can an actor ask for? After completing the first season of *New Amsterdam,* it is hard to enunciate the different emotions I am feeling. I am experiencing a great sense of accomplishment and excitement. Howsoever, I may be excited about this series,I do feel an underlying sense of vacuum—as I am going to be away, once again, from my country for another nine months. I am eagerly looking forward to the second series—which has just been announced. I recall, when I walked back three blocks on the last day of shooting for this season, I was stopped by seven people, all Americans who recognised me and paid tribute to my character, Dr Vijay Kapoor. Audience feedback is always so special to me and when they told me how much they loved me in the show and how they identified with Dr Kapoor, I was both humbled and filled with pride.

One of the requirements even before the shooting starts for the pilot is to sign a contract for seven years. There was no way I could have done that. If this had happened 20 or 15 or even 10 years back, I would've signed for seven years. But not in the year 2018. *I am aware that I am 63 years old,* I thought to myself. *I can't give away seven years of my life to a series abroad.* So, we came to a mutual understanding that I would be available for three years. However, having spent almost one year with the cast, writers, directors, producers and the unit hands, I couldn't have asked for a better family outside India. When I get time I do catch up with my dear friends, the Dandonas— Kamal, Chummu and their son Rajiv. They give me a great feel . . . a great sense of belonging.

Today, I am enjoying leading the life of a New Yorker, whatever that means. When I met the Mayor of NYC, Bill Blasio, he said, 'It is a great honour to have you based here as a New Yorker.' He went on to say that he and his wife Chirlane are huge fans of my role in *New Amsterdam* since it captures the spirit of the city and the message of serving others.

I wake up every morning and take a walk around Riverside Park. It has been amazing to be living this novel routine. I often wonder as to who would have thought that an underprivileged, unknown boy from Shimla would be living in a high-rise apartment with a spectacular view of the New York skyline, enjoying life in the Big Apple. Truly, in life, *kucch bhi ho sakta hai!*

Today, after 35 years in the industry, as I have relocated to New York, I have no new Hindi film on hand for the first time in my life. I would've never ever thought that one day, I would make such a statement openly. And I am not insecure or distressed about it. Yes, today I feel my work has come a full circle. I am busy with the shooting of *New Amsterdam*. The series has already become a big hit

As this book is about to get into printing, another kucch bhi ho sakta hai moment knocks at my door. The Academy of Motion Picture Arts and Sciences has invited me to be their member. Who would have thought that a boy from Shimla would one day be a part of The Academy? I am honoured and deeply humbled.

I can now openly, gladly and proudly say that this is the best stage of my life. I am working on this book—my autobiography— every weekend or any day when we don't shoot or when I am not required on the sets. And through it, I am reinventing myself. How many people at this stage get to start their life from the beginning and with so much promise? As I revisit my life, I am facing a gamut of emotions, happiness, sadness, pride and so much more. I remember a dialogue from Mahesh Bhatt's film *Daddy*, 'Yaad karne par khushi bhi ghum deti hai' (When revisiting old memories, even happy memories bring sadness).

As I complete my autobiography, I hope it inspires people from all walks of life who read it to reflect and embrace the lessons unknowingly learnt in the life I have lived to the fullest. Lessons of optimism, hope, promise, success, wonder and the infinite possibilities of a life well experienced. I myself have been motivated by countless inspirational tales such as—Kirk Douglas's autobiography the *Ragman's Son, Lust for Life* by Vincent van Gogh and many others including Charlie Chaplin & Maxim Gorky. It would make me immensely happy if my life story is equally inspirational—a guiding light and a beacon call to one and all that anything is possible in a lifetime. Glean the simple lesson from your life and environment and dress yourself in the cloak of wisdom from the parents that give birth to you, the family that supports you and the friends and community you build along the path to success. Aspire, Reach and Achieve.

The pace of my life and career has changed. In the early years, I was always in a hurry. Now I just want to pace myself and enjoy life in the sense that I don't want to plan things too much. I want to live for today . . . live in the moment. In that sense, I am still a struggler and I want to live that life all over again so as to learn . . . to immerse myself fully in everything. Believe me, it's a great feeling. Something that gives me a euphoric sensation! Each and every day!

But this is certainly not the end. There are still many new horizons to capture. And that too in this one life! The possibilities are endless and my future script has not even been written yet.

My Life is not Bound, not Limited, not Defined.
My Life is Free, Infinite and Immeasurable.

NOTES AND REFERENCES

1. Mohandas K Gandhi: *Third Class in Indian Railways*, Floating Press, Ranchi, 25 September 1917.
2. Henry Sharp: *Goodbye India*, Oxford University Press, London, 1945.
3. A stanza from the song beginning *Dil kahe ruk ja re ruk ja*, from Raghunath Jhalani's 1970 Hindi film *Man Ki Aankhen*, rendered by Mohammed Rafi and set to tune by the duo of Laxmikant Pyarelal.
4. This song is from the 1963 film *Dil Ek Mandir*, directed by C. V. Sridhar. The lyrics have been penned by the eminent poet Shailendra and the tune composed by the Shankar-Jaikishan duo.
5. Harikishen Giri Goswami (born on 24 July 1937) took on the screen name Manoj Kumar after the character played by the thespian Dilip Kumar (born as Yousuf Khan; more about him later) in the 1949 film *Shabnam*, whom he greatly admired. Manoj Kumar went to produce, direct and act in a string of hit films, beginning with Fashion in 1957. In the later years, most of his movies were based on patriotic themes, such as *Shaheed* (1965), *Upkar* (1967), *Purab Aur Paschim* (1970), *Roti, Kapda Aur Makaan* (1974) and *Kranti* (1981).
6. Penned by Hasrat Jaipuri, tuned by Shankar Jaikishan and sung by Mohammed Rafi, the song is an evergreen number from the film *Sangam*, popular to this day.
7. *Mere Desh Ki Dharti*, a patriotic song from 1967 film *Upkar*, it was written by Indeevar, sung by Mahendra Kapoor and composed by Kalyanji-Anandji.
8. The opening lines of the mesmerising melody from the 1959 Guru Dutt Hindi film *Kagaz Ke Phool*, written by Kaifi Azmi, composed by Sachin Dev Burman and sung by Geeta Dutt.
9. Attributed to the playwright Sudraka (who lived in the third or fifth century A.D.).
10. Ashok Chopra, quoting Neelam Mansingh: *A Scrapbook of Memories–My Life with the Rich, the Famous and the Scandalous*, HarperCollins Publishers India, 2015.

11. The first stanza of the evergreen number from Dilip Kumar and Meena Kumari's 1953-film *Footpath* which was directed by Zia Sarhadi. The lyrics were by Majrooh Sultanpuri and Sardar Jafri with music by Khayyam. This soulful melody was picturised on 'tragedy king' Dilip Kumar.

12. Ben Kingsley (born as Krishna Pandit Bhanji) played the title role of Mahatma Gandhi and, deservedly, bagged an Oscar.

13. Muhammad Ali Jinnah, the founder of Pakistan.

14. Since Khan Abdul Ghaffar Khan hailed from the North-West Frontier Province (NWFP) and was an ardent follower of Mahatma Gandhi, he was known as the 'Frontier Gandhi'.

15. Rohini Hattangadi by then had become famous for playing the role of Kasturba Gandhi (Mahatma's wife) in Sir Richard Attenborough's *Gandhi* (1982). She went on to carve a distinct niche for herself in Indian cinema.

16. Sanjeev Kumar (born as Harihar Jethalal Jariwala; 9 July 1938 to 6 November 1985) was a versatile actor who essayed a wide variety of roles and won numerous awards. He is remembered for his impeccable performances in movies such as *Khilona* (1970), *Koshish* (1972), *Naya Din Nayi Raat* (1974; in which he played nine different characters), *Aandhi*, *Sholay* and *Mausam* (all three 1975 releases), *Trishul* (1978) and *Angoor* (1982).

17. Pali Hill is a locality in western Mumbai, along the sea coast. Many celebrities from the cinema world resided, and still reside, there.

18. Two lines from the qawwali in the 1960 Shanker Mukherjee directed *Mahal*, featuring Deva Anand and Asha Parekh, with music by Kalyanji-Anandji, penned by the prolific Anand Bakshi and rendered by Mohammed Rafi and chorus.

19. Navin Nischol (11 April 1946 to 19 March 2011) made his debut as a hero in Mohan Kumar's *Sawan Bhadon* (1970) and went on to prove his talent through films such as *Buddha Mil Gaya* (1971), *Victoria No. 203* (1972), *Dharma* (1973) and *Dhund* (also 1973). His performance in *Hanste Zakhm* (1973) was superb as was composer Madan Mohan's music. He and I shared screen space in the 2006 movie *Khosla Ka Ghosla*. His last movie was *Break Ke Baad* (2010).

20. Naseeruddin Shah (born 20 July 1950) was the 'dominant face' of what has been called 'parallel cinema', which was based on neo-realism. He later blended smoothly into commercial cinema. He is also a theatre personality. He and I have featured together in several movies. He too has bagged numerous awards.

21. The opening line of a song from Manoj Kumar's 1972 film *Shor*, penned by Raj Kavi Inderjit Singh Tulsi, composed by Laxmikant Pyarelal and sung by Manna Dey, Mahendra Kapoor, Shyama Chittar and chorus.

22. The first three words of the Aarti—a very common and important prayer that is sung on a daily basis as also during ceremonies.

23. Kazuo Ishiguro: *My Twentieth Century Evening and Other Small Breakthroughs–The Nobel Lecture*, Faber & Faber, London, 2017.

24. The state had been ruled for decades by one family: Sheikh Abdullah (1948 to 1953 and 1975 to 1982), his son Farooq Abdullah (1982 to 1984; 1986 to 1990 and 1996 to 2002) and then his (Farooq's) son Omar Abdullah (2009 to 2015).

25. On 9 February 2016, a group of Jawaharlal Nehru University students organised an event on the campus to protest against the hanging of Afzal Guru. The event was held despite the university withdrawing permission. The event witnessed clashes between various student groups. Anti-India slogans were also raised at the event. The slogans were castigated by several political leaders and some students of JNU.

26. *Om Tryambakam Yajaamahe Sugandhim Pushtti-Vardhanam Urvaarukam Iva Bandhanaan Mrityor-Mukshiya Maamrtaat.* (We meditate focusing on the three-eyed God [Lord Shiva] who permeates and nourishes all life. May we be liberated from death for the sake of immortality, even as the cucumber is delivered from bondage to the creeper.)

INDEX

ACKNOWLEDGEMENTS

In a book about my life, acknowledgements cannot be just to those who helped me with my autobiography but to the Truths which set me on the path to Success. I want to acknowledge that I was born into a poor Kashmiri family in Shimla and that my parents shifted from Srinagar to Shimla. I want to acknowledge the fact that I lived in a large joint family of 14 people in two rooms with three generations of Khers; we had very little money, yet we were always happy.

I want to acknowledge that when I asked my grandfather the reason for our happiness, he said that when one was poor, the cheapest luxury was happiness! There was so little living space that we used to always collide into each other. I want to acknowledge that when I asked my grandfather about how to handle this irritant, he told me to hug the person we had just bumped into and all irritation would be dispelled.

In a similar vein, I want to acknowledge the failures which led to my successes. It was because of these adversities and reverses that I now have a story to tell . . . This book details my life, the way it happened, how it happened and when it happened. Just the way it unfolded. My journey, so far, wouldn't be complete without the love and support, and even the let-downs, of a number of people. I want to thank them all. My grandparents who knew my dreams were seamless, and despite our humble origins, encouraged it. My mother, Dulari Kher, for being my silent strength. Pushkarnath Kher, my father, for being an ordinary man and, yet, an extraordinary person. Raju, my brother, for being my Laxman, despite me not being Ram. Kirron Kher, for being the mirror and anchor in my life. Sikandar, for completing the family that I have. P. L. Kher, for helping me discover the magic of books.

My gurus, my drama schoolteachers, Balwant Gargi, Amal Allana, Raj Bisaria, and the emperor of theatre, Alkazi Saab, for building, in me, an unbreakable foundation of knowledge. Sunita Kapoor, for giving me a second home. All the chawl owners in Mumbai who put a roof over my head in my meagre days. Ashok Panjabi, H.D. Pathak and P. R. Rane who had my back in my early days. Datta Sawant, my selfless assistant. Mahesh Bhatt, my break-giver, my mentor, my godfather. Rajshri Productions, for placing their faith in me at a time when they didn't need to. Dr Agarwal for giving me love and health. Ashok Pandit, my unconditional support. Herman Dsouza, for keeping my life in order. Ruth Young, my international agent, for believing in me. My US manager, Lisa Wright. As with my previous book, Atul Kasbekar, once again, shot with his mind's eye and through the eye of his camera, to give me the beauty of a cover photograph as only he can do. Ashok Chopra and the Hay House team, for bringing out the author in me in my first book and, now, giving my autobiography the platform it deserves. My friend Sailesh Kottary, for spending so much time with me in understanding the complex strands of my life and preparing a matrix. My friend and former journalist, Lalita Dilip, who met me after a long time in the US, for lending another perspective to my story. The producers and directors of the films which I have been part of. Feroz Khan and Ashok Patole for shaping my life-changing play, *Kucch Bhi Ho Sakta Hai*. The amazing city of Mumbai that ensured that I didn't fall short of opportunities to help me rise above each failure. My community, the Kashmiri Pandits, who gave me my identity and, through their resilience, shaped my attitude in life. My acting institute, Actor Prepares, that keeps me grounded and helps me learn my craft even today. I want to thank all my saddest failures, without which I wouldn't have had successes beyond the realms of my imagination . . . and, finally, I want to thank myself for living life the way I did.

I want my autobiography to be read of a man who has achieved everything and now is a compendium of his success. I want it to be read of someone who has failed and peaked, on innumerable occasions, and post the release of this book will keep wanting to peak and fail. This is not the summary of my life; it is just the interval! Remember, we all are born ordinary just till the time we add the little 'extra' to it.

This is me, Anupam Kher, the small-town boy, the loser, the fighter and the winner all in one. See you on the other side.